■ Stereotype Threat

Stereotype Threat

Theory, Process, and Application

Michael Inzlicht

AND

Toni Schmader

OXFORD
UNIVERSITY PRESS

Oxford University Press, Inc., publishes works that further Oxford University's
objective of excellence in research, scholarship, and education.

Oxford New York
Auckland   Cape Town   Dar es Salaam   Hong Kong   Karachi
Kuala Lumpur   Madrid   Melbourne   Mexico City   Nairobi
New Delhi   Shanghai   Taipei   Toronto

With offices in
Argentina   Austria   Brazil   Chile   Czech Republic   France   Greece
Guatemala   Hungary   Italy   Japan   Poland   Portugal   Singapore
South Korea   Switzerland   Thailand   Turkey   Ukraine   Vietnam

Published by Oxford University Press, Inc.
198 Madison Avenue, New York, New York 10016

www.oup.com

Oxford is a registered trademark of Oxford University Press, Inc.

Library of Congress Cataloging-in-Publication Data

Stereotype threat: theory, process, and application/[edited by] Michael Inzlicht, Toni Schmader.
    p. cm.
Includes bibliographical references and index.
ISBN 978-0-19-973244-9 (hbk) 1. Stereotypes (Social psychology) 2. Group identity.
3. Discrimination. I. Inzlicht, Michael, 1972- II. Schmader, Toni, 1972-
HM1096.S7398 2011
303.3'85—dc22   2011004094

For Naomi, Jonah, and Jaffa, whose group hugs and kisses have sustained me.

—MI

For Matt and Hazen and all the love, patience, and laughter they provide.

—TS

■ ACKNOWLEDGMENTS

There are a number of organizations and people who deserve special thanks in helping us make this book a reality. We would like to thank the universities for whom we have worked while editing this book: the Universities of Toronto, Arizona, and British Columbia. We would also like to thank the many granting agencies who have supported us over the years: the British Columbia Knowledge Development Fund, the Canada Foundation for Innovation, the National Academy of Education, the National Institute of Mental Health, the National Science Foundation, the Ontario Ministry of Research and Innovation, the Social Sciences and Humanities Research Council, and the Spencer Foundation. Next, and perhaps more importantly, we would like to acknowledge the people who have helped make this happen. We would like to thank Lori Handelman for wooing us with her charm and convincing us to sign with Oxford University Press. Also at Oxford, we are indebted to Abby Gross and Joanna Ng for shepherding the project to its completion. We are indebted to our graduate students and post-docs who have been patient when we haven't responded as quickly as we would have liked and who have made us look better than we deserve. Thank you: Alyssa Croft, Chad Forbes, Jennifer Gutsell, Will Hall, Jacob Hirsh, Mike Johns, Sonia Kang, Lisa Legault, Marchelle Scarnier, Shona Tritt, Alexa Tullett, Shen Zhang, and Jessica Whitehead. We are also thankful for all our wonderful undergraduate students, who are too many to mention by name, although a few do stand out for special thanks: Jeff Wong, Timour Al-Khindi, and Winnifred Ip. Finally, we would like to thank all the contributors to this volume. It is their fascinating words that you will be reading, and it is they, not us, who deserve the lion's share of praise.

■ CONTENTS

■ CONTRIBUTORS

Joshua Aronson
Department of Applied Psychology
Steinhardt School of Culture,
   Education, and Human Development
New York University
New York, NY

Sian Beilock
Department of Psychology
University of Chicago
Chicago, IL

Priyanka B. Carr
Department of Psychology
Stanford University
Palo Alto, CA

Aina Chalabaev
Department of Psychology
University of Nice-Sophia Antipolis
Nice, France

Alison L. Chasteen
Department of Psychology
University of Toronto
Toronto, ON, Canada

Geoffrey L. Cohen
School of Education
Department of Psychology
Stanford University
Palo Alto, CA

Jean-Claude Croizet
Department of Psychology
University of Poitiers
Poitiers, France

Thomas Dee
Batten School of Leadership and
   Public Policy
Department of Economics
University of Virginia
Charlottesville, VA

Julio Garcia
Department of Psychology and
   Neuroscience
University of Colorado at Boulder
Boulder, CO

Jennifer N. Gutsell
Department of Psychology
University of Toronto
Toronto, ON, Canada

C. Keith Harrison
College of Business Administration
University of Central Florida
Orlando, FL

Geoffrey C. Ho
Anderson School of Management
University of California, Los Angeles
Los Angeles, CA

Michael Inzlicht
Department of Psychology
University of Toronto
Toronto, ON, Canada

Jeremy Jamieson
Department of Psychology
Harvard University
Cambridge, MA

Sonia K. Kang
Rotman School of Management
University of Toronto
Toronto, ON, Canada

Laura J. Kray
Haas School of Business
University of California, Berkeley
Berkeley, CA

Christine Logel
Department of Social Development
  Studies
Renison University College, University
  of Waterloo
Waterloo, ON, Canada

David M. Marx
Department of Psychology
San Diego State University
San Diego, CA

Wendy Berry Mendes
Department of Psychiatry
University of California,
  San Francisco
San Francisco, CA

Mathias Millet
Department of Sociology
University of Poitiers
Poitiers, France

Mary C. Murphy
Department of Psychology
University of Illinois at Chicago
Chicago, IL

Jennifer Peach
Department of Psychology
University of Waterloo
Waterloo, ON, Canada

Todd L. Pittinsky
Department of Technology & Society
Stony Brook University
Stony Brook, NY

Valerie Purdie-Vaughns
Department of Psychology
Institute for Research on African
  American Studies
Columbia University
New York, NY

Jessica D. Remedios
Department of Psychology
University of Toronto
Toronto, ON, Canada

Jennifer A. Richeson
Department of Psychology
Institute for Policy Research
Northwestern University
Evanston, IL

Ann Marie Ryan
Department of Psychology
Michigan State University
East Lansing, MI

Paul R. Sackett
Department of Psychology
University of Minnesota
Minneapolis, MN

Toni Schmader
Department of Psychology
University of British Columbia
Vancouver, BC

Jenessa R. Shapiro
Department of Psychology
University of California, Los Angeles
Los Angeles, CA

J. Nicole Shelton
Department of Psychology
Princeton University
Princeton, NJ

Margaret J. Shih
Anderson School of Management
University of California, Los Angeles
Los Angeles, CA

Aiwa Shirako
Haas School of Business
University of California, Berkeley
Berkeley, CA

Steven J. Spencer
Department of Psychology
University of Waterloo
Waterloo, ON, Canada

Claude M. Steele
Department of Psychology
Columbia University
New York, NY

Jeff Stone
Department of Psychology
University of Arizona
Tucscon, AZ

Valerie Jones Taylor
Department of Psychology
Princeton University
Princeton, NJ

Alexa M. Tullett
Department of Psychology
University of Toronto
Toronto, ON, Canada

Gregory M. Walton
Department of Psychology
Stanford University
Palo Alto, CA

■ Stereotype Threat

1 Introduction

■ MICHAEL INZLICHT AND
TONI SCHMADER

Stereotype threat is one of the most widely studied social psychological concepts of the past 20 years. In this introductory chapter, we provide a broad overview of the theory and introduce the goals of this volume. The significance of the theory lies in its ability to offer a more optimistic account of group differences in performance. By side-stepping the nature–nurture debate entirely, stereotype threat seeks to identify how factors in the immediate performance situation contribute to—if not create—the appearance of systematic differences in ability. Interest in these effects is not restricted to academic circles but has gained broad recognition in the popular press with applications beyond education to intergroup interactions, organizational behavior, and clinical diagnoses. We review the four main sections of the book: an examination of basic processes that trigger and mediate how negative stereotypes impair performance, a discussion of recent theoretical extensions to the original formulation of the theory, a review of the variety of groups in which stereotype threat has been documented, and a description of how the theory can be applied to alleviate the debilitating effects that negative stereotypes can have in academic contexts. The book is intended for anyone with an interest in the behavioral science of performance, whether from an academic, organizational, or social policy perspective. To facilitate application of basic theory to the field, each chapter provides policy recommendations stemming from the research reviewed. To inspire future research, we conclude the chapter with a review of unanswered questions that await further inquiry.

Keywords: Stereotype threat, stigma, academic performance, black–white test score gap, male–female science gap

The 21st century has brought with it unparalleled levels of diversity in the classroom and the workforce. It is now not uncommon to see in elementary, high school, and university classrooms—not to mention boardrooms and factory floors—a global mixture of ethnicities, races, genders, and religious affiliations. This is the case in countries all over the globe, and is only enhanced by technological advances that enable global communication, collaboration, and education. In addition, many countries have come to embrace not only the idea of basic human rights but also egalitarian principles of equal opportunity extended to each and every member of that society. With these increases in academic and economic opportunities came the promise of not only greater intergroup harmony, but also the elimination of group disparities in academic performance, career opportunities, and levels of advancement. This promise has not been met.

Even a quick glance at national statistics reveals sobering results. According to the most recent data collected by the U.S.-based National Assessment of Educational Progress (2009), blacks and Latinos continue to trail whites in standardized measures of reading and mathematics at all age levels. Although this achievement gap has narrowed since these data were first collected in 1973, the race gap has not changed in any significant way since about 1990. Despite ever-increasing opportunities, then, measurable progress has not been made in performance in nearly two decades. Lest one concludes that this is an American phenomenon, data indicate that similar gaps exist worldwide, whether black–white achievement gaps in Canada (Duffy, 2004), socioeconomic gaps in France (Croizet & Millet, 2011, Chapter 12, this volume), Christian–Muslim gaps in the Netherlands (Levels & Dronkers, 2008), or Ashkenazi–Sephardic gaps in Israel (Peleg & Adler, 1977).

Data reveal some similarities in the gender gap in math and science achievement and engagement. Although there is only a narrow gender gap in standard measures of math achievement in high school (National Assessment of Educational Progress, 2009), this gap is large and significant on university entrance tests like the Scholastic Assessment Test (SAT College Board, 2010). What is more problematic, perhaps, is that this gender gap has not diminished since 1994, despite women now being better high school students overall, over-representing men in the top 10% of their 2010 classes. Women also remain a minority in the fields of science, technology, engineering, and mathematics, earning about 25% of the highest degrees in these fields despite approaching equality with men in the fields of medicine, business, and law. Even in fields in which women are more evenly represented, there is still a dearth of women in top leadership positions (Eagly & Carli, 2007).

▦ WHAT CAUSES THE ACHIEVEMENT GAP?

Standard explanations for these disparities, vehemently debated in the scientific community and popular press, typically invoke either nature or nurture, either biological and genetic explanations, or ones based on culture and socialization. In their controversial book, *The Bell Curve*, for example, Herrnstein and Murray (1994) claim that the race gap in academic achievement has at its root real biological differences that contribute to variation in IQ. Blacks and Latinos, in other words, perform worse than whites because they are genetically endowed with inferior intelligence. Similar suggestions have been made to explain women's under-representation in math and sciences (Benbow & Stanley, 1982), with Harvard University president Lawrence Summers' controversial allusions to women's inferior intrinsic aptitude being only the most high-profile of recent examples.

On the nurture side of the debate is the view that racial, ethnic, and religious minorities and women are products of sociocultural environments that frustrate the development of the appropriate skills, values, and motivation needed for success. For instance, being raised in a low-income family—which is highly associated with race—often means having less access to educational resources, in addition to limited access to health care and nutrition, both of which contribute to lower academic performance (e.g. Kleinman et al., 2002; Kozol, 1991; see Croizet & Millet, 2011, Chapter 12, this volume). Cultural and socialization pressures may also contribute to the gap. Mothers, for example, are more likely to encourage their sons than daughters to work hard in math and science, despite evidence indicating that their daughters are as skilled in these domains as their sons (Eccles, Jacobs, & Harold, 1990).

Although these existing explanations differ along a continuum of nature versus nurture, they share a presumption that a majority of our population, due to their gender, racial, or ethnic background, lacks the potential to achieve academic and career success to the same degree as their white (and Asian) male counterparts. The message coming from these explanations, in other words, is that, whether due to biology or the accrued effects of upbringing, people belonging to marginalized groups have less ability. These explanations also share an assumption that the evidence most often the subject of debate—scores on standardized tests of intelligence or achievement—is a valid and unbiased indicator of a person's true ability. Indeed, the assessment literature has taken great pains to eliminate cultural bias in the selection and construction of test items, and research suggests that race differences persist even after controlling for socioeconomic status (Loehlin, Lindzey, & Spuhler, 1975).

But the theory that is the focus of the present volume assumes that even culturally fair and valid measures can still be subject to variables that systematically impair performance for some individuals and not others. Even if we could match students on genetic predispositions, educational background, and personal values, *something* in the situation itself—be that the testing center, the laboratory, or the boardroom— holds marginalized groups back from reaching their full potential.

This *something* is the existence of social stereotypes. During the past 15 years, research suggests that the mere existence of stereotypes asserting the intellectual inferiority of marginalized groups creates a threatening intellectual environment for stigmatized individuals—a climate in which anything they say or do could be interpreted through the lens of low expectations. This *stereotype threat* (Steele, 1997) can ultimately interfere with intellectual functioning and academic engagement, setting the stage for later differences in educational attainment, career choice, and job advancement. The edited volume you have in your hand presents a focused look on this situational explanation, on stereotype threat.

■ STEREOTYPE THREAT

Stereotype threat (Steele & Aronson, 1995) is defined as a situational predicament in which individuals are at risk, by dint of their actions or behaviors, of confirming negative stereotypes about their group. It is the resulting sense that one might be judged in terms of a negative stereotype that is "in the air" (Steele, 1997). For example, because African Americans are well aware of the negative stereotypes impugning their intellectual ability, whenever they are in a situation requiring them to display said ability—say, a standardized testing situation—they may fear confirming the stereotype. Ironically, this fear of stereotype confirmation can hijack the cognitive systems required for optimal performance and result in low test performance (Schmader, Johns, & Forbes, 2008; see Schmader & Beilock, 2011, Chapter 3, this volume). In the original studies documenting this effect, Steele and Aronson (1995) endeavored to show that if situations themselves are creating or magnifying group differences in performance, then black college students should perform much better when the situation is cast in a less stereotype relevant way. Indeed, African Americans in their sample performed much better on a set of verbal ability problems when they were described as a simple laboratory task than when they were described as a diagnostic measure of intelligence.

Research over the past 15 years has shown, time and time again, that stereotype threat contributes to low performance not only among African Americans (Steele & Aronson, 1995), but also Latinos (Gonzales, Blanton, & Williams, 2002) and the poor in standardized testing (Croizet & Millet, 2011, Chapter 12, this volume), women in math and science (Logel, Peach & Spencer, 2011, Chapter 10, this volume), the elderly in memory (Chasteen, Kang, & Remedios, 2011, Chapter 13, this volume), and whites in athletics (Stone, Chalabaev, & Harrison, 2011, Chapter 14, this volume). This is a robust phenomenon, then, well-replicated in different groups, on different tasks, and in different countries. Even groups that are not traditionally marginalized in society (e.g., white men) can exhibit these effects if they are led to believe that their performance on a math test is being used to examine Asian superiority at math (Aronson et al., 1999).

The phenomenon of stereotype threat has proved to be incredibly popular in academic psychology as well as among the lay public. The first empirical article on stereotype threat was published in the *Journal of Personality and Social Psychology* in 1995, by Claude Steele and Joshua Aronson and is now widely hailed as a modern classic. For example, when the editors of *Psychological Inquiry* asked prominent social psychologists to nominate articles published in the 1990s that are now considered classics of the field, more than one contributor nominated the Steele and Aronson (1995) paper (Devine & Brodish, 2003; Fiske, 2003). And it is no wonder. Since the appearance of this first paper, stereotype threat has become one of the most vigorously explored topics of the past decade in social psychology. Searching for metrics of impact in October 2010 confirms the importance of this seminal work. According to *PsycInfo*, the Steele and Aronson article has been cited over 1,200 times, with over 450 separate publications having "stereotype threat" as keywords. A Google search with the keywords "stereotype threat" generates 66,000 unique hits; an entire website is devoted to summarizing the empirical science on the topic (www.ReducingStereotypeThreat.org), and dozens of symposia have been centered on the topic of stereotype threat in conferences worldwide. There is no indication that this frantic rate of citation will abate; to the contrary, it is likely to increase.

But the interest in stereotype threat is not confined to academic debates among social psychologists. The audience for this research is broad and extends beyond academic psychology to other disciplines and beyond the walls of academia altogether to members of the public. The work has been the subject of essays in the *Atlantic Monthly* and *New Yorker*, featured in a segment on the television show *20/20*, and discussed in articles in the *New York Times*, *Washington Post*, *Los Angeles Times*, and the *Wall Street Journal*, among others. It has also sparked research in other disciplines on issues ranging from race differences in athletic performance to the best methods for administering diagnostic tests when studying cognitive deficits due to aging, disease, or drug use. In 2005, when the National Academies of Science held a convocation to discuss research on Biological, Social, and Organizational Contributions to Science and Engineering Success, stereotype threat was one of the topics of interest.

Why has this topic been of so much interest? According to Fiske (2003), one of the reasons an idea takes hold is that it makes people uncomfortable, pointing to a natural hole in the literature that people did not realize even existed. There are other reasons, of course. Part of the enthusiasm, we believe, stems from the fact that the theory of stereotype threat avoids the nature versus nurture trap by suggesting that situations themselves can bring about apparent group differences in performance. Although the existence of stereotype threat does not preclude other factors that could also contribute to group differences in performance, it avoids labeling people with trait-like, immutable abilities, which, for underperforming groups, can only lead to frustration and disidentification (Dweck, 1999). Instead, it points to the power of the situation—the very basis of much social-psychological theorizing–by suggesting that the mere existence and awareness of cultural stereotypes creates a fundamentally different experience for those who are stereotyped to be less competent, an experience that systematically impairs their ability to perform up to their potential. The appealing consequence of this situational approach is that the performance of under-represented groups can be increased, sometimes dramatically, by relatively simple interventions designed to remove those threats. So, now we can do something about underperformance. Although we cannot change people's biology or upbringing, we can change the situations they find themselves in. And more and more, research is doing just this, finding that even subtle changes to situations can have profound effects on the real-life performance of traditionally underperforming groups (see Cohen, Purdie-Vaughns, & Garcia, 2011, Chapter 18, this volume).

Certainly another aspect of its appeal is the phenomenon's broad applicability. Not long after publication of this first paper, researchers started noticing that the theory could be applied to many different groups and to many different situations. So, there is now evidence that stereotype threat could be used to explain the performance not only of blacks and women in school, but also of gay daycare workers

(Bosson, Haymovitz, & Pinel, 2004), female automobile drivers (Yeung & Von Hippel, 2008), and white athletes (Stone, Chalabev, & Harrison, 2011, Chapter 14, this volume). We also know that threat can be elicited in a broad range of situational cues, from the mere presence of men in a room (Inzlicht & Ben-Zeev, 2000) to the content of television commercials (Davies, Spencer, Quinn, & Gerhardstein, 2002; see Murphy & Jones Taylor, 2011, Chapter 2, this volume). This broad applicability then spawned more research, the most important of which may be how and why stereotype threat operates as it does, exploring not only the psychological mechanisms (Schmader & Beilock, 2011, Chapter 3, this volume), but also the biological ones (Berry Mendes & Jamieson, 2011, Chapter 4, this volume). Despite this broad appeal, however, not one single book or edited volume has been devoted to stereotype. Not until now, that is.

■ ORGANIZATION OF THE BOOK

Stereotype Threat: Theory, Process, and Application offers to fill this need by examining this popular topic not only at the level of basic processes and theory, but also at the level of application in the real world. It provides a contemporary and systematic treatment of research on the impact of negative stereotypes and devalued social identities on performance, engagement, sense of belonging, and self-control. We believe that now is the right time for such an edited volume. Work on the theory is sufficiently mature—we have insights into the mechanics of the process, including issues of mediation and moderation—and so perhaps the time has come to take a step back to reflect on what we have accomplished thus far and how to move forward in the future. It is our hope that this volume will afford you the opportunity to do just that.

Stereotype Threat: Theory, Process, and Application is organized into four sections, containing three to six chapters each. The first section, *Basic Processes*, introduces definitions and conceptualizations of stereotype threat, including issues related to environmental triggers, questions of mechanism, and the biology and neuroscience of threat. Section two, *Theoretical Extensions*, explores how the initial theory has been refined to acknowledge stereotype threats (plural) as opposed to threat (singular), how threat affects a sense of belonging, how it has implications that extend beyond the stereotyped domain, and the comparison of performance impairments due to motivational versus automated processes. Section three, *Manifestations of Stereotype Threat*, shows the breadth of the theory by exploring many of the different groups and performances to which the phenomenon of stereotype threat has been applied, including women in math and the workplace, athletes, the elderly, and even whites trying to control their prejudice. Section four, *Stereotype Threat in the Real World*, examines issues of applied importance, taking a critical approach to understanding the extent to which stereotype threat has real-world consequences outside the lab, and the personal and institutional strategies needed to reduce stereotype threat and unlock the hidden potential of those who are socially stigmatized. Finally, the originator of the theory, Claude Steele, provides a final essay in which he reflects upon the theory, from its origin to its implication.

■ INTENDED AUDIENCE AND SPECIAL FEATURES

We edited this book thinking that it would have a number of audiences. First, this book is for an academic audience, for whom it can serve as a handbook for not only social, developmental, and organizational psychologists, but also for other social scientists, such as sociologists and education researchers. This book could serve as a text in both undergraduate and graduate seminars in social psychology, education, public policy, organizational behavior, and sociology. We hope that it will also act as a source book for psychologists interested in conducting research on stereotype and social identity threat. Second, this book is also for those people who are involved in creating public policy, be that in education, immigration, or business practice. Each chapter of this book has a government policy audience in mind, with an explicit discussion of the effective strategies for equipping students and workers with tools they can use to combat the negative effects of stereotypes and suggestions for specific methods and interventions that bridge the gap between theory and practice. Finally, this book is for people on the ground, the teachers and managers who want to provide a safe classroom and workplace so that their students and employees can thrive and flourish.

This book incorporates a number of special features that we think you will appreciate. First, all the chapters in this book are short, very short. Taking a page from the enormous success of the journal *Psychological Science*, we have asked (and sometimes cajoled!) authors to keep their word count down. We do this because we believe that authors do their best writing and thinking when they need to get to their main points quickly. We think you'll agree that the authors have succeeded here, with the chapters being a real pleasure to read. All chapters also include short abstracts, so that even casual readers can quickly peruse chapters to find what they're looking for. Abstracts are useful, and we're unsure why it is not common custom to include them in edited books. Finally, each chapter contains what we are calling "policy boxes." These contain short paragraphs, written in plain language, describing the public policy implications of the research described in the chapter. These policy boxes are self-contained units in which the reader can quickly get a snapshot of the policy implications for each chapter, without having to dig too deeply. We hope that these will be especially useful to policy makers, to teachers and managers, and to undergraduate students.

■ FUTURE DIRECTIONS

Over a decade of research on the phenomenon of stereotype threat has taught us a great deal about when and where it arises, the mechanisms that underlie its effects, and the ways to alleviate it. You can think of this book as a "halftime report" on the state of that research, but let's also spend a few minutes mapping out the strategy for the next stage of inquiry. Of course, doing so requires a recognition that many interesting lines of research are already under way that we simply didn't have the time or space to include in this volume.

First, stereotype threat has its roots as a theory applied to educational outcomes and experiences, specifically when it comes to test performance. But there is a need for more research examining other ways in which the threat of academic inferiority shapes processes of identification and motivation, ultimately affecting people's decisions of when to enter and exit certain academic spheres. Such research needs to explore when situations of threat motivate additional effort in an attempt to disconfirm the stereotype (Forbes & Schmader, 2010; Jamieson & Harkins, 2007) as opposed to a withdrawal of effort as a means of self-handicapping (Keller, 2002; Stone, 2002) or a decision to avoid that domain altogether (Cheryan, Plaut, Davies, & Steele, 2009). Emerging models of the role of motivation might further capitalize by considering how people negotiate a threatened sense of identity (Pronin, Steele, & Ross, 2004; Rosenthal & Crisp, 2006; Rydell, McConnell, & Beilock, 2009; von Hippel et al., 2005). In essence, this also touches on the need for more research to distinguish self-reputational threat ("I don't want to be seen stereotypically") from group-reputational threat ("I don't want to contribute to a stereotype about my group"), a distinction nicely laid out in Shapiro's chapter (2011, Chapter 5, this volume; see also Steele, 2011, Chapter 19, this volume).

Another future direction for research on stereotype threat as it is studied in educational contexts is to consider the role it plays not just in demonstrating performance on tests, but also in learning new information. Rydell and colleagues (Rydell, Rydell, & Boucher, 2010; Rydell, Shiffrin, Boucher, Van Loo, & Rydell, 2010) have recent research showing learning impairments under threat that can be distinguished from effects on performance. Other recent work reveals that young girls' (but not boys') math performance is predicted by the math anxiety of their female teachers (Beilock, Gunderson, Ramirez, & Levine, 2010). So, gender stereotypes may affect not only how academic content and strategies are learned, but also how emotional reactions to that content are learned as well. The positive implication, however, should be that successful role models might better model effective coping strategies that counteract threat. Delineating the ways in which threat affects learning is an exciting new area of inquiry.

A third direction for future research is to expand upon our understanding of the physiological and neurological mechanisms that underlie acute experiences of threat. Mendes and Jamieson (2011, Chapter 4, this volume) provide the foundational overview of research in this area. But more work is needed to then consider how chronic exposure to stereotype threatening contexts could lead to negative health consequences as a result of frequent activation of a stress response. Such work would have implications across of a range of situations as the threat of negative stereotypes can be encountered in any cross-group interaction (Richeson & Shelton, 2011, Chapter 15, this volume). New research in this area could be informed by parallel inquiries into the health consequences of having lower socioeconomic status (Miller, Chen, & Cole, 2009), as some of these effects might be partly accounted for by lack of resources but partly by those processes that are the focus of the volume.

Finally, as research on stereotype threat expands outward from an original focus on academic testing, there is a greater need to understand the other consequences of the basic psychological processes elicited in threat situations. Inzlicht, Tullett, and Gutsell (2011, Chapter 7, this volume) identify how the impairments to basic executive-level cognitive processes can then have implications for decision making and the control of negative or maladaptive impulses. These broader effects on self-regulatory processes have profound implications for how stereotype threat can be applied to a variety of domains in which threat effects have not yet been investigated. For example, in health care interactions, does threat experienced by stigmatized patients discussing treatment with nonstigmatized doctors impair their interpretation of, as well as their ability and motivation to follow, a recommended change in health behavior? In close relationships, does the experience of stereotype threat lead to interpersonal conflict that can counteract the potential for social support from a partner? In an organizational context, how does the experience of stereotype threat affect decision making in ways that can impair productivity? Work on these broader consequences might also consider the unique ways in which threat might be experienced by those with concealable stigmas (Quinn, Kahng, & Crocker, 2004; Smart & Wegner, 1999). And most importantly, once identifying these effects, what remedies can be transported from the foundational work on academic interventions to alleviate threat in these broader contexts?

To sum up, research on stereotype threat continues to be a vibrant growth industry for academic research. The power of the original theory to explain the experience of being socially devalued and negatively stereotyped is still being fully realized. It is our sincere hope that reading through the compelling chapters of this book will spark your interest in expanding the theoretical and practical implications of these ideas.

References

Aronson, J., Lustina, M. J., Good, C., Keough, K., Steele, C. M., & Brown, J. (1999). When white men can't do math: Necessary and sufficient factors in stereotype threat. *Journal of Experimental Social Psychology, 35,* 29–46.

Beilock, S. L., Gunderson, E. A., Ramirez, G., & Levine, S. C. (2010). Female teachers' math anxiety affects girls' math achievement. *Proceedings of the National Academy of Sciences, USA, 107*(5), 1060–1063.

Bosson, J. K., Haymovitz, E. L., & Pinel, E. C. (2004). When saying and doing diverge: The effects of stereotype threat on self-reported versus non-verbal anxiety. *Journal of Experimental Social Psychology, 40,* 247–255.

College Board (2010). 2010 SAT Trends. Retrieved from http://professionals.collegeboard. com/data-reports-research/sat/cb-seniors-2010/tables

Benbow, C. P., & Stanley, J. C. (1982). Consequences in high school and college of sex differences in mathematical reasoning ability: A longitudinal perspective. *American Educational Research Journal, 19,* 598–622.

Berry Mendes, W., & Jamieson, J. (2011). Embodied stereotype threat: Exploring brain and body mechanisms underlying performance impairments. In M. Inzlicht & T. Schmader (Eds.), *Stereotype threat: Theory, process, and application.* New York: Oxford University Press.

Chasteen, A. L., Kang, S. K., & Remedios, J. D. (2011). Aging and stereotype threat: Development, process, and interventions. In M. Inzlicht & T. Schmader (Eds.), *Stereotype threat: Theory, process, and application.* New York: Oxford University Press.

Cheryan, S., Plaut, V. C., Davies, P., & Steele, C. M. (2009). Ambient belonging: How stereotypical environments impact gender participation in computer science. *Journal of Personality and Social Psychology, 97,* 1045–1060.

Cohen, G. L., Purdie-Vaughns, V., & Garcia, J. (2011). An identity threat perspective on intervention. In M. Inzlicht & T. Schmader (Eds.), *Stereotype threat: Theory, process, and application.* New York: Oxford University Press.

Croizet, J. C., & Millet, M. (2011). Social class and test performance: From stereotype threat to symbolic violence and vice versa. In M. In M. Inzlicht & T. Schmader (Eds.), *Stereotype threat: Theory, process, and application.* New York: Oxford University Press.

Davies, P. G., Spencer, S. J., Quinn, D. M., & Gerhardstein, R. (2002). Consuming images: How television commercials that elicit stereotype threat can restrain women academically and professionally. *Personality and Social Psychology Bulletin, 28,* 1615–1628.

Devine, P. G., & Brodish, A. B. (2003). Modern classics in social psychology. *Psychological Inquiry, 14,* 196–202.

Dweck, C. S. (1999). Self-Theories: Their role in motivation, personality and development. Philadelphia: Taylor and Francis/Psychology Press.

Duffy, A. (2004, October 3). Black students still poorly served: Study. *Toronto Star,* A1–A11.

Eagly, A. H., & Carli, L. L. (2007). *Through the labyrinth: The truth about how women become leaders.* Boston: Harvard Business School Press.

Eccles, J. S., Jacobs, J. E., Harold, R. D. (1990). Gender role stereotypes, expectancy effects, and parents' socialization of gender differences. *Journal of Social Issues, 46,* 183–201.

Fiske, S. T. (2003). The discomfort index: How to spot a really good idea whose time has come. *Psychological Inquiry, 14,* 203–208.

Forbes, C. E., & Schmader, T. (2010). Retraining attitudes and stereotypes to affect motivation and cognitive capacity under stereotype threat. *Journal of Personality and Social Psychology, 99,* 740–754.

Gonzales, P. M., Blanton, H., & Williams, K. J. (2002). The effect of stereotype threat and double-minority status on the test performance of Latino women. *Personality and Social Psychology Bulletin, 28,* 659–670.

Herrnstein, R. J., & Murray, C. (1994). *The bell curve: Intelligence and class structure in American life.* New York: Free Press.

Logel, C., Peach, J., & Spencer, S. J. (2011). Threatening gender and race: Different manifestations of stereotype threat. In M. In M. Inzlicht & T. Schmader (Eds.), *Stereotype threat: Theory, process, and application.* New York: Oxford University Press.

Levels, M., & Dronkers, J. (2008). Educational performance of native and immigrant children from various countries of origin. *Ethnic and Racial Studies, 31,* 1404–1425.

Jamieson, J. P., & Harkins, S. G. (2007). Mere effort and stereotype threat performance effects. *Journal of Personality and Social Psychology, 93,* 544–564.

Keller, J. (2002). Blatant stereotype threat and women's math performance: Self-handicapping as a strategic means to cope with obtrusive negative performance expectations. *Sex Roles, 47,* 193–198.

Kleinman, R. E., Hall, S., Korzec-Ramirez, D., Patton, K., Pagano, M. E., & Murphy, J. M. (2002). Diet, breakfast, and academic performance in children. *Annals of Nutrition & Metabolism, 46,* 24–30.

Kozol, J. (1991). *Savage inequalities: Children in America's schools.* New York: Crown Publishing.

Inzlicht, M., & Ben-Zeev, T. (2000). A threatening intellectual environment: Why females are susceptible to experiencing problem-solving deficits in the presence of males. *Psychological Science, 11,* 365–371.

Inzlicht, M., Tullett, A. M., & Gutsell, J. N. (2011). Threat spillover: The short-term and long-term effects of coping with threats to social identity. In M. Inzlicht & T. Schmader (Eds.), *Stereotype threat: Theory, process, and application.* New York: Oxford University Press.

Loehlin, J. C., Lindzey, G., & Spuhler, J. N. (1975). *Race differences in intelligence.* New York: Freeman.

Mendes, W. B., & Jamieson (2011). Embodied stereotype threat: Exploring brain and body mechanisms underlying performance impairments. In M. Inzlicht & T. Schmader (Eds.), *Stereotype threat: Theory, process, and application.* New York: Oxford University Press.

Miller, G. E., Chen, E., & Cole, S. (2009). Health psychology: Developing biologically plausible models linking the social world and physical health. *Annual Review of Psychology, 60,* 501–524.

Murphy, M. C., & Jones Taylor, V. (2011). The role of situational cues in signaling and maintaining stereotype threat. In M. Inzlicht & T. Schmader (Eds.), *Stereotype threat: Theory, process, and application.* New York: Oxford University Press.

National Assessment of Educational Progress. (2009). Nation's Report Card. Retrieved from http://nationsreportcard.gov/ltt_2008/ltt0004.asp

Peleg, R., & Adler, C. (1977). Compensatory education in Israel: Conceptions, attitudes, and trends. *American Psychologist, 32,* 945–958.

Pronin, E., Steele, C., & Ross, L. (2004). Identity bifurcation in response to stereotype threat: Women and mathematics. *Journal of Experimental Social Psychology, 40,* 152–168.

Quinn, D. M., Kahng, S. K., & Crocker, J. (2004). Discreditable: Stigma effects of revealing a mental illness history on test performance. *Personality and Social Psychology Bulletin, 30,* 803–815.

Richeson, J. A., & Shelton, J. N. (2011). Stereotype threat in interracial interactions. In M. Inzlicht & T. Schmader (Eds.), *Stereotype threat: Theory, process, and application.* New York: Oxford University Press.

Rosenthal, H. E. S., & Crisp, R. J. (2006). Reducing stereotype threat by blurring intergroup boundaries. *Personality and Social Psychology Bulletin, 32,* 501–511.

Rydell, R. J., McConnell, A. R., & Beilock, S. L. (2009). Multiple social identities and stereotype threat: Imbalance, accessibility, and working memory. *Journal of Personality and Social Psychology, 96,* 949–966.

Rydell, R. J., Rydell, M. T., & Boucher, K. L. (2010). The effect of negative performance stereotypes on learning. *Journal of Personality and Social Psychology, 99,* 883–896.

Rydell, R. J., Shiffrin, R., Boucher, K. L., Van Loo, K., & Rydell, M. T. (2010). Stereotype threat prevents perceptual learning. *Proceedings of the National Academy of Sciences (USA), 107,* 14042–14047.

Schmader, T., & Beilock, S. (2011). An integration of processes that underlie stereotype threat. In M. Inzlicht & T. Schmader (Eds.), *Stereotype threat: Theory, process, and application.* New York: Oxford University Press.

Schmader, T., Johns, M., & Forbes, C. (2008). An integrated process model of stereotype threat effects on performance. *Psychological Review, 115,* 336–356.

Shapiro, J. (2011). Types of threats: From stereotype threat to stereotype threats. In M. Inzlicht & T. Schmader, (Eds.), *Stereotype threat: Theory, process, and application.* New York: Oxford University Press.

Smart, L., & Wegner, D. M. (1999). Covering up what can't be seen: Concealable stigmas and mental control. *Journal of Personality and Social Psychology, 77,* 474–486.

Steele, C. M. (1997). A threat in the air: How stereotypes shape intellectual identity and performance. *American Psychologist, 52,* 613–629.

Steele, C. M. (2011). Extending and applying stereotype threat research: A brief essay. In M. Inzlicht & T. Schmader, (Eds.), *Stereotype threat: Theory, process, and application.* New York: Oxford University Press.

Steele, C. M., & Aronson, J. (1995). Stereotype threat and the intellectual test performance of African Americans. *Journal of Personality and Social Psychology, 69,* 797–811.

Stone, J. (2002). Battling doubt by avoiding practice: The Effect of stereotype threat on self-handicapping in white athletes. *Personality and Social Psychology Bulletin, 28,* 1667–1678.

Stone, J., Chalabaev, A., & Harrison, C. K. (2011). The impact of stereotype threat on performance in sports. In M. In M. Inzlicht & T. Schmader (Eds.), *Stereotype threat: Theory, process, and application.* New York: Oxford University Press.

von Hippel, W., von Hippel, C., Conway, L., Preacher, K. J., Schooler, J. W., & Radvansky, G. A. (2005). Coping with stereotype threat: Denial as an impression management strategy. *Journal of Personality and Social Psychology, 89,* 22–35.

Yeung, N. C. J., & Von Hippel, C. (2008). Stereotype threat increases the likelihood that female drivers in a simulator run over jaywalkers. *Accident Analysis & Prevention, 40,* 667–674.

■ PART ONE

Basic Processes

2

The Role of Situational Cues in Signaling and Maintaining Stereotype Threat

■ MARY C. MURPHY AND
VALERIE JONES TAYLOR

This chapter focuses on how stereotype threat is produced and sustained through threatening situational cues in an environment—such as its organization, features, and physical characteristics—that suggest the possible mistreatment or devaluation of stigmatized individuals. First, we illustrate how threatening situational cues engender a vigilance process whereby stigmatized individuals direct attention toward additional cues to determine the value and meaning of their social identity in a setting. We review how both explicit and subtle situational cues elicit stereotype threat, particularly among racial minorities in academic settings and women in science, technology, engineering, and math (STEM) domains. We propose that the meaning people assign to those cues ultimately affects whether they will become vulnerable to—or protected against—stereotype threat. Further, we suggest that situational cues are meaningful to the extent that they elicit identity-related concerns, such as concerns for belonging, institutional fairness, or of being marginalized in a setting. Finally, we explore how "identity-safe" cues in a setting can eliminate stereotype threat by reducing identity threat concerns and signaling to stigmatized individuals that their social identity will not be a liability to their outcomes. Understanding how situational cues trigger and diffuse identity threat offers hope for changing the dynamics of social identity threat and ultimately points toward a new wave of identity threat research—investigating the interactive and contextual nature of identity-safe cues to create environments that are welcoming and comfortable for all groups.

Keywords: Stereotype threat, situational cues, environment, stereotype activation, stereotype maintenance

From an observer's standpoint, the situations of a boy and a girl in a math classroom or of a Black student and a White student in any classroom are essentially the same. The teacher is the same; the textbooks are the same; and in better classrooms, these students are treated the same. Is it possible, then, that they could still experience the classroom differently, so differently in fact as to significantly affect their performance and achievement there? This is the central question. CLAUDE M. STEELE (1997)

As Steele describes, the initial aim of stereotype threat research was to examine those factors suppressing the intellectual performance of black students and women in math, science, and engineering (Steele, 2011, Chapter 19, this volume). These groups were of particular interest because it was clear—based upon longstanding national data—that both were reliably underperforming in the classroom relative to their intellectual abilities, as indexed by the Scholastic Assessment Test (SAT). That is, at every level of preparation—matched with their white and male peers—standardized tests consistently *over-predicted* their achievement in school (Steele, 2010; Walton & Spencer, 2009). Because these data equated racial minorities and women's SAT scores with those of their nonstereotyped counterparts, academic ability and preparation seemed an unlikely explanation for this achievement gap. What else, then, was depressing their academic performance? Intrigued by these data, Steele and colleagues (Spencer, Steele, & Quinn, 1999; Steele & Aronson, 1995) began to investigate whether contending with negative stereotypes, themselves, might be restricting the academic performance of these groups.

■ STEREOTYPE THREAT: A PERSON IN CONTEXT

Since the original studies, stereotype threat research has shifted the paradigm regarding how social psychologists think about—and investigate—causes of group differences in academic performance. Rather than theorizing about these causes as rooted in one's culture or lack of preparation, stereotype threat theory posited that these differences might be attributed to features of the situation. The insight was this: When situational cues in a setting make a stereotype salient and relevant to one's actions, the resulting psychological pressure to disprove the stereotype might depress academic performance.

Since the seminal investigation in 1995, nearly 400 studies have documented stereotype threat, investigating those factors that trigger and temper its effects, and revealing the processes by which it influences psychological and behavioral outcomes. In this chapter, we focus specifically on how stereotype threat is produced and sustained through situational cues in the environment. We propose that the meaning(s) people derive from situational cues ultimately affects whether they become vulnerable to—or protected against—stereotype threat. Finally, we describe how situational cues can create an atmosphere of identity safety for stigmatized groups, alleviating stereotype threat effects.

The Role of Cues and Vigilance in Stereotype Threat

Drawing from social identity theory (Tajfel & Turner, 1986), stereotype threat theory begins with the assumption that each person has multiple social identities (e.g., gender, age, race/ethnicity, socioeconomic status, etc.). When situational cues signal an identity's value or importance in a setting, that particular group membership becomes more salient than the others and a vigilance process is initiated.

During the vigilance phase of stereotype threat, people's attention is directed to other situational cues in the environment to determine whether the identity may be a liability. Two appraisals are possible. If cues in the social environment *disconfirm* the possibility that one's social identity will likely be a source of stigma, devaluation, or mistreatment, vigilance relaxes. Performance and functioning, then, are contingent only on the task at hand (Cohen & Garcia, 2008). However, if situational cues *confirm* the possibility that one's social identity is likely to be negatively evaluated, vigilance increases. Consequently, even seemingly innocuous situational cues—like an instructor's race or sex—can become imbued with meaning as people try to discern the probability of being devalued in a setting (Kaiser, Vick, & Major, 2006; Wout, Shih, Jackson, & Sellers, 2009).

Our own research investigated this vigilance process by examining how attention is drawn to relatively innocuous cues in a math, science, and engineering (MSE) environment, in which long-standing gender stereotypes abound (Murphy, Steele, & Gross, 2007). In this study, male and female MSE majors watched a video advertising a prestigious MSE summer conference, that depicted a gender ratio of either three men to one woman (the ratio typically found in American MSE settings; National Science Foundation [NSF], 2009), or a balanced gender ratio of 1:1. Among other outcomes, we measured participants' psychological and physiological vigilance as they watched the video. Sadly, women majors who watched the 3:1 video reported less belonging in MSE and expressed little desire to attend the conference; moreover, they were highly vigilant compared to women who watched the gender-balanced video and men who watched either video. These women remembered more details of the conference video, such as past conference activities. They also had faster heartbeats and sweatier palms—indications of physiological vigilance and stress. Even more interesting, the cue focused women's attention on their broader social environment. That is, women who watched the gender-unbalanced video remembered more MSE-related cues planted in the lab room, including MSE textbooks, *Science* and *Nature* journals, and posters of Einstein and the periodic table, than did the other groups. Thus, the situational cue of numeric representation caused these MSE women to engage a vigilance process—deploying attention to situational cues, both within the video and their local environment, to determine the value of their gender identity in the MSE conference setting.

Of course, individuals differ with regard to the likelihood and intensity that they engage the vigilance process. Some people constantly scan almost every environment for situational cues that signal their identity's value—for example, they may be particularly sensitive to identity-based rejection (e.g., Mendoza-Denton, Downey, Purdie, Davis, & Pietrzak, 2002) or highly conscious of the stigma associated with their identity (Pinel, 1999, 2004). For others, the vigilance process may begin only when cues disambiguate the likelihood of identity-based judgments. Similarly, people have different thresholds by which firm appraisals of identity threat are made. Some individuals require just one strong situational cue, such as a coworker's sexist comment, whereas others might experience threat only when multiple cues converge. Furthermore, certain situational cues will be less threatening for people not personally invested in particular domains (e.g., women who avoid MSE). Indeed, research finds that the degree to which one identifies with a domain moderates stereotype threat effects (e.g., Aronson, Lustina, Good, Keough, Steele, & Brown, 1999). Likewise, people who are more identified with their stereotyped social group are also more vulnerable to stereotype threat effects (Schmader, 2002; Wout, Danso, Jackson, & Spencer, 2008).

These experiences with situational cues—and the unfolding stereotype threat processes that result (Schmader & Beilock, 2011, Chapter 3, this volume)—can influence people's desire to identify with, and persist in, professional and academic domains (Jones, 2009; Nussbaum & Steele, 2007; Osborne, 1997; Steele, 1997). Moreover, these vigilance processes may shape people's experiences in the future— steering their attention toward similar situational cues in new environments.

It is clear, then, that the psychological and behavioral experiences of stereotype threat are grounded in an environment's situational cues. In the next section, we provide an abbreviated review of those situational cues that have been shown to produce stereotype threat effects.

Situational Cues in Academic Settings

Perhaps because of the compelling nature of the original underperformance question, the majority of stereotype threat studies have examined the effects of situational cues on women's math performance or racial minorities' academic performance. The primary goal of these studies has been to investigate the processes that govern or modulate these performance effects.

Grounded in the original theory and research (Steele, 1997; Steele & Aronson, 1995), two cues—the diagnosticity of a test and the relevance of a stereotype to people's test performance—reliably produce stereotype threat among groups whose intellectual abilities are negatively stereotyped. In particular, the cue of diagnosticity signals to people that the test they are about to take is a valid predictor of their intellectual abilities (e.g., Johns, Inzlicht, & Schmader, 2008; Steele & Aronson, 1995; Taylor & Walton, 2011). The diagnosticity cue makes it clear that one's intelligence and competence is on the line and will be evaluated.

Studies that evoke stereotype relevance either explicitly refer to group stereotypes or more subtly suggest that stereotypes may be relevant to one's performance. For example, in studies examining stereotype threat among women in math, experimenters often inform participants that men are known to outperform women on the impending math test (e.g., Beilock, Rydell, & McConnell, 2007; Keller, 2002) or that women's performances will be compared to men's to determine whether the gender stereotype is true (e.g., Delgado & Prieto, 2008; Rosenthal, Crisp, & Suen, 2007). Others mention that the experiment's purpose is to examine gender differences in mathematical performance (e.g., Brown & Pinel, 2003; Johns, Schmader, & Marten, 2005) or to determine whether gender differences actually exist (McIntyre, Paulson, & Lord, 2003). Finally, in some studies participants are told that gender differences have been documented on the upcoming math test—leaving people to infer the direction of the gender difference (e.g., O'Brien & Crandall, 2003; Spencer et al., 1999).

Research has shown that linking one's identity to one's performance or future potential subtly suggests diagnosticity and relevance. For instance, indicating one's race or gender on demographic questions increases the salience of stereotypes related to those group memberships and reduces performance, both in the lab and in the world (e.g., Danaher & Crandall, 2008; Schmader & Johns, 2003; Steele & Aronson, 1995). Highlighting the potential for evaluation also intensifies stereotype threat. Telling participants that they will receive performance feedback following the test (e.g., Martens, Johns, Greenberg, & Schimel, 2006; Steele & Aronson, 1995; Schmader & Johns, 2003) or that the test will "reveal their strengths and weaknesses," for example, amplifies threat (e.g., Johns et al., 2008; Marx & Stapel, 2006; Steele & Aronson, 1995). Stereotypes thereby are made relevant by emphasizing a test's importance, explicitly linking it to other, presumably more important abilities, such as one's general intelligence or future academic potential (e.g., Rydell, McConnell, & Beilock, 2009; Seibt & Förster, 2004).

Yet, stereotype relevance does not require heavy-handed experimental manipulations. Studies have shown that when a test is notoriously important—such as when it predicts future academic opportunities or scholarships—no additional cue is necessary to induce stereotype threat. For example, when stereotyped students hoping to attend graduate school take the GRE (Schmader, Forbes, Zhang, & Mendes, 2009), or when college-bound women take the AP Math Exam (Danaher & Crandall, 2008), both show stereotype threat underperformance. Thus, all that appears necessary for stereotype threat effects to emerge, particularly in high-stakes testing situations of personal importance, is that individuals are both aware of the stereotype and aware that the performance task is diagnostic of the ability in question (Kray, Galinsky, & Thompson, 2002).

Beyond these cues, research has shown that the organization of a setting significantly moderates stereotype threat effects. For example, several studies have revealed that the number of whites or men in a setting can significantly affect the performance of racial minorities and women, respectively (Inzlicht & Ben-Zeev, 2000, 2003; Sekaquaptewa & Thompson, 2002, 2003). In one experiment that manipulated the cue of numeric representation, women took a math test in a room with two other test-takers—either with two other females, one male and one female, or with two males. The effect of number was clear: With each man added to the setting, women showed a linear decrease in math performance, whereas men remained unaffected by the cue (Inzlicht & Ben-Zeev, 2000). In other research, the mere presence of men or whites administering math and intellectual ability tests caused underperformance among women and racial minorities (Marx & Goff, 2005; Marx & Roman, 2002; Wout et al., 2009). Thus, the physical arrangements and mere presence of certain groups within a setting are subtle, but powerful, situational cues affecting stigmatized individuals (Steele, Spencer, & Aronson, 2002).

Of course, stereotype threat occurs among other groups and in other situations besides women in math and African Americans in academics. In fact, all people have social identities that—given a particular collection of cues—trigger stereotype threat. For example, Latinos, negatively stereotyped as intellectually inferior, can underperform on math and spatial ability tasks (Gonzales, Blanton, & Williams, 2002), low-income students may underperform when their socioeconomic background is highlighted (e.g., Croizet & Claire, 1998; Croizet & Millet, 2011, Chapter 12, this volume), and even white men's math performance can become vulnerable when compared to that of Asian Americans (Aronson et al., 1999). Thus, people from all social groups—including those who do not belong to traditionally stereotyped groups—can be affected by identity-threatening cues and experience the cognitive, behavioral, and emotional disruptions of stereotype threat.

In fact, some research demonstrates just how insidious commonplace cues can be. In a set of studies investigating the effects of the media, Davies and colleagues showed women and men three different sets of prime-time TV commercials (Davies, Spencer, Quinn, & Gerhardstein, 2005; Davies, Spencer, & Steele, 2002). One set included neutral commercials that advertised products unrelated to gender (e.g., a cellular phone, an insurance company). Another set featured gender-stereotypic depictions of women (e.g., a woman fantasizes about being chosen homecoming queen), whereas a third set featured counterstereotypic depictions of women (e.g., an attractive woman impresses a man with her car knowledge). Results revealed that, relative to the neutral ads, the stereotypic ads activated gender stereotypes and reduced women's inclinations to occupy leadership roles (Davies et al., 2005). Moreover, the stereotypic commercials depressed women's subsequent performance on a nondiagnostic math test, whereas men and women who watched the counterstereotypic commercials performed equally well. Women exposed to the stereotypic commercials even indicated less interest in pursuing quantitative domains as a career, preferring instead to apply their skills to verbal domains in which the potential for gender stereotyping is reduced (Davies et al., 2002). These clever studies demonstrate the far-reaching effects of subtle situational cues—affecting outcomes as varied as performance, task choice, and career aspirations.

A final set of studies reveals that other people's behavior can also trigger stereotype threat. Researchers hypothesized that women might use men's body language as an indicator of the potential for negative treatment and stereotyping (Logel, Walton, Spencer, Iserman, von Hippel, & Bell, 2009). In a set of experiments, male confederates either did or did not display certain behavioral cues to their female partners—scanning their female conversation partner's body, showing confident and dominant facial expressions, and displaying open body postures (i.e., shoulders back, knees far apart). They found that the confederate's sexist behaviors were enough to disrupt the performance of even highly skilled female engineering majors on an engineering test. Furthermore, women who interacted with the sexist confederate cognitively suppressed concerns about gender stereotypes in anticipation of their test performance—actively trying to manage these negative stereotypes before taking the test. This cognitive suppression ironically led to their subpar performance as it depleted the cognitive resources required to excel on the test. Thus, subtle situational cues—found in both the media and in the behaviors of others—can launch the stereotype threat process and interfere with the performance, aspirations, and cognitive processes of stigmatized individuals.

■ SITUATIONAL CUES AND SOCIAL IDENTITY CONCERNS

More recent research on the effects of social identity threat suggests that situational cues become meaningful to people to the extent that they imply some contingency between the cue and one's outcomes in a setting (Murphy & Steele, 2010; Purdie-Vaughns, Steele, Davies, Ditlmann, & Crosby, 2008; Steele, 2010). Take for example, the situational cue of student segregation in a high school cafeteria. When a freshman walks into the cafeteria and sees its organization by social identities—the jocks are sitting together, as are the nerds, the artsy kids, the African American students, the Asian students, the Latino students—this cue presents a contingency for his behavior. Suddenly, he is aware of his group membership more than he was before, and he feels pressure to sit with the group that he most identifies with so that he can feel comfortable. Thus, when situational cues direct or restrict one's behavior along the lines of social identity, those cues are likely to be perceived as meaningful.

But what particular meanings do situational cues hold for stigmatized individuals? We suggest that members of stigmatized social groups—by nature of their stigmatized status—have multiple concerns in the settings they encounter. Research has shown that stigmatized individuals experience more uncertainty in novel situations than do unstigmatized individuals—unsure whether others will judge them according to their identity, or whether their stigma will be a burden that impinges on their outcomes (Crocker & Major, 1989; Crocker, Major, & Steele, 1998; Crocker, Voelkl, Testa, & Major, 1991). Indeed, stigma carries with it additional burdens besides that of being reduced to a stereotype; people wonder how their identity will matter for many social and personal outcomes. These concerns constitute a more general social identity threat—a threat that arises when situational cues signal that one's social identity is meaningfully tied to one's outcomes in a setting. For example, a black student might be concerned that a predominantly Caucasian fraternity, looking to "diversify," accepted him primarily because of his race. Whereas a female manager may wonder whether she got a promotion because her company wanted to increase the representation of women at the management level. The situational cues tied to one's outcomes or interpersonal treatments are likely to be those that have the most impact on people's psychological and behavioral outcomes. Below, we provide an illustrative list of these concerns and describe how particular situational cues might speak to these concerns.

- *Stereotype threat concerns.* These concerns derive from situational cues that speak to the possibility that one's behavior will be interpreted through the lens of negative group stereotypes—that one might inadvertently confirm a stereotype about one's group to oneself or to others (Steele, 1997; Steele & Aronson, 1995). Cues that speak to stereotype threat concerns—such as task diagnosticity and stereotype relevance—reveal to people whether the stereotypes tied to their social identity will be central to their evaluation and treatment in a setting.

- *Belonging concerns.* Stigmatized individuals also search for cues to belonging. Belonging to various social groups is a fundamental human need (Baumeister & Leary, 1995), but a sense of belonging is particularly important for stigmatized groups whose stigma implies that they might be seen as unsuitable in certain settings (Dovidio, Major, & Crocker, 2000). To date, identity-threat research has focused on several aspects of belonging. From feeling that one is comfortable—and can be oneself—within a social setting (e.g., Murphy & Steele, 2010) to a more interpersonal sense of fit and belonging that relies on the perceived acceptance by others (e.g., Walton & Cohen, 2007), belonging is crucial to stigmatized group members. Belonging concerns can be triggered by physical cues in a social environment, such as the presence or absence of other identity mates (Inzlicht & Ben-Zeev, 2000), or posters on a wall and items in a room that together create an ambiance suggesting that one's group does or does not belong in a setting (e.g., Cheryan, Plaut, Davies, & Steele, 2009).

- *Authenticity concerns.* Stigmatized individuals are also vigilant to cues that indicate the likelihood that they can be authentic in a setting (Shelton, 2003; Shelton & Richeson, 2006). Some situational cues suggest that others may treat them as an exemplar of their social group, rather than as an individual. Often, the pressure to represent one's group in such settings can cause a person to feel inauthentic and "fake."

- *Trust and fairness concerns.* Generally, people want reassurance that their social identity will not restrict their opportunities. Cues that speak to whether stigmatized individuals have fair chances for advancement and benefits are particularly important. Thus, stigmatized individuals often look for cues to interpersonal trust: "Can I trust those in my environment?" (Purdie-Vaughns et al., 2008). They also look for cues about whether the setting at large—at an institutional level—is worthy of trust: "Will the institution give my social group, and me, a fair chance?"

- *Discrimination and devaluation concerns.* Stigmatized individuals often look for evidence regarding whether they will be negatively treated, disrespected, discriminated against, or harassed on the basis of their social identity (Kaiser & Miller, 2001; Major, Quinton, & McCoy, 2002).

- *Marginalization, "ghettoization," and social exclusion concerns.* These include concerns that one's beliefs, values, and cultural practices might be seen as strange, abnormal, or not compatible with mainstream practices. Thus, stigmatized individuals are vigilant to cues about whether their group may be marginalized or pushed to the periphery of social environments—either physically or culturally segregated. Similarly, stigmatized individuals are vigilant to cues about whether their social identity is—or historically has been—excluded from particular social environments.

Situational cues vary in the number and types of social identity concerns that they trigger. Some situational cues may speak to a single concern; however, most cues—especially subtle, ambiguous ones—are likely to speak to many concerns at once. Moreover, it is likely that different concerns have varying impacts on one's psychological, emotional, and behavioral functioning. More research into the particular concerns that situational cues raise—and their interaction with personality characteristics such as rejection sensitivity—are needed to better understand how they shape people's vigilance to other features of an environment and affect their outcomes.

Policy Box

Identity-threatening cues in environments, including subtle cues in classrooms and workplaces, initiate a vigilance process among stigmatized individuals that affects their psychological and behavioral functioning and dampens their performance. Identity-safe cues, however, reverse this process by signaling to people that their social identity is valued. Understanding how these processes may cause disparate outcomes for stigmatized groups is particularly important for educators and employers who interact with diverse populations on a daily basis. Our recommendations are threefold. First, organizational leaders should evaluate classrooms and work settings for the degree of identity threat that exists for stigmatized groups, especially in settings where disparate outcomes for stigmatized group members are apparent. Although different groups may have different concerns, anonymous climate surveys, opinion polls, and focus groups conducted by third parties will clarify these potentially multifaceted concerns and identify the organizational, physical, or ideological cues that signal identity threat. Second, organizational leaders should change these subtle, but threatening, cues in classrooms and workplaces and develop materials that utilize identity-safe cues. Finally, organizations should create and maintain committees charged with offering support, resources, and recommendations on how to sustain and reshape environments to remain identity safe as they diversify and grow. These recommendations, while not financially burdensome, will require thoughtful consideration to address the concerns of multiple social groups and diversifying organizations. The aim of these recommendations is to reverse the destructive effects of identity-threatening cues and to reshape settings so that all groups feel welcome and assured that their identity will not limit their performance or future outcomes.

■ CREATING AND SUSTAINING IDENTITY-SAFE SETTINGS

One of the early goals of stereotype threat research was not only to reveal the cues and processes that negatively impact stigmatized group members, but to also develop strategies to remove threat from valued settings such as schools and workplaces (Steele et al., 2002). A hopeful implication of stereotype threat theory is that, by changing the situational cues in an environment, one might dampen the identity threat there. Although some settings are replete with threatening situational cues, others contain few that indicate the potential for stereotyping, devaluation, or exclusion. Instead, these "identity-safe" settings contain identity-affirming cues—which signal to people that their social identity is affirmatively welcomed, respected, and poses no barrier for them (Davies et al., 2005; Markus, Steele, & Steele, 2000). Theoretically, situational cues should be effective in reducing stereotype threat to the extent that they adequately target people's social identity concerns and disconfirm the possibility that one's identity will impinge on one's outcomes in a setting. In what follows, we describe several identity-safe cues and discuss how the meanings ascribed to these cues set the stage for appraisals of threat or safety (see also, Cohen, Purdie-Vaughns, & Garcia, 2011, Chapter 18, this volume).

Cues to Identity Safety in Academic Settings

As with identity-threat cues, most identity-safe cues have been investigated among racial minorities in academic settings and women in math. These focus on alleviating the threat signaled by diagnosticity and stereotype relevance. Just as identity-threat cues vary in their explicitness, so do identity-safe cues. In studies of racial minorities, for example, threat in an academic setting is reduced by explicitly stating that the upcoming test is nondiagnostic of intelligence—that is, it cannot adequately predict participants' academic abilities (e.g., Ho & Sidanius, 2010; Steele & Aronson, 1995). To disarm the evaluation apprehension associated with stereotype threat, researchers might not use the label "test" at all—introducing the task instead as a "puzzle" or "problem-solving exercise" (e.g., Brown & Day, 2006). Studies also make stereotypes irrelevant to the task at hand by explicitly stating that the upcoming test has shown no racial differences or that it is an unbiased, "culturally fair" test (e.g., Blascovich, Spencer, Quinn, & Steele, 2001). Similar manipulations serve to alleviate stereotype threat among women in math settings (e.g., Spencer et al., 1999; Wout et al., 2008).

A series of stereotype threat meta-analyses demonstrated that the manner in which stereotypes are made relevant or irrelevant to performance influences people's perceptions of threat or safety (Walton & Cohen, 2003), and that the effectiveness of identity-safe cues varies by social group (Nguyen & Ryan, 2008). Among studies that manipulate stereotype relevance in testing settings, those that explicitly refute the link between the test and the stereotype show the most reduction in stereotype threat compared to those that do not. Thus, it seems that people link evaluative tests to negative group stereotypes more or less automatically and that it takes an explicit rebuttal of the stereotype's relevance to eliminate stereotype threat (Walton & Cohen, 2003). Complementing this work, a second meta-analysis (Nguyen & Ryan, 2008) revealed even more fine-grained results. Among women in math, explicit stereotype threat reduction strategies—such as telling participants that a test is not gender-biased—were more effective than were subtle ones, such as showing women in nonstereotypical roles (i.e., exposure to female role models). However, among minority students, subtle strategies to reduce stereotype threat—such as describing a standardized test as a problem-solving exercise—were more effective than explicit strategies, such as stating that blacks outperform whites. More research that investigates the potential differences between social identity concerns that arise for women and racial minorities is needed so that we may understand these different responses to identity-threat and identity-safe cues.

Adding Identity-safe Cues to a Setting

Rather than reframing tests as nondiagnostic of ability or irrelevant to one's performance, it is possible to introduce additional (identity-safe) cues to neutralize an otherwise threatening environment. "Critical mass"—or the number of identity mates that it takes for individuals to feel they will not be judged according to their social identity (Steele, 2010)—is a potent identity-safe cue. If stigmatized individuals perceive a critical mass of their identities, identity threat is put to rest. For example, adding more female students to a math test setting reduces the concerns that solo women have about representing their group (Inzlicht & Ben-Zeev, 2000). Likewise, including a black experimenter in a study reduces African American students' concerns that they will be negatively stereotyped while taking an intelligence test (e.g., Danso & Esses, 2001; Marx & Goff, 2005; Wout et al., 2009). Thus, sharing group membership with key individuals in a setting—such as a professor in a classroom—is yet another powerful situational cue that limits the perceived likelihood that these individuals will apply stereotypes to fellow ingroup members (Wout et al., 2009).

Like the cues above, most successful stereotype threat interventions focus on disconfirming stigmatized individuals' social identity concerns. For example, black students may not only be concerned that their intellectual abilities will be negatively stereotyped; they may also be concerned about not "fitting in" due to the low numbers of black students on college campuses. To target such belonging uncertainty, Walton and Cohen (2007) provided an alternative attribution for the social and academic hardships that students may experience in their freshman year. They manipulated situational cues aimed at helping students realize that the concerns they had about fitting in at college were normal, widely experienced, and decreased with time. This short, 1-hour intervention protected black students' academic outcomes in their freshman year and buffered their grades through their senior year (Walton & Carr, 2011, Chapter 6, this volume). Thus, brief exposures to cues that directly target people's social identity concerns by decoupling their identity from their negative experiences in a setting protect them from the pernicious effects of stereotype threat.

Some Limits and Caveats to Creating Identity-safe Settings

In this chapter, we propose that to effectively reduce stereotype and social identity threat, situational cues must address the concerns of ṣtigmatized individuals in a particular setting. Certain cues, then, are likely to be more effective in reducing threat than others. Researchers must pay attention to how cues operate in concert to create an environment of safety. When people are appraising identity threat, one cue can shape the interpretation of another.

A few studies have examined this interactive nature of situational cues. In one experiment, black professionals were asked to evaluate a company based on a brochure in which two cues (numeric representation and a diversity policy) were manipulated (Purdie-Vaughns et al., 2008). A policy that explicitly valued diversity led black participants to overlook the low number of minorities in the company, a cue that otherwise troubled them. Similarly, depicting large numbers of minorities in the company led them to overlook concerns they would otherwise have had about a color-blind diversity policy. The meaning of one cue, then, depended on what other cues were also present. This interactive nature of situational cues makes it imperative that researchers assess the full range of cues in a setting, as changes in one cue may not alleviate the threat associated with another cue (Purdie-Vaughns et al., 2008.

■ FUTURE DIRECTIONS

Stereotype threat theory suggests that to understand an individual's psychology and behavior, researchers must pay attention to context. Understanding the situational cues in a setting and the meaning(s) ascribed to them is foundational to understanding stigmatized groups' outcomes. The exact same situation—by virtue of the different meanings implied by situational cues—can be experienced in completely different ways by different groups of people. Threatening situational cues induce a vigilance process that directs attention to other features of a setting, so that people can determine whether a setting is aligned against their social identity. The appraisals that result from an assessment of situational cues crucially shape people's sense of belonging, trust, motivation, and performance. Although stereotype threat research has investigated many identity-threat and identity-safe cues within academic environments, stereotypes and broader social identity threats are relevant to many more settings. Additional work is needed to examine how identity-threatening cues affect people's particular social identity concerns. Similarly, investigations of how stereotype threat concerns are similar to, and different from, broader social identity threats such as concerns for belonging or marginalization are needed.

■ CONCLUSION

Stereotype threat research has illuminated why certain social groups underperform relative to their talents. By locating the problem in the situation, stereotype threat theory offers the hope that, by understanding the cues that trigger and diffuse identity threat, we might create and reshape environments that are welcoming and comfortable to all groups.

◼ ACKNOWLEDGMENTS

Preparation of this chapter was supported by a National Science Foundation Grant (HRD-0936613) awarded to Mary Murphy and a National Science Foundation Minority Postdoctoral Fellowship (SMA-0905695) awarded to Valerie Jones Taylor.

References

Aronson, J., Lustina, M. J., Good, C., Keough, K., Steele, C. M., & Brown, J. (1999). When White men can't do math: Necessary and sufficient factors in stereotype threat. *Journal of Experimental Social Psychology, 35*, 29–46.

Baumeister, R. F., & Leary, M. R. (1995). The need to belong: Desire for interpersonal attachments as a fundamental human motivation. *Psychological Bulletin, 117*, 497–529.

Blascovich, J., Spencer, S. J., Quinn, D., & Steele, C. M. (2001). African Americans and high blood pressure: The role of stereotype threat. *Psychological Science, 12*, 225–229.

Beilock, S. L., Rydell, R. J., & McConnell, A. R. (2007). Stereotype threat and working memory: Mechanisms, alleviation, and spillover. *Journal of Experimental Psychology: General, 136*, 256–276.

Brown, R. P., & Day, E. A. (2006). The difference isn't black and white: Stereotype threat and the race gap on Raven's Advanced Progressive Matrices. *Journal of Applied Psychology, 91*, 979–985.

Brown, R. P., & Pinel, E. C. (2003). Stigma on my mind: Individual differences in the experience of stereotype threat. *Journal of Experimental Social Psychology, 39*, 626–633.

Cheryan, S., Plaut, V. C., Davies, P. G., & Steele, C. M. (2009). Ambient belonging: How stereotypical cues impact gender participation in computer science. *Journal of Personality and Social Psychology, 97*, 1045–1060.

Cohen, G. L., & Garcia, J. (2008). Identity, belonging, and achievement: A model, interventions, implications. *Current Directions in Psychological Science, 17*, 365–369.

Cohen, G. L., Purdie-Vaughns, V., & Garcia, J. (2011). An identity threat perspective on intervention. In M. Inzlicht, & T. Schmader (Eds.), *Stereotype threat: Theory, process, and application.* New York: Oxford University Press.

Crocker, J., & Major, B. (1989). Social stigma and self-esteem: The self-protective properties of stigma. *Psychological Review, 96*, 608–630.

Crocker, J., Major, B., & Steele, C. (1998). Social stigma. In D. T. Gilbert, S. T. Fiske, & G. Lindzey (Eds.), *The handbook of social psychology* Vols. 1 and 2 (4th ed., pp. 504–553). New York: McGraw-Hill.

Crocker, J., Voelkl, K., Testa, M., & Major, B. (1991). Social stigma: The affective consequences of attributional ambiguity. *Journal of Personality and Social Psychology, 60*, 218–228.

Croizet, J. C., & Claire, T. (1998). Extending the concept of stereotype threat to social class: The intellectual underperformance of students from low socioeconomic backgrounds. *Personality and Social Psychology Bulletin, 24*, 588–594.

Croizet, J. C., & Millet, M. (2011). Social class and test performance: From stereotype threat to symbolic violence and vice versa. In M. Inzlicht, & T. Schmader (Eds.), *Stereotype threat: Theory, process, and application.* New York: Oxford University Press.

Danaher, K., & Crandall, C. S. (2008). Stereotype threat in applied settings re-examined. *Journal of Applied Social Psychology, 38*, 1639–1655.

Danso, H. A., & Esses, V. A. (2001). Black experimenters and the intellectual test performance of White participants: The tables are turned. *Journal of Experimental Social Psychology, 37,* 158–165.

Davies, P. G., Spencer, S. J., Quinn, D. M., & Gerhardstein, R. (2002). Consuming images: How television commercials that elicit stereotype threat can restrain women academically and professionally. *Personality and Social Psychology Bulletin, 28,* 1615–1628.

Davies, P. G., Spencer, S. J., & Steele, C. M. (2005). Clearing the air: Identity safety moderates the effects of stereotype threat on women's leadership aspirations. *Journal of Personality and Social Psychology, 88,* 276–287.

Delgado, A. R., & Prieto, G. (2008). Stereotype threat as validity threat: The anxiety-sex-threat interaction. *Intelligence, 36,* 635–640.

Dovidio, J. F., Major, B., & Crocker, J. (2000). Stigma: Introduction and overview. In T. Heatherton, R. E. Kleck, M. R. Hebl, & J. G. Hull (Eds.), *The social psychology of stigma* (pp. 1–28). New York: Guilford Press.

Gonzales, P. M., Blanton, H., & Williams, K. (2002). The effects of stereotype threat and double-minority status on the test performance of Latino women. *Personality and Social Psychology Bulletin, 28,* 659–670.

Ho, A. K., & Sidanius, J. (2010). Preserving positive identities: Public and private regard for one's ingroup and susceptibility to stereotype threat. *Group Processes and Intergroup Relations, 13,* 55–67.

Inzlicht, M., & Ben-Zeev, T. (2000). A threatening intellectual environment: Why females are susceptible to experiencing problem-solving deficits in the presence of males. *Psychological Science, 11,* 365–371.

Inzlicht, M., & Ben-Zeev, T. (2003). Do high-achieving female students underperform in private? The implications of threatening environments on intellectual processing. *Journal of Educational Psychology, 95,* 796–805.

Johns, M., Inzlicht, M., & Schmader, T. (2008). Stereotype threat and executive resource depletion: Examining the influence of emotion regulation. *Journal of Experimental Psychology: General, 137,* 691–705.

Johns, M., Schmader, T., & Marten, A. (2005). Knowing is half the battle: Teaching stereotype threat as a means of improving women's math performance. *Psychological Science, 16,* 175–179.

Jones, V. (2009). The pressure to work harder: The effect of numeric underrepresentation on academic motivation. *Unpublished doctoral dissertation,* Stanford University.

Kaiser, C. R., & Miller, C. T. (2001). Reacting to impending discrimination: Compensation for prejudice and attributions to discrimination. *Personality and Social Psychology Bulletin, 27,* 1357–1367.

Kaiser, C. R., Vick, S. B., & Major, B. (2006). Prejudice expectations moderate preconscious attention to cues that are threatening to social identity. *Psychological Science, 17,* 332–338.

Keller, J. (2002). Blatant stereotype threat and women's math performance: Self-handicapping as a strategic means to cope with obtrusive negative performance expectations. *Sex Roles, 47,* 193–198.

Kray, L. J., Galinsky, A. D., & Thompson, L. (2002). Reversing the gender gap in negotiations: An exploration of stereotype regeneration. *Organizational Behavior and Human Decision Processes, 87,* 386–409.

Logel, C., Walton, G. M., Spencer, S. J., Iserman, E. C., von Hippel, W., & Bell, A. E. (2009). Interacting with sexist men triggers social identity threat among female engineers. *Journal of Personality and Social Psychology, 96,* 1089–1103.

Major, B., Quinton, W. J., & McCoy, S. K. (2002). Antecedents and consequences of attributions to discrimination: Theoretical and empirical advances. In M. P. Zanna (Ed.), *Advances in experimental social psychology* Vol. 34 (pp. 251–330). San Diego: Academic Press.

Markus, H. R., Steele, C. M., & Steele, D. M. (2000). Colorblindness as a barrier to inclusion: Assimilation and nonimmigrant minorities. *Daedalus, 129*, 233–259.

Martens, A., Johns, M., Greenberg, J., & Schimel, J. (2006). Combating stereotype threat: The effect of self-affirmation on women's intellectual performance. *Journal of Experimental Social Psychology, 42*, 236–243.

Marx, D. M., & Goff, P. A. (2005). Clearing the air: The effect of experimenter race on target's test performance and subjective experience. *British Journal of Social Psychology, 44*, 645–657.

Marx, D. M., & Roman, J. S. (2002). Female role models: Protecting women's math test performance. *Personality and Social Psychology Bulletin, 28*, 1183–1193.

Marx, D. M., & Stapel, D. (2006). Distinguishing stereotype threat from priming effects: On the role of the social self and threat-based concerns. *Journal of Personality and Social Psychology, 91*, 243–254.

McIntyre, R. B., Paulson, R. M., & Lord, C. G. (2003). Alleviating women's mathematics stereotype threat through salience of group achievements. *Journal of Experimental Social Psychology, 39*, 83–90.

Mendoza-Denton, R., Purdie, V. J., Downey, G., Davis, A., & Pietrzak, J. (2002). Sensitivity to status-based rejection: Implications for African American students' college experience. *Journal of Personality and Social Psychology, 83*, 896–918.

Murphy, M. C., & Steele, C. M. (2010). *The importance of context: Understanding the effects of situational cues on perceived identity contingencies and sense of belonging.* Manuscript submitted for review.

Murphy, M. C., Steele, C. M., & Gross, J. J. (2007). Signaling threat: How situational cues affect women in math, science, and engineering settings. *Psychological Science, 18*, 879–885.

National Science Foundation (NSF), Division of Science Resources Statistics. (2009). *Women, minorities, and persons with disabilities in science and engineering: 2009* (NSF 09–305). Arlington, VA: Author. Retrieved from http://www.nsf.gov/statistics/wmpd/

Nguyen, H. D., & Ryan, A. M. (2008). Does stereotype threat affect test performance of minorities and women? A meta-analysis of experimental evidence. *Journal of Applied Psychology, 93*, 1314–1334.

Nussbaum, A. D., & Steele, C. M. (2007). Situational disengagement and persistence in the face of adversity. *Journal of Experimental Social Psychology, 43*, 127–134.

O'Brien, L. T., & Crandall, C. S. (2003). Stereotype threat and arousal: Effects on women's math performance. *Personality and Social Psychology Bulletin, 29*, 782–789.

Osborne, J. W. (1997). Race and academic disidentification. *Journal of Educational Psychology, 89*, 728–735.

Pinel, E. C. (1999). Stigma consciousness: The psychological legacy of social stereotypes. *Journal of Personality and Social Psychology, 76*, 114–128.

Pinel, E. C. (2004). You're just saying that because I'm a woman: Stigma consciousness and attributions to discrimination. *Self and Identity, 3*, 39–51.

Purdie-Vaughns. V., Steele, C. M., Davies, P. G., Ditlmann, R., & Crosby, J. R. (2008). Social identity contingencies: How diversity cues signal threat or safety for African Americans in mainstream institutions. *Journal of Personality and Social Psychology, 94*, 615–630.

Rosenthal, H. E. S., Crisp, R. J., & Suen, M. W. (2007). Improving performance expectancies in stereotypic domains: Task relevance and the reduction of stereotype threat. *European Journal of Social Psychology, 37*, 586–597.

Rydell, R. J., McConnell, A. R., & Beilock, S. L. (2009). Multiple social identities and stereotype threat: Imbalance, accessibility, and working memory. *Journal of Personality and Social Psychology, 96*, 949–966.

Schmader, T. (2002). Gender identification moderates stereotype threat effects on women's math performance. *Journal of Experimental Social Psychology, 38*, 194–201.

Schmader, T., & Beilock, S. (2011). An integration of processes that underlie stereotype threat. In M. Inzlicht, & T. Schmader (Eds.), *Stereotype threat: Theory, process, and application*. New York: Oxford University Press.

Schmader, T., Forbes, C. E., Zhang, S., & Mendes, W. B. (2009). A metacognitive perspective on the cognitive deficits experienced in intellectually threatening environments. *Personality and Social Psychology Bulletin, 35*, 584–596.

Schmader, T., & Johns, M. (2003). Converging evidence that stereotype threat reduces working memory capacity. *Journal of Personality and Social Psychology, 85*, 440–452.

Seibt, B., & Förster, J. (2004). Stereotype threat and performance: How self-stereotypes influence processing by inducing regulatory foci. *Journal of Personality and Social Psychology, 87*, 38–56.

Sekaquaptewa, D., & Thompson, M. (2002). The differential effects of solo status on members of high and low status groups. *Personality and Social Psychology Bulletin, 28*, 694–707.

Sekaquaptewa, D., & Thompson, M. (2003). Solo status, stereotype threat, and performance expectancies: Their effects on women's performance. *Journal of Experimental Social Psychology, 39*, 68–74.

Shelton, J. N. (2003). Interpersonal concerns in social encounters between majority and minority group members. *Group Processes and Intergroup Relations, 6*, 171–186.

Shelton, J. N., & Richeson, J. A. (2006). Interracial interactions: A relational approach. In M. P. Zanna (Ed), *Advances in experimental social psychology* Vol. 38 (pp. 121–181). San Diego: Elsevier Academic Press.

Spencer, S. J., Steele, C. M., & Quinn, D. M. (1999). Stereotype threat and women's math performance. *Journal of Experimental Social Psychology, 35*, 4–28.

Steele, C. M. (1997). A threat in the air: How stereotypes shape intellectual identity and performance. *American Psychologist, 52*, 613–629.

Steele, C. M. (2010). *Whistling Vivaldi: And other clues to how stereotypes affect us*. New York: W. W. Norton & Company, Inc.

Steele, C. M. (2011). Extending and applying stereotype threat research: A brief essay. In M. Inzlicht, & T. Schmader (Eds.), *Stereotype threat: Theory, process, and application*. New York: Oxford University Press.

Steele, C. M., & Aronson, J. (1995). Stereotype threat and the intellectual test performance of African Americans. *Journal of Personality and Social Psychology, 69*, 797–811.

Steele, C. M., Spencer, S. J., & Aronson, J. (2002). Contending with group image: The psychology of stereotype and social identity threat. In M. P. Zanna (Ed.), *Advances in experimental social psychology* Vol. 34 (pp. 379–440). San Diego, CA: Academic Press.

Tajfel, H., & Turner, J. C. (1986). The social identity theory of intergroup behavior. In S. Worchel, & W. G. Austin (Eds.), *The psychology of intergroup relations* (pp. 7–24). Chicago: Nelson-Hall.

Taylor, V. J., & Walton, G. M. (2011). Stereotype threat undermines academic learning. *Personality and Social Psychology Bulletin, 37,* 1055–1067.

Walton, G. M., & Carr, P. B. (2011). Social belonging and the motivation and intellectual achievement of negatively stereotyped students. In M. Inzlicht, & T. Schmader (Eds.), *Stereotype threat: Theory, process, and application.* New York: Oxford University Press.

Walton, G. M., & Cohen, G. L. (2003). Stereotype lift. *Journal of Experimental Social Psychology, 39,* 456–467.

Walton, G. M., & Cohen, G. L. (2007). A question of belonging: Race, social fit, and achievement. *Journal of Personality and Social Psychology, 92,* 82–96.

Walton, G. M., & Spencer, S. J. (2009). Latent ability: Grades and test scores systematically underestimate the intellectual ability of negatively stereotyped students. *Psychological Science, 20,* 1132–1139.

Wout, D., Danso, H., Jackson, J., & Spencer, S. (2008). The many faces of stereotype threat: Group- and self-threat. *Journal of Experimental Social Psychology, 44,* 792–799.

Wout, D., Shih, M. J., Jackson, J. S., & Sellers, R. M. (2009). Targets as perceivers: How people determine when they will be negatively stereotyped. *Journal of Personality and Social Psychology, 96,* 349–362.

3 An Integration of Processes that Underlie Stereotype Threat

■ TONI SCHMADER AND SIAN BEILOCK

The theory of stereotype threat has captivated those who have long struggled to understand why some groups of people seem to systematically underperform in certain domains. But although early research on the theory provided dramatic examples that even very subtle reminders of being negatively stereotyped could impair performance, it has been only recently that research has identified the processes by which these performance impairments occur. In this chapter, we provide a summary of how situations of stereotype threat set in motion both automatic processes that activate a sense of uncertainty and cue increased vigilance toward the situation, one's performance, and oneself; as well as controlled processes aimed at interpreting and regulating the resulting negative thoughts and feelings that the negative stereotype can induce. By articulating the integration of these component cognitive and emotional processes, we are then able to identify how policy changes and interventions can combat stereotype threat both by facilitating changes to people's stereotypes and by providing individuals with the tools they need to better cope with the threat.

Keywords: Stereotype threat, working memory, automatic and controlled processes, self-regulation

Steele and Aronson's (1995) discovery that performance could be easily manipulated by merely how a task is described or who is present in the room was astonishing. Just how is it that being surrounded by male test-takers can lead women to do worse on a math test? Why does the mere knowledge that a task will be used to measure intelligence impair the performance of black but not white college students? Many cues in our immediate environment can signal in subtle and not so subtle ways our cultural "fit" within that context (Murphy & Jones Taylor, 2011, Chapter 2, this volume). Whereas the first wave of research on stereotype threat established that these cues exist and can affect performance and behavior for a wide range of groups on a wide range of tasks, questions were soon raised about the process by which these effects occur. Although this thirst for process information is partly a manifestation of a current zeitgeist for breaking open phenomena to see how they work, it also stems from a very practical need to identify how these effects can be reduced.

Early stereotype threat research searched for evidence that those who show performance decrements when they are negatively stereotyped also report feeling more anxious, more concern about being evaluated negatively, or lower expectations for how they would do (Spencer, Steele, & Quinn, 1999; Stangor, Carr, & Kiang, 1998). Yet, although these effects emerged in a few studies, they remained elusive in other work. The early dearth of evidence for threat-based mediators led to some speculation that stereotype threat effects were not due to threat at all (Wheeler & Petty, 2001). Rather, it was argued that situations can prime negative stereotypes that individuals (even those who are not the target of the stereotype) then automatically assimilate into their behavior (Marx, 2011, Chapter 8, this volume).

From our perspective, both anxiety and negative stereotype activation are overly simplistic explanations for stereotype threat. It is not just the case that individuals feel anxious when they are stereotyped and that is why they underperform. Furthermore, it is not just the case that stereotypes are activated and automatically induce stereotype-consistent behavior. The phenomenon is more complex. It involves both cognitive and affective components and engages both automatic and controlled processes. Schmader, Johns, and Forbes (2008) outlined an integration of processes that underlie stereotype threat. Likewise, Beilock and colleagues (e.g., Beilock, 2008; Beilock, Jellison, Rydell, McConnell, & Carr, 2006; Beilock, Rydell, & McConnell, 2007) have proposed connections between stereotype threat mechanisms. The goal of this chapter is to summarize some of what we know about the ways in which stereotype threat reduces performance by focusing specifically on articulating the automatic and controlled effects stemming from the experience of being targeted by negative stereotypes.

▪ STEREOTYPE THREAT IS WHAT STEREOTYPE THREAT DOES

Understanding what stereotype threat is as a phenomenon requires insight into what it does psychologically. By definition, stereotype threat characterizes a concern that one might inadvertently confirm an unwanted belief about one's group. As a result, those who experience stereotype threat have a motivation to avoid enacting any behavior that might be seen as stereotypical. For example, blacks anticipating having their intelligence assessed report less liking for stereotypically black music and sports (Steele & Aronson, 1995), and women majoring in math and science disciplines report dressing and behaving in less feminine ways (Pronin, Steele, & Ross, 2004). But this focus on preventing any form of stereotype confirmation does not simply affect behavioral preferences, it also prompts more subtle changes in how one processes information at both an automatic and a controlled level. As we will review, these shifts in processing have important implications for performance that help us understand exactly why negative stereotypes can have such pernicious effects for those who are targeted by them. Although situations of stereotype threat clearly cue physiological responses as well, we focus our review on cognitive, neural, and affective mechanisms, and refer the reader to Mendes and Jamieson (2011, Chapter 4, this volume) for an excellent review of the physiological concomitants of stereotype threat.

Automatic Activation of Threat

An interesting and often understated feature of stereotype threat is its ability to affect performance without a person's conscious awareness of the stereotype having been activated. Although we do not deny that stereotype threat can be acutely experienced in a very conscious way, such awareness is not always necessary. Rather, many of the processes instigated by being the target of negative stereotypes happen automatically, outside of conscious awareness, and result in outcomes in direct opposition to the person's explicit goals and intentions.

First, situations that cue stereotype threat activate a schema of that stereotype. This was demonstrated directly by Steele and Aronson (1995), who found that black college students expecting to take an intelligence test were more likely than their white peers to complete word fragments like R_C_ with the word RACE instead of reasonable alternatives like RICE, ROCK, or RICH. Such evidence reveals that a cue as simple as the way a task is described can bring the stereotype to mind. However, activating the stereotype might lead to stereotype threat only to the extent that it cues an imbalance between three relevant propositions: "I am a member of Group G, Group G is expected to do poorly at Domain D, but I do well at Domain D" (see Figure 3.1). As Schmader et al. (2008) contend, it is the logical inconsistency among these propositions that is what actually constitutes stereotype

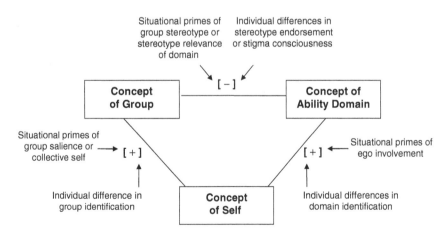

Figure 3.1 Stereotype threat as a cognitive imbalance triggered by person and/or situation factors. Adapted from Schmader, T., Johns, M., & Forbes, C. (2008). An integrated process model of stereotype threat effects on performance. Psychological Review, 115, 336–356, with permission of the publisher.

threat. This implies that stereotype threat will be experienced most strongly in those situations and for those individuals most likely to activate all three ideas simultaneously (for confirmatory evidence, see Rydell, McConnell, & Beilock, 2010).

Ultimately, the cognitive imbalance referred to above elicits other automatic but downstream consequences. As humans have a fundamental motive for cognitive consistency (Festinger, 1957), the immediate reaction is a sense of uncertainty and self-doubt since one clear resolution to the imbalance is to activate a more negative association between oneself and the domain (Johns & Schmader, 2010). Several studies have documented these thoughts of doubt (Beilock, Rydell, & McConnell, 2007; Steele & Aronson, 1995; Cadinu, Maass, Rosabianca, & Kiesner, 2005), and others have shown that once doubt has been activated (even if outside of awareness), it can color the interpretation of one's experience in ways that disrupt cognitive abilities (Schmader, Forbes, Zhang, & Mendes, 2009).

Our perspective emphasizes uncertainty not as an end state but as a phenomenological driver of additional processing aimed at resolving the inconsistency of one's thought processes. As a result, situations of stereotype threat raise competing possible outcomes ("I could do poorly as the stereotype predicts," or "I could do well, consistent with my goals and past experience"), and one's attention becomes focused on cues that might provide evidence for or against either alternative. Because the underlying goal, however, is to avoid confirmation of the stereotype, one's attention is likely to be oversensitive in its detection of any sign that could indicate that unwanted outcome. As a result, cues that might be otherwise innocuous, such as feeling anxious during an interview or making a simple arithmetic error while solving math problems, can be overinterpreted as a sign of failure.

Evidence for this increased vigilance for negative cues comes from a recent study by Forbes, Schmader, and Allen (2008). In this experiment, patterns of brain activity were assessed in minority college students who thought that their intelligence was being assessed using neurological measurements. The researchers were most interested in measuring activity in the anterior cingulate cortex (ACC) by analyzing error related negativity (ERN), observed as a negative deflection in an event-related potential occurring 50–100 ms after making an incorrect response (Gehring, Goss, Coles, Meyer, & Donchin, 1993). Past research has confirmed that individuals show larger ERNs to errors when they are particularly motivated to avoid mistakes or when they are being evaluated (e.g., Hajcak, McDonald, & Simons, 2003). Not surprisingly, then, results revealed that minority college students who were invested in doing well academically exhibited greater vigilance (i.e., larger ERNs) to the errors they made during a simple response time task when they believed that their intelligence was being assessed compared to when the task was described more neutrally.

In addition to an automatic detection of errors and bias from others, people also become more vigilant to signs of threat in their environment (Kaiser, Vick, & Major, 2006) as well as to their own internal experience. For example, in one study, women expecting to take a difficult math test (as opposed to a more neutrally described problem-solving task) exhibited an automatic attentional shift toward anxiety-related words, betraying the emotional state they were likely experiencing at the time (Johns, Inzlicht, & Schmader, 2008).

In sum, situations of stereotype threat bring to mind thoughts about one's relation to a valued domain that conflict with one's relation to a valued group that is stereotyped to do poorly. This cognitive inconsistency triggers certain automatic effects, including a sense of uncertainty and increased vigilance toward cues that might help one to detect, with the goal of avoiding, behavior that could confirm the stereotype. As we will see, these automatic effects are complemented by more controlled processes aimed at managing one's behavior, thoughts, and emotions.

Explicit Efforts to Manage the Situation and One's Response

As is quite evident from the discussion thus far, stereotype threat can affect our thoughts and behavior via automatic processes that run largely outside conscious awareness. However, this is not the entire story. The automatic processes that negative self-relevant stereotypes set in motion are accompanied by a number of controlled processes that can, in turn, affect performance—often for the worse but, sometimes, even for the better.

Increased Effort at the Task

A core tenet of stereotype threat theory is that it increases one's motivation to disconfirm the stereotype. Interestingly, however, increased effort is not purely a controlled or explicit process. Jamieson and Harkins (2007) articulate this idea in their mere effort account of stereotype threat. From this perspective, when people are threatened by how they might be evaluated, their increased drive to perform well increases activation of the prepotent or dominant response to the task. The problem is that one's dominant response is not always the best response to achieve success. Performance will be enhanced if the task is one that relies on a cognitively simple or well-learned thought process or behavior. But, as we will discuss in more detail below, performance will be impaired when the task is more cognitively challenging.

Research has uncovered evidence that stereotype threat increases arousal in a way that can facilitate a dominant response. For example, Ben-Zeev, Fein, and Inzlicht (2005; see also O'Brien & Crandall, 2003) demonstrated that women were faster to write their name repeatedly when they were expecting to take a math test that had revealed gender differences in the past compared to when they did not receive threatening instructions about the upcoming test. Presumably, the increased arousal due to stereotype threat facilitated a dominant response of name writing in an automatic way.

Jamieson and Harkins' (2007) mere effort account expands upon this idea of an automatic activation of a prepotent response to suggest that stereotype threat also increases one's efforts to counter that response when it is identified as an error—efforts that are likely to be more explicit and controlled in nature. To demonstrate these ideas, Jamieson and Harkins (2007) employed an antisaccade task in which people try to inhibit an automatic tendency to look toward, or saccade to, a stimulus cue that flashes to the left or the right of a central fixation point on a computer screen. On antisaccade trials, participants are explicitly instructed to look away from this cue and toward the opposite side of the screen, where a target that they have to identify will briefly appear. To be successful at this identification task, individuals must inhibit their prepotent saccade to the cue or at least quickly correct for an automatic saccade in order to see and identify the target before it disappears from the screen.

Several interesting results emerged from Jamieson and Harkins' (2007) research with this task. First, they showed that women who were told the task was related to visuospatial and math ability were more likely to saccade toward the distracting cue on trials in which they needed to inhibit this reflex, a result that is consistent with the idea that threat increases a prepotent response pattern. But they also demonstrated that women under stereotype threat were faster to launch a corrective saccade—to correct their mistake by reversing their gaze direction in time to identify the target on the opposite side of the screen. This corrective response pattern, likely stemming from their enhanced motivation to do well, seems to rely on a more controlled mode of processing, given that it was eliminated by giving women an additional cognitive load in one study.

In sum, stereotype threat enhances one's motivation to do well, but effort is not purely a function of controlled processing. Arousal or increased drive cues prepotent responses in a fairly automatic way. But when errors are identified, the motivation to disconfirm the stereotype can cue more controlled attempts to correct one's mistake.

Decreased Working Memory

Perhaps the greatest paradox of stereotype threat is that it can simultaneously increase motivation while also decreasing performance, particularly when one is performing a task that requires the mental manipulation of complex information. Indeed, Ben-Zeev and colleagues (2005) found that, in contrast to an easy name writing task, women under threat did worse than those who were not threatened on a difficult name writing task (in which people were asked to write their name backward as many times as they could for 20 seconds).

Several researchers have proposed that performance is impaired on these kinds of tasks because stereotype threat taxes working memory capacity (Beilock, 2008; Beilock et al., 2007; Schmader & Johns, 2003). Working memory can be thought of as a short-term memory system that is involved in the control, regulation, and active maintenance of a limited amount of information with immediate relevance to the task at hand (Miyake & Shah, 1999). It is also thought to allow one to focus attention on information relevant to that task, while inhibiting other irrelevant or distracting cues (Engle, 2002). Because working memory is integral to performance on sustained, effortful, and/or complex processing tasks, performance on such tasks will suffer if one's working memory resources are temporarily depleted or used for another purpose.

Support for stereotype threat's impact on working memory capacity comes from work by Schmader and Johns (2003). The researchers had women complete a working memory task and a difficult math task under control conditions or following the activation of a stereotype regarding gender differences in quantitative ability. They found that women in the stereotype threat condition showed reduced working memory capacity and poorer math test performance relative to the control group. Furthermore, working memory capacity mediated the link between stereotype threat and poorer math performance, supporting a causal relationship. Other research soon followed that confirmed the general idea that individuals under threat are mentally overloaded (Beilock et al., 2007; Croizet, Despres, Gauzins, Hugeut, & Leyens, 2004) and cognitively depleted (Inzlicht, McKay, & Aronson, 2006).

But how exactly might this working memory compromise occur? To answer this question, one must delve a little deeper into the various controlled processes regulated by working memory. Although a number of prominent working memory models differ on both structural and functional dimensions (Miyake & Shah, 1999), one of the most common is Baddeley's (2000) multicomponent model. According to this framework, a domain-general central executive controls and coordinates the information active in working memory. Some of this information is represented and maintained in domain-specific short-term stores, such as the phonological loop for acoustic/verbal information and the visual–spatial sketchpad for visual images. A fourth component, a multimodal episodic buffer, serves to bind information from the phonological loop, the visual–spatial sketchpad, and long-term memory into a unitary episodic representation. Using this analysis, we consider a couple of ways in which stereotype threat can affect working memory.

The Depleting Effects of Task Ruminations

One notable means by which working memory can be impaired when one is targeted by negative stereotypes is by saturating central executive and phonological loop resources with internal worries about one's performance (Beilock, 2008). Steele, Spencer, and Aronson (2002) suggested that stereotype threat is accompanied by explicit and verbalizable "concerns about how one will be perceived, doubts about one's ability, and thoughts about the stereotype … " (p. 392). Work by Cadinu et al. (2005) supports this idea. Women performing difficult math problems after being told that gender differences in math exist had more negative math-related thoughts and performed more poorly than did women who did not receive this information. These task worries partially mediated their impaired performance on the test (see also Beilock et al., 2007).

If stereotype threat induces distracting thoughts and worries, these internal ruminations should most heavily tax the phonological aspect of working memory thought to support inner speech and thinking in the service of complex cognitive activities (Miyake & Shah, 1999; Rapee, 1993). Moreover, signs of stereotype threat should occur most strongly for tasks that rely on verbal working memory resources in addition to general executive components. Consistent with this idea, Beilock et al. (2007) observed that women who were reminded about gender differences in math showed increased worries and negative thoughts about the situation compared to those who were not, and this translated to poor performance on difficult math problems thought to rely heavily on verbal working memory resources (but not on similar problems that were more spatial in nature).

Additional research has suggested that thoughts of doubt might be particularly detrimental to working memory when they occur in the presence of general arousal or anxiety (Schmader et al., 2009). Earlier, we suggested that stereotype threat automatically cues a sense of self-uncertainty stemming from an imbalanced set of thought processes activated in situations of threat. But that sense of uncertainty, we believe, then elicits more controlled processes aimed at interpreting and ruminating about one's performance. Although feeling somewhat anxious or aroused in a performance situation could be seen as understandable to sustain attention and engagement, if interpreted in light of self-doubt, that arousal is translated into the sort of worry likely to consume the phonological loop and deplete working memory. In a series of studies, Schmader and colleagues demonstrated that working memory deficits under stereotype threat are greatest for those who are generally most anxious, but only if they are also primed with thoughts of doubt. Anxious arousal actually predicted better working memory under stereotype threat when individuals were primed with confidence or had a dispositional tendency to reappraise negative emotions in a more positive way.

It is important to note that a heavy involvement of verbal resources in stereotype threat impairment does not exclude other subcomponents of the working memory system from being implicated. Rather, stereotype threat not only affects the functioning of the phonological loop (via verbal thoughts and worries), it can also hijack central executive functioning via attempts to suppress such thoughts. This leaves open the possibility that tasks that do not rely on phonological resources can still be impaired by stereotype threat.

Efforts To Regulate Thoughts and Emotions

As mentioned above, the central executive component of working memory provides one with the ability to focus attention and regulate thought processes. When solving complex cognitive problems, this central executive selects what information is relevant, engages in the online process of logical computation or critical thinking, and makes deliberative choices between alternative options. However, this powerful tool for controlled processing of information plays double duty for those experiencing stereotype threat. Because the experience of threat activates a goal to avoid confirmation of the stereotype, and the experience of self-doubt or anxiety is often interpreted as a sign of failure, efforts are made to detect and suppress these negative thoughts and feelings and push them out of mind. Research on self-regulatory control reveals that such suppression processes are cognitively depleting as they rely on the same central executive processes needed for other types of problem solving (Baumeister, Muraven, & Tice, 2000; Richards & Gross, 2000).

Evidence that people are ego depleted after experiencing stereotype threat comes from research by Inzlicht and colleagues (Inzlicht et al., 2006), who showed that situational reminders of one's stigmatized status led minority students expecting to take an intelligence test to perform more poorly on a Stroop interference task in one study and led women expecting to have their math ability assessed to have greater difficulty squeezing a hand-grip. Together, these effects point to general reductions in self-regulatory abilities when one is anticipating being evaluated through the lens of a stereotype. Other research has since demonstrated that these kinds of effects might occur because people under threat are actively trying to regulate the negative thoughts and feelings that have been activated by the stereotype.

For example, in one set of studies, Logel, Iserman, Davies, Quinn, and Spencer (2009) revealed that women who experience stereotype threat related to their math abilities attempt to suppress gender stereotypes, and presumably as a result, exhibit an ironic rebound in activation of these concepts later. Interestingly, when women were given a thought, either about themselves or something completely arbitrary, to replace the distracting thoughts about the stereotype, these rebound effects were attenuated and their math performance improved. In other research, Carr and Steele (2009) replicated this stereotype suppression effect and showed that the more women under threat try to suppress a negative performance stereotype, the more likely they were to perseverate on an incorrect problem-solving strategy, when switching to a different strategy would be more successful. Given that the central executive plays an important role in task switching (Crinella & Yu, 1999), this research provides some indirect evidence that effortful suppression processes underlie performance impairments.

In addition to suppressing thoughts of the stereotype, it has also been argued that stereotype threat might more commonly lead to attempts to suppress negative emotions. For example, Johns et al. (2008) provided evidence that when women and minorities experience stereotype threat, they are motivated to avoid appearing anxious, and their efforts to regulate that anxiety lead to deficits in working memory capacity. Earlier, we mentioned that, in one of these studies, women expecting to take a difficult math test had their attention automatically drawn toward anxiety-related stimuli in a dot probe paradigm. In this paradigm, participants have to identify the location of a dot as above or below a fixation point. Prior to each trial, however, two words are flashed on the screen for one second, one in the upper and one in the lower position. If people are anxious (as they tend to be under stereotype threat), their attention tends to be pulled toward the anxiety-related word, and they are faster to identify the dot if it is in that same position (and slower if the subsequent dot is in the other position).

However, the effect was only exhibited when women didn't know what this task was meant to assess. When they knew how the task could reveal their anxiety, they showed evidence of anxiety suppression: They were faster to identify the dot when it was in the same position as the neutral word, suggesting that they were actively trying to avoid appearing anxious. Interestingly, the more their reaction times revealed a motivation to suppress anxiety, the lower their working memory on a subsequent task. Another study revealed similar low levels of inhibitory control among women in two conditions: a standard stereotype threat condition and a threat condition in which they were explicitly instructed to suppress their emotional reactions, compared to third threat condition in which women were instructed to remain objective during the tasks. Again, this result suggests that stereotype threat might elicit spontaneous efforts to suppress one's emotional reactions during a performance situation. Because the cognitive mechanism used for this kind of regulatory control is the same one needed to do well on complex cognitive tasks, performance suffers.

Finally, recent advances in our ability to examine neurological function during a situation of stereotype threat also point to the involvement of brain regions that most typically underlie emotion regulation. For example, a study by Krendl and colleagues (2008) revealed greater activation in the ventral anterior cingulate cortex among women experiencing stereotype threat compared to those in a control condition. Activation in this same region was found in work by Wraga, Helt, Jacobs, and Sullivan (2007), who created stereotype threat in women about their spatial abilities relative to men. Given evidence that this region is activated in other situations involving social evaluation and emotion regulation, these results provide converging evidence for these processes being activated when people experience stereotype threat.

Threat Depends on the Task

Stereotype threat can impact performance in a variety of ways that are both controlled and automatic in nature. But, to truly understand the threat phenomenon, one cannot just consider the cognitive and neural mechanisms by which it occurs. Some of the processes that result from stereotype threat—a vigilance-based mindset and explicit monitoring of one's performance—have different effects on performance depending on the situation and task at hand.

As we have already seen from the work presented above, on simple tasks in which one's dominant response is the optimal response, or on tasks in which people have time to correct their prepotent response and know what that correction should be, performance can be enhanced rather than harmed under threat (Jamieson & Harkins, 2007). In the case of the antisaccade task used by Jamieson and Harkins, for example, increased vigilance is beneficial. However, this is not always true.

For instance, Beilock and colleagues (2006) examined stereotype threat's impact on expert golf putting, a skill that, unlike the antisaccade task, is harmed when too much attention is allocated to performance and not when working memory is impaired. Beilock et al. found that well-learned golf putting is susceptible to stereotype threat, but that giving expert golfers a secondary task eliminates stereotype threat–induced impairment. Distracting attention away from the stereotyped behavior eliminated the harmful impact of negative stereotype activation, suggesting that performance degradation under threat can occur when too much attention is allocated to processes that usually run more automatically. That is, unlike in the antisaccade task, increased vigilance to the task is not always a good thing.

Thus, it seems as if stereotype threat can alter performance in multiple ways. It populates working memory with worries, and it entices the performer to try to pay attention to step-by-step control, possibly resulting from motivation to succeed. Whether or not such effects will be beneficial or detrimental depends on the nature of the task being performed.

Policy Box

Understanding the mechanisms that underlie the experience of stereotype threat yields insight into the ways in which threat can be reduced. Our focus on examining the automatic and controlled components to threat-induced performance impairments points to two broad types of interventions: those that seek to change situations that would induce threat in the first place, and those that provide individuals with coping strategies to contend with stereotype threat when it is triggered. Armed with this framework, education and organizational policies should be aimed at two key solutions. First, affirmative action policies are an efficacious approach not only because they involve targeted efforts to recruit and retain those individuals whose past performance on standardized tests might under-represent their true ability, but also because they provide the next generation with role models that build an important cognitive association between the stigmatized group and success in the domain. This is the most critical step in breaking down stereotypes. In addition, efforts need to be made to educate the public about how stereotypes subtly impair performance. Broad understanding of these mechanisms is essential not only for justifying the continuing need of affirmative action policy, but also to provide those who experience stereotype threat with a new awareness of their phenomenological experience and the appraisals they need to cope with the threats imposed by negative stereotypes.

■ A GUIDE FOR REDUCING STEREOTYPE THREAT EFFECTS ON PERFORMANCE

As we have reviewed, situations that remind us that we are negatively stereotyped set in motion a sequence of automatic and controlled processes that roughly correspond to the detection of threat to one's identity and subsequent efforts to cope with that threat. So, now that we understand how these impairments come about, the critical question is whether that information can inform how stereotype threat is reduced or eliminated. Following from our analysis, we consider two broad categories of remedies: those that decrease the activation of threat in the first place and those that increase one's ability to cope with the threat after it has been perceived. Because other chapters will provide a more exhaustive review of remedies (see Aronson & Dee, 2011, Chapter 17, this volume; Cohen, Purdie-Vaughns, & Garcia, 2011, Chapter 18, this volume), our goal here is merely to relate these effects to the processes we have outlined.

Threat Inoculations

One way to combat the experience of stereotype threat is to reduce the likelihood that such threatening cognitions get activated in the first place, leading to the cognitive imbalance discussed earlier. Most obviously, as stereotypes change and become less prevalent in a culture, the ability for situations to cue those beliefs is diminished. For example, structural changes that balance the representation of people in different occupations and roles can effectively erode the automatic associations that people have (Dasgupta & Asgari, 2004). In fact, the direct retraining of implicit stereotypes can boost women's working memory and increase their math performance even under stereotype threat (Forbes & Schmader, 2010). Many students report a belief that stereotypes (at least as they pertain to gender roles) will diminish over the coming years (Diekman & Eagly, 2000), giving us some reason for optimism. But even if the larger cultural stereotypes are slow to change, situations can be modified to include threat inoculations. The presence of role models (Marx & Roman, 2002) or affirmations of other good qualities of one's group (McIntyre, Paulson, & Lord, 2003) can dull the threatening sting that the stereotype might normally have.

Because stereotype threat results from an imbalance of thoughts activated in the situation, the likelihood that the threatening stereotype will be applied to oneself is also dependent on one's perceived identification with the stereotyped group (Schmader, 2002). Not surprisingly then, individuals cope with stereotype threat by distancing themselves from activities that would signal a stereotypical connection to the group (Pronin et al., 2004; Steele & Aronson, 1995). But strengthening one's confidence in the domain might also be effective at reducing the automatic activation of threat (Schmader et al., 2009).

Working from the idea that threat is triggered from an activated imbalance of thoughts that impugn the identity of oneself and/or one's group, we can infer that threat can also be alleviated by manipulations that allow one to tolerate specific instances of dissonance by affirming the self. As discussed by Cohen et al. (2011, Chapter 18, this volume), a simple affirmation of one's own values can lead to a dramatic increase in grades and academic motivation among minority college students (Cohen, Garcia, Apfel, & Master, 2006). Reminders of the complexity in one's self-concept can also diffuse the threat of being targeted by a stereotype (Gresky, Ten Eyck, Lord, & McIntyre, 2005; Rosenthal & Crisp, 2006).

A Better Way to Cope

If threat itself cannot be reduced, interventions can facilitate more effective ways of coping with stereotype threat. At first glance, it might seem that problem-focused coping strategies are always called for. But, as we have already discussed, too much effort or conscious attention to the task can sometimes further compromise performance (Beilock et al., 2006; Jamieson & Harkins, 2007). A better approach than trying to channel more controlled processing to the task at hand is to figure out how to channel fewer cognitive resources to ineffective emotion-focused coping efforts. The explicit processes of monitoring one's performance and suppressing unwanted thoughts and feelings both stem from an initial appraisal that errors, anxiety, and self-doubt are all evidence that one is confirming a negative stereotype about one's group. Changing this appraisal can effectively eliminate the need for these additional processes. Several pieces of evidence now point to these effects.

First, it is notable that individuals who generally report a tendency to reframe their negative feelings in a more positive way show a positive relationship between sympathetic nervous system activation and task performance in a stereotype threatening domain (Schmader et al., 2009). For them, anxiety seems to be reframed as a challenge rather than a threat. But even if a person doesn't have a natural disposition to reappraise threats, he or she can be taught that anxiety is not necessarily a sign of failure, and with this reappraisal show less of effortful anxiety suppression, greater working memory, and as a consequence better test performance (Johns et al., 2008).

In addition to helping individuals reappraise what anxiety means, interventions can inform individuals about where anxiety comes from. When women were taught about stereotype threat and its ability to induce anxiety and impair performance, they performed at the same level as their male counterparts and significantly better than women merely expecting to take a diagnostic math test (Johns, Schmader, & Martens, 2005). Knowing that anxiety is an indication of cultural stereotypes rather than an indication of one's own ability seems to enable people to distance themselves from these negative feelings and perform better as a result. Having knowledge of these effects really does grant the power to overcome them.

■ CONCLUSION

As we have reviewed, being the target of negative stereotypes in a domain that one cares about elicits a host of processes at both implicit and explicit levels. Stereotypes are automatically activated that call into question, at an implicit level, one's association to the domain. The resulting cognitive imbalance cues uncertainty that drives vigilance toward any cue that might signal that one is confirming the stereotype. It is when these cues are detected that more explicit and controlled processes kick in. These include added efforts to correct mistakes; explicit monitoring, worrying, and rumination about one's performance; and active efforts to suppress these negative thoughts and feelings that are assumed to distract from the task at hand.

Fortunately, an understanding of these mechanisms allows us to identify solutions. Indeed, research has uncovered a host of solutions. Some of these reduce the experience of threat in the first place by affecting the initial cognitions that prompt a cognitive imbalance between self, group, and domain. Others help establish performance skills that are impervious to threat or free up working memory for use at cognitively complex tasks by helping individuals reappraise the situation and their reaction to it in a less negative or self-relevant way. Finally, other strategies help individuals keep skills that normally operate outside working memory running smoothly without too much explicit control.

It used to be standard language in research papers that little is known about what mediates the effect of stereotype threat on performance. This is no longer the case. Research has revealed a great deal about the underlying mechanisms, and we are optimistic that the knowledge gained from this research can help educators, administrators, and individuals combat the pernicious effects that negative stereotypes can have on performance. In fact, knowing that these effects exist and how they work seems to be one means of diffusing their effects. The future of research, then, is not only to delve deeper in search of more mediators, but to expand outward to show how the knowledge we have gained from this basic science approach can be applied in the field to create practical interventions that enable individuals to truly perform up to their potential.

References

Aronson, J., & Dee, T. (2011). Stereotype threat in the real world. In M. Inzlicht, & T. Schmader (Eds.), *Stereotype threat: Theory, process, and application*. New York: Oxford University Press.

Baddeley, A. D. (2000). The episodic buffer: A new component of working memory? *Trends in Cognitive Sciences, 4*, 417–423.

Baumeister, R. F., Muraven, M., & Tice, D. M. (2000). Ego depletion: A resource model of volition, self-regulation, and controlled processing. *Social Cognition, 18*, 130–150.

Beilock, S. L. (2008). Math performance in stressful situations. *Current Directions in Psychological Science, 17*, 339–343.

Beilock, S. L., Jellison, W. A., Rydell, R. J., McConnell, A. R., & Carr, T. H. (2006). On the causal mechanisms of stereotype threat: Can skills that don't rely heavily on working memory still be threatened? *Personality and Social Psychology Bulletin, 32*, 1059–1071.

Beilock, S. L., Rydell, R. J., & McConnell, A. R. (2007). Stereotype threat and working memory: Mechanisms, alleviations, and spillover. *Journal of Experimental Psychology: General, 136*, 256–276.

Ben-Zeev, T., Fein, S., & Inzlicht, M. (2005). Arousal and stereotype threat. *Journal of Experimental Social psychology, 41*, 174–181.

Cadinu, M., Maass, A., Rosabianca, A., & Kiesner, J. (2005). Why do women underperform under stereotype threat? Evidence for the role of negative thinking. *Psychological Science, 16*, 572–578.

Carr, P. B., & Steele, C. M. (2009). Stereotype threat and inflexible perseverance in problem solving. *Journal of Experimental Social Psychology, 45*, 853–859.

Cohen, G. L., Garcia, J., Apfel, N., & Master, A. (2006). Reducing the racial achievement gap: A social-psychological intervention. *Science, 313*, 1307–1310.

Cohen, G. L., Purdie-Vaughns, V., & Garcia, J. (2011). An identity threat perspective on intervention. In M. Inzlicht, & T. Schmader (Eds.), *Stereotype threat: Theory, process, and application*. New York: Oxford University Press.

Crinella, F. M., & Yu, J. (1999). Brain mechanisms and intelligence: Psychometric g and executive function. *Intelligence, 27*, 299–327.

Croizet, J. C., Despres, G., Gauzins, M., Hugeut, P., & Leyens, J. (2004). Stereotype threat undermines performance by triggering a disruptive mental load. *Personality and Social Psychology Bulletin, 30*, 721–731.

Dasgupta, N., & Asgari, S. (2004). Seeing is believing: Exposure to counterstereotypic women leaders and its effect on automatic gender stereotyping. *Journal of Experimental Social Psychology, 40*, 642–658.

Diekman, A. B., & Eagly, A. H. (2000). Stereotypes as dynamic constructs: Women and men of the past, present, and future. *Personality and Social Psychology Bulletin, 26*, 1171–1188.

Engle, R. W. (2002). Working memory capacity as executive attention. *Current Directions in Psychological Science, 11*, 19–23.

Festinger, L. (1957). *A theory of cognitive dissonance.* Stanford, CA: Stanford University.

Forbes, C. E., & Schmader, T. (2010). Retraining implicit attitudes and stereotypes to distinguish motivation from performance in a stereotype threatening domain. *Journal of Personality and Social Psychology.99*, 740–754.

Forbes, C., Schmader, T., & Allen, J. J. B. (2008). The role of devaluing and discounting in performance monitoring: A neurophysiological study of minorities under threat. Social Cognitive Affective Neuroscience, 3, 253-261.

Gehring, W. J., Goss, B., Coles, M. G. H., Meyer, D. E., & Donchin, E. (1993). A neural system for error detection and compensation. *Psychological Science, 4*, 385–390.

Gresky, D. M., Ten Eyck, L. L., Lord, C. G., & McIntyre, R. B. (2005). Effects of salient multiple identities on women's performance under mathematics stereotype threat. *Sex Roles, 53*, 703–716.

Hajcak, G., McDonald, N., & Simons, R. F (2003). Anxiety and error-related brain activity. *Biological Psychology, 64*, 77–90.

Inzlicht, M., McKay, L., & Aronson, J. (2006). Stigma as ego depletion: How being the target of prejudice affects self-control. *Psychological Science, 17*, 262–269.

Jamieson, J. P., & Harkins, S. G. (2007). Mere effort and stereotype threat performance effects. *Journal of Personality and Social Psychology, 93*, 544–564.

Johns, M. J., Inzlicht, M., & Schmader, T. (2008). Stereotype threat and executive resource depletion: Examining the influence of emotion regulation. *Journal of Experimental Psychology: General, 137*, 691–705.

Johns, M., & Schmader, T. (2010). Meta-cognitive regulation as a reaction to the uncertainty of stereotype threat. In R. M. Arkin, K. C. Oleson, & P. J. Carroll (Eds.), The uncertain self: A handbook of perspectives from social and personality psychology (pp. 176-192). Lawrence Erlbaum Associates.

Johns, M., Schmader, T., & Martens, A. (2005). Knowing is half the battle: Teaching stereotype threat as a means of improving women's math performance. *Psychological Science, 16*, 175–179.

Kaiser, C. R., Vick, S. B., & Major, B. (2006). Prejudice expectations moderate preconscious attention to cues that are threatening to social identity. *Psychological Science, 17*, 332–338.

Krendl, A. C., Richeson, J. A., Kelley, W. M., & Heatherton, T. F. (2008). The negative consequences of threat: An fMRI investigation of the neural mechanisms underlying women's underperformance in math. *Psychological Science,19*, 168–175.

Logel, C., Iserman, E. C., Davies, P. G., Quinn, D. M., & Spencer, S. J. (2009). The perils of double consciousness: The role of thought suppression in stereotype threat. *Journal of Experimental Social Psychology, 45*, 299–312.

Martens, A., Johns, M., Greenberg, J., & Schimel, J. (2006). Combating stereotype threat: The effects of self-affirmation on women's math performance. *Journal of Experimental Social Psychology, 42,* 236–243.

Marx, D. M., & Roman, J. S. (2002). Female role models: Protecting women's math test performance. *Personality and Social Psychology Bulletin, 28,* 1183–1193.

Marx, D. M. (2011). Differentiating theories: A comparison of stereotype threat and stereotype priming effects. In M. Inzlicht, & T. Schmader (Eds.), *Stereotype threat: Theory, process, and application.* New York: Oxford University Press.

McIntyre, R. B., Paulson, R. M., & Lord, C. G. (2003). Alleviating women's mathematics stereotype threat through salience of group achievements. *Journal of Experimental Social Psychology, 39,* 83–90.

Mendes, W. B., & Jamieson, J. (2011). Embodied stereotype threat: Exploring brain and body mechanisms underlying performance impairments. In M. Inzlicht, & T. Schmader (Eds.), *Stereotype threat: Theory, process, and application.* New York: Oxford University Press.

Miyake, A., & Shah, P. (1999). *Models of working memory: Mechanisms of active maintenance and executive control.* New York: Cambridge University Press.

Murphy, M., & Jones, V. D. (2011). The role of situational cues in signaling and maintaining stereotype threat. In M. Inzlicht, & T. Schmader (Eds.), *Stereotype threat: Theory, process, and application.* New York: Oxford University Press.

O'Brien, L. T., & Crandall, C. S. (2003). Stereotype threat and arousal: Effects on women's math performance. *Personality and Social Psychology Bulletin, 29,* 782–789.

Pronin, E., Steele, C. M., & Ross, L. (2004). Identity bifurcation in response to stereotype threat: Women and mathematics. *Journal of Experimental Social Psychology, 40,* 152–168.

Rapee, R. M. (1993). The utilization of working memory by worry. *Behavioral Research Therapy, 31,* 617–620.

Richards, J. M., & Gross, J. J. (2000). Emotion regulation and memory: The cognitive costs of keeping one's cool. *Journal of Personality and Social Psychology, 79,* 410–424.

Rosenthal, H. E. S., & Crisp, R. J. (2006). Reducing stereotype threat by blurring intergroup boundaries. *Personality and Social Psychology Bulletin, 32,* 501–511.

Rydell, R. J., McConnell, A. R., & Beilock, S. L. (2010). Multiple social identities and stereotype threat: Imbalance, accessibility, and working memory. *Journal of Personality and Social Psychology, 96,* 949–966.

Schmader, T. (2002). Gender identification moderates stereotype threat effects on women's math performance. *Journal of Experimental Social Psychology, 38,* 194–201.

Schmader, T., Forbes, C. E., Zhang, S., & Mendes, W. B. (2009). A meta-cognitive perspective on cognitive deficits experienced in intellectually threatening environments. *Personality and Social Psychology Bulletin, 35,* 584–596.

Schmader, T., & Johns, M. (2003). Converging evidence that stereotype threat reduces working memory capacity. *Journal of Personality and Social Psychology, 85,* 440–452.

Schmader, T., Johns, M., & Forbes, C. (2008). An integrated process model of stereotype threat effects on performance. *Psychological Review, 115,* 336–356.

Spencer, S. J., Steele, C. M., & Quinn, D. M. (1999). Stereotype threat and women's math performance. *Journal of Experimental Social Psychology, 35,* 4–28.

Stangor, C., Carr, C., & Kiang, L. (1998). Activating stereotypes undermines task performance expectations. *Journal of Personality and Social Psychology, 75,* 1191–1197.

Steele, C. M., & Aronson, J. (1995). Stereotype threat and the intellectual test performance of African Americans. *Journal of Personality and Social Psychology, 69,* 797–811.

Steele, C. M., Spencer, S. J., & Aronson, J. (2002). Contending with images of one's group: The psychology of stereotype and social identity threat. In M. Zanna (Ed.), *Advances in experimental social psychology*. San Diego: Academic Press.

Wheeler, S. C., & Petty, R. E. (2001). The effects of stereotype activation on behavior: A review of possible mechanisms. *Psychological Bulletin, 127,* 797–826.

Wraga, M., Helt, M., Jacobs, E., & Sullivan, K. (2007). Neural basis of stereotype-induced shifts in women's mental rotation performance. *Social Cognition and Affective Neuroscience, 2,* 12–19.

4 Embodied Stereotype Threat

Exploring Brain and Body Mechanisms
Underlying Performance Impairments

■ WENDY BERRY MENDES AND
JEREMY JAMIESON

In this chapter, we explore brain and body mechanisms that link the experience of stereotype threat to changes in cognitive and behavioral performance. We begin by identifying a model of causal sequences of stereotype threat: psychological states associated with stereotype threat, neurobiological responses triggered by these psychological states, and cognitive and behavioral outcomes that are influenced by the neurobiological states. We explore this theoretical path analysis throughout the chapter, focusing on two broad psychological states often implicated in stereotype-threat processes: stress arousal and vigilance. To explore stress arousal as an explanation for stereotype threat performance effects, we highlight the biology underlying stress systems, stress typologies, and temporal trajectories of stress responses. We highlight how these neurobiological changes can influence cognitive and behavioral outcomes, and review existing stereotype threat research that explores these neurobiological responses. We then examine the broad category of vigilance in stereotype threat processes, and again highlight extant stereotype threat literature exploring neurobiological changes associated with vigilance. The intent of the chapter is to provide a neurobiological framework to assist stereotype threat researchers in identifying possible brain and body mechanisms that may be directly or indirectly implicated in performance changes engendered by stereotype threat.

Keywords: Stereotype threat, biological mechanisms, autonomic nervous system, neuroscience, challenge, threat, stress

Performance changes brought on by stereotype threat appear to be reliable and robust across many domains. Indeed, so reliable are stereotype threat effects on performance that much of the current research on this topic focuses on *why* it happens rather than *if* or *when*. In the search for the answer (or answers) to how negative stereotypes influence performance changes, researchers have identified several candidate mechanisms. In an influential review paper, Schmader, Johns, and Forbes (2008) present a process model in which they implicate three mechanisms that may underlie impairments in working memory brought on by stereotype threat: stress arousal, vigilance, and self-regulation. In this chapter, we capitalize on two of these mechanisms—stress arousal and vigilance—to explore how knowledge of negative stereotypes affects performance via brain and bodily mechanisms. That is, we delve under the skin to bring to light biological and neuroscience evidence that illuminates if, when, and how the body and brain responses can be viewed as direct or indirect causal effects on performance changes as a result of stereotype threat.

We explore these mechanisms by first describing what is known about how the underlying neurobiology is initiated by psychological states, which allows us to identify when we might expect a neurobiological response to be implicated in stereotype threat performance effects. We then examine the empirical evidence linking these brain and bodily responses to cognitive and behavioral outcomes, which sharpens our understanding of which types of tasks might be more susceptible to performance decrements and what the time course of the impairment might be. We then narrow our attention to stereotype threat research and review the extant literature with a focus on interpreting these data, given what we know about the underlying biology. We end with speculations on future directions and possible interventions targeted at mind–body effects to reduce performance impairments that follow from stereotype threat.

The overall model that we explore in this chapter in presented in Figure 4.1 and is referenced throughout. The figure presents three columns: psychological states, neurobiological responses, and performance outcomes. We present this figure as a theoretical path analysis that examines putative relationships between psychology and neurobiology, and then between neurobiology and cognitive and physical outcomes. The arrows connecting the columns represent the amount of empirical data supporting the relationships, with thicker arrows indicating a larger and more reliable body of work based on a qualitative review of the literature.

What might be most striking about Figure 4.1 is the number and strength of arrows connecting psychological states with neurobiological changes (i.e., left side of Figure 4.1) relative to the connections between the neurobiological changes and the performance outcomes (i.e., right side of Figure 4.1). Related to this, the theoretical path analysis suggests neurobiological responses as mediators linking psychological states of stereotype threat and performance outcomes; however, as we review the literature, we will see that a paucity of studies link neurobiological responses to performance outcomes, and even fewer studies demonstrate neurobiological mediation. We discuss why this may be the case and suggest studies to explore possible direct and indirect neurobiological mechanisms involved in stereotype processes.

It also is important to note that, due to space constraints, several potentially important factors are not discussed in this chapter. For example, Figure 4.1 presents the stereotype path as initiating with psychological states, which then triggers neurobiological responses. This assumes that psychology always precedes biology, and thus ignores the importance of individual differences in the neurobiological milieu that may make one more likely to experience a psychological state. We touch on this point when we discuss stereotype threat as a chronic stressor that may,

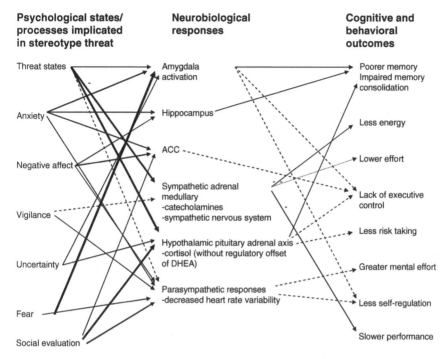

Figure 4.1 The left side of the figure depicts relationships between psychological states and processes associated with neurobiological changes. The right side of the figure indicates relationships between the neurobiological changes and cognitive or physical outcomes. The thickness of the arrow represents the greater quality and quantity of data supporting the link. All arrows represent positive associations unless indicated with a minus (-) sign.

over time, result in dysregulated hypothalamic-pituitary-adrenal cortical (HPA) functioning, but the importance of individual differences in neurobiology and how that influences stereotype processes is worthy of its own chapter and is not explored in depth here.

■ STRESS AROUSAL

Possibly the first thing that comes to mind when one thinks about stress arousal and academic performance is *test anxiety*—the idea that, when facing an important test, one's excessive worry over performance can instigate a cascade of bodily changes that can directly undermine performance. Stereotype threat theory suggests that this "stress" or "anxiety" might be behind performance impairment (Ben-Zeev, Fein, & Inzlicht, 2005; O'Brien & Crandall, 2003), but stress and anxiety are fuzzy constructs and require greater precision in exactly what is meant by these terms to be of value in understanding their roles in stereotype threat. For example, there are two critical distinctions of stress arousal: acute versus chronic, and adaptive versus mal-adaptive. Here, we highlight that not all stress responses are created equal, and by drawing these distinctions we can derive more specific hypotheses regarding the effects of *stress arousal* as a potential explanation for performance impairments brought on by stereotype threat.

Stress Systems

There are two primary stress systems: the *sympathetic-adrenal-medullary* (SAM) and *hypothalamic-pituitary-adrenal cortical* (HPA) axes. At the risk of oversimplification, one can think of the SAM system as activating during fight-or-flight situations, whereas the HPA system is more conservative and requires more intense affective or physical states to disrupt its diurnal cycle. When the SAM system is activated, epinephrine is released from the adrenal medulla, which contributes to several changes in the body such as increasing heart rate, dilating pupils, and inhibiting the gastrointestinal tract. HPA activation is initiated in the hypothalamus, which releases corticotropin releasing hormone (CRH), triggering the anterior pituitary to release adrenocorticotropin hormone (ACTH), which then travels to the adrenal cortex and stimulates the adrenal cortex to release hormones, especially cortisol.

Acute Versus Chronic Stress Arousal

The distinctions in the time course and intensity required to activate these systems are critical to both understanding how stereotype threat operates in people's daily lives as well as to how scientists approach studying stereotype threat processes in the lab. When considering how stress arousal may explain stereotype threat effects on performance in one's daily life, it is useful to first draw the distinction between environmental triggers that are *acute* versus *chronic*. For example, an acute environmental trigger would be one that occurs with little warning, such as being a student who is called upon in a classroom. In this split second, the SAM system could respond with a cascade of physiological changes that could impair (or enhance) cognitive performance, but implicating the full cascade of HPA-axis stress responses with cortisol as the end product is not likely to be a candidate for understanding performance outcomes because of the time course of HPA activation. Thus, acute situations are more likely to be mediated by changes in SAM, especially when they occur with little warning.

Stereotype threat as a chronic stressor would look very different. For example, consider a college engineering course that is well into the semester and comprises primarily male students, is taught by a male professor, and the classroom walls are lined with pictures of famous engineers, all of whom happen to be male. For a female engineering student in the course, especially one who is sensitive to these stereotype threat triggers, each class session might result in incrementally more "stress," which would accumulate over time. She might wake up the morning of the class feeling anxious, be preoccupied with thoughts about her performance on the way to class, and sit in class thinking that at any moment she will be called upon and be in jeopardy of being negatively evaluated by the professor and the other class members. This scenario describes a *chronic stressor* and, to the extent that the environment was perceived as socially evaluative and *threatening*, we would expect over-activation of the HPA axis. Evidence of *hyper-responsiveness* of the HPA would be indicated by higher waking cortisol the day of the engineering class, less habituation of HPA responses to the classroom, and slower recovery following the end of the class. Interestingly, if this environment repeated over years, rather than months, eventually the HPA responses would likely be dysregulated and possibly show *hyporesponsiveness*, or a flattened diurnal cycle. It is interesting to speculate that hyporesponsiveness may be associated with the psychological disengagement in stereotyped academic domains seen among stigmatized group members (Davies, Spencer, Quinn, & Gerhardstein, 2002). From a chronic stress perspective, we would anticipate that an overactive HPA response would influence low-affinity receptors in the hippocampus and begin to impair memory (Figure 4.1). Individuals who perceive their environment as an unremitting source of stereotype threat may develop an overactive HPA response, which may impair both learning and recall of knowledge.

The above section may lead the casual reader to infer that acute stress activates SAM and chronic stress activates HPA, but this would be a faulty conclusion. HPA activation most certainly can occur during acute stress, and indeed a large literature examining cortisol as an end product of acute stress states relies almost exclusively on cortisol as the primary measure of stress (see Dickerson & Kemeny, 2004, for a review). Our point here is that acute HPA activation as an explanation for performance impairments brought on by stereotype threat is probably more likely to occur during anticipated important, but isolated, events like a standardized test (e.g., SAT, GRE, MCAT), an oral presentation, or a job interview.

Adaptive Versus Maladaptive Stress Responses

Independent of the acute versus chronic distinction of stress arousal, not all stress responses are created equal. Indeed, it is problematic to think of stress as a unidimensional construct that ranges from low to high, with high stress interpreted as maladaptive. There are at least two problems with this conception. First, this view of stress fails to acknowledge that some stress responses are benign and, indeed, part of the adaptive response required because reactivity mobilizes energy to cope with the task at hand. The second problem is that low levels of "stress arousal" may actually indicate withdrawal or disengagement from a task, which would manifest itself in low stress arousal but also poor performance. For both of these problems, a detailed understanding of stress system typologies allows us to understand both the psychological states that bring about stereotype threat, and also how neurobiological responses may contribute to performance impairments.

Challenge and Threat Theory

Several theories have differentiated adaptive stress from maladaptive stress (e.g., Dienstbier, 1989). *Challenge and threat theory* (Blascovich & Mendes, 2010), for example, integrates appraisals and psychophysiological theories and makes predictions regarding distinctions in cardiovascular reactivity resulting from appraisal processes. The basic tenets of this theory are that an individual's perceptions of how demanding a task is can be offset by his assessment of the personal and situational resources he has to meet the tasks demands (see Lazarus & Folkman, 1991). For example, imagine a student taking a final exam for an important class. That exam could vary on many dimensions, such as its difficulty, its grading structure, and the number and types of questions. All of those features can be appraised in terms of the "demands" of the exam, and different students will assess those demands differently. But simply how demanding the test is does not necessarily predict responses to taking the exam. Individuals also can assess their resources to complete the exam. How much did they study, do they have natural ability in this domain, do they have dispositional styles that make them more optimistic (and hence more likely to persevere on difficult questions), or were they allowed to bring in notes that have the information they need to answer some of the questions? All of these components would be considered resources. Challenge and threat theory maintains that responses to stressful situations are a combination of individuals' assessments of available resources relative to task demands: When resources are higher than demands, individuals are more likely to experience *challenge*, whereas when demands exceed resources, individuals experience *threat*.

Importantly, these psychological states of challenge and threat can be differentiated by changes in physiological responses that are concomitant with the experiences. Specifically, challenge states tend to be associated with greater SAM activation and are characterized by increases in ventricular contractility, cardiac efficiency (i.e., greater cardiac output), and vasodilation in the arterioles, which together provides greater blood flow to the brain and periphery. Similar to challenge states, threat states also are characterized by an increase in sympathetic activation, but in contrast to challenge, threat states consist of less efficient cardiac responses and vasoconstriction. These patterns may be critical in understanding stereotype threat processes because these physiological states can either facilitate (in challenge) or impair (in threat) performance.

Stress Typologies Influence Cognition

The distinction of adaptive and maladaptive stress allows for a more nuanced understanding of how stress influences performance. For example, in Dienstbier's (1989) review of physiologically "tough" patterns, he questioned the commonly held belief that "arousal" would be related to cognitive or behavioral performance in a curvilinear relation (similar to the Yerkes-Dodson principle). Numerous studies show strong linear relations, with no evidence of curvilinear effects, between SAM activation and cognitive and physical performance. Most typically, greater cate-cholamine increases from baseline are associated with better math performance among students (Dienstbier, 1989; Jamieson, Mendes, Blackstock, & Schmader, 2010), and physical performance also yields a similar finding: Greater increases in catecholamines are associated with better technical competence among military paratroopers in training (Ursin, Baade, & Levine, 1978).

Profiles associated with challenge and threat responses have also been associated with performance outcomes. In a number of experiments, individuals who experi-enced "challenge" performed better at cognitive tasks, such as word-finding and pattern recognition tasks (e.g., Blascovich, Mendes, Hunter, & Salomon, 1999), which is consistent with the linear relationship between sympathetic nervous system activation and performance. In one recent study in which participants were randomly assigned to experience challenge *or* threat states, those in the challenge condition provided more accurate answers in an anchor-and-adjustment decision-making task (Kassam, Koslov, & Mendes, 2009). Importantly, the cardiovascular responses differentiating challenge from threat *mediated* the relationship between the psychological state and the decision-making outcome, implicating bodily changes brought on by challenge to be associated with improved decision-making outcomes.

In contrast, there is evidence for the inverted U-relation (Yerkes-Dodson) when considering HPA activation—specifically cortisol responses—on performance. For example, memory is improved when there are small increases in cortisol, but is impaired at higher levels of cortisol (Lovallo & Thomas, 2000). The inverted-U relation may be explained by different receptors in the hippocampus, which has high-affinity and low-affinity receptors for cortisol. At low levels of cortisol produc-tion, high-affinity receptors are activated, which can improve memory. However, at higher levels of cortisol production, or when cortisol is chronically activated, the low-affinity receptors are activated, which can impair memory (Reul & de Kloet, 1985). Taken together, we expect that during active tasks, SAM activation more often has a linear relationship with cognitive and behavioral performance measures, whereas HPA activation shows an inverted-U between arousal and performance.

Stereotype Threat Studies

These biological processes provide us with a framework to understanding when and how stereotype threat might influence performance, especially given the previous distinction between acute and chronic stress and adaptive versus maladaptive stress responses. For example, an adaptive response to acute stress would be characterized by a strong sympathetic response in which we would expect improved cognitive and physical performance, especially on tasks that benefit from effort and perseverance but less relevant for tasks that are retrieval based (Figure 4.1). Therefore, the predic-tion would be that if a negative stereotype is activated and this resulted in a shift to greater perceived demands relative to resources, then we would expect to observe a psychological threat state. However, if resources are already high or are increased, then the negative stereotype might not result in impaired performance. Thus, this theory might be useful to understand when primed negative stereotypes do not impair performance or assist in developing interventions to combat existing negative stereotypes.

Since the first conceptualization of stereotype threat, arousal/anxiety has been hypothesized to be part of the process through which performance is impaired (Steele & Aronson, 1995). However, there is little work that actually measures biological responses during performance situations associated with stereotype threat, although several research traditions implicate stress without measuring it; for example, misattribution of arousal paradigms (Ben-Zeev et al., 2005). We reviewed the literature to identify published studies that directly measured physiological responses associated with "stress" (Table 4.1).

One of the first studies to provide evidence that stress arousal was associated with the experience of stereotype threat examined blood pressure changes during

TABLE 4.1 *Summary of empirical papers exploring neurobiological consequences of stereotype threat*

Author(s)	Year	Target Group	Neurobiological Measure	Performance Measure	Mediation Found
Blascovich, Spencer, Quinn, & Steele	2001	African-Americans	Mean arterial blood pressure	Remote associates test	Not reported
Croizet, Despres, Gauzin, Huguet, Leyens, & Meot	2004	Academic major	HRV	Raven progressive matrices test	Yes
Derks, Inzlicht, & Kang	2008	Women	EEG	Stroop & automatic face evaluation	Yes
Forbes, Schmader, & Allen	2008	Latinos/African Americans	EEG	Flanker task	Not reported
Inzlicht & Kang	2010	Women	EEG	Stroop	Yes
Josephs, Newman, Brown, & Beer	2003	Women	Testosterone	Quantitative GRE	Not reported
Krendl, Richeson, Kelley, & Heatherton	2008	Women	fMRI	Mixed math: arithmetic & modular arithmetic	Not reported
Matheson & Cole	2004	College identity	Cortisol	None reported	
Murphy, Steele, & Gross	2007	Women	Sympathetic activation	Recall test	Not reported
Osborne	2007	Women	Sympathetic activation/blood pressure	Quantitative GRE	Not reported
Vick, Seery, Weisbuch, & Blascovich	2008	Women	Cardiovascular reactivity	Quantitative GRE: just comparison problems	Not reported
Wraga, Helt, Jacobs, & Sullivan	2006	Women	fMRI	Mental rotation task	Yes

HRV, heart rate variability; EEG, electroencephalogram; fMRI, functional magnetic resonance imaging two 5-minute blocks of the remote associates task (RAT) in which European American and African American participants were randomly assigned to either a "tests are racially biased" condition or a "tests are unbiased" condition (Blascovich, Spencer, Quinn, & Steele, 2001). African American participants assigned to the biased test condition (the stereotype threat manipulation) exhibited greater mean arterial blood pressure relative to the other three conditions. Importantly, however, race by condition did not show a robust interaction until the second block of the task. This finding is not surprising, given the temporal trajectories of adaptive and maladaptive stress responses—sluggish habituation for maladaptive stress, but quick habituation for adaptive stress responses. There was no evidence, however, that the physiological response *mediated* performance effects: The authors reported controlling for performance, and the performance covariate did not reduce the effect of race or condition on blood pressure reactivity. Although not a formal test of mediation, it does suggest that blood pressure changes could not be directly linked—at least not in a linear sense—to performance decrements.

More recently, Vick, Seery, Blascovich, and Weisbuch (2008) examined physiological responses associated with challenge and threat among men and women who were assigned to either a "gender-biased" or "gender-fair" math task. The authors observed a sex-by-condition interaction for cardiac output and total peripheral resistance. Examining the mean responses from this study it appears that when a math test was described as gender-fair, women exhibited the adaptive (challenge) profile more so than did men. In contrast, when the test was described as gender-biased, women exhibited threat profiles relative to men. What is notable about these findings is that the interaction between sex and condition seems to be driven by the large *challenge* response of male participants in the "gender-biased" condition, a pattern consistent Walton and Cohen's (2003) stereotype lift meta-analysis that suggest dominant groups perform better under "biased" test conditions. However, there were no reports of performance differences, so it is not possible to determine if the physiological responses explained performance decrements or if there were any performance decrements observed as a function of stereotype threat.

We have highlighted these papers that have explicitly tested physiological reactivity associated with stress in standard stereotype threat studies with a more complete list presented in Table 4.1. Although the studies we review showed some support that the state of stereotype threat results in more maladaptive stress (or threat) as we have defined here, none of them reported evidence that the changes in physiological reactivity could explain performance decrements, even though, as we outlined earlier, there is evidence to hypothesize that physiological reactivity may be part of the causal link to performance decrements. Indeed, in our search of the literature, we could not find any published papers in which stress arousal, measured with a neurobiological response, even partially mediated the link between stereotype threat manipulations and cognitive performance (in the next section, we examine vigilance processes that have shown mediation). We believe there are at least four reasons why this may be the case: timing of physiology relative to performance, types of tasks employed, stress arousal measures, and measurement issues.

The first critical factor is the timing of the "stress" response and the performance change. Temporal activation of stress responses differs between adaptive and maladaptive stress responses. If a stereotype threat manipulation occurs and this activates the HPA responses, it might take as long as 10 minutes or more for increasing levels of cortisol to affect neural regions. In contrast, an adaptive stress response characterized by strong sympathetic activation might show its greatest effects on performance very early in a task and might dissipate after only a minute or two of a test. In other words, timing of the physiological response and performance outcome must be considered in terms of their temporal activation and shut off. Another factor is the type of task being performed. As we outlined, memory and information retrieval are more likely to be influenced by chronic stress and "threat" responses, whereas execution, effort, and perseverance may be impaired as a result of blunted sympathetic activation.

The third factor is the stress arousal measure. Examining physiological responses that only present one component of the stress response (e.g., cortisol as opposed to cortisol and counter-regulatory hormones) or measures that represent combined influences of different physiological systems (heart rate that is dually innervated by sympathetic and parasympathetic branches) is likely to obscure relationships between physiology and performance. Finally, a typical mediational analysis assumes linear relationships between a mediator (in this case, physiology) and an outcome (performance). But this analytic approach might be misguided for two reasons. First, the relationship between the neurobiological response and the performance variable may not be linear but rather curvilinear, so higher-order trends should always be tested. More problematic is that neurobiological responses, like those reviewed here, may be released in pulsatile patterns, which would obscure linear relations and render standard generalized linear model (GLM) techniques inappropriate.

Strategies to Combat Maladaptive Stress Arousal

Several successful interventions have been developed to counteract performance impairments believed to be linked to stereotype threat (see Cohen, Purdie-Vaughs, & Garcia, 2011, Chapter 18, this volume). If stress arousal is directly (or even indirectly) responsible for performance impairments associated with stereotype threat, what can the literature on stress and emotion regulation teach us about combating stereotype threat effects on performance? One potentially useful strategy capitalizes on reappraising "anxiety" or "arousal" (Jamieson et al., 2010; Johns, Schmader, & Martens, 2005; Schmader, Forbes, Zhang, & Mendes, 2009). This approach emphasizes the idea that even though arousal is multidimensional, the precise assessment of one's internal states can be ambiguous, which allows for flexibility in terms of labeling one's stress state.

For example, the effectiveness of reappraising arousal was examined among a group of college students preparing to take the Graduate Records Examination (GRE; Jamieson, et al., 2010). In this study, participants were randomly assigned to either a reappraisal condition or a control condition. The reappraisal condition informed participants about challenge states; that is, they were told that the arousal they were feeling before they took the GRE actually was signaling that their body was preparing for action and would be associated with better performance. The control condition was not provided this reappraisal strategy. Participants provided saliva samples at baseline (prior to the manipulation) and immediately before taking the GRE math and verbal sections that were assayed for salivary alpha amylase (sAA), a proxy for SAM activation. Results showed that participants in the reappraisal condition had a greater increase in sAA and performed better on the GRE-math section than did participants in the control condition. Correlations between sAA levels and GRE-math performance showed the expected positive relationship—the greater the increase in sAA from baseline to the math task was associated with better math performance. Furthermore, the effects of reappraisal were evident when participants took the actual GRE. Between 1 and 3 months later, participants returned to the lab after they had taken the actual GRE and brought in their score reports. Participants who had been in the reappraisal condition had obtained higher GRE-math scores than did those in the control condition.

This study highlights several important points from this chapter. First, consistent with the adaptive stress profile, the greater the sympathetic activation, the better the performance with no indications of a curvilinear pattern between "arousal" and performance. Second, the effects were not observed with the GRE verbal section. This may be due to the types of questions from the math compared to verbal sections. The math section requires active execution, which like physical exercise, is enhanced at higher levels of sympathetic activation. Verbal problems are often recall or comprehension questions that do not benefit from sympathetic activation in the same way. Finally, the study demonstrates the importance of labeling one's physical state, which may influence subsequent reactivity thus suggesting flexibility of stress responses. Importantly, the reappraisal strategy employed was not one that tried to dampen or minimize the reactivity, but rather accentuate the "arousal" component as a beneficial state. We believe that exploiting stress and emotion regulation techniques to modify and enhance physiological responses associated with stress may prove to be a useful intervention for stereotype threat research.

■ VIGILANCE

The experience of stereotype threat requires stigmatized individuals to reconcile environmental cues associated with their stigmatized status while simultaneously marshalling the cognitive resources necessary to perform well on tasks. Thus, another possible mechanism of stereotype threat performance decrements is vigilance—the process of excessively monitoring the environment for threat cues while at the same time attending to the task at hand. This perspective suggests that the experience of stereotype threat occupies or diverts attentional resources, thereby debilitating performance on higher-order tasks, which may be responsible for performance decrements (e.g., Schmader et al., 2008). There are several brain and bodily responses associated with vigilance that may shed light on this possible mechanism. Here, we review responses from measures obtained from parasympathetic reactivity, electroencephalogram (EEG) and, more specifically, event-related potentials (ERP) and functional magnetic resonance imaging (fMRI).

Parasympathetic Reactivity

In the first half of this chapter, we reviewed stress arousal as a mechanism of stereotype threat effects, and we focused on activation of the sympathetic nervous system (SNS), ignoring a large part of the autonomic nervous system: the parasympathetic system (PNS). Given that these two systems can operate independently (Berntson, Cacioppo, & Quigley, 1993), our distinction was not merely didactic but rather dictated by the role that the SNS serves in stress and the PNS serves in attention or vigilance.

The PNS is most often measured with high-frequency heart rate variability (HRV), which is presumed to measure the activity of the vagus nerve, a cranial nerve originating in the medulla, which innervates a number of organs including the heart. Heart rate variability appears to be sensitive to a variety of psychological states, but is not particularly specific. However, accumulating evidence suggests that decreases in HRV during active tasks are associated with greater attentional control or effort (Croizet et al., 2004; Porges, 2007). Indeed, cognitive psychophysiologists infer decreases in HRV as an index of attention or mental effort (Tattersall & Hockey, 1995). In the anchoring-adjustment study we described earlier (Kassam et al., 2009), the strongest physiological predictor of performance was HRV changes: The greater the decreases in HRV during the decision-making task, the better the performance (Kassam et al., 2009).

Just as few stereotype threat studies have examined the physiological underpinnings of stress, there is also a dearth of research on the biological mechanisms underlying vigilance. In one study of stereotype threat, Croizet et al. (2004) examined changes in HRV during a stereotype threat paradigm, relying on the interpretation that decreases in HRV would index mental effort. They found that participants assigned to a stereotype threat prime showed greater decreases in HRV and poorer performance than did those in the control condition, and that HRV changes mediated the relationship from the condition to the performance effects. This work provides some evidence that changes in parasympathetic activity may mediate the relationship between stereotype threat and performance; however, HRV decreases may index processes other than vigilance and performance monitoring, such as conscious control (Kassam et al., 2009), anxiety or depression (Porges, 2007), or pessimism (Oveis et al., 2009) to name a few. Although there may be great promise with exploiting HRV changes as a possible mechanism underlying stereotype threat, some caution is warranted. It might be difficult to determine if vigilance-induced decreases in HRV will facilitate or impair performance. In the Croizet article, for example, the argument was that stereotype threat induced-vigilance directed attention away from the task; however, if attentional control could be marshaled toward the task and away from the environmental triggers of the stereotype threat, then one might expect HRV decreases to be associated with performance enhancements.

Electroencephalogram

Other noninvasive techniques can be used to measure vigilance and attentional processes in stereotype threat. For example, researchers have used evoked EEG signals, which measure electrical activity along the scalp via a network of sensors. Of specific interest for stereotype threat researchers interested in vigilance processes are ERPs—the average of a short epoch of EEG waveform data directly following an event (e.g., a response, stimulus onset, etc.). The high temporal resolution of ERP signals allows researchers to study the impact of psychological states on individuals' allocation of attention, not just at conscious levels, but also at early processing stages. Thus, EEG methods help researchers determine how psychological states, like stereotype threat, impact low-level processes that are difficult to measure with standard behavioral methods.

To study vigilance processes, researchers have examined ERP signals measured at electrodes located in the medial-frontal area of the scalp. Broadly, medial-frontal ERP waves index vigilance and attention, especially when an error has been made or some other anxiety-provoking event has occurred. A specific type of medial-frontal ERP signal that stereotype threat researchers have focused on is the error-related negativity (ERN) component. The ERN signal is a negative-going deflection in the ERP waveform that is most pronounced at the frontocentral region on the midline of the scalp 30–180 ms after an error has been made, and ERN amplitudes are larger after performance errors than after correct responses. The magnitude of ERN responses are used to index vigilance (i.e., error detection) and performance monitoring processes (Nieuwenhuis, Ridderinkhof, Blom, Band, & Kok, 2001), as well as affective responses such as defensive motivation (Hajcak & Foti, 2008). Thus, ERN methods are not only useful for studying the cognitive effects of threat, but may also provide insight into participants' affective responses to stereotype threat (e.g., anxiety and/or motivation) because the ERN signal originates in the ACC (Ullsperger & von Cramon, 2003), an area thought to underlie emotion regulation.

Along similar lines, other social neuroscience research has found evidence that stereotype threat leads participants to monitor their performance for mistakes. More specifically, Forbes et al. (2008) measured ERPs to explore early-stage motivational processes in performance monitoring and also examined the moderating effect of domain identification. For minority participants who valued academics, the experience of stereotype threat led to an increased ERN response, which suggests that these participants were vigilant for performance-related stimuli and were more efficient in responding to them. This increase in vigilance is indicative of increased motivation to perform well under threat in domain-identified targets. However, Forbes and colleagues observed a very different pattern for minority participants who did not value academic success. Specially, rather than devoting attentional resources to performance monitoring, devaluing academics negatively predicted

ERN amplitude under threat. This finding suggests that stigmatized individuals who no longer care about performance in stereotyped domains are not vigilant for potential errors, and instead disengage during performance.

Electroencephalogram methods have also been used to study self-regulation and spillover processes under stereotype threat. Like the aforementioned work by Forbes et al. (2008), work by Inzlicht and Kang (2010) suggests that the experience of threat leads to hypervigilance, thereby debilitating self-regulation. In that work, threatened females exhibited higher-amplitude medial-frontal ERP waves in response to Stroop errors (naming the incorrect color), as well as during correct high-conflict ("blue" printed in red ink) and correct low-conflict Stroop trials ("blue" printed in blue ink). On the other hand, males did not exhibit this increased ERP amplitude for low-conflict trials. Threatened females increased monitoring of every type of trial, even on low-conflict trials not requiring vigilance, indicating that female participants under threat may lose self-regulatory capacity.

Functional Magnetic Resonance Imaging

Although EEG methods provide high temporal resolution, they are less able to localize an effect in the brain. However, advances in neuroimaging methods have allowed researchers to spatially localize processes related to attention and vigilance noninvasively. To study the brain regions underlying psychological states, researchers often measure blood oxygenation level–dependent (BOLD) signals obtained via fMRI. The logic behind BOLD signals is that changes in brain activity lead to changes in blood flow to active brain regions in response to a thought, action, and/or psychological experience. The BOLD signals provide a measure of neural activation that can be measured online while participants are experiencing the psychological state of interest. Thus, fMRI techniques can help inform researchers as to the brain regions underlying attention allocation and vigilance processes under conditions of stereotype threat.

The few stereotype threat studies that have used fMRI methods have observed activation in the ACC (e.g., Krendl, Richeson, Kelley, & Heatherton, 2008; Wraga, Helt, Jacobs, & Sullivan, 2007). Several fMRI studies suggest that the ACC, specifically the ventral ACC, is activated by the experience of physical pain (e.g., Rainville, Duncan, Price, Carrier, & Bushnell, 1997), emotional distress (Eisenberger, Lieberman, & Williams, 2003), or emotion regulation (e.g., Bush, Luu, & Posner, 2000). Particularly relevant for stereotype threat researchers is the acute sensitivity of ventral ACC regions to social feedback, especially social rejection (Eisenberger et al., 2003). That is, when threatened by the salience of stereotype-related cues, stigmatized individuals may respond with increased activity in the ventral ACC.

Research using fMRI techniques has suggested that the experience of stereotype threat decreases participants' recruitment of attention resources. In some recent research, Krendl and colleagues (2008) observed that women not subject to stereotype threat exhibited activation in prefrontal and parietal areas, indicative of the recruitment of attentional resources, during math performance. However, when women were subject to stereotype threat, they exhibited less prefrontal and parietal activity, and instead demonstrated increased activity in the ventral stream of the ACC. This finding was corroborated and extended in additional work by Wraga and colleagues (2007), who found that stereotype threat increased activation in the ventral ACC, and that this activation predicted threatened participants' performance decrements on a mental rotation task. Thus, previous research provides some initial evidence that the experience of stereotype threat shifts how women utilize attentional resources. When not subject to threat, women recruited resources from prefrontal regions associated with attention, but when threatened, females exhibited greater activation in monitoring, correction, and emotion regulation areas. Therefore, rather than focusing on task performance, threat caused women to recruit additional systems associated with performance monitoring and emotion regulation, potentially decreasing the amount of cognitive resources available for task performance.

Policy Box

In this chapter, we highlight brain and bodily changes associated with the experience of stereotype threat and how those changes might affect cognitive performance. This leads to the question: Can changing bodily states alter cognitive performance? *Embodied cognition* is an area of growing research interest in psychology and neuroscience. It examines how bodily responses can influence cognitive processes. For example, if you hold a pencil in your mouth with your teeth (rather than your lips) this will activate the smiling muscles and—without even realizing it—you may find the morning comic strip funnier than you typically do. The idea behind this effect is that the smiling muscles are sending information to your brain that you are happy and hence the comics seem funnier. These same processes can be observed with *adaptive* stress profiles and cognition. Adaptive stress profiles are associated with increased sympathetic activation and increased blood flow to the brain and body, which can increase cognitive performance. These profiles can be brought on by psychological stress, but also with aerobic exercise. Acute effects of exercise and, of course, long-lasting effects of conditioning, may buffer impairments in cognition by maintaining increased blood flow to the brain and body. Indeed, in a recent longitudinal medical study, individuals with greater cardiac output (a cardiac index of oxygenated blood pumped from the heart) had lower risk of cognitive declines in older age and reduced risk of Alzheimer's disease. In addition to the large body of evidence showing exercise is beneficial for physical and mental health, there is also reason to believe that exercise can be beneficial for cognitive performance. Policy makers should be mindful that physical education in schools may have direct links to performance in the classroom.

■ CONCLUSION

In this chapter, we reviewed various literature that would further our understanding of stereotype threat processes. As many of the mechanisms that are believed to underlie stereotype threat processes have neurobiological concomitants, we explored the process of stereotype threat from two angles. First, we examined how different psychological and affective states associated with stereotype threat were linked to various neurobiological changes. The second angle examined how these various neurobiological changes might be associated with performance changes. We summarized this approach early in the chapter, in Figure 4.1, but also highlighted that there are stronger links between the psychological states and the neurobiological changes than there are links between the neurobiological changes and the performance outcomes. Although we do believe that neurobiology may prove to be a useful candidate mechanism for stereotype threat, clearly much remains unknown regarding how biological changes influence performance and the multiple pathways that complicate these links. This review is meant to be both humbling in terms of how much is yet unknown about links between biology and performance, but also, we hope, inspiring as researchers continue to search for explanations of stereotype threat effects. Our intent was to offer possible avenues for researchers to explore biological mechanisms, but also words of caution in that not all stress responses are created equal, and that many neurobiological responses have yet to show reliable influences on cognition. There is certainly more work to be done, but by exploring brain and body mechanisms associated with stereotype threat, we believe that the puzzle of how negative stereotypes influence performance can be revealed.

References

Ben-Zeev, T., Fein, S., & Inzlicht, M. (2005). Stereotype threat and arousal. *Journal of Experimental Social Psychology, 41,* 174–181.

Berntson, G. G., Cacioppo, J. T., & Quigley, K. S. (1993). Cardiac psychophysiology and autonomic space in humans: Empirical perspectives and conceptual implications. *Psychological Bulletin, 114,* 296–322.

Blascovich, J., & Mendes, W. B. (2010). Social psychophysiology and embodiment. In S. T. Fiske, & Gilbert, D. T. (Eds.), *The handbook of social psychology* (5th ed.). New York: Wiley.

Blascovich, J., Mendes, W. B., Hunter, S. B., & Salomon, K. (1999). Social "facilitation" as challenge and threat. *Journal of Personality and Social Psychology, 77,* 68–77.

Blascovich, J., Spencer, S., Quinn, D., & Steele, C. (2001). African-Americans and high blood pressure: The role of stereotype threat. *Psychological Science, 12,* 225–229.

Bush, G., Luu, P., & Posner, M. I. (2000). Cognitive and emotional influences in anterior cingulate cortex. *Trends in Cognitive Sciences, 4*(6), 215–222.

Cohen, G. L., Purdie-Vaughns, V., & Garcia, J. (2011). An identity threat perspective on intervention. In M. Inzlicht, & T. Schmader (Eds.), *Stereotype threat: Theory, process, and application.* New York: Oxford University Press.

Croizet, J., Despres, G., Gauzin, M., Huguet, P., Levens, J., & Meot, A. (2004). Stereotype threat undermines intellectual performance by triggering a disruptive mental load. *Personality and Social Psychology Bulletin, 30,* 721–731.

Davies, P. G., Spencer, S. J., Quinn, D. M., & Gerhardstein, R. (2002). Consuming images: How television commercials that elicit stereotype threat can restrain women academically and professionally. *Personality and Social Psychology Bulletin, 28*(12), 1615–1628.

Derks, B., Inzlicht, M., & Kang, S. (2008). The neuroscience of stigma and stereotype threat. *Group Processes and Intergroup Relations, 11,* 163–181.

Dickerson, S. S., & Kemeny, M. E. (2004). Acute stressors and cortisol responses: A theoretical integration and synthesis of laboratory research. *Psychological Bulletin, 130*(3), 355–391.

Dienstbier, R. A. (1989). Arousal and physiological toughness: Implications for mental and physical health. *Psychological Review, 96*, 84–100.

Eisenberger, N. I., Lieberman, M. D., & Williams, K. D. (2003). Does rejection hurt? An fmri study of social exclusion. *Science, 302*, 290–292.

Forbes, C., Schmader, T., & Allen, J. J. B. (2008). Error monitoring in an intellectually threatening environment. *Social Cognitive Affective Neuroscience, 3*, 253–261.

Hajcak, G., & Foti, D. (2008). Errors are aversive: Defensive motivation and the error-related negativity. *Psychological Science, 19*, 103–108.

Inzlicht, M., & Kang, S. K. (2010). Stereotype threat spillover: How coping with threats to social identity affects aggression, eating, decision-making, and attention. *Journal of Personality and Social Psychology, 99*, 467–481.

Jamieson, J., Mendes, W. B., Blackstock, E., & Schmader, T. (2010). Turning the knots in your stomach into bows: Reappraising arousal improves performance on the GRE. *Journal of Experimental Social Psychology, 46*, 208–212.

Johns, M., Schmader, T., & Martens, A. (2005). Knowing is half the battle: Teaching stereotype threat as a means of improving women's math performance. *Psychological Science, 16*(3), 175–179.

Josephs, R. A., Newman, M. L., Brown, R. P., & Beer, J. M. (2003). Status, testosterone, and human intellectual performance: Stereotype threat as status concern. *Psychological Science, 14*, 158–163.

Kassam, K., Koslov, K., & Mendes, W. B. (2009). Decisions under distress: Stress profiles influence anchoring and adjustment. *Psychological Science, 20*, 1394–1399.

Krendl, A. C., Richeson, J. A., Kelley, W. M., & Heatherton, T. F. (2008). The negative consequences of threat: An fmri investigation of the neural mechanisms underlying women's underperformance in math. *Psychological Science, 19*, 168–175.

Lazarus, R., & Folkman, S. (1991). The concept of coping. *Stress and coping: An* anthology (3rd ed.). New York: Columbia University Press.

Lovallo, W. R., & Thomas, T. L. (2000). Stress hormones in psychophysiological research: Emotional, behavioral, and cognitive implications. In J. T. Cacioppo, L. G. Tassinary, & G. G. Berntson (Eds.), *Handbook of psychophysiology* (2nd ed., pp. 342–367). New York: Cambridge University Press.

Matheson, K., & Cole, B. (2004). Coping with a threatened group identity: Psychological and neuroendocrine responses. *Journal of Experimental Social Psychology, 40*, 777–786.

Murphy, M. C., Steele, C. M., & Gross, J. J. (2007). Signaling threat how situational cues affect women in math, science, and engineering settings. *Psychological Science, 18*, 879–888.

Nieuwenhuis, S., Ridderinkhof, K. R., Blom, J., Band, G. P. H., & Kok, A. (2001). Error-related brain potentials are differentially related to awareness of response errors: Evidence from an antisaccade task. *Psychophysiology, 38*, 752–760.

O'Brien, L. T., & Crandall, C. S. (2003). Stereotype threat and arousal: Effects on women's math performance. *Personality and Social Psychology Bulletin, 29*(6), 782–789.

Osborne, J. W. (2007). Linking stereotype threat and anxiety. *Educational Psychology, 27*(1), 135–154.

Oveis, C., Cohen, A. B., Gruber, J., Shiota, M. N., Haidt, J., & Kelter, D. (2009). Resting respiratory sinus arrhythmia is associated with tonic positive emotionality. *Emotion, 9*, 265–270.

Porges, S. W. (2007). The polyvagal perspective. *Biological Psychology, 74*(2), 116–143.

Rainville, P., Duncan, G. H., Price, D. D., Carrier, B., & Bushnell, M. C. (1997). Pain affect encoded in human anterior cingulate but not somatosensory cortex. *Science, 277*(5328), 968–971.

Reul, J., & de Kloet, E. (1985). Two receptor systems for corticosterone in rat brain: Microdistribution and differential occupation. *Endocrinology, 117*, 2505–2511.

Schmader, T., Forbes, C. E., Zhang, S., & Mendes, W. B. (2009). A meta-cognitive perspective on cognitive deficits experienced in intellectually threatening environments. *Personality and Social Psychology Bulletin, 35*, 584–596.

Schmader, T., Johns, M., & Forbes, C. (2008). An integrated process model of stereotype threat effects on performance. *Psychological Review, 115*, 336–356.

Steele, C. M., & Aronson, J. (1995). Stereotype threat and the intellectual test performance of African-Americans. *Journal of Personality and Social Psychology, 69*, 797–811.

Tattersall, A. J., & Hockey, G. R. J. (1995). Level of operator control and changes in heart rate variability during simulated flight maintenance. *Human Factors, 37*(4), 682–698.

Ullsperger, M., & von Cramon, D. Y. (2003). Error monitoring using external feedback: Specific roles of the habenular complex, the reward system, and the cingulate motor area revealed by functional magnetic resonance imaging. *Journal of Neuroscience, 23*, 4308–4314.

Ursin, H., Baade, E., & Levine, S. (1978). *Psychobiology of stress: A study of coping men.* New York: Academic Press.

Vick, S. B., Seery, M. D., Blascovich, J., & Weisbuch, M. (2008). The effect of gender stereotype activation on challenge and threat motivational states. *Journal of Experimental Social Psychology, 44*, 624–630.

Walton, G. M., & Cohen, G. L. (2003). Stereotype lift. *Journal of Experimental Social Psychology, 39*, 456–467.

Wraga, M., Helt, M., Jacobs, E., & Sullivan, K. (2007). Neural basis of stereotype-induced shifts in women's mental rotation performance. *Social Cognitive and Affective Neuroscience, 2*, 12–19.

PART TWO

Theoretical Extensions

5 Types of Threats

From Stereotype Threat to Stereotype Threats

■ JENESSA R. SHAPIRO

The psychological experience of stereotype threat—a concern about being seen through the lens of a negative stereotype—can undermine motivation and performance in stereotype-relevant fields (Steele, Spencer, & Aronson, 2002). However, a key question remains: What exactly is stereotype threat a threat to, or a fear of? A close look at this important literature reveals that "stereotype threat" is often employed to describe and explain distinct processes and phenomena. The present chapter reviews a new approach to stereotype threat: the Multi-Threat Framework (Shapiro & Neuberg, 2007). In contrast to previous research, the Multi-Threat Framework articulates six qualitatively distinct stereotype threats that emerge from the intersection of two dimensions—the target of the stereotype threat (who will one's stereo-type-relevant actions reflect upon: the self or one's group) and the source of the stereotype threat (who will judge these stereotype-relevant actions: the self, outgroup others, or ingroup others). Each of these stereotype threats have different eliciting conditions and moderators, are mediated by some-what different processes, are experienced to different degrees by different negatively stereotyped groups, are coped with and compensated for in different ways, and require different interventions to overcome. The chapter focuses on the diversity of situational and individual difference factors that moderate an individual's susceptibility to the different types of stereotype threats, as these factors shed light on when each of the stereotypes threats will emerge and how to best remediate the negative consequences of these stereotype threats.

Keywords: Stereotype threat, stigma, academic performance, group identi-fication, domain identification

Stereotype threat is the concern that one's performance or actions can be seen through the lens of a negative stereotype (e.g., Aronson, Lustina, Good, Keough, Steele, & Brown, 1999; Shapiro & Neuberg, 2007; Steele, 1997; Steele, Spencer, & Aronson, 2002), a concern that disrupts and undermines performance in the nega-tively stereotyped domain (Schmader & Beilock, 2011, Chapter 3, this volume). For example, in stereotype threatening situations, women underperform in math and sci-ence (e.g., Spencer, Steele, & Quinn, 1999), ethnic/racial minority students under-perform on academic tasks (e.g., Steele & Aronson, 1995), and men underperform on measures of social sensitivity (Koenig & Eagly, 2005). The past 15 years have seen an explosion of stereotype threat research with hundreds of studies examining different stereotypes, different groups, and different boundary conditions, revealing the far-reaching influence of this phenomenon. However, a question that has yet to be fully explored is what specifically underlies stereotype threat. That is, if stereotype threat is a concern about being seen as stereotypic, in whose mind might an individual be concerned about confirming these stereotypes? One's own mind? Someone else's mind? Both at the same time? In addition, whose ability might this performance reflect upon? One's own? One's group's? Both? Joshua Aronson and colleagues asked a similar set of questions:

> Is stereotype threat self-threatening because it arouses a fear of being a bad ambassador of one's group to mainstream society? Or is it more simply the apprehension about appearing incompetent—for the sake of one's own reputation? Or, alternatively, is it merely the result of worrying that one might lack ability? Or is it some combination of these concerns? These are important questions that will have to await the results of future research for answers.
>
> —(Aronson et al., 1999, p. 43)

Although these questions were proposed over a decade ago, very little research has addressed them. Recently, we argued that these distinctions are important for a complete understanding of stereotype threat. Thus, we proposed a *Multi-Threat Framework* consisting of six core, qualitatively distinct stereotype threats that are elicited by different conditions, can differentially characterize the experiences of individuals contending with different stereotyped characteristics, are mediated and moderated by somewhat different mechanisms, and will require different interventions to overcome (Shapiro & Neuberg, 2007; Shapiro, 2011). In this chapter, I will review the Multi-Threat Framework with particular attention to the diversity of situational and individual difference factors that influence susceptibility to the different types of stereotype threats.

■ THE MULTI-THREAT FRAMEWORK

The Multi-Threat Framework outlines six core stereotype threats that emerge from a consideration of two dimensions—the target of the stereotype threat (who does this action reflect upon: the self or one's group) and the source of the stereotype threat (who will draw conclusions regarding this action: the self, outgroup others, or ingroup others). The intersection of these dimensions results in stereotype-based threats to one's personal self-concept (i.e., "What if I come to learn this stereotype is true of me?"), to one's group concept ("What if I come to learn this stereotype is true of my group?"), to one's personal reputation in the eyes of outgroup others ("What if outgroup others come to see me as stereotypic?"), to one's personal reputation in eyes of ingroup others ("What if ingroup others come to see me as stereotypic?"), to one's group's reputation in the eyes of outgroup others ("What if others come to see my group as stereotypic?"), and to one's group's reputation in the eyes of ingroup others ("What if ingroup others come to see my group as stereotypic?"); see Table 5.1.

TABLE 5.1 *Six qualitatively distinct stereotype threats emerge from the intersection of two dimensions: Source of the threat and target of the threat*

			Target of the Threat	
			Self	Group
	Self		**Self-Concept Threat** Fear that my behavior will confirm, **in my own mind**, that the negative stereotypes held of my group **are true of me**	**Group-Concept Threat** Fear that my behavior will confirm, in **my own mind**, that the negative stereotypes held of my group **are true of my group**
Source of the Threat	Other	Outgroup members	**Own-Reputation Threat (Outgroup)** Fear that my behavior will confirm, **in the minds of outgroup members**, that the negative stereotypes held of my group **are true of me**, and I will therefore be judged or treated badly by outgroup members	**Group-Reputation Threat (Outgroup)** Fear that my behavior will confirm, **in the minds of outgroup members**, that the negative stereotypes held of my group **are true of my group**, and my group will therefore be judged or treated badly by outgroup members
		Ingroup members	**Own-Reputation Threat (Ingroup)** Fear that my behavior will confirm, **in the minds of ingroup members**, that the negative stereotypes held of my group **are true of me**, and I will therefore be judged or treated badly by ingroup members	**Group-Reputation Threat (Ingroup)** Fear that my behavior will confirm, **in the minds of ingroup members**, that the negative stereotypes held of my group **are true of my group**, and my group will therefore be judged or treated badly by ingroup members

Adapted from Shapiro, J. R., & Neuberg, S. L. (2007). From stereotype threat to stereotype threats: Implications of a Multi-Threat Framework for causes, moderators, mediators, consequences, and interventions. *Personality and Social Psychology Review*, 11(2), 107–130.

In this section, each stereotype threat is defined and the constellation of factors that give rise to each stereotype threat is explored (see Table 5.2). It is important to note that each of the eliciting conditions is necessary but not sufficient for the emergence of each stereotype threat. That is, the entire profile of eliciting conditions yields a particular stereotype threat. In addition, although some eliciting conditions increase risk for more than one stereotype threat, each combination of conditions is unique—no two stereotype threats share the same combination of eliciting conditions.

Self-Concept Threat (self-as-target, self-as-source stereotype threat) is the fear of stereotypic characterization in "one's own eyes"—the fear of seeing oneself as actually possessing the negative stereotypic trait. For example, Michelle might fear a poor performance on a chemistry exam will support the hypothesis lurking within the recesses of her own mind that she is indeed, by virtue of her gender, less capable than her male classmates in scientific domains. Thus, Michelle's risk for Self-Concept Threat increases to the extent that she identifies with the negatively stereotyped

TABLE 5.2 *Profile of eliciting conditions necessary to yield each of the proposed stereotype threats*

In order for one to experience _____ Threat, the following need to be true:	Self-Concept	Group-Concept	Own-Reputation (Outgroup)	Group-Reputation (Outgroup)	Own-Reputation (Ingroup)	Group-Reputation (Ingroup)
Need to identify with the stereotyped domain	X					
Need to believe that the stereotype might be true of oneself	X					
Need to care about the implications of one's stereotype-relevant actions for the way one sees oneself	X					
Need to recognize that one belongs to the group	X	X		X	X	X
Need to believe one's stereotype-relevant actions are public to outgroup others			X	X		
Need to believe the stereotype-relevant actions are linked to oneself			X		X	
Need to care about the implications of one's stereotype-relevant actions for the way outgroup others see oneself			X			
Need to believe that outgroup others think the stereotype might be true of oneself			X			
Need to believe that outgroup others recognize one belongs to the group			X	X		
Need to believe the stereotype might be true of the group		X				
Need to care about the implications of one's stereotype-relevant actions for the way one sees the group		X				
Need to see oneself as representing the group		X		X		X
Need to identify with the group		X		X	X	X
Need to believe that outgroup others think the stereotype might be true of the group				X		
Need to care about the implications of one's stereotype-relevant actions for the way outgroup others see the group				X		
Need to believe the stereotype-relevant actions are linked to the group				X		X
Need to believe one's stereotype-relevant actions are public to ingroup others					X	X
Need to believe that ingroup others recognize one belongs to the group					X	X
Need to care about the implications of one's stereotype-relevant actions for the way ingroup others see oneself					X	
Need to believe that ingroup others think the stereotype might be true of oneself					X	
Need to believe that ingroup others think the stereotype might be true of the group						X
Need to care about the implications of one's stereotype-relevant actions for the way ingroup others see the group						X

Adapted from Shapiro, J. R., & Neuberg, S. L. (2007). From stereotype threat to stereotype threats: Implications of a Multi-Threat Framework for causes, moderators, mediators, consequences, and interventions. *Personality and Social Psychology Review, 11*(2), 107–130.

domain (e.g., sees science as a central, important part of her identity) and believes the negative stereotype could be true (i.e., if Michelle believes there is no credibility to the stereotype, there would be no reason to fear possessing this negative trait). Note that for Self-Concept Threat to emerge, identifying with the negatively stereotyped group (e.g., seeing one's gender as a central, important part of her identity) should not be necessary—regardless of whether Michelle sees her gender as an important social identity, she can still fear that a performance could reveal she is stereotypic. Furthermore, a stereotype-relevant performance need not be public for Self-Concept Threat to emerge: Because this threat is rooted in perceptions of one's Self-Concept, this threat should emerge as a function of private concerns regarding the stereotype's applicability to the self.

Group-Concept Threat (group-as-target, self-as-source stereotype threat) is the fear of seeing one's group as possessing the negative stereotypic trait—the fear that one's performance will confirm in one's own mind that this group is legitimately devalued. Thus, Michelle might fear an inadequate performance on a chemistry exam will confirm in her own mind that women have less scientific ability than men. Thus, risk for Group-Concept Threat increases to the extent that one identifies with one's group, sees oneself as a representative of the group (otherwise one's personal failures should not reflect the group's abilities), and cares about the implications of one's views of the group for the self. In addition, similar to Self-Concept Threat, to the extent that one believes the stereotype could be true, risk for Group-Concept Threat increases. Note that public performance should not be necessary, nor should domain identification be important for Group-Concept Threat to occur. That is, as long as Michelle cares about seeing women in a positive light, the importance she places on the domain of competence for herself is irrelevant.

Own-Reputation Threat (Outgroup, Ingroup) (self-as-target, other-as-source stereotype threat) is the fear of stereotypic characterization in the eyes of others—the fear of being judged or treated poorly by others because they may see one as negatively stereotypical. For example, Michelle may fear that a poor performance on a chemistry exam would enable an employer, coworker, teacher, or friend to judge her based on negative stereotypes about women's scientific ability and thereby treat her in an unfavorable manner. Thus, in contrast to Self-Concept Threat, Own-Reputation Threat is a more public stereotype threat that emerges when one believes an audience can identify whether one belongs to the stereotyped group.

Thus, Michelle's risk for Own-Reputation Threat increases to the extent that she believes (a) an audience holds the negative stereotypes (one cannot confirm a negative stereotype in the minds of others if these others are not believed to hold the stereotype as a reasonable hypothesis) and (b) there are important stereotype-relevant implications for the way in which the audience perceives her. That is, if Michelle knows her performance will remain private or her performance will be publicly available but not linked to her personally, her risk for Own-Reputation Threat should be very low. Note that domain identification should not put one at risk for Own-Reputation Threat; as long as Michelle cares about the implications of her behavior for how others see her, she is at risk for Own-Reputation Threat.

For *Own-Reputation Threat (Outgroup)* to emerge, the evaluative other must be a member of an outgroup (e.g., a male, in Michelle's case). Given that the focus of this stereotype threat is on personal evaluation, identification with one's group is not required: Michelle would not need to see her gender as a central identity to worry that outgroup others could view her performance through the lens of the negative stereotype. *Own-Reputation Threat (Ingroup)* emerges when an ingroup member is the evaluative other (e.g., a woman, in Michelle's case). Thus, to the extent that Michelle identifies with the negatively stereotyped group (her gender), her risk for Own-Reputation Threat (Ingroup) should increase. That is, if Michelle does not identity with her gender, she is unlikely to care about how a stereotype-relevant action will be seen by an ingroup member.

Finally, *Group-Reputation Threat (Outgroup, Ingroup)* (group-as-target, other-as-source stereotype threat) is the fear of reinforcing negative stereotypes about one's group in the minds of others—the fear of being a bad ambassador for one's group. Michelle's concern here would be that a poor performance on the exam would reinforce, in another's mind, the negative stereotypes about women as a whole and their scientific ability. Thus, to experience Group-Reputation Threat, one's performance in the stereotyped domain must be visible to others and visibly linked to the stereotyped group. Furthermore, risk for Group-Reputation Threat increases to the extent that one believes others think the stereotype is, or could be, true. If Michelle, for instance, takes a chemistry test but does not provide any personal or demographic information, she should not fear poorly representing her group, as there will be no way to link her performance to the group. In addition, identifying with the negatively stereotyped group increases one's risk for Group-Reputation Threat; if one does not see the group as a central identity, one is unlikely to care about letting this group down. Again, note that domain identification should not be necessary to elicit Group-Reputation Threat—regardless of her own investment in the domain, as long as Michelle cares about the implications of her behavior for how others see women, she is at risk for Group-Reputation Threat. For *Group-Reputation Threat (Outgroup)* to occur, the evaluative other must be a member of an outgroup. In contrast, for *Group-Reputation Threat (Ingroup)* to occur, the evaluative other must be a member of the ingroup.

Independence and Co-occurrence of Stereotype Threats

Given that qualitatively different constellations of conditions elicit each of the stereotype threats, each stereotype threat can be experienced independently of the others. For example, a woman who identifies with the domain of math but wonders whether the negative stereotypes about women and math may indeed be true is at risk for Self-Concept Threat, but none of the other stereotype threats if she does not care how other people see, judge, or treat her, and if she never performs math-relevant tasks publicly. In contrast, a woman who believes men hold negative math-relevant stereotypes about women and believes she will be personally linked to her math performance will be at risk for Own-Reputation Threat (Outgroup) but no other stereotype threats if she cares very little about her group (i.e., has low group identification) and about math (i.e., has low domain identification).

Although the stereotype threats can be experienced independently of one another, they can (and often will) co-occur, and in a manner predictable by the Multi-Threat Framework. Specifically, because some of the stereotype threats share common eliciting conditions, they should be more likely to co-occur than threats that share fewer (if any) eliciting conditions. For example, being highly identified with a particular negatively stereotyped group is relevant to all of the stereotype threats that have the ingroup as the target or as the source of the stereotype threat. Thus, an individual who is highly identified with her group should have an increased likelihood of experiencing multiple group-as-target and ingroup-as-source stereotype threats, depending on the other situation- and individual-level variables present. Additionally, if this group-identified individual is also highly identified with the domain—as is the case with a large proportion of stereotype threat research because of its focus on racial/ethnic minority college students engaging in academic tasks—this individual will be at risk for experiencing most of the stereotype threats. In sum, although the stereotype threats can be experienced independently of one another, they can, and often will, be experienced jointly.

Different Threats Moderated and Mediated by Different Factors

The different situational (e.g., private vs. public nature of one's performance) and dispositional (e.g., group identification) factors that give rise to the stereotype threats demonstrate that different variables facilitate or inhibit the experience of different stereotype threats. Thus, the factors listed in Table 5.2 can be seen as elicitors or moderators of each of the stereotype threats. In addition to these factors, the experience of the various stereotype threats should also be moderated by other, more general, constructs that relate specifically to each of the stereotype threats. For example, self-as-target stereotype threats (Self-Concept Threat, Own-Reputation Threat [Outgroup, Ingroup]) should be moderated to some extent by variables that more generally tie into the desire to be seen positively by oneself or others (e.g., self-esteem level and stability, need to belong; Crocker & Wolfe, 2001; Kernis, Paradise, Whitaker, Wheatman, & Goldman, 2000; Leary, Kelly, Cottrell, & Schreindorfer, 2006), whereas group-as-target stereotype threats (Group-Concept Threat, Group-Reputation Threat [Ingroup, Outgroup]) should be moderated to some extent by variables that more generally tie into the desire for one's group to be seen positively (e.g., situations that activate collectivism, private or public regard for the group, private or public collective self esteem; Luhtanen & Crocker, 1992; Sellers, Rowley, Chavous, Shelton, & Smith, 1997). Other-as-source stereotype threats (Own-Reputation Threat [Outgroup, Ingroup], Group-Reputation Threat [Outgroup, Ingroup]) should be moderated by variables that more generally tie into the desire for public social approval (e.g., self-monitoring, public self-consciousness; Briggs, Cheek, & Buss, 1980; Gangestad & Snyder, 2000; Inzlicht, Aronson, Good, & McKay, 2006; Scheier &

Carver, 1985), whereas self-as-source stereotype threats should tie into the desire for private approval (e.g., private self-consciousness; Briggs et al., 1980).

Although each of these stereotype threats is proposed to yield a similar behavioral outcome in most negatively stereotyped domains—underperformance relative to one's ability—the factors that mediate the relationship between each of the stereotype threats and this outcome should differ. Research reveals that a complex meditational chain accounts for stereotype threat-induced performance decrements: Earlier-in-the-stream mediators such as negative intrusive thoughts and negative emotional reactions degrade what is considered the most proximate cause of performance decrements—working memory efficiency (Schmader & Beilock, 2011, Chapter 3, this volume; Schmader, Johns, & Forbes, 2008). Although reduced working memory should similarly undermine performance across all stereotype threats, the earlier-in-the-stream mediators should differ between stereotype threats. For instance, group-based intrusive thoughts should emerge in the group-as-target stereotype threats and serve to tax working memory, whereas self-based intrusive thoughts should emerge in the self-as-target stereotype threats, and these thoughts should tax working memory.

In addition to reducing working memory efficiency, intrusive thoughts tend to require management. Research reveals the exertion of self-control to regulate and manage these intrusive thoughts and negative emotions consequently depletes many of the resources essential to effectively accomplishing any tasks—the stereotyped task or other tasks—that require conscious effort (e.g., Inzlicht, McKay, & Aronson, 2006; Johns, Inzlicht, & Schmader, 2008; McGlone & Aronson, 2007). Although regulation will likely emerge across all the stereotype threats and some of the emotions being regulated will likely be similar across the stereotype threats (e.g., dejection, anxiety; see, for example, Bosson, Haymovitz, & Pinel, 2004; Keller & Dauenheimer, 2003), a distinct set of emotions are likely to arise in the context of specific stereotype threats. For instance, anticipatory shame and guilt—two social emotions—may arise when experiencing Group-Reputation Threat (Outgroup), Own-Reputation Threat (Ingroup), and Group-Reputation Threat (Ingroup) because in each of these cases, one has the potential to let down ingroup members. In contrast, anticipatory anger may arise when experiencing Own-Reputation Threat (Outgroup), as this is the emotion experienced when one perceives oneself to have been treated unfairly.

■ IMPLICATIONS OF THE MULTI-THREAT FRAMEWORK

The Multi-Threat Framework articulates six unique stereotype threats that are elicited by qualitatively distinct factors. Although similarities exist between the stereotype threats in terms of implications for performance in the negatively stereotyped domain, differentiating between the stereotype threats has important implications, including identifying risk for stereotype threats, understanding how people will cope with and compensate for the experience of stereotype threats, and developing interventions.

Experience of Stereotype Threat by Different Groups

As described earlier, risk for the different stereotype threats should vary across individuals in predictable ways as a function of the presence or absence of the factors that serve to elicit each of the stereotype threats. Thus, identifying the situation- and individual-level factors present in a given context offers insight into stereotype threat risk. However, this should also have implications for stereotype threat risk across individuals contending with different stigmatizable identities. Consistent with this prediction, one set of studies revealed that individuals contending with stereotypes about their race/ethnicity, weight, religion, mental health, or physical disability reported experiencing different patterns of stereotype threats (Shapiro, 2011). That is, differences between stigmatizable characteristics, such as the ability to conceal this characteristic, the perceived controllability of this characteristic, and the way in which a stigmatized characteristic changes over time, shape the experience of possessing a given stigma (Crocker & Major, 1989; Crocker, Major, & Steele, 1998; Frable, Blackstone, & Scherbaum, 1990; Goffman, 1963; Hebl & Dovidio, 2005; Jones et al., 1984). Furthermore, many aspects of one's environment, socialization, development, and interactions shape one's relationships with a stigmatizable characteristic (Crocker & Major, 1989; Steele et al., 2002). As a result, as we describe in more detail below, to the extent that these experiences create systematic variability in stereotype threat elicitors between negatively stereotyped groups, overall risk for the stereotype threats should vary between groups as well.

For the other-as-source stereotype threats to emerge—Own-Reputation Threat (Outgroup), Group-Reputation Threat (Outgroup), Own-Reputation Threat (Ingroup), Group-Reputation Threat (Ingroup)—one must believe another individual can identify one's group membership. That is, if the evaluative other has no knowledge of one's status as a member of the negatively stereotyped group, there would be no reason to fear this person might apply the stereotypes to one's performance. Thus, to the extent that one's stigmatizable characteristic is effectively concealed—as it often is, for example, for those who can be stigmatized on the basis of sexual orientation, mental illness, religion, or political ideology—one should be less susceptible to experiencing the other-as-source stereotype threats, but should remain susceptible to the self-as-source threats (e.g., Bosson et al., 2004).

As a second example, although a great deal of variability exists within groups across factors such as group identification and stereotype endorsement (factors that elicit some of the stereotype threats), research finds variability between groups on these factors as well (Shapiro, 2011). For instance, an individual can recognize that he or she possesses a negatively stereotyped characteristic, or that others can label him or her as a member of a particular group, without psychologically identifying with the group (e.g., Crocker & Major, 1989; Lickel et al., 2000). Previous research finds that, compared to groups based on race or religion, group identification is relatively low among individuals who are obese or have a mental illness (Corrigan, 2004; Crocker & Major, 1989; Cohen, 2009; Sellers, Smith, Shelton, Rowley, & Chavous, 1998). In contrast, compared to individuals considering the negative stereotypes associated with their mental illness or weight, groups based on race or religion are less likely to endorse the negative stereotypes or entertain the notion that the negative stereotypes could in fact be true (Crandall & Biernat, 1990; Rusch, Todd, Bodenhausen, Olschewski, & Corrigan, 2010; Quinn & Crocker, 1999; Rusch, Corrigan, Todd, & Bodenhausen, 2010; Teachman, Wilson, & Komarovskaya, 2006). These differences in group identification and stereotype endorsement likely emerge for a number of different reasons; we will review some of these reasons here.

First, there is variability between some groups in when one comes to learn he or she possesses a particular stigmatizable characteristic—a dimension of stigma that likely contributes to differences in group identification and stereotype endorsement (Crocker & Major, 1989; Jones et al., 1984). For example, characteristics like weight or mental illness often emerge later in life. Indeed, some mental illnesses show no symptoms prior to 18 years of age, are triggered by stressful events that take place later in life, etc. In contrast, group memberships based on race (and often religion) are usually salient from an early age (due to skin color, family practices, early socialization). Research finds that children are aware of many racial stereotypes by the age of 4 or 5 (e.g., Aboud, 1988) and are able to correctly label their own and others' race by the age of 6 (e.g., Aboud, 1988; Madge, 1976). These differences have implications for group identification—having access to information about one's race early in one's developmental trajectory allows children to develop their self-concepts with knowledge of this identity, increasing the likelihood that this identity will be integrated into, and seen as central to, one's self-concept (e.g., Akiba, Szalacha, & Garcia Coll, 2004; Alvarez, Cameron, Garfinkle, Ruble, & Fuligni, 2001; Cohen, 2009; Turner & Spears Brown, 2007). In contrast, learning of, or acquiring, a stigmatizable characteristic later in life (such as mental illness) often means considering this identity after one has established or solidified one's self-concept, suggesting that these identities are more likely to be seen as peripheral to one's self-concept or primary social identities.

Differences in stigma acquisition should also have implications for stereotype endorsement. When stigmas are acquired later in life, this leaves many years to learn and endorse negative stereotypes associated with these characteristics and to devalue these groups *before* they become personally relevant (e.g., Link, 1987; Link et al., 1989). In contrast, when stigma acquisition occurs early in life, one's understanding of the self and the stereotype can be developed in tandem. This allows one to engage in, and benefit from, self-protective strategies that limit the internalization of the negative stereotypes and the likelihood of endorsing the stereotypes, such as attributing negative feedback to prejudice, selectively comparing one's outcomes with other individuals with the same stigmatizable characteristic, and selectively valuing and devaluing attributes on which one's group does well or poorly (respectively) (e.g., Crocker & Major, 1989).

Variability also exists between groups on the extent to which one's stigmatizable identity is seen as controllable (e.g., Schwarzer & Weiner, 1991; Weiner, 1993; Weiner, Perry, & Magnusson, 1988)—a factor that has implications for stereotype endorsement. Characteristics like obesity and mental illness are often seen as controllable or personally remediable (e.g., Crandall, 1994; Crocker et al., 1998; DeJong, 1993; Weiner et al., 1988), both by those who possess these stigmatizable characteristics and nonstigmatized observers (e.g., Quinn & Crocker, 1999; Rusch, Corrigan, Todd, & Bodenhausen, 2010; Rusch, Todd, Bodenhausen, Olschewski, & Corrigan, 2010). Thus, perceptions that one's stigmatizable status is controllable likely contribute to the tendency for individuals to endorse these stereotypes and see stereotypes and prejudices as legitimate (Corrigan & Watson, 2002; Rusch, Lieb, Bohus, & Corrigan, 2006; Watson, Corrigan, Larson, & Sells, 2007).

As detailed earlier in this chapter, group identification and stereotype endorsement are two factors that are differentially necessary for the emergence of group-as-target and self-as-source stereotype threats. Specifically, low group identification reduces risk for group-as-target stereotype threats. In contrast, believing there is no credibility to the stereotypes reduces risk for self-as-source stereotype threats. As a result, risk for these particular stereotype threats should vary to the extent that individuals possessing particular stigmatizable characteristics are more or less likely to identify with the stereotyped group or endorse the negative stereotypes. For example, individuals with group memberships that tend not to elicit stereotype endorsement (e.g., race/ethnicity, religion) should have a lower risk for self-as-source stereotype threats (concerns that a performance would confirm, in an individual's own mind, that she or her group is stereotypic) compared to other-as-source stereotype threats (concerns that a performance would confirm in another's mind that she or her group is stereotypic). In contrast, individuals with group memberships that tend not to elicit group identification (e.g., mental illness, being overweight) should have a lower risk for group-as-target stereotype threats (concerns that a performance could poorly represent the group) compared to self-as-target stereotype threats (concerns that a performance could confirm she is stereotypic). This is indeed what research reveals; different patterns of stereotype threats emerge between individuals contending with negative stereotypes associated with their race/ethnicity, religion, weight, and mental health, in ways that are predictable from the Multi-Threat Framework (Shapiro, 2011).

The variability in stereotype threat risk between negatively stereotyped groups highlights the importance of differentiating between stereotype threats and understanding the factors that give rise to each of the stereotype threats. In general, a great deal of stereotype threat research focuses on racial minority groups, groups that tend to elicit relatively high levels of group identification and relatively low levels of stereotype endorsement. If stereotype threat is a singular construct, this research should generalize to any negatively stereotyped group. However, to the extent that different negatively stereotyped groups are at risk for different stereotype threats, a focus on a subset of negatively stereotyped groups may inadvertently converge on a subset of stereotype threats. As a result, many findings from the extant literature may not generalize to less commonly studied groups. Furthermore, to the extent that manipulations and measures of stereotype threat are assumed to function similarly and are translated from one program of research to another, from one group to another, or even within a group between individuals who vary on the stereotype threat elicitors, these studies may yield null findings, suggesting no risk for stereotype threat. As a result, some groups may be excluded from stereotype threat research or overlooked for interventions because they are perceived to have low risk for stereotype threat when in fact they may only have low risk for the *one particular form* of stereotype threat captured by the selected paradigm.

Different Coping and Compensatory Strategies in Response to Different Stereotype Threats

Although performance or behaviors in the negatively stereotyped domain should be similarly harmed across the stereotype threats, people will likely cope with each of these stereotype threats in distinct ways (Shapiro & Neuberg, 2007). Research exploring the ways in which individuals spontaneously cope with and compensate for the experience of stereotype threat reveals that stereotype threat can lead to self-handicapping, or putting disruptive obstacles in the way of one's success (e.g., Keller, 2002; Stone, 2002); disidentifying from, disengaging from, or devaluing the stereotyped domain (e.g., Major & Schmader, 1998; Nussbaum & Steele, 2007); and reducing one's aspirations to pursue stereotype-relevant careers (e.g., Davies, Spencer, Quinn, & Gerhardstein, 2002). Although many strategies—such as trying to perform in ways that disprove the negative stereotype—may be universally employed in the face of stereotype threats, a close consideration of the diversity of cognitive and behavioral coping and compensatory strategies, and a recognition that these strategies logically serve somewhat different functions, suggests that different strategies are likely to be employed (and to be differentially successful) in response to the experience of the different stereotype threats.

For example, self-as-source stereotype threats focus on one's own views of the self (Self-Concept Threat) and of one's group (Group-Concept Threat), and thus likely engage coping strategies aimed at preserving a positive self-view or group view (e.g., self-handicapping, the discounting of feedback, excuse generation, devaluing the domain, affirming in another domain). In contrast, the other-as-source stereotype threats focus on ingroup and outgroup others' views of the self or the group, and thus often require public remediation strategies (e.g., publicly self-handicapping, publicly discounting feedback, public excuse generation). Another difference between self-as-source and other-as-source stereotype threats detailed earlier in this chapter is the emotions that accompany these stereotype threats. That is, other-as-source threats likely elicit anger, an emotional reaction that tends to emerge when one believes one is being treated unfairly, whereas self-as-source stereotype threats likely elicit shame. Thus, these emotional reactions can spur different types of strategies. For example, in circumstances in which individuals feel they have sufficient resources (e.g., very talented female engineers), anger may be more likely to elicit challenge responses that fuel more successful performances (e.g., Crisp, Bache, & Maitner, 2009; Kray, Reb, Galinksy, & Thompson, 2004).

To cope with group-as-target stereotype threats, one might engage in strategies that reduce one's attachment to the group: By reducing the extent to which the group itself is related to the individual's self-worth—by, for example, disassociating, disengaging, or ultimately disidentifying with the group—one can reduce the discomfort one might otherwise anticipate prior to a stereotype-relevant performance. One might also cope by directly distancing oneself as a representative of the group (e.g., by pointing to other group members more suited for the role as representative, communicating compensatory information regarding own or other group members' successes). For the self-as-target stereotype threats, one might also reject or otherwise distance oneself from the stereotyped group in an attempt to shed the possibility of being evaluated in terms of the group's stereotyped abilities. However, given that identification with the group does not contribute to the experience of self-as-target stereotype threats, individuals experiencing self-as-target stereotype threats may also engage the group, or pull themselves closer to the group, as a source of support (e.g., turning to the ingroup for social comparison purposes, solidarity, positive affirmation, and corroboration of suspicions that the evaluative situation may have been biased; Crocker & Major, 1998).

Policy Box

Whereas previous research conceptualizes stereotype threat as a singular threat, the Multi-Threat Framework distinguishes between multiple unique forms of stereotype threats. That is, stereotype-relevant tasks can elicit concerns regarding who one's performance will reflect upon—oneself or the group's—and who will judge this performance—oneself or another person (e.g., a boss, teacher, coworker). Each of these concerns represents a unique stereotype threat that is elicited by different variables, emerges to different degrees for different individuals and different groups, and is exacerbated by different factors. The pragmatic significance here is twofold. First, because different factors give rise to each stereotype threat, it is easy to overlook stereotype threats. For example, to the extent that stereotype threat is conceptualized as a concern rooted in how a test might reflect upon women as a whole, a test that does not request gender may be deemed stereotype threat-free and used for important high-stakes tests. However, to the extent that other cues make gender salient (e.g., demographic composition of the room), this situation can still yield stereotype threats rooted in concerns about what the test can confirm in the test-taker's mind. Second, these stereotype threats will require different interventions. That is, an intervention designed to reduce one form of stereotype threat—for example, attempting to reduce concerns regarding performance implications for one's group's abilities by establishing support-oriented groups/societies for women in domains in which they are under-represented—will do very little to reduce other stereotype threats present in the situation—for example, increasing concerns about the implications of a test for one's own abilities by making salient the dearth of women.

Intervention

One of the most important implications of considering multiple, qualitatively distinct stereotype threats is that no single condition (or set of conditions) contributes to the experience of all stereotype threats (see Table 5.2). As a result, an intervention that effectively mitigates one stereotype threat is unlikely to effectively mitigate another because these threats are elicited by different factors. This suggests that, to be effective, interventions must target the specific stereotype threat undermining performance or eliciting harmful coping strategies. The Multi-Threat Framework offers insight into the development of stereotype threat-reducing interventions. First, to the extent that one can identify the specific form of stereotype threat experienced by individuals or groups of individuals, one can tailor an intervention to target the most relevant eliciting circumstances. For example, because each of the eliciting variables in Table 5.2 is conceptualized as necessary, but not sufficient, for each of the stereotype threats to emerge, eliminating a single one should eliminate risk for a particular stereotype threat. Second, to the extent that one desires to combat several forms of stereotype threat with a single intervention, the intervention will need to be multipronged: Several specific sets of conditions will need to be altered. For instance, if one can convince an individual that those evaluating her math performance will never know her identity, she should not experience Own-Reputation Threat (Outgroup). That is, even if the other conditions for eliciting this stereotype threat are present—she is aware others know her gender, she knows others believe women lack mathematical talent, and she cares deeply that others not see her perform poorly in math—she will nonetheless not experience the threat if she is convinced that her identity cannot be linked to her performance. This is not to say that she will not experience one of the other forms of stereotype threat; she very well might, as the intervention suggested above is irrelevant to most of the other threats. Thus, the Multi-Threat Framework suggests there is not a single, simple intervention: Qualitatively different interventions will need to target the different factors that elicit each of the stereotype threats or the different mechanisms that underlie each of the stereotype threats.

▪ CONCLUSION

Stereotype threat has traditionally been conceptualized as a singular construct, experienced similarly across situations, groups, and individuals. In contrast, the Multi-Threat Framework breaks down this phenomenon into qualitatively distinct stereotype threats and offers a structure by which to understand the antecedents and consequences of these unique stereotype threats. We believe that differentiating among these more specific stereotype threats will be critical to understanding when stereotype threats will emerge, the experiences of members of different negatively stereotyped groups, how these stereotype threats are coped with and compensated for across situations, and most importantly, how to develop the strongest interventions. Thus, we feel that future stereotype threat research will benefit, both theoretically and pragmatically, from a consideration of these different stereotype threats.

▪ ACKNOWLEDGMENTS

This research was supported by a National Institutes of Health/National Institute of General Medical Sciences grant (grant number: RC1GM09071) and a National

Science Foundation grant (grant number: BCS0956321) awarded to Jenessa R. Shapiro. The author would like to thank Toni Schmader and Christine Chu for their helpful comments on an earlier version of this manuscript.

References

Aboud, F. E. (1988). *Children and prejudice.* New York: Basil Blackwell.

Akiba, D., Szalacha, L. A., & Garcia Coll, C. T. (2004). Multiplicity of ethnic identification during middle childhood: Conceptual and methodological considerations. *New Directions for Child and Adolescent Development, 104,* 45–60.

Alvarez, J. M., Cameron, J., Garfinkle, G. S., Ruble, D. N., & Fuligni, A. J. (2001, April). *Identity development in immigrant children.* Paper presented at the biennial meeting of the Society for Research in Child Development, Minneapolis, MN.

Aronson, J., Lustina, M. J., Good, C., Keough, K., Steele, C. M., & Brown, J. (1999). When White men can't do math: Necessary and sufficient factors in stereotype threat. *Journal of Experimental Social Psychology, 35,* 29–46.

Bosson, J. K., Haymovitz, E. L., & Pinel, E. C. (2004). When saying and doing diverge. *Journal of Experimental Social Psychology, 40,* 247–255.

Briggs, S. R., Cheek, J. M., & Buss, A. H. (1980). Other directedness questionnaire. *Journal of Personality and Social Psychology, 38,* 679–686.

Cohen, A. B. (2009). Many forms of culture. *American Psychologist, 64,* 94–204.

Corrigan, P. (2004). How stigma interferes with mental health care. *American Psychologist, 59,* 614–625.

Corrigan, P., & Watson, A. (2002). The paradox of self-stigma and mental illness. *Clinical Psychology: Science and Practice, 9,* 35–53.

Crandall, C. S. (1994). Prejudice against fat people: Ideology and self-interest. *Journal of Personality and Social Psychology, 66,* 882–894.

Crandall, C. S., & Biernat, M. (1990). The ideology of anti-fat attitudes. *Journal of Applied Social Psychology, 20,* 227–243.

Crisp, R. J., Bache, L. M., & Maitner, A. T. (2009). Dynamics of social comparison in counter-stereotypic domains: Stereotype boost, not stereotype threat, for women engineering majors. *Social Influence, 4,* 171–184.

Crocker, J., & Major, B. (1989). Social stigma and self-esteem: The self-protective properties of stigma. *Psychological Review, 96,* 608–630.

Crocker, J., Major, B., & Steele, C. M. (1998). Social stigma. In D. Gilbert, S. T. Fiske, & G. Lindzey (Eds.), *The handbook of social psychology* Vol. 2 (4th ed., pp. 504–553). Boston: McGraw Hill.

Crocker, J., & Wolfe, C. T. (2001). Contingencies of self-worth. *Psychological Review, 108,* 593–623.

Davies, P. G., Spencer, S. J., Quinn, D. M., & Gerhardstein, R. (2002). Consuming images: How television commercials that elicit stereotype threat can restrain women academically and professionally. *Personality and Social Psychology Bulletin, 28,* 1615–1628.

DeJong, W. (1993). Obesity as a characterological stigma: The issue of responsibility and judgments of task performance. *Psychological Reports, 73,* 963–970.

Frable, D., Blackstone, T., & Scherbaum, C. (1990). Marginal and mindful: Deviants in social interactions. *Journal of Personality and Social Psychology, 59,* 140–149.

Gangestad, S. W., & Snyder, M. (2000). Self-monitoring: Appraisal and reappraisal. *Psychological Bulletin, 126*, 530–555.

Goffman, E. (1963). *Notes on the management of spoiled identity*. New York: Simon & Schuster.

Hebl, M. R., & Dovidio, J. F. (2005). Promoting the "social" in the examination of social stigmas. *Personality and Social Psychology Review, 9*, 156–182.

Inzlicht, M., Aronson, J., Good, C., & McKay, L. (2006). A particular resiliency to threatening environments. *Journal of Experimental Social Psychology, 42*, 323–336.

Inzlicht, M., McKay, L., & Aronson, J. (2006). Stigma as ego depletion - How being the target of prejudice affects self-control. *Psychological Science, 17*, 262–269.

Johns, M., Inzlicht, M., & Schmader, T. (2008). Stereotype threat and executive resource depletion: Examining the influence of emotion regulation. *Journal of Experimental Psychology-General, 137*, 691–705.

Jones, E., Farina, A., Hastorf, A., Markus, H., Miller, D., & Scott, R. (1984). *Social stigma: The psychology of marked relationships*. New York: Freeman.

Keller, J. (2002). Blatant stereotype threat and women's math performance: Self-handicapping as a strategic means to cope with obtrusive negative performance expectations. *Sex Roles, 47*, 193–198.

Keller, J., & Dauenheimer, D. (2003). Stereotype threat in the classroom: Dejection mediates the disrupting threat effect on women's math performance. *Personality and Social Psychology Bulletin, 29*, 371–381.

Kernis, M. H., Paradise, A. W., Whitaker, D. J., Wheatman, S. R., & Goldman, B. N. (2000). Master of one's psychological domain? Not likely if one's self-esteem is unstable. *Personality and Social Psychology Bulletin, 26*, 1297–1305.

Koenig, A. M., & Eagly, A. H. (2005). Stereotype threat in men on a test of social sensitivity. *Sex Roles, 52*, 489–496.

Kray, L. J., Reb, J., Galinsky, A. D., & Thomson, L. (2004). Stereotype reactance at the bargaining table: The effect of stereotype activation and power on claiming and creating value. *Personality and Social Psychology Bulletin, 30*, 399–411.

Leary, M. R., Kelly, K. M., Cottrell, C. A., & Schreindorfer, L. S. (2006). *Individual differences in the need to belong: Mapping the nomological network*. Unpublished manuscript, Wake Forest University.

Lickel, B., Hamilton, D. L., Wieczorkowska, G., Lewis, A., Sherman, S. J., & Uhles, A. N. (2000). Varieties of groups and the perception of group entitativity. *Journal of Personality and Social Psychology, 78*, 223–246.

Link, B. G. (1987). Understanding labeling effects in the area of mental disorders: An assessment of the effects of expectations of rejection. *American Sociological Review, 52*, 96–112.

Link, B. G., Cullen, F. T., Struening, E., Shrout, P. E., & Dohrenwend, B. P. (1989). A modified labeling theory approach to mental disorders: An empirical assessment. *American Sociological Review, 54*, 400–423.

Luhtanen, R., & Crocker, J. (1992). A collective self-esteem scale: Self-evaluation of one's social identity. *Personality and Social Psychology Bulletin, 18*, 302–318.

Madge, N. J. (1976). Context and the expressed ethnic preferences of infant school children. *Journal of Child Psychology and Psychiatry, 17*, 337–344.

Major, B., & Schmader, T. (1998). Coping with stigma through psychological disengagement. In J. Swim, & C. Stangor (Eds.), *Prejudice: The target's perspective*. San Diego: Academic Press.

McGlone, M. S., & Aronson, J. (2006). Stereotype threat, identity salience, and spatial reasoning. *Journal of Applied Developmental Psychology, 27*, 486–493.

Nussbaum, D. A., & Steele, C. M. (2007). Situational disengagement and persistence in the face of adversity. *Journal of Experimental Social Psychology, 43*, 127–134.

Quinn, D. M., & Crocker, J. (1999). When ideology hurts: Effects of belief in the Protestant ethic and feeling overweight on the psychological well-being of women. *Journal of Personality and Social Psychology, 77*, 402–414.

Rusch, N., Corrigan, P. W., Todd, A. R., & Bodenhausen, G. V. (2010). Implicit self-stigma in people with mental illness. *Journal of Nervous and Mental Disease, 198*, 150–153.

Rusch, N., Lieb, K., Bohus, M., & Corrigan, P. W. (2006). Self-stigma, empowerment, and perceived legitimacy of discrimination among women with mental illness. *Psychiatric Services, 57*, 399–402.

Rusch, N., Todd, A. R., Bodenhausen, G. V., Olschewski, M., & Corrigan, P. W. (2010). Automatically activated shame reactions and perceived legitimacy of discrimination: A longitudinal study among people with mental illness. *Journal of Behavior Therapy and Experimental Psychiatry, 41*, 60–63.

Scheier, M. F., & Carver, C. S. (1985). The Self-consciousness Scale: A revised version for use with general populations. *Journal of Applied Social Psychology, 15*, 687–699.

Schmader, T., & Beilock, S. L. (2011). Mechanisms: An integration of processes that underlie stereotype threat. In T. Schmader, & M. Inzlicht (Eds.), *Stereotype threat: Theory, process, and application.* New York: Oxford University Press.

Schmader, T., Johns, M., & Forbes, C. (2008). An integrated process model of stereotype threat effects on performance. *Psychological Review, 115*, 336–356.

Schwarzer, R., & Weiner, B. (1991). Stigma controllability and coping as predictors of emotions and social support. *Journal of Social and Personal Relationships, 8*, 133–140.

Sellers, R. M., Rowley, S. A. J., Chavous, T. M., Shelton, J. N., & Smith, M. (1997). Multidimensional inventory of black identity: Preliminary investigation of reliability and construct validity. *Journal of Personality and Social Psychology, 73*, 805–815.

Sellers, R. M., Smith, M. A., Shelton, J. N., Rowley, S. A. J., & Chavous, T. M. (1998). Multidimensional model of racial identity: A reconceptualization of Black racial identity. *Personality and Social Psychology Review, 2*, 18–39.

Shapiro, J. R. (2011). Different groups, different threats: A multi-threat approach to the experience of stereotype threats. *Personality and Social Psychology Bulletin, 37*, 464–480.

Shapiro, J. R., & Neuberg, S. L. (2007). From stereotype threat to stereotype threats: Implications of a multi-threat framework for causes, moderators, mediators, consequences, and interventions. *Personality and Social Psychology Review, 11*, 107–130.

Spencer, S. J., Steele, C. M., & Quinn, D. M. (1999). Stereotype threat and women's math performance. *Journal of Experimental Social Psychology, 35*, 4–28.

Steele, C. M. (1997). A threat in the air: How stereotypes shape intellectual identity and performance. *American Psychologist, 52*, 613–629.

Steele, C. M., & Aronson, J. (1995). Stereotype threat and the intellectual test performance of Blacks. *Journal of Personality and Social Psychology, 69*, 797–811.

Steele, C. M., Spencer, S. J., & Aronson, J. (2002). Contending with group image: The psychology of stereotype and social identity threat. In M. P. Zanna (Ed.), *Advances in experimental social psychology* Vol. 34 (pp. 379–440). San Diego: Academic Press.

Stone, J. (2002). Battling doubt by avoiding practice: The effects of stereotype threat on self-handicapping in White athletes. *Personality and Social Psychology Bulletin, 12*, 1667–1678.

Teachman, B. A., Wilson, J. G., & Komarovskaya, I. (2006). Implicit and explicit stigma of mental illness in diagnosed and healthy samples. *Journal of Social and Clinical Psychology, 25*, 75–95.

Turner, K. L., & Brown, C. S. (2007). The importance of gender and ethnic identities across individuals and contexts. *Social Development, 16*, 700–719.

Watson, A. C., Corrigan, P., Larson, J. E., & Sells, M. (2007). Self-stigma in people with mental illness. *Schizophrenia Bulletin, 33*, 1312–1318.

Weiner, B. (1993). On sin versus sickness: A theory of perceived responsibility and social motivation. *American Psychologist, 48*, 957–965.

Weiner, B., Perry, R. P., & Magnusson, J. (1988). An attributional analysis of reactions to stigmas. *Journal of Personality and Social Psychology, 55*, 738–748.

6

Social Belonging and the Motivation and Intellectual Achievement of Negatively Stereotyped Students

■ GREGORY M. WALTON AND
PRIYANKA B. CARR

An important consequence of negative stereotypes that impugn non-Asian ethnic minorities' intellectual ability and women's mathematical ability is to convey to the targets of these stereotypes that they are not seen as individuals, that they may not be fully valued or respected—that they may not belong—in academic settings. In this chapter, we review research demonstrating that people who contend with numeric under-representation and with negative stereotypes in mainstream academic and professional arenas are vigilant for cues that could communicate they do not belong or are not fully included in these settings. When encountered, such cues can undermine people's sense of belonging, motivation, and achievement. Further, this chapter reviews effective remedies—strategies to buttress students' sense of social belonging in academic environments. These strategies aim to forestall negative attributions for social events in school—to lead students to see social adversity as normal and nondiagnostic of a lack of belonging. As tested in randomized intervention field experiments, variants of this intervention have improved school outcomes among black college students, black middle school students, and female engineering students, even over long periods of time. A 1-hour-long social-belonging intervention delivered in students' freshman year improved black students' college grades from sophomore through senior year, and reduced the achievement gap between black and white students over this period by 52%. Implications for psychological process, for stereotype threat, and for efforts to ameliorate social inequality are discussed.

Keywords: Stereotype threat, need for belonging, academic performance, black–white test score gap

In the spring of 1985, a promising young African American student graduated from Princeton University and wrote her senior thesis on the experiences of African Americans on campus. She introduced the topic from personal experience:

My experiences at Princeton have made me far more aware of my "Blackness" than ever before... no matter how liberal and open-minded some of my White professors

and classmates try to be toward me, I sometimes feel like a visitor on campus; as if
I really don't belong. . . it often seems as if, to them, I will always be Black first and
a student second.

—(Robinson, 1985, p. 2)

This was Michelle Robinson, who would later become Michelle Obama and First Lady
of the United States. Sonia Sotomayor, the first Latina on the United States Supreme
Court, described her own experience at Princeton a decade earlier in strikingly similar
terms. She writes of feeling like "a visitor landing in an alien country" and says, "I have
spent my years since Princeton, while at law school, and in my various professional
jobs, not feeling completely a part of the worlds I inhabit" (Lewis, 2009).

Such feelings appear to be common. In an insightful book, *The Rage of a Privileged
Class*, Ellis Cose tells the stories of dozens of successful African Americans who
questioned their belonging in mainstream settings. One partner at a law firm tells of
arriving at work early one day and, as he searched for his key at the office door,
having his credentials questioned by a young white associate. The partner "found
himself growing angrier and angrier: 'Because of his color, he felt he had the right to
check me out'" (Cose, 1993, pp. 48–49).

Incidents like this illustrate why even highly successful ethnic minorities may
come to feel that they do not belong in mainstream settings. Such experiences may
convey to them that they are not viewed as individuals with distinct interests, per-
sonalities, and talents but as token representatives of a group that is stereotyped as
less qualified, less able, and less worthy than others. It is hardly surprising that, in the
face of experiences like these, African Americans might feel that they are seen as, as
Michelle Robinson put it, "Black first and a student second."

This chapter reviews research exploring how negative stereotypes affect people's
feelings of social belonging in mainstream school and work settings and, over time,
their motivation, participation, and achievement in these settings. Of course,
Michelle Robinson, Sonia Sotomayor, and many other ethnic minorities have had
extraordinarily successful careers in mainstream settings. But many talented ethnic
minorities do not; gaps in academic achievement and professional success between
white and non-Asian ethnic minorities, as well as between men and women in quantitative fields, remain a pressing social problem in the United States and many other
countries (Hyde, Fennema, & Lamon, 1990; Jencks & Phillips, 1998). Research
investigating negatively stereotyped individuals' social experiences in mainstream
settings can provide novel insights into factors that contribute to inequality between
marginalized and nonmarginalized groups, and suggest new reforms to reduce these
disparities. We close this chapter with a review of interventions to boost students'
sense of social belonging in school, and the effects these interventions have on the
academic achievement of negatively stereotyped students.

We begin with the proposition that social belonging and the experience of being
negatively stereotyped are fundamentally antithetical. By *social belonging*, we mean
people's perception of the quality of their social relationships in a setting—whether
others in that setting include, value, and respect one (see Baumeister & Leary,

1995). A basic tenet of social belonging is that one belongs, at least in part, as an individual—that one's individual qualities, characteristics, and contributions are recognized and valued by others in the setting. Negative stereotypes, such as stereotypes about African Americans' intellectual abilities and women's quantitative skills, convey to their targets that they could be devalued in these settings, that their contributions might not be recognized, and that perhaps they will not belong. Given that social belonging is essential for sustained, high levels of motivation and achievement (see Walton & Cohen, 2011a), these social-relational worries can have a large negative effect on stereotyped students' school performance. However, as will be seen, interventions that buttress stereotyped students' feelings of belonging in school can generate large and long-lasting improvements in academic outcomes (e.g., Walton & Cohen, 2011b).

This chapter is divided into three sections. First, we discuss research investigating how cues that signal the presence of negative stereotypes affect targets' sense of belonging and motivation in school and work environments. Second, we discuss how social-relational concerns impair intellectual performance in laboratory settings, especially in the context of research investigating stereotype threat. Third, we discuss research examining students' sense of social belonging in field settings, including interventions designed to buttress students' feelings of belonging in school.

■ HINTS OF STEREOTYPES AFFECT SOCIAL BELONGING AND MOTIVATION

For people who work or study in settings in which their group is targeted by negative stereotypes, the world can look very different from how it appears to others (Steele, 2010). People targeted by negative stereotypes face the possibility that others in the setting could view them as representatives of a devalued group rather than as individuals—"as Black first, and a student second." The prospect that one could be excluded or devalued simply because of one's group identity can cause people to be vigilant for cues that might suggest whether others will include and value them in mainstream settings (Walton & Cohen, 2007). When confronted with negative cues, people may question their belonging and lose motivation. People who are not negatively stereotyped in a setting simply do not have to deal with this concern. They might worry about their belonging as a consequence of individual factors, but they need not worry that they will be reduced to a negative group stereotype.

In one line of research investigating these processes, Purdie-Vaughns, Steele, Davies, Ditlmann, and Crosby (2008) examined African American professionals' trust in a company. Participants read a brochure ostensibly published by a consulting firm depicting either a diverse or a nondiverse workforce. Crossed with this manipulation, half of the brochures described a "color-blind" philosophy, which emphasized that the company trained its "diverse workforce to embrace their similarities" (p. 618). The other half described a "value-diversity" philosophy, which emphasized that, "embracing our diversity enriches our culture" (p. 619).

The researchers then asked participants how much they trusted the company and how comfortable they would feel in it. On their own, neither the nondiverse company nor the color-blindness ideology led African American professionals to distrust the company. But together they carried a threatening meaning: In combination with a lack of diversity, the color-blindness message seemed to convey to participants not fairness but a willful ignorance of the concerns that arise from a stigmatized identity. In this condition, participants distrusted the company, anticipated feeling uncomfortable in it, and expressed greater concern about being devalued in the company because of their race.

Another study examined women's response to threatening cues in math, science, and engineering (MSE) environments (Murphy, Steele, & Gross, 2007). Male and female MSE majors watched a video of an MSE conference that depicted either equal numbers of men and women or more men than women. As predicted, although men were unaffected by the gender ratio manipulation, women who viewed the gender-unbalanced video exhibited heightened vigilance on both cognitive and physiological indices. They recalled more details from the video and exhibited greater cardiovascular reactivity. Moreover, women in this condition reported a lower sense of belonging in the conference and less interest in participating in it.

A third line of research found that physical objects alone can signal to people that they do not belong (Cheryan, Plaut, Davies, & Steele, 2009). Men and women participated in the study in a room in the university computer science department. In one condition, the room was filled with objects pretesting had identified as stereotypical of computer scientists (e.g., junk food, a Star Trek poster). In the other condition, the objects were nonstereotypical (e.g., healthy snacks, a nature poster). In the stereotypical condition, men reported greater interest in pursuing computer science than did women. But in the nonsterotypical condition, women's interest increased and, if anything, exceeded men's. Subsequent studies found that the stereotypical objects activated a masculine representation of computer science, that this representation undermined women's sense of belonging in the field, and this, in turn, decreased women's interest in pursuing the field.

Why are people who contend with negative stereotypes in academic or professional settings so closely attuned to subtle cues about who belongs and who does not? They are, we suggest, because contending with negative stereotypes can reasonably cause people to feel uncertain about their social belonging (Walton & Cohen, 2007). In this state of *belonging uncertainty*, even small cues or events can appear to be proof of a lack of belonging. To test this idea more directly, in one study, black and white students were asked to list either two friends who would fit in well in a field of study or eight friends (Walton & Cohen, 2007, Experiment 1). The researchers reasoned that listing eight friends is difficult, and that students who feel uncertain of their belonging in the field might interpret this difficulty as meaning that they do not belong and could not succeed in the field (see Schwarz et al., 1991). This prediction was confirmed. Although white students showed no effect of the manipulation, black students evaluated their belonging and prospects of success in the field far lower in the list-eight-friends condition than in the list-two-friends condition or in a condition in which they had not been asked to list any friends. Moreover, black students seemed to interpret difficulty listing friends as evidence that their group, too, would fare poorly in the field. Given the opportunity to advise peers choosing among academic majors, black students in the list-eight-friends condition discouraged a black peer (but not white peers) from pursuing the field at hand. We return to this research and to the idea of belonging uncertainty later in discussing interventions to buttress students' sense of social belonging in school.

The research reviewed in this section shows that people whose group is negatively stereotyped in a setting are sensitive to cues—like numeric under-representation, diversity ideologies, stereotypical physical objects, and difficulty calling to mind friends in the field—that suggest that they and their group might not belong in that setting. These cues undermine people's sense of belonging and motivation. In the next section, we review research suggesting that worries about social belonging also contribute to decrements in intellectual performance associated with stereotype threat.

▦ SOCIAL BELONGING AND INTELLECTUAL PERFORMANCE

Since the first stereotype threat studies were conducted, researchers have investigated whether stereotype threat undermines people's performance expectancies and sense of self-efficacy (e.g., "I/we can't do it"; Stangor, Carr, & Kiang, 1998), if it raises concerns about being devalued by others in light of the stereotype (e.g., "They think I/we can't do it"; Steele, 2010), or if it triggers both intrapsychic and interpersonal fears (Shapiro, 2011, Chapter 5, this volume). Many classic stereotype-threat manipulations arguably confound these processes. For instance, describing a test as nonevaluative (Steele & Aronson, 1995) could either boost people's confidence in their ability to perform well or reduce apprehension that their performance could be interpreted through the lens of a negative stereotype. To what extent do social-relational worries contribute to stereotype threat?

Stereotype Threat and Social Belonging

Research finds both that cues that evoke specifically social-relational concerns can trigger stereotype threat and that cues that remedy these concerns can prevent stereotype threat. For instance, in the first case, research shows that interacting with a sexist man, which can be devaluing for women, can cause women to experience stereotype threat. In one series of studies, male and female engineering students discussed an engineering-related news article (Logel et al., 2009). Both had previously completed a subtle measure of sexism and, after the interaction, both took a challenging engineering test. Men's performance did not vary with their own or their partner's level of sexism, and women's performance did not vary with their own level of sexism. But the man's level of sexism mattered a great deal for women. More sexist men sat closer to the woman, looked at her body more, held a more open posture, and generally behaved in a more dominant and boorish manner. These behaviors may predictably convey to women that they are not taken seriously in the conversation about engineering. Women who interacted with these sexist men as compared to less sexist men, or with confederates trained to behave in the sexist rather than nonsexist manner, performed worse on a subsequent engineering test. Moreover, consistent with a stereotype threat account, interacting with the sexist man undermined performance only on the engineering test and not on an English test, and was associated with the suppression of concerns about gender stereotypes, a mediator of stereotype threat.

In another, ingenious study, Quinn (2009) zeroed in on interpersonal processes by examining a group in which group membership is invisible—people with a history of mental illness. Quinn assigned students who did and did not have a history of mental illness to one of three conditions. One group of participants completed a background questionnaire that contained no reference to mental illness. In another, the questionnaire asked participants to indicate which, if any, of various psychological problems and physical disorders (e.g., severe frostbite) they had experienced. Here, participants' history of mental illness was both salient to themselves and revealed to the researchers. In the third group, the questionnaire asked participants to indicate only whether they had experienced one of the various psychological and physical maladies listed but did not ask them to specify which one. In this condition, participants' mental illness history was salient to themselves but not revealed to others.

Participants then took a test of "reasoning ability"—a domain in which people with mental illness are negatively stereotyped. Quinn reasoned that to the extent that stereotype threat results from an intrapsychic process, both the second and third conditions—in which participants had been reminded of their history of mental illness—should undermine performance. But if stereotype threat results primarily from an interpersonal process, only the condition in which participants believed they had revealed this history publicly should undermine performance. The latter prediction was confirmed. Both when participants were not reminded of their mental illness history and when participants were reminded of this history but did not reveal it, no decrement in performance occurred. But when students revealed their history of mental illness, their scores dropped precipitously and they performed worse than students with no history of mental illness. The results from both the Logel et al. and Quinn studies suggest that worries about interpersonal perception and evaluation contribute to the performance decrements associated with stereotype threat.

Research using brain imaging corroborates this conclusion (Krendl, Richeson, Kelley, & Heatherton, 2008). In this study, women completed a series of math problems under stereotype threat or not while undergoing functional magnetic resonance imaging (fMRI). Women under stereotype threat performed worse than women not under stereotype threat and, in addition, showed less activation over time of brain regions associated with mathematical computation and learning (e.g., left parietal and prefrontal cortex). Further, women under stereotype threat showed greater activation over time in brain regions associated with social and emotional processing and, especially, with the processing of negative social information (e.g., the ventral anterior cingulate cortex). Consistent with the behavioral evidence, the results suggest that stereotype threat is, in part, a social threat—an apprehension that one could be perceived and devalued in light of a negative stereotype about one's group.

Of course, stereotype threat can also cause damaging intrapsychic processes. For instance, people may try to disprove the stereotype to themselves (Shapiro, 2011, Chapter 5, this volume; see also Inzlicht & Ben-Zeev, 2003). Indeed, stereotype threat operates through multiple mechanisms (Schmader & Beilock, 2011, Chapter 3, this volume). Nonetheless, the interpersonal aspect of stereotype threat suggests novel remedies to improve performance. Testing these remedies both provides important theory-tests and may pave the way for practical strategies to reduce inequality in education.

One strategy is to change the social climate in testing situations directly to forestall interpersonal concerns. In a series of studies, we tested whether evoking a psychological sense of working *with* a man on a test—even on a test completed individually—would forestall apprehension about being viewed stereotypically and thus mitigate stereotype threat among women (Carr, Walton, & Dweck, in preparation). Men and women completed a difficult, ostensibly evaluative math test— conditions that evoke stereotype threat. Using a manipulation we have previously validated (Carr & Walton, under review), we led some participants to feel as though they were working on the test *with* a male confederate, even though in all cases participants worked on the test individually. All participants were led to believe that they had been randomly assigned to receive a tip on the math problems. In the working-together condition, participants received a tip ostensibly authored by the male confederate and written for the participant. The tip read, "Hey [participant's name], Here's something I find helpful . . . I hope it helps you too!– [confederate's name]." Although the content of the tip was not substantively helpful, the exchange was designed to create in participants a sense of working together on the test. In the control condition, participants received the same tip but it was attributed to a computer bank. The results were striking. In the control condition, women performed worse than men (2.18 vs. 3.25 correct). But when led to feel they were working with others, women if anything outscored men (3.68 vs. 2.94 correct). This study suggests that subtle cues that evoke a positive social climate in testing environments can reduce stereotype threat. It is intriguing to speculate about what other kinds of social-relational cues—such as respectful non-verbal behavior—could reduce worries about being seen stereotypically in otherwise threatening academic settings (cf. Logel et al., 2009).

Another remedy is suggested by research on individuation. If stereotype threat leads people to feel they are perceived through the lens of a negative stereotype rather than valued as individuals, then cues that convey to people that their individual characteristics are recognized and valued might prevent stereotype threat. In one study testing this idea, women were asked to describe their personal preferences (e.g., favorite food) before completing a math test in conditions that otherwise trigger stereotype threat (Ambady, Paik, Steele, Owen-Smith, & Mitchell, 2004). The individuating questions led to better performance. A follow-up study found that individuation prevented stereotype threat even when it was negatively valenced (i.e., women listed three positive and four negative personal traits; for a related study, see Gresky, Eyck, Lord, & McIntyre, 2005).

Of course, individuation manipulations may operate through multiple mechanisms, both intrapsychic and interpersonal. If these manipulations in fact mitigate concerns about being viewed through the lens of a stereotype, an intriguing possibility is that they should be more effective when participants believe that the experimenter or evaluator has requested and/or will read their individuating information rather than that the request for individuating information is pro forma or that this information is not of interest. If found, such results would suggest that individuating procedures assure participants that they are seen as individuals rather than as token group members.

This analysis also implies a novel interpretation for the effects of value-affirmation exercises on stereotype threat. Both laboratory experiments (e.g., Martens, Johns, Greenberg, & Schimel, 2006) and intervention field experiments (e.g., Cohen, Garcia, Purdie-Vaughns, Apfel, & Brzustowski, 2009; Cohen, Purdie-Vaughns, & Garcia, 2011, Chapter 18, this volume) show that value-affirmations—in which people write for several minutes about personally important values (e.g., a sense of humor, relationships with friends or family)—can reduce stereotype threat and improve intellectual performance among people from negatively stereotyped groups. For instance, in a series of striking field experiments, Cohen and colleagues (2009) found that a few brief (15–20 minute) value-affirmation exercises improved black middle school students' grades in core academic classes over 2 years, in 7th and 8th grade.

Value-affirmations are thought to buttress people's self-integrity—their view of themselves as good, virtuous, and efficacious—and so to reduce stress in threatening situations (Sherman & Cohen, 2006). But it is also possible that value-affirmations signal to people that their personal values are recognized and respected in a setting, reducing fears of being viewed stereotypically and buttressing their sense of social belonging. Consistent with this possibility, value-affirmations can cause people to experience positive other-directed emotions, such as feelings of love and connectedness (Crocker, Niiya, & Mischkowski, 2008). In addition, content analyses of student essays from value-affirmation interventions indicate that students who wrote about issues of social belonging (e.g., about how a value brought them closer to others) gained more in terms of improvement in grade point average (GPA) than students who did not write about issues of social belonging (Shnabel, Purdie-Vaughns, Cook, Garcia, & Cohen, 2011). The effects of value-affirmations on academic achievement are likely to be multiply mediated, perhaps especially in field settings (Cohen et al., 2009). But to the extent that social-relational processes contribute to these effects, value-affirmations may be more effective when students are led to write about their values in ways that connect them to others. A related question is whether a seemingly minor feature of past value-affirmation interventions—that students believe that their essays have been requested by and will be read by their teacher—increases the effectiveness of these interventions (in fact, in past studies teachers remain blind to students' essays and condition assignment to forestall teacher expectancy effects). This hypothesis awaits test.

Stereotype Lift and Social Belonging

Finally, some research suggests that social-relational processes also contribute to *stereotype lift*—the performance boost experienced by nonstereotyped students when they know that an outgroup is negatively stereotyped on a task (Walton & Cohen, 2003). If apprehensions about how one is viewed and whether one is valued contribute to stereotype threat, a sense of assurance that one will be viewed positively and valued might contribute to stereotype lift. In one study, white students took a test said to be evaluative of intellectual ability or that was said, in addition, to be fair for different racial groups (Walton, Thomas, & Cohen, 2003). Participants exhibited stereotype lift—they scored better when the test was described only as evaluative. Additional measures suggest that the manipulation assured participants of their social standing. In the evaluative condition, participants reported more confidence that they would be viewed well by others (higher social state self-esteem) and less worry about proving their ability by performing well (lower performance goals). Moreover, these patterns and the performance results were stronger the more participants activated race-related concepts as assessed by a word completion measure (Steele & Aronson, 1995). The more participants thought about race and could benefit from negative stereotypes about an outgroup, it seems, the more they could relax and feel assured they would be well-received in the setting and the better they performed.

The Quinn (2009) study provides complementary evidence that social-relational processes contribute to stereotype lift. Just as the performance of students with a history of mental illness dropped only when they had disclosed this history (but not when they were reminded of it), so the performance of students without a history of mental illness rose only when they had disclosed its absence (but not when they were reminded of its absence).

Policy Box

Most reforms in education end at the classroom door or, at most, the teacher's chair. They do not directly target students' experience. Reforms like more equitable school funding, new governance structures, better curricula or pedagogical approaches, merit pay, new accountability systems, and so forth emphasize structural factors and/or incentives. Although these factors can create opportunities to learn, as important is whether students take up such opportunities. A central task of education reform should be to address psychological barriers to learning (Yeager & Walton, 2011); for example, to mitigate the worries of a student who sits in the back of the class feeling isolated and lonely, wondering whether her classmates or teacher view her through the lens of a negative group stereotype. Only when psychological concerns have been addressed will students be able to fully avail themselves of leaning opportunities in class.

The research reviewed here shows that members of marginalized groups may chronically wonder whether they belong in mainstream school settings. This worry causes negative social events in school to loom large in meaning, undermining students' motivation and achievement and contributing to group differences. This process is fundamentally psychological; it necessitates a psychological remedy. Educational reforms should build on existing small-scale psychological interventions to develop ways to buttress a sense of belonging in school among large numbers of students—to create a climate of belonging. It will be challenging to do so. But psychological interventions hold great promise. They can fuel engagement and performance and produce a cascade of benefits. And without them, students may be unable to take full advantage of learning opportunities created through effective structural reforms.

■ SOCIAL BELONGING IN FIELD SETTINGS

The research described above suggests the potential importance of social belonging in shaping the experiences and achievement of people from negatively stereotyped groups in mainstream school and work settings. But this research was all conducted in laboratory settings. How does social belonging affect the real-world academic experiences and achievement of negatively stereotyped students? Research investigating this question comes in two forms: correlational longitudinal research and intervention field experiments.

Correlational Longitudinal Research

Longitudinal research shows that worries about negative stereotypes and devaluation can lead students to feel that they do not belong in mainstream academic environments and this can undermine their academic outcomes over time. For instance, in a classic study, Mendoza-Denton, Downey, Purdie, Davis, and Pietrzak (2002) tracked African American students' experiences in the first few years at an elite, predominantly white college. They assessed individual differences in students' sensitivity to race-based rejection (RS-Race)—the anxious expectation of being rejected on the basis of race. African American students who were high in RS-Race experienced a lower sense of belonging in the university and showed a semester-by-semester decline in grades over the first 2 years of college. By contrast, students low in RS-Race maintained a steady level of academic performance. Further, high levels of RS-Race seemed to interfere with students' ability to engage effectively with the academic environment—for instance, African American students high in RS-Race experienced greater anxiety about discussing academic problems with instructors and attended fewer review sessions than did peers low in RS-Race.

A second longitudinal study explored feelings of belonging among women enrolled in a challenging college calculus course (Good, Rattan, & Dweck, under review). This study found that women who believed that others in their class endorsed negative gender stereotypes and who believed that math ability is fixed rather than expandable experienced a lower sense of belonging in mathematics over time. This lowered sense of belonging, in turn, was associated with less interest in pursuing math and with worse math grades.

Intervention Field Experiments

If worries about social belonging undermine the achievement of negatively stereo-typed students, would buttressing students' sense of belonging improve their out-comes? As will be seen, even brief social belonging interventions can yield strikingly large and long-lasting benefits for stereotyped students in real-world school settings (e.g., Walton & Cohen, 2011). This contrasts with many large, costly interventions in education that have little or no effects, or effects that dissipate rapidly with time. In general, psychological interventions can exert positive effects long after their delivery because they change the trajectory of students' experiences in a school setting over time—they curtail negative cyclical processes that undermine outcomes over time and set in motion positive cyclical processes that improve outcomes over time (for a review, see Yeager & Walton, 2011; e.g., Aronson, Fried, & Good, 2002; Blackwell, Trzesniewski, & Dweck, 2007; Cohen et al., 2009; Wilson, Damiani, & Shelton, 2002). For instance, a student who comes to feel secure in her social belonging in school may anticipate better interactions with peers and instructors. This expectation may improve interactions with others and help the student form the kind of strong social bonds that sustain high levels of motivation and achieve-ment in school. The capability of brief psychological interventions to initiate power-ful self-reinforcing processes that improve students' outcomes over time makes their applied promise especially exciting. In addition, the way in which these processes unfold over time raise significant new empirical and theoretical questions.

The *social belonging intervention* was developed in response to research indicating that ethnic minority students' experience in academic environments is particularly labile (e.g., Aronson & Inzlicht, 2004; Mendoza-Denton et al., 2002). For instance, as described above, minority students may experience a state of belonging uncer-tainty (Walton & Cohen, 2007) in which negative social events—such as critical feedback or feelings of isolation—carry a more global and threatening meaning to minority students than to others. Such events may lead minority student to question their belonging on campus in general and undermine their motivation.

The social belonging intervention was designed to prevent such deleterious global conclusions. To do so, the intervention provides students an alternative, non-threatening explanation for negative social events in school (Walton & Cohen, 2007, 2011b). It conveys to students that worries about belonging and negative social experiences are normal at first in a new school and not reflective of an actual lack of belonging on their part or the part of their social group. Further, the intervention conveys that such experiences dissipate with time, such that with time they, like other students, will come to feel at home in the school (cf. Wilson et al., 2002).

The intervention was first tested among black and white first-year college students attending a selective university Walton & Cohen, 2007, 2011b). Students read the results of a survey of ethnically diverse upper-year students at their school. The survey indicated that negative social events and feelings of nonbelonging are normal in the transition to college, experienced by students of all ethnicities, and dissipate with time. These materials were designed to lead students to attribute these difficulties to the challenges of the transition to college, rather than to a lack of belonging on their part or the part of their ethnic group. The message was reinforced using "saying is believing" procedures: Students wrote an essay about the process of change in students' experiences in college over time and then delivered their essay as a speech to a video camera. They were told that the video would be shown during freshman orientation the next year to help future students better adjust to the college environment (cf. Aronson et al., 2002). In the control condition, the procedure was the same but the information students were exposed to was irrelevant to issues of belonging (e.g., change in students' social-political attitudes). In total, the treatment lasted approximately 1 hour.

For white students, who have little cause to doubt their belonging in school on account of their race, the treatment had little effect. However, the treatment had powerful benefits for black students. In the week following its delivery, the treatment buffered black students' sense of social belonging against negative social events. Whereas in the control condition black students' sense of fit or belonging in school dropped sharply on socially adverse days, in the treatment condition, it stayed high even on adverse days (see Figure 6.1). The treatment also increased black students' self-reported achievement behaviors; for instance, black students reported studying nearly an hour and a half longer each day in the treatment condition than in the control condition (Walton & Cohen, 2007).

Most important were effects on academic achievement, as assessed by official school records. The next semester, black students in the treatment group had grades that were one-third of a grade point higher, both as compared both to the randomized control group and to all black students campus-wide but who had not participated in the study (Walton & Cohen, 2007). Again white students were unaffected.

Subsequent analyses tracked students' academic outcomes through senior year (Walton & Cohen, 2011b). These analyses combined students in the original sample

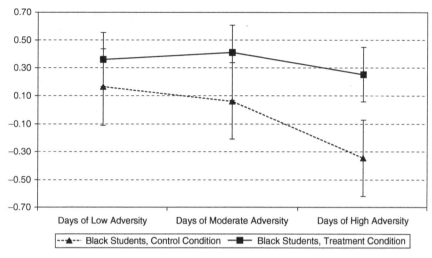

Figure 6.1 Black students' sense of fit or belonging on days of low, moderate, and high adversity in Walton and Cohen (2007). Error bars represent +1/−1 standard errors.

with students in a second cohort. They compared the belonging-treatment to multiple randomized control groups and to the campus-wide comparison group. The treatment effect continued and significantly increased black students' grades over this 3-year period. Whereas in the control condition black students' grades showed no growth over time—no improvement from freshman through senior year—black students in the belonging-treatment condition showed a steady semester-by-semester rise in GPA (see Figure 6.2; Walton & Cohen, 2011b). Overall, the social belonging intervention administered in the spring of students' freshman year cut by half the white–black gap in raw GPA from sophomore through senior year.

Mediation analyses suggest how the intervention raised black students' grades. As noted, in the week following the intervention, black students' feelings of belonging became less vulnerable to adversity on campus: Adverse social events no longer carried a global or symbolic meaning to black students. This reduction in the contingency of black students' feelings of belonging—not the mean level of belonging students reported—statistically mediated the long-term gain in black students' GPA (Walton & Cohen, 2011b). The intervention improved outcomes by securing black students' belonging against adversity, not simply by raising their levels of belonging.

Subsequent research has tested variants of the social-belonging intervention in diverse populations. One study delivered the treatment to ethnically diverse 6th grade students entering middle school (Walton, Cohen, Garcia, Apfel, & Master, in preparation). Regular surveys conducted over the subsequent 3 years showed that, as compared to a randomized control group, the treatment reduced black students' self-reported uncertainty about social belonging over this period and eliminated the

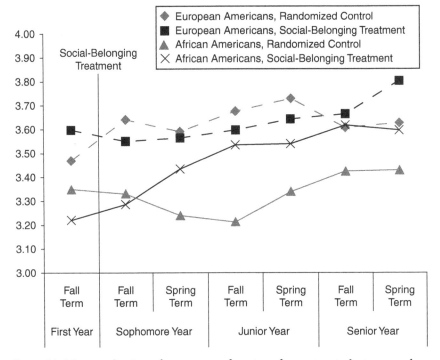

Figure 6.2 Mean academic performance as a function of semester, student race, and experimental condition (raw means) in Walton and Cohen (2011b).

emergence of high levels of perceived stereotype threat in 7th grade. The treatment also improved black students' grades in 8th grade and attenuated an increase in disciplinary incidents among black boys over middle school.

A third study tested the belonging-intervention among men and women entering a selective university engineering program (Logel, Walton, Peach, Spencer, & Zanna, in press; Walton, Logel, Peach, & Spencer, in preparation). Because participants in this study were enrolled in different engineering majors, this study provided an opportunity to test how the effects of the intervention were moderated by context. Some students were enrolled in relatively diverse majors (e.g., environmental engineering), in which 25% or more of students were women. Other students were enrolled in male-dominated majors (e.g., electrical engineering), in which fewer than 20% of students were female. If women experience the greatest level of threat in male-dominated majors (Murphy et al., 2007), the intervention could be most needed and thus most effective for students enrolled in these majors.

The primary outcome was first-term grades, combining across two cohorts of students. Among students enrolled in gender-diverse majors, there was no gender difference in first-term GPA in the control condition and no effect of the intervention. The absence of a gender difference mimics the pattern found on pretreatment measures: Men and women entered the university with similarly high levels of preparation and prior achievement. The results imply that, in these majors, women did not experience high levels of threat.

By contrast, in male-dominated majors, there was a large gender difference in first-term GPA in the control condition—men outperformed women. This gender difference emerged even though men and women again entered the university with identical high levels of preparation and prior achievement, suggesting that in these majors women experienced high levels of threat that undermined their performance. And, here, the belonging intervention had a large effect. It raised women's grades and fully eliminated the gender difference in GPA. Moreover, this effect was mediated by a change in women's feelings about the belonging of their group in engineering as assessed at an implicit level. The belonging-treatment led women to associate "most people like" and "female engineers" more easily along an implicit association test (IAT)-like reaction time task, and this mediated the treatment effect on grades.

These results illustrate how contexts can give rise to threats that undermine negatively stereotyped and under-represented students' feelings of belonging in academic environments, even students who are highly skilled and qualified, and how addressing worries about belonging can improve students' outcomes.

■ CONCLUSION

Many factors that contribute to inequality in education are exceedingly difficult to remedy, such as high levels of poverty in many ethnic minority communities, inequality in school funding and teacher quality, and so forth (Jencks & Phillips, 1998). In this context, brief social-psychological interventions are especially promising. The research reviewed in this chapter illustrates how negative intellectual stereotypes can undermine minority-group students' feelings of belonging in mainstream settings and their motivation and achievement. Further, this research shows that strategies to allay concerns about belonging can improve minority-group students' outcomes even over months and years. An important implication of this research, and of research on stereotype threat more broadly, is that students from negatively stereotyped groups have an enormous amount of untapped intellectual potential in school, which can be hidden by psychological threats (Walton & Spencer, 2009). It is important to understand that interventions to remove psychological threats are not "magic bullets" (Yeager & Walton, 2011). For instance, they do not provide students learning opportunities where none exist; instead, they open students up to learning opportunities that are present in their academic environment. Nonetheless, this research provides hope that effective remedies to allay worries about belonging, if implemented at a large scale, could remove one barrier to high levels of academic achievement among ethnic minority students and women in quantitative fields—and help the young Michelle Robinsons and Sonia Sotomayors attending school today reach their potential.

In addition, this research underscores important theoretical lessons. For instance, whereas much past research in social psychology emphasizes the role of individual factors such as self-efficacy and autonomy in high levels of motivation and achievement, the research reviewed here illustrates the profound importance of students' feelings of belonging and connectedness to others in creating and sustaining achievement (Walton & Cohen, 2011a).

To date, interventions to buttress students' sense of belonging in school have targeted students' own experiences and perceptions. In closing, we suggest that, in some circumstances, it may also be necessary to improve the school environment itself, for instance to reduce prejudice that is present there or to help teachers or administrators support students' sense of belonging at key times (e.g., in transitions) more effectively. Research testing such interventions can pose challenges; for instance, the environment (e.g., classroom) may become the unit of analysis for statistical purposes. But when aspects of the environment itself undermine women and minorities' experience and achievement (see Logel et al., 2009), it may be necessary to improve the objective environment.

References

Ambady, N., Paik, S. K., Steele, J., Owen-Smith, A., & Mitchell, J. P. (2004). Deflecting negative self-relevant stereotype activation: The effects of individuation. *Journal of Experimental Social Psychology, 40,* 401–408.

Aronson, J., Fried, C. B., & Good, C. (2002). Reducing the effect of stereotype threat on African American college students by shaping theories of intelligence. *Journal of Experimental Social Psychology, 38,* 113–125.

Aronson, J., & Inzlicht, M. (2004). The ups and downs of attributional ambiguity: Stereotype vulnerability and the academic self-knowledge of African American college students. *Psychological Science, 15,* 829–836.

Baumeister, R., & Leary, M. (1995). The need to belong: Desire for interpersonal attachments as a fundamental human motivation. *Psychological Bulletin, 117,* 497–529.

Blackwell, L. S., Trzesniewski, K. H., & Dweck, C. S. (2007). Implicit theories of intelligence predict achievement across an adolescent transition: A longitudinal study and an intervention. *Child Development, 78,* 246–263.

Carr, P. B., Walton, G. M., & Dweck C. S. (in preparation). *A sense of working together forestalls stereotype threat.*

Carr, P. B. & Walton, G. M. (under review). A sense of working together fuels intrinsic motivation.

Cohen, G. L., Garcia, J., Purdie-Vaughns, V., Apfel, N., & Brzustoski, P. (2009). Recursive processes in self-affirmation: Intervening to close the minority achievement gap. *Science, 324,* 400–403.

Cohen, G. L., Purdie-Vaughns, V., & Garcia, J. (2011). An identity threat perspective on intervention. In M. Inzlicht, & T. Schmader (Eds.), *Stereotype threat: Theory process, and application.* New York: Oxford University Press.

Cheryan, S., Plaut, V. C., Davies, P. G., & Steele, C. (2009). Ambient belonging: How stereotypical cues impact gender participation in computer science. *Journal of Personality and Social Psychology, 97,* 1045–1060.

Cose, E. (1993). *The rage of a privileged class.* New York: Harper Collins.

Crocker, J., Niiya, Y., & Mischkowski, D. (2008). Why does writing about important values reduce defensiveness? Self-affirmation and the role of positive other-directed feelings. *Psychological Science, 19,* 740–747.

Good, C., Rattan, A., & Dweck, C. S. (under review). *Why do women opt out? Sense of belonging and women's representation in mathematics.*

Gresky, D. M., Eyck, L. L. T., Lord, C. G., & McIntyre, R. B. (2005). Effects of salient multiple identities on women's performance under mathematics stereotype threat. *Sex Roles, 53,* 703–716.

Hyde, J. S., Fennema, E., & Lamon, S. J. (1990). Gender differences in mathematics performance: A meta-analysis. *Psychological Bulletin, 107,* 139–155.

Inzlicht, M., & Ben-Zeev, T. (2003). Do high-achieving female students underperform in private? The implications of threatening environments on intellectual processing. *Journal of Educational Psychology, 95,* 796–805.

Jencks, C., & Phillips, M. (Eds.). (1998). *The Black-White test score gap.* Washington, DC: Brookings Institution Press.

Krendl, A. C., Richeson, J. A., Kelley, W. M., & Heatherton, T. F. (2008). The negative consequences of threat: A functional magnetic resonance imaging investigation of the neural mechanisms underlying women's underperformance in math. *Psychological Science, 19,* 168–175.

Lewis, N. A. (2009, May 27). Woman in the news: A "kid from the Bronx" with hopes and doubts. *New York Times,* p. A1. Retrieved August 24, 2009 from http://query.nytimes.com/gst/fullpage.html?res=9903E7D81439F934A15756C0A96F9C8B63&sec=&spon=&pagewanted=all.

Logel, C., Walton, G. M., Peach, J., Spencer, S. J., & Zanna, M. P. (in press). Unleashing latent ability: Creating stereotype-safe environments for college admissions. *Educational Psychologist.*

Logel, C., Walton, G. M., Spencer, S. J., Iserman, E. C., von Hippel, W., & Bell, A. (2009). Interacting with sexist men triggers social identity threat among female engineers. *Journal of Personality and Social Psychology, 96,* 1089–1103.

Martens, A., Johns, M., Greenberg, J., & Schimel, J. (2006). Combating stereotype threat: The effect of self-affirmation on women's intellectual performance. *Journal of Experimental Social Psychology, 42,* 236–243.

Mendoza-Denton, R., Downey, G., Purdie, V. J., Davis, A., & Pietrzak, J. (2002). Sensitivity to status-based rejection: Implications for African American students' college experience. *Journal of Personality and Social Psychology, 83,* 896–918.

Murphy, M. C., Steele, C. M., & Gross, J. J. (2007). Signaling threat: How situational cues affect women in math, science, and engineering settings. *Psychological Science, 18,* 879–885.

Purdie-Vaughns, V., Steele, C. M., Davies, P. G., Ditlmann, R., & Crosby, J. R. (2008). Social identity contingencies: How diversity cues signal threat or safety for African Americans in mainstream institutions. *Journal of Personality and Social Psychology, 94,* 615–630.

Quinn, D. M. (2009). *Understanding the predicament of stereotype threat: Evidence that the threat is social.* Unpublished manuscript, University of Connecticut, Storrs, CT.

Robinson, M. L. (1985). *Princeton-educated Blacks and the Black community.* Unpublished senior thesis, Princeton University, Princeton, NJ.

Schmader, T., & Beilock, S. (2011). An integration of processes that underlie stereotype threat M. Inzlicht, & T. Schmader (Eds.), *Stereotype threat: Theory process, and application.* New York: Oxford University Press.

Shnabel, N., Purdie-Vaughns, V., Cook, J., Garcia, J., & Cohen, G. (2011). *Demystifying values-affirmation interventions: Writing about social-belonging is a key to buffering against stereotype threat.*

Schwarz, N., Bless, H., Strack, F., Klumpp, G., Rittenauer-Schatka, H., & Simons, A. (1991). Ease of retrieval as information: Another look at the availability heuristic. *Journal of Personality and Social Psychology, 61*, 195–202.

Shapiro, J. (2011). From stereotype threat to stereotype threats. In M. Inzlicht, & T. Schmader (Eds.), *Stereotype threat: Theory process, and application.* New York: Oxford University Press.

Sherman, D. K., & Cohen, G. L. (2006). The psychology of self-defense: Self-affirmation theory. In M. P. Zanna (Ed.), *Advances in experimental social psychology* Vol. 38 (pp. 183–242). San Diego: Academic Press

Stangor, C., Carr, C., & Kiang, L. (1998). Activating stereotypes undermines task performance expectations. *Journal of Personality and Social Psychology, 75*, 1191–1197.

Steele, C. M. (2010). *Whistling Vivaldi and other clues to how stereotypes affect us.* New York: Norton.

Steele, C. M., & Aronson, J. (1995). Stereotype threat and the intellectual test performance of African Americans. *Journal of Personality and Social Psychology, 69*, 797–811.

Walton, G. M., & Cohen, G. L. (2003). Stereotype lift. *Journal of Experimental Social Psychology, 39*, 456–467.

Walton, G. M., & Cohen, G. L. (2007). A question of belonging: Race, social fit, and achievement. *Journal of Personality and Social Psychology, 92*, 82–96.

Walton, G. M., & Cohen, G. L. (2011a). Sharing motivation. In D. Dunning (Ed.), *Social Motivation.* (pp. 79–101). New York: Psychology Press.

Walton, G. M., & Cohen, G. L. (2011b). A brief social-belonging intervention improves academic and health outcomes among minority students. *Science, 331*, 1447–1451.

Walton, G. M., Cohen, G. L., Garcia, J., Apfel, N., & Master A. (in preparation). *A brief intervention to buttress middle school students' sense of social-belonging: Effects by race and gender.* Manuscript in preparation.

Walton, G. M., Logel, C., Peach, J., & Spencer, S. (in preparation). Two interventions to boost women's achievement in engineering: Social-belonging and self-affirmation-training.

Walton, G. M., & Spencer, S. J. (2009). Latent ability: Grades and test scores systematically underestimate the intellectual ability of negatively stereotyped students. *Psychological Science, 20*, 1132–1139.

Walton, G. M., Thomas, N., & Cohen, G. L. (2003). *Social-relational processes in stereotype lift.* Unpublished data, Yale University, New Haven, CT.

Wilson, T. D., Damiani, M., & Shelton, N. (2002). Improving the academic performance of college students with brief attributional interventions. In J. Aronson (Ed.), *Improving academic achievement: Impact of psychological factors on education* (pp. 91–110). Oxford, UK: Academic Press.

Yeager, D. S. & Walton, G. M. (2011). Social-psychological interventions in education: They're not magic. *Review of Educational Research, 81*, 267–301.

7 Stereotype Threat Spillover

The Short- and Long-term Effects of Coping with Threats to Social Identity

■ MICHAEL INZLICHT,

ALEXA M. TULLETT, AND

JENNIFER N. GUTSELL

Experiencing prejudice has consequences. When people feel like they are being judged by a negative stereotype about their group, they perform poorly in the domain in which the stereotype applies—a phenomenon known as stereotype threat. Unfortunately, the effects of stereotype threat do not end in the threatening environment, but also spill over into other domains, where they can have further detrimental consequences. In this chapter, we present a model detailing the social-psychological processes whereby someone confronted with a negative stereotype comes to suffer effects in areas unrelated to the source of threat, an experience we call *stereotype threat spillover*. This model is based on identity-threat models of stigma, process models of stereotype threat, and theories of stress and coping. We first describe some of the short-term effects of spillover, including aggression, risky decision-making, and overeating. We then discuss long-term effects, including both physical health problems like obesity and hypertension, as well as mental health issues, such as depression and anxiety. We end on a positive note when we outline traits and offer strategies that allow individuals to overcome the negative outcomes set in motion by the powerful experience of prejudice.

Keywords: Stereotype threat, spillover, self-control, ego-depletion, eating, aggression, decision making, health

In their now classic paper, Steele and Aronson (1995) laid out the foundations of a phenomenon that came to be known as *stereotype threat*, the apprehension that targets feel when they think that negative stereotypes about their group will act as a lens through which their behaviors will be judged. According to Steele and Aronson, one of the reasons the black students tend to perform worse on standardized tests of performance compared to white students is that stereotypes are "in the air" (Steele, 1997), arousing deep-seated fears and distracting them from doing as well as they could.

Nearly two decades of research have followed this landmark paper and have confirmed this basic view. As this edited volume attests, the basic phenomenon of stereotype threat is robust, occurring for many groups and in many stereotyped domains, from women in science (Logel, Peach, & Spencer, 2011, Chapter 10, this volume) to indigent students in France (Croizet & Millet, 2011, Chapter 12, this volume), from the elderly (Chasteen, Kang, & Remedios, 2011, Chapter 13, this volume) to white athletes (Stone, Chalabaev, & Harrison, 2011, Chapter 14, this volume). What's more, performance is hurt by a broader category of events— it can occur whenever cues hint that one's social identity is devalued and marginalized, when one feels like the victim of a *social identity threat* (Steele, Spencer, & Aronson, 2002).

Whether we are talking about stereotype threat or social identity threat, the point here is that it can affect performance whenever people find themselves in threatening environments (Inzlicht & Ben-Zeev, 2000). In this chapter, however, we ask what happens *after* people leave threatening environments. In short, we ask if coping with the stress of negative stereotypes can spill over into a variety of other domains. Classic research on stereotype threat is mute to such questions.

Here, we present theory and research that allows for an expansion of this theory to cover not only domains in which people are denigrated and unwelcome, but also areas that are stereotype-free. We start by sketching a model detailing the steps involved in coping with stereotype and social identity threat. In this model, we conceive of stereotype threat as a stressor similar to those other stressors that targets of prejudice need to deal with, like economic hardships and poor housing (Allison, 1998; Miller & Kaiser, 2001; Major & O'Brien, 2005). Once appraised, stereotype and social identity threat result in involuntary stress reactions, like physiological arousal and cognitive distraction, and volitional coping responses, like thought suppression and attempts at emotion regulation (Schmader & Beilock, 2011, Chapter 3, this volume). The central thesis of this chapter is that both of these types of reactions, voluntary and involuntary, can consume self-regulatory resources, leaving people less able to control and regulate themselves in instances in which self-control is required (Muraven & Baumeister, 2000). Even if participants perform adequately in a stereotyped domain, we suggest that the act of coping is difficult and can leave people in a depleted state that outlasts the threatening situation. Moreover, stress can have direct effects on a whole host of outcomes, which together with depletion can result in both short- and long-term consequences.

Short-term, coping with stereotype threat can affect people in a number of non-stereotyped domains. We review empirical work indicating that after women cope with the negative stereotypes about their math ability, they become more aggressive, eat more unhealthy foods, and have a tougher time paying attention. Critically, we present work revealing how such effects are implemented in the brain. The long-term consequences are just as disquieting, with theoretical and empirical links between threats to social identity and poor mental health (e.g., depression and anxiety), poor physical health (e.g., obesity and hypertension), and unhealthy behaviors (e.g., ignoring medical advice, drug use, etc.). Stereotype threat, however, does not always spill over and cause havoc in such a wide variety of domains. We end with a hopeful note, reviewing work suggesting that spillover is not inevitable, but can be overcome with things like active coping, social support, and the cultivation of resilience. Rather than offering a comprehensive analysis of the effects of coping with stigma and discrimination (see Miller & Kaiser, 2001; Major & O'Brien, 2005; Pascoe & Smart Richman, 2009), this chapter presents a working model of how and why the experience of stereotype threat can spill over into nonstereotyped domains, especially domains in which self-control is required. We begin by describing our working model.

■ A STRESS AND COPING MODEL OF STEREOTYPE THREAT SPILLOVER

Figure 7.1 presents a model detailing the social-psychological processes whereby someone confronted with a negative stereotype comes to suffer short- and long-term effects in areas unrelated to the source of threat, an experience we call *stereotype threat spillover*. This model is based on identity-threat models of stigma

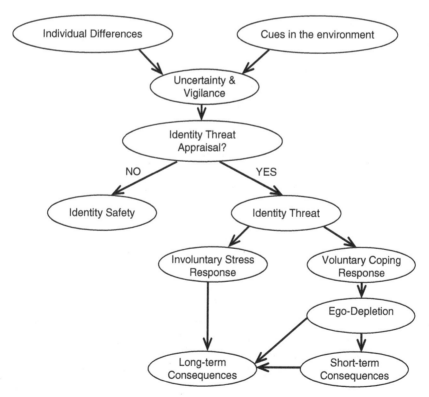

Figure 7.1 A stress and coping model of stereotype threat

(Major & O'Brien, 2005), process models of stereotype threat (Schmader, Johns, & Forbes, 2008), and theories of stress and coping (Compas et al., 2001; Lazarus & Folkman, 1984). Briefly, this model assumes that targets of prejudice are more at risk of facing social identity stress than are nontargets (see Figure 7.1). In the short-term, this stress prompts efforts to cope, draining energy required for other things, including making sound decisions and regulating emotions. In the long-term, this increased stress can directly and indirectly lead to physical and mental health problems, such as hypertension, obesity, and depression (Pascoe & Smart Richman, 2009).

The model begins with a classic person-by-situation interaction. Situations and environments vary, with some being more threatening and some, less (Murphy & Jones Taylor, 2011, Chapter 2, this volume). Threatening environments can be thought of as settings in which people come to suspect that they could be devalued, stigmatized, or discriminated against because of a particular social identity (Steele et al., 2002). For example, threatening environments could include situations in which one is outnumbered by nonstigmatized outgroups, say when a women finds herself as one of only a handful of women in her engineering lecture hall (Inzlicht & Ben-Zeev, 2000). What is interesting about potentially threatening environments is that they don't need to arouse feelings of rejection explicitly, but may contain subtle, seemingly innocuous cues. The number and position of male and female bathrooms in the executive floor of a bank building may be enough to send messages of acceptance or rejection and start the cascade of physiological stress and coping responses (Murphy, Steele, & Gross, 2007).

People differ in the extent to which they are aware of and bothered by negative stereotypes about their groups—a construct known as *stigma-consciousness* (Pinel, 1999) or *group-based rejection-sensitivity* (e.g., Mendoza-Denton, Downey, Purdie, Davis, & Pietrzak, 2002). These individuals are vigilant for cues signaling that they are being viewed stereotypically and are therefore more likely to appraise situations as threatening. Other individual differences that contribute to identity-threat appraisals include the extent to which people regard their devalued identity as a central part of themselves (Schmader, 2002) and how strongly they identify with domains in which their group is negatively stereotyped (Aronson et al., 1999). Moreover, even the type of threat that people experience can vary from person to person (Shapiro, 2011, Chapter 5, this volume).

The point here is that situations and persons differ, and in specific situations, specific people will become uncertain about their standing and vigilant for cues that signal that their group is devalued (Crocker & Major, 1989). States of uncertainty are significant because they are felt very keenly and are sometimes more aversive than states of certain negativity (Hirsh & Inzlicht, 2008). This could be why targets of prejudice are sometimes more affected by ambiguous cues of threat than by overt ones (e.g., Major, Quinton, & Schmader, 2003; Mendoza-Denton, Shaw-Taylor, Chen, & Chang, 2009).

Once uncertain, people become acutely aware of cues that indicate whether their social-identity is in fact being threatened (Inzlicht, Kaiser, & Major, 2006; Kaiser,

Vick, & Major, 2006). If cues are not present, or if individuals are not sensitive to those that are there (Feldman-Barrett & Swim, 1998), they may not make identity-threat appraisals or experience further consequences. These "identity–safe" environments convey to individuals that their stigmatized social identities pose no barrier (Davies, Spencer, & Steele, 2005). On the other hand, if cues that confirm stereotype relevance are present in the environment, or if individuals are sensitive to discrimination, they may make threat appraisals, setting in motion a chain of stress and coping responses.

As soon as an identity-threat appraisal is made, people experience a physiological stress response characterized by increases in arousal (Ben-Zeev, Fein, & Inzlicht, 2005; Blascovich, Spencer, Quinn, & Steele, 2001) and distracting thoughts (Cadinu, Maass, Rosabianca, & Kiesner, 2005) that consume limited working memory capacity (Beilock, Rydell, & McConnell, 2007; Schmader & Johns, 2003). These involuntary stress responses are accompanied by voluntary coping strategies. Essentially, individuals are motivated to disconfirm negative stereotypes. On an academic test, for example, targets of prejudice are motivated to perform well and expend great effort to do so (Jamieson & Harkins, 2007). However, once an individual confronts the possibility of failing, they may cope by suppressing harmful thoughts and denying uncomfortable emotions (Johns, Inzlicht, & Schmader, 2008; Logel, Iserman, Davies, Quinn, & Spencer, 2009).

According to the integrated process model of stereotype threat, the proximal mediator of the threat–performance link is loss of executive control (Schmader et al., 2008). The one thing all of the other putative mediators have in common is that they tax executive control, the cornerstone resource needed for skilled performance in virtually any challenging information-processing task. The more executive control is used to manage the effects of stereotypes and identity threats, the less executive control remains for the central performance task—and the less that remains after people leave the threatening environment. Stereotype threat, therefore, leads to processing inefficiencies via depleted executive control.

What is striking about this stress and coping account is that it suggests that people can perform well when confronted by the stress of stereotypes, but would need to expend a good amount of energy and effort to do so (e.g., Inzlicht, Aronson, Good, & McKay, 2006). Whether people underperform or not, the key feature of this model is that this extra compensatory coping effort can result in a state knows as *ego depletion* (Muraven & Baumeister, 2000), affecting people long after they have left the threatening environment (Inzlicht, McKay, & Aronson, 2006). Ego depletion refers to a state of compromised reserves of self-control, of having little mental energy to overcome environmental temptations and override urges, emotions, and automatic response tendencies. Empirical studies have confirmed that self-control is a limited, easily exhausted resource, with prior acts of self-control depleting the self-control available for subsequent tasks (Baumeister & Heatherton, 1996; Muraven & Baumeister, 2000; Muraven, Tice, & Baumeister, 1998).

Managing the stress of negative stereotypes involves coping strategies that are dependent on executive resources, and because these resources are finite, coping could result in poorer self-control even after the stereotype stressor is no longer "in the air" (Beilock et al., 2007; Inzlicht et al. 2006). In the short term, this state of ego depletion can lead to all sorts of maladaptive behaviors. In the long term, the effects of these behaviors can accrue and have significant consequences, especially to the state of people's health. Chronic exposure to the stress of dealing with a devalued social identity can also have direct effects on health, an issue we return to after detailing the short-term consequences of stereotype threat spillover.

■ SHORT-TERM CONSEQUENCES OF STEREOTYPE THREAT SPILLOVER

Since coping with stereotype threat is ego depleting, it has the potential to affect any domain requiring self-control. Several experimental investigations have now confirmed that, after leaving a threatening environment, people continue to exhibit maladaptive behaviors in domains unrelated to the original threat. In particular, Inzlicht and Kang (2010) have conducted a number of studies indicating that stereotype threat can lead to aggression, overeating, risky decision making, and problems maintaining attention.

In their first study, Inzlicht and Kang (2010) examined whether coping with stereotype threat could lead to aggressive behavior among women. Although aggressive impulses are various and common, the ability to control such impulses is critical and is compromised by ego depletion (DeWall, Baumeister, Stillman, & Gailliot, 2007; Stucke & Baumeister, 2006). To the extent that coping with stereotype threat results in ego depletion, it should also result in unrestrained aggression. Female participants took a difficult math test and half of them received instructions to reappraise the situation and test neutrally and objectively, as if they were professional test evaluators. Such reappraisal instructions eliminate the need to suppress thoughts and emotions in order to cope with the threat, thereby saving participants' self-control resources (Richards & Gross, 2000). The other half of participants were given no further instruction about how to cope with the situation and presumably engaged in the resource-depleting coping strategy typical of those under threat—suppressing emotions and cognitions (Johns et al., 2008; Logel et al., 2009. Then, when no longer in the threatening situation, participants completed a competitive reaction time task against their partner. In this task, whoever responded quicker to a stimulus was allowed to send a burst of white noise to the slower partner. Aggression was operationalized as the intensity and duration of white noise blasts delivered to the partner. Results revealed stereotype threat spillover: Women who coped with stereotype threat "naturally" engaged in more aggressive behavior than did those who were encouraged to reappraise the situation. People normally restrain their aggressive impulses, but the women who coped with threat did not.

Using the same suppression versus reappraisal manipulation, a second study investigated whether stereotype threat can spill over into the domain of eating behavior (Inzlicht & Kang2010). As in the first study, female participants took a difficult math test while reappraising or not. They were then asked to take part in an ostensibly unrelated "taste test" of three ice cream flavors and were allowed to eat as much of the ice cream as they wanted. Restraining the impulse to indulge in eating this fattening but tempting food requires participants' self-control resources and, consequently, ego-depleted participants should be less able to deny themselves the ice cream (Vohs & Heatherton, 2000). The results confirmed this prediction. Participants in the threat group—those who presumably suppressed their emotions and thoughts—ate significantly more ice cream than did participants in the non-threat, reappraisal group.

The third study looked at yet another important domain: decision making. Previous research suggests that ego depletion hampers the deliberate aspects of the decision-making process (Kahneman, 2003; Masicampo & Baumeister, 2008). In the study, participants were reminded of a time they experienced identity threat before (threat) or after (control) the main dependent variable, a lottery task. In this task, they had the choice between two lotteries, one of them very risky but with a high payoff, and the other one far less risky but with a lower payoff. The expected utility of the second lottery was higher, so rationally, the second, low-risk lottery was the better choice. Again, the results revealed a spillover effect: Identity-threatened participants, who were limited to the automatic, intuitive decision system, selected the risky lottery more often than did control participants.

Although these three studies provide good evidence that stereotype threat can spill over and affect behavior in other, nonstereotyped domains, they cannot inform us of the mechanism. To shed light on the neural processes underlying the observed effects, in their last study Inzlicht and Kang (2010) looked at the activity in the anterior cingulate cortex (ACC), a brain region that is richly interconnected with both limbic and prefrontal areas of the brain, and is critical for self-control (Bush, Luu, & Posner, 2000). In electroencephalographic (EEG) studies, activation of the ACC is associated with a medial-frontal negative event-related potential (ERP), sensitive to errors, conflict, and uncertainty (Gehring, Goss, Coles, & Meyer, 1993). These ERPs are a product of affective responses to one's performance (Luu, Collins, & Tucker, 2000) and act as neural "'distress signals'" sent by the ACC indicating when attention, vigilance, and control are needed (Bartholow et al., 2005, p. 41). Recent work suggests that self-control depletion could be caused by hypoactive performance monitoring (Inzlicht & Gutsell, 2007) or by inefficient performance-monitoring; for example, increased performance monitoring for the wrong type of event, like ones not requiring attention or vigilance. If stereotype threat consumes executive resources, it should not only result in poor executive control, this effect should be mediated by disruptions to this ACC performance-monitoring system.

Male and female participants in the final Inzlicht and Kang study (2010) took a diagnostic math test and were required to cope "naturally" or encouraged to reappraise their emotions. After the test, participants completed a Stroop color naming task, designed to tap cognitive inhibition processes, while their ACC activity was recorded with EEG. As expected, threatened female participants performed worse on the Stroop task than did male or nonthreatened female participants.

Moreover, these control participants showed a normal pattern of brain activity—ERP amplitudes were high after trials that required behavioral inhibition and low after those that did not. The ACC activation of threatened participants, however, deviated from this adaptive pattern: ERP amplitudes were high whether inhibition was necessary or not. Curiously, it was especially high after trials that did not require inhibition. Importantly, this inefficient pattern of ACC activity significantly mediated the negative effects of stereotype threat on performance in the Stroop task. Hence, threatened participants appear to be more vigilant and anxious after all trial types and tend to waste their efforts in situations that do not require vigilance. Having experienced stereotype threat, it seems, affects the ACC-based performance monitoring system in a way that renders it inefficient and thus impairs effective self-control.

The studies described above touch on many domains of human behavior affected by resource depletion, and future studies will likely add to the list of domains affected by stereotype threat spillover. Depletion leaves people unable to restrain their urges and impulses, and as such can affect a large variety of human behavior. This draws a dark picture for those targeted by negative stereotypes. Fortunately, there are ways to cope and means to strengthen self-control. We will detail some of these remedies, but first we discuss potential long-term effects of dealing with the stress of negative stereotypes.

Policy Box

Stereotype threat spillover is the phenomenon whereby coping with stigma can contribute to a host of lingering effects in both the short- and long-term, from overeating to obesity, from aggressive behavior to poor physical health. These ill effects come about directly, through the increased burden of living with stigma, or indirectly through misdirected efforts to cope with this burden. The implications are clear: People belonging to marginalized groups regularly find themselves in situations that make their lives more difficult. Can governments and social service agencies do anything to ease this burden? If spillover comes about because of the interplay between stress and coping, policy should focus on both. The most obvious solution is to buffer targets' exposure to stress by changing the social climate, for example through public education and diversity training. However, such measures are not only slow-moving, their efficacy is not clear. Instead, we advocate for policy that focuses on helping the stigmatized cope. One example would be to offer workshops and seminars in schools and workplaces on adaptive coping techniques, such as problem-focused coping and emotion reappraisal techniques. If many of the short-term problems are caused by self-control failure, helping people develop more efficient self-control resources by "practicing" self-control could also be of use. For example, mindfulness-based stress reduction techniques, now offered in almost every major city in North America, have shown great promise in not only helping people deal with stress, but also in honing their skills at attentional control. Such interventions, we believe, empower victims, helping them take control of the outcomes they experience.

■ LONG-TERM HEALTH EFFECTS OF STEREOTYPE THREAT SPILLOVER

In addition to the immediate consequences of stereotype threat that become evident as soon as a person exits the threatening environment, there is also mounting evidence to suggest that social identity threat can have long-term detrimental effects on health. As described above, perceiving discrimination—a clear threat to social identity—can cause people to feel stress and to cope with that stress. These experiences of stress and coping can then result in physical, psychological, and behavioral changes that can have marked effects on health outcomes (Pascoe & Smart Richman, 2009). Links between perceived discrimination and health have been documented in a number of reviews that demonstrated that both mental and physical health can be adversely affected by experiences of discrimination (i.e., Paradies, 2006; Pascoe & Smart Richman, 2009; Williams & Mohammed, 2009). Stereotype threat spillover, then, may provide a new lens through which to understand how these problems arise, and perhaps also how they can be avoided.

Mental Health Outcomes

An impressive body of work has investigated the effects of perceived discrimination on mental health, with a particular focus on depression. For Koreans in Toronto (Noh, Kaspar, & Wickrama, 2007), mainland Chinese teens in Hong Kong (Lam, Tsoi, & Chan, 2005), blacks in the United States (Lincoln, Chatters, Taylor, & Jackson, 2007), and a considerable number of other minority groups (see Williams & Mohammed, 2009, for review), cross-sectional evidence shows that the more discrimination a person experiences, the more likely he or she is to exhibit depressive symptoms. In addition, some longitudinal work has shown that perceived discrimination predicts depressive symptoms down the road (Brody et al., 2006; Greene, Way, & Pahl, 2006).

Related research has shown that mental health outcomes as varied as anxiety (Banks, Kohn-Wood, & Spencer, 2006; Bhui et al., 2005), rebellious behavior (Brook, Brook, Balka, & Rosenberg, 2006) post-traumatic stress disorder (Khaylis, Waelde, & Bruce, 2007), and reduced general well-being (Sujoldzic, Peternel, Kulenovic, & Terzic, 2006) are all associated with discrimination. In a comprehensive meta-analysis, Pascoe and Smart Richman (2009) found a significant correlation between perceived discrimination and a wide variety of mental health indices. Furthermore, the discrimination-health link still holds when factors such as socioeconomic status, education, and employment are controlled for (Pascoe & Smart Richman, 2009). Although much of the work in this area has been correlational and thus has not addressed the causal processes involved, the longitudinal work that has been done suggests that it is perceived discrimination that is affecting mental health and not the other way around. Possible mediators of this process will be discussed below and lend credence to this interpretation. Overall, even though there are clear self-protective properties to having a stigmatized identity (e.g., Crocker & Major, 1989), it appears that social identity threat can cause people's mental health to worsen, a result that seems to hold for physical health as well.

Physical Health Outcomes

As with mental health, a link appears to exist between perceived discrimination and reduced physical health. Various studies demonstrate that increases in diseases and risk factors such as obesity (Inzlicht & Kang, 2010), hypertension (Davis, Liu, Quarells, Din-Dzietharn, & M.A.H.D.S. Group, 2005; Roberts, Vines, Kaufman, & James, 2007), and self-reported poor health (Harris et al., 2006; Larson, Gillies, Howard, & Coffin, 2007) accompany higher levels of perceived discrimination. In one longitudinal study, breast cancer incidence was found to be higher among women who reported frequent everyday discrimination, even when controlling for breast cancer risk factors (Taylor et al., 2007). In the same meta-analysis mentioned above, a significant correlation between perceived discrimination and physical health was found, although the results were not as strong as they were for mental health outcomes (Pascoe & Smart Richman, 2009). The evidence, then, strongly supports the conclusion that social-identity threat has detrimental effects on a wide variety of both mental and physical health outcomes. What remains is the question of how this relationship might come about.

How Does Social-identity Threat Affect Health?

According to the model outlined above, people have two immediate reactions to discrimination: an involuntary stress response and a voluntary coping response. Through their effects on health risk factors and health behavior, stress and coping may act as mediators of the relationship between perceived discrimination and health, and thus may help to illuminate the process by which negative health effects take root.

Investigations into the physiological effects of perceived racism show that racism increases the amount of stress one experiences and can contribute directly to physiological effects such as increased blood pressure, heart rate, and negative emotional reactivity that are indicators of stress-related diseases (Harrell, Hall, & Taliaferro, 2003). Repeated exposure to stress can also influence health by contributing to *allostatic load*, the cumulative physiological toll on the body that occurs as a result of experiencing and adapting to stressful events (e.g., Stewart, 2006). Furthermore, stress can also have a negative impact on psychological factors such as negative affectivity, and as such can have detrimental consequences for mental, as well as physical health (Watson & Pennebaker, 1989).

In addition to the direct effects of stress, efforts to cope with that stress can also, perhaps paradoxically, have an indirect negative impact on health. One of the primary ways that these coping strategies can take their toll is through ego depletion. As described earlier in this chapter, efforts to control thoughts, feelings, and behavior can result in a lack of resources necessary for other tasks (Baumeister, Faber, &

Wallace, 1999; Inzlicht et al., 2006). Because of ego depletion and reduced self-control capacity, people may show a tendency to participate in fewer healthy behaviors and more unhealthy behaviors (Pascoe & Smart Richman, 2009). For example, higher levels of self-reported discrimination have been linked to increases in smoking (Landrine & Klonoff, 1996), drug use (Martin, Tuch, & Roman, 2003; Yen, Ragland, Grenier, & Fisher, 1999; Gibbons et al., 2007), and unhealthy eating (Mulia, 2008), as well as decreases in seeking and following medical advice (Casagrande, Gary, LaVeist, Gaskin, & Cooper, 2007; Facione & Facione, 2007). Moreover, experimentally introducing stereotype threat causes women to eat more, providing additional evidence to suggest that coping with negative stereotypes results in ego depletion and can thus prompt individuals to make unhealthier choices (Inzlicht & Kang, 2010).

■ CONCLUSION

The main goal of this chapter was to extend the theory of stereotype threat, to include effects that may occur after people leave threatening environments, when stereotypes are no longer "in the air" (Steele, 1997). We presented a working model of what we have called *stereotype threat spillover*, to demonstrate how threat can have residual effects not only in domains in which people are denigrated and unwelcome, but also in areas that are stereotype-free. This model asserts that targets of prejudice face social identity threat, which can result in involuntary stress reactions, like anxiety and cognitive distraction, and volitional coping responses, like trying to suppress stereotypes and emotions. In the short term, this stress means that individuals will spend their limited energies to cope, leaving them with less energy to do other things, including eating a balanced meal and making sound decisions. Over the long term, this increased stress can directly and indirectly lead to physical and mental health problems, such as subjective well-being, anxiety, and the risk of certain cancers.

We would like to end on a positive note. Although the preceding evidence might paint a dark picture, implying that experiencing stereotype threat can have a wide range of residual effects on volitional control and have real consequences for mental and physical health, it is important to note that this phenomenon does not occur for all people in all situations. A number of factors confer resilience to targets of negative stereotypes, and a number of interventions can increase adaptive coping and therefore reduce spillover. People who have more social support (Noh & Kaspar, 2003), who use problem-focused as opposed to emotion-focused coping (King, 2005), and who appraise discriminatory situations as less central in their lives (Noh et al., 2007) are less likely to experience the ill health that may befall others in the same situations. Similarly, although identifying with one's stigmatized group leaves one more vulnerable to stereotype threat (Schmader, 2002), it also confers resilience from its ego-threatening effects by protecting self-esteem (Crocker & Major, 1989). People who are good at projecting a positive image during social interactions, those who are good at understanding and adapting to various social situations, are also resilient and appear to cope quite well to the threat of stereotypes (Inzlicht, Aronson, Good, & McKay, 2006).

In addition to the now long list of interventions that could help people overcome stereotype threat (e.g., Cohen, Purdie-Vaughs, & Garcia, 2011, Chapter 18, this volume), we might be able to add an intervention derived from research on ego depletion—practice. Some research indicates that people who practice, or "exercise," self-control can improve and expand their executive resources (Muraven, Baumeister, & Tice, 1999). In the case of stereotype threat spillover, this might mean that people who practice adaptive coping strategies, for example those who consciously practice emotion reappraisal, might be better able to deal with stereotype stress and, importantly, have enough executive resources remaining so that when they leave the threatening environment, they don't leave in a depleted state. The good news is that stereotype threat spillover is not destiny; although social identity stress poses a very real threat to volitional control and mental and physical health, there are approaches and strategies that may be effective in preventing these threats from materializing.

References

Allison, K. W. (1998). Stress and oppressed social category membership. In J. K. Swim, & C. Stangor (Eds.), *Prejudice: The target's perspective* (pp. 145–170). San Diego: Academic Press.

Aronson, J., Lustina, M. J., Good, C., Keough, K., Steele, C. M., & Brown, J. (1999). When White men can't do math: Necessary and sufficient factors in stereotype threat. *Journal of Experimental Social Psychology, 35,* 29–46.

Banks, K. H., Kohn-Wood, L. P., & Spencer, M. (2006). An examination of the African American experience of everyday discrimination and symptoms of psychological distress. *Community Mental Health Journal, 42,* 555–570.

Bartholow, B. D., Pearson, M. A., Dickter, C. L., Fabiani, M., Gratton, G., & Sher, K. H. (2005). Strategic control and medial frontal negativity: Beyond errors and response conflict. Psychophysiology, 42, 33–42.

Baumeister, R. F., Faber, J. E., & Wallace, H. M. (1999). Coping and ego-depletion: Recovery after the coping process. In C. R. Snyder (Ed.), *Coping: The psychology of what works* (pp. 50–69). New York: Oxford University Press.

Baumeister, R. F., & Heatherton, T. F. (1996). Self-regulation failure: An overview. *Psychological Inquiry, 7,* 1–15.

Beilock, S. L., Ryell, R. J., & McConnell, A. R. (2007). Stereotype threat and working memory: Mechanisms, alleviation, and spillover. *Journal of Experimental Psychology: General, 136,* 256–276.

Ben-Zeev, T., Fein, S., & Inzlicht, M. (2005). Stereotype threat and arousal. *Journal of Experimental Social Psychology, 41,* 174–181.

Bhui, K., Stansfeld, S., McKenzie, K., Karlsen, S., Nazroo, J., & Weich, S. (2005). Racial/ Ethnic discrimination and common mental disorders among workers: Findings from the EMPIRIC study of ethnic minority groups in the United Kingdom. *American Journal of Public Health, 95,* 496–501.

Blascovich, J., Spencer, S. J., Quinn, D., & Steele, C. (2001). African Americans and high blood pressure: The role of stereotype threat. *Psychological Science, 12,* 225–229.

Brody, G. H., Chen, Y., Murry, V. M., Ge, X., Simons, R. L., Gibbons, F. X., et al. (2006). Perceived discrimination and the adjustment of African American youths: A five-year longitudinal analysis with contextual moderation effects. *Child Development, 77,* 1170–1189.

Brook, J. S., Brook, D. W., Balka, E. B., & Rosenberg, G. (2006). Predictors of rebellious behavior in childhood: Parental drug use, peers, school environment, and child personality. *Journal of Addictive Diseases, 25,* 77–87.

Bush, G., Luu, P., & Posner, M. I. (2000). Cognitive and emotional influences in anterior cingulate cortex. *Trends in Cognitive Sciences, 4,* 215–222.

Cadinu, M., Maass, A., Rosabianca, A., & Kiesner, J. (2005). Why do women underperform under stereotype threat? *Psychological Science, 16,* 572–578.

Casagrande, S. S., Gary, T. L., LaVeist, T. A., Gaskin, D. J., & Cooper, L. A. (2007). Perceived discrimination and adherence to medical care in a racially integrated community. *Journal of General Internal Medicine, 22*(3), 389–395.

Chasteen, A. L., Kang, S. K., & Remedios, J. D. (2011). Aging and stereotype threat: Development, process, and interventions. In M. Inzlicht, & T. Schmader (Eds.), *Stereotype threat: Theory, process, and application.* New York: Oxford University Press.

Cohen, G. L., Purdie-Vaughns, V., & Garcia, J. (2011). An identity threat perspective on intervention. In M. Inzlicht, & T. Schmader (Eds.), *Stereotype threat: Theory, process, and application.* New York: Oxford University Press.

Compas, B. E., Connor-Smith, J. K., Saltzman, H., Thomsen, A. H., & Wadsworth, M. E. (2001). Coping with stress during childhood and adolescence: Problems, progress, and potential in theory and research. *Psychological Bulletin, 127,* 87–127.

Crocker, J., & Major, B. (1989). Social stigma and self-esteem: The self-protective properties of stigma. *Psychological Review, 96,* 608–630.

Croizet, J. C., & Millet, M. (2011). Social class and test Performance: From stereotype threat to symbolic violence and vice versa. In M. Inzlicht, & T. Schmader (Eds.), *Stereotype threat: Theory, process, and application.* New York: Oxford University Press.

Davies, P. G., Spencer, S. J., & Steele, C. M. (2005). Clearing the air: Identity safety moderates the effects of stereotype threat on women's leadership aspirations. *Journal of Personality and Social Psychology, 88,* 276–287.

Davis, S. K., Liu, Y., Quarells, R. C., Din-Dzietharn, R., & M.A.H.D.S. Group. (2005). Stress-related racial discrimination and hypertension likelihood in a population-based sample of African Americans: The Metro Atlanta Heart Disease Study. *Ethnicity and Disease, 15*(4), 585–593.

Dewall, C. N., Baumeister, R. F., Stillman, T. F., & Gailliot, M. T. (2007). Violence restrained: Effects of self-regulation and its depletion on aggression. *Journal of Experimental Social Psychology, 43,* 62–76.

Facione, N. C., & Facione, P. A. (2007). Perceived prejudice in healthcare and women's health protective behavior. *Nursing Research, 56,* 175–184.

Feldman-Barrett, L. F., & Swim, J. (1998). Appraisals of prejudice: A signal detection framework. In J. Swim, & C. Stangor (Eds.), *Prejudice: The target's perspective* (pp. 11–36). New York: Academic Press.

Gehring, W. J., Goss, B., Coles, M. G., & Meyer, D. E. (1993). A neural system for error detection and compensation. *Psychological Science, 4,* 385–390.

Gibbons, F. X., Yeh, H. C., Gerrard, M., Cleveland, M. J., Cutrona, C., Simons, R. L., & Brody, G. H. (2007). Early experience with racial discrimination and conduct disorder as predictors of subsequent drug use: A critical period analysis. *Drug and Alcohol Dependence, 88*(Suppl 1), 27–37.

Greene, M. L., Way, N., & Pahl, K. (2006). Trajectories of perceived adult and peer discrimination among Black, Latino, and Asian American adolescents: Patterns and psychological correlates. *Developmental Psychology, 42*, 218–238.

Harrell, J. P., Hall, S., & Taliaferro, J. (2003). Physiological responses to racism and discrimination: An assessment of the evidence. *American Journal of Public Health, 93*, 243–248.

Harris, R., Tobias, M., Jeffreys, M., Waldegrave, K., Karlsen, S., & Nazroo, J. (2006). Effects of self-reported racial discrimination and deprivation on Māori health and inequalities in New Zealand: Cross-sectional study. *Lancet, 367*(9527), 2005–2009.

Hirsh, J. B., & Inzlicht, M. (2008). The devil you know: Neuroticism predicts neural response to uncertainty. *Psychological Science, 19*, 962–967.

Inzlicht, M., Aronson, J., Good, C., & McKay, L. (2006). A particular resiliency to threatening environments. *Journal of Experimental Social Psychology, 42*, 323–336.

Inzlicht, M., & Ben-Zeev, T. (2000). A threatening intellectual environment: Why females are susceptible to experiencing problem-solving deficits in the presence of males. *Psychological Science, 11*, 365–371.

Inzlicht, M., & Gutsell, J. N. (2007). Running on empty: Neural signals for self-control failure. *Psychological Science, 18*, 933–937.

Inzlicht, M., Kaiser, C. R., & Major, B. (2008). The face of chauvinism: How prejudice expectations shape perceptions of facial affect. *Journal of Experimental Social Psychology, 44*, 758–766.

Inzlicht, M., & Kang, S. K. (2010). Stereotype threat spillover: How coping with threats to social identity affects aggression, eating, decision-making, and attention. *Journal of Personality and Social Psychology, 99*, 467–481.

Inzlicht, M., McKay, L., & Aronson, J. (2006). Stigma as ego depletion: How being the target of prejudice affects self-control. *Psychological Science, 17*, 262–269.

Jamieson, J. P., & Harkins, S. G. (2007). Mere effort and stereotype threat performance effects. *Journal of Personality and Social Psychology, 93*, 544–564.

Johns, M., Inzlicht, M., & Schmader, T. (2008). Stereotype threat and executive resource depletion: The influence of emotion regulation. *Journal of Experimental Psychology: General, 137*, 691–705.

Kahneman, D. (2003). A perspective on judgment and choice: Mapping bounded rationality. *American Psychologist, 58*, 697–720.

Kaiser, C. R., Vick, S. B., & Major, B. (2006). Prejudice expectations moderate preconscious attention to social identity threatening cues. *Psychological Science, 17*, 332–338.

Khaylis, A., Waelde, L., & Bruce, E. (2007). The role of ethnic identity in the relationship of race-related stress to PTSD symptoms among young adults. *Journal of Trauma & Dissociation, 8*, 91–105.

King, K. R. (2005). Why is discrimination stressful? The mediating role of cognitive appraisal. *Cultural Diversity and Ethnic Minority Psychology, 11*, 202–212.

Lam, A. M. C., Tsoi, K. W., & Chan, T. S. (2005). Adolescent Chinese immigrants in Hong Kong: A comparison with locally born students and factors associated with their psychological well-being. *International Journal of Adolescent Medicine and Health, 17*, 157–168.

Landrine, H., & Klonoff, E. A. (1996). The schedule of racist events: A measure of racial discrimination and a study of its negative physical and mental health consequences. *Journal of Black Psychology, 22*, 144–168.

Larson, A., Gillies, M., Howard, P. J., & Coffin, J. (2007). It's enough to make you sick: The impact of racism on the health of Aboriginal Australians. *Australian and New Zealand Journal of Public Health, 31*(4), 322–329.

Lazarus, R. S., & Folkman, S. (1984). Transactional theory and research on emotions and coping. *European Journal of Personality, 13,* 141–169.

Lincoln, K. D., Chatters, L. M., Taylor, R. J., & Jackson, J. S. (2007). Profiles of depressive symptoms among African Americans and Caribbean Blacks. *Social Science & Medicine, 65,* 200–213.

Logel, C., Iserman, E. C., Davies, P. G., Quinn, D. M., & Spencer, S. J. (2009). The perils of double consciousness: The role of thought suppression in stereotype threat. *Journal of Experimental Social Psychology, 45,* 299–312.

Logel, C., Peach, J., & Spencer, S. J. (2011). Threatening gender and race: Different manifestations of stereotype threat. In M. Inzlicht, & T. Schmader (Eds.), *Stereotype threat: Theory, process, and application.* New York: Oxford University Press.

Luu, P., Collins, P., & Tucker, D. M. (2000). Mood, personality and self-monitoring: Negative affect and emotionality in relation to frontal lobe mechanisms of error monitoring. *Journal of Experimental Psychology: General, 129,* 43–60.

Major, B., & O'Brien, L. T. (2005). The social psychology of stigma. *Annual Review of Psychology, 56,* 393–421.

Major B., Quinton W. J., & Schmader, T. (2003). Attributions to discrimination and self-esteem: Impact of social identification and group ambiguity. *Journal of Experimental Social Psychology, 39,* 220–231.

Martin, J. K., Tuch, S. A., & Roman, P. M. (2003). Problem drinking patterns among African Americans: The impacts of reports of discrimination, perceptions of prejudice, and "risky" coping strategies. *Journal of Health and Social Behavior. Special Issue: Race, Ethnicity and Mental Health, 44,* 408–425.

Masicampo, E. J., & Baumeister, R. F. (2008). Toward a physiology of dual-process reasoning and judgment: Lemonade, willpower, and expensive rule-based analysis. *Psychological Science, 19,* 255–260.

Mendoza-Denton, R., Downey, G., Purdie, V. J., Davis, A., & Pietrzak, J. (2002). Sensitivity to status-based rejection: Implications for African American students' college experience. *Journal of Personality and Social Psychology, 83,* 896–918.

Mendoza-Denton, R., Shaw-Taylor, L., Chen, S., & Chang, E. (2009). Ironic effects of explicit gender prejudice on women's test performance. *Journal of Experimental Social Psychology, 45,* 275–278.

Miller, C. T., & Kaiser, C. R. (2001). A theoretical perspective on coping with stigma. *Journal of Social Issues, 57,* 73–92.

Mulia, N. (2008). Social disadvantage, stress, and alcohol use among Black, Hispanic, and White Americans: Findings from the 2005 U.S. national alcohol survey. *Journal of Studies on Alcohol and Drugs, 69,* 824.

Muraven, M., & Baumeister, R. F. (2000). Self-regulation and depletion of limited resources: Does self-control resemble a muscle? *Self, 126,* 247–259.

Muraven, M., Baumeister, R. F., & Tice, D. M. (1999). Longitudinal improvement of self-regulation through practice: Building self-control strength through repeated exercise. *Journal of Social Psychology, 139,* 446–457.

Muraven, M., Tice, D. M., & Baumeister, R. F. (1998). Self-control as limited resource: Regulatory depletion patterns. *Journal of Personality and Social Psychology, 74,* 774–789.

Murphy, M. C., & Jones Taylor, V. (2011). The role of situational cues in signaling and maintaining stereotype threat. In M. Inzlicht, & T. Schmader (Eds.), *Stereotype threat: Theory, process, and application.* New York: Oxford University Press.

Murphy, M. C., Steele, C. M., & Gross, J. J. (2007). Signaling threat: How situational cues affect women in math, science, and engineering settings. *Psychological Science, 18,* 879–885.

Noh, S., & Kaspar, V. (2003). Perceived discrimination and depression: Moderating effects of coping, acculturation, and ethnic support. *American Journal of Public Health, 93,* 232–238.

Noh, S., Kaspar, V., & Wickrama, K. A. S. (2007). Overt and subtle racial discrimination and mental health: Preliminary findings for Korean immigrants. *American Journal of Public Health, 97*(7), 1269–1274.

Paradies, Y. C. (2006). Defining, conceptualizing and characterizing racism in health research. *Critical Public Health, 16,* 143–157.

Pascoe, E. A., & Smart Richman, L. (2009). Perceived discrimination and health: A meta-analytic review. *Psychological Bulletin, 135,* 531–554.

Pinel, E. C. (1999). Stigma consciousness: The psychological legacy of social stereotypes. *Journal of Personality and Social Psychology, 76,* 114–128.

Roberts, C. B., Vines, A. I., Kaufman, J. S., & James, S. A. (2007). Cross-sectional association between perceived discrimination and hypertension in African-American men and women: The Pitt County Study. *American Journal of Epidemiology, 167*(5), 624–632.

Schmader, T. (2002). Gender identification moderates stereotype threat effects on women's' math performance. *Journal of Experimental Social Psychology, 38,* 194–201.

Schmader, T., & Beilock, S. (2011). An integration of processes that underlie stereotype threat. In M. Inzlicht, & T. Schmader (Eds.), *Stereotype threat: Theory, process, and application.* New York: Oxford University Press.

Schmader, T., & Johns, M. (2003). Converging evidence that stereotype threat reduces working memory capacity. *Journal of Personality and Social Psychology, 85,* 440–452.

Schmader, T., Johns, M., & Forbes, C. (2008). An integrated process model of stereotype threat effects on performance. *Psychological Review, 115,* 336–356.

Shapiro, J. R. (2011). Types of threats: From stereotype threat to stereotype threats. In M. Inzlicht, & T. Schmader (Eds.), *Stereotype threat: Theory, process, and application.* New York: Oxford University Press.

Steele, C. M. (1997). A threat in the air: How stereotypes shape intellectual identity and performance. *American Psychologist, 52,* 613–629.

Steele, C. M., & Aronson, J. (1995). Stereotype threat and the intellectual test performance of African Americans. *Journal of Personality and Social Psychology, 69,* 797–811.

Steele, C. M., Spencer, S. J., & Aronson, J. (2002). Contending with group image: The psychology of stereotype and social identity threat. *Advances in Experimental Social Psychology, 34,* 379–440.

Stewart, J. A. (2006). The detrimental effects of allostasis: Allostatic load as a measure of cumulative stress. *Journal of Physiological Anthropology, 25,* 133–145.

Stone, J., Chalabaev, A., & Harrison, C. K. (2011). The impact of stereotype threat on performance in sports. In M. Inzlicht, & T. Schmader (Eds.), *Stereotype threat: Theory, process, and application.* New York: Oxford University Press.

Stucke, T. S., & Baumeister, R. F. (2006). Ego depletion and aggressive behaviour: Is the inhibition of aggression a limited resource? *European Journal of Social Psychology, 36,* 1–13.

Sujoldzic, A., Peternel, L., Kulenovic, T., & Terzic, R. (2006). Social determinants of health—a comparative study of Bosnian adolescents in different cultural contexts. *Collegium Antropologicum, 30,* 703–711.

Taylor, T. R., Williams, C. D., Makambi, K. H., Mouton, C., Harrell, J. P., Cozier, Y., et al. (2007). Racial discrimination and breast cancer incidence in US black women: The black women's health study. *American Journal of Epidemiology, 166,* 46–54.

Vohs, K. D., & Heatherton, T. F. (2000). Self-regulatory failure: A resource-depletion approach. *Psychological Science, 11,* 249–254.

Watson, D., & Pennebaker, J. W. (1989). Health complaints, stress, and distress: Exploring the central role of negative affectivity. *Psychological Review, 96,* 234–254.

Williams, D. R., & Mohammed, S. A. (2009). Discrimination and racial disparities in health: Evidence and needed research. *Journal of Behavioral Medicine, 32,* 20–47.

Yen, I. H., Ragland, D. R., Grenier B. A., & Fisher, J. M. (1999). Workplace discrimination and alcohol consumption: Findings from the San Francisco Muni health and safety study. *Ethnicity & Disease, 9*(1), 70–80.

8 Differentiating Theories

*A Comparison of Stereotype Threat and
Stereotype Priming Effects[1,2]*

■ DAVID M. MARX

It has been argued that merely priming negative stereotypic traits is sufficient to cause stereotype threat. This chapter discusses theory and research
that challenges this assumption by highlighting how one's stereotyped social
identity and the concerns about confirming a negative self and/or group-
relevant stereotype can help distinguish between stereotype threat and
priming effects. Specifically, we discuss how stereotype threat is not the
product of some automatic perception–behavior link, but is in fact a "hot"
motivational phenomenon, which is based on the concern that targets of
negative stereotypes have about confirming the group-relevant stereotype—what we refer to as the "knowing-and-being" account of stereotype
threat. In the first part of this chapter, we outline the theoretical rationale
for our knowing-and-being account and then detail research that supports
this account. Following this, we discuss how typical priming procedures
may be used to create a stereotype threat–like experience, provided that
the priming procedure activates one's stereotyped identity and not simply
the stereotypes associated with that identity. In closing, we provide a brief
summary of the policy implications for this research.

Keywords: Stereotype threat, priming, social identity, motivation

Imagine the following situation. It is the first day of the fall semester, and students
are strolling into an advanced-level math class bleary-eyed from getting up early after
a summer of sleeping in. Naturally, most students in this type of class risk feeling
discouraged or upset if they perform poorly. However, certain students, such as
women or ethnic-minority students, face an additional pressure because of negative
stereotypes alleging their group's intellectual inferiority, a predicament known as
stereotype threat (Steele, 1997; Steele & Aronson, 1995). Because of this predicament, these students often perform worse than they otherwise would due to the
pressure posed by the negative group-relevant stereotype. Such stereotype threat
effects have now been documented among a wide range of groups and performance
domains (see e.g., Chasteen, Kang, & Remedios, 2011, Chapter 13, this volume;
Croizet & Millet, 2011, Chapter 12, this volume; Shapiro, 2011, Chapter 5, this
volume; Stone, Chalabaev, & Harrison, 2011, Chapter 14, this volume).

Clearly, stereotype threat is ubiquitous, far-reaching, and detrimental to the performance and achievement of those who experience it. Yet, only recently have researchers begun to clarify how stereotype threat may differ from other processes that also involve the effects of stereotype activation on behavior—namely, stereotype priming effects. The primary purpose of this chapter is to present a theoretical account and a discussion of research aimed at differentiating these two processes of stereotype-based behavior. This differentiation seems particularly important because knowing what process is at work refines existing theory while also helping pinpoint when interventions against the debilitating effects of stereotypes may be especially beneficial. In this chapter, we also provide additional insights into the relationship between stereotype threat and typical priming procedures because this priming issue may be less about whether to prime or not to prime and more about what is primed in the first place.

■ DISTINGUISHING BETWEEN STEREOTYPE THREAT AND PRIMING EFFECTS

Although stereotype threat and stereotype priming effects share certain aspects, they are, in fact, distinct effects that involve different processes. The similarities essentially boil down to stereotype activation—in either case, no activation, no effect. The differences involve the self-relevance of the stereotype and the concerns that arise when stereotyped targets make the connection between the stereotype and how they may be judged if they perform poorly on a stereotype-relevant task. In this section, we first provide a brief overview of priming effects and then describe in more detail the similarities and differences between stereotype priming and stereotype threat effects.

Overview of Priming Effects

Many explanations have been proposed for priming effects, such as ideomotor action (e.g., Dijksterhuis & Bargh, 2001; Herr, 1986; Higgins, 1989; James, 1890/1950), the active-self account (DeMarree, Wheeler, & Petty, 2005; Wheeler, DeMarree, & Petty, 2007; Wheeler & Petty, 2001), or motivated preparation to act (Cesario, Plaks, & Higgins, 2006); however, it is generally agreed upon that the prime activates knowledge structures that guide behavior in ways consistent with the activated knowledge. Indeed, it has been routinely shown that the most accessible traits, knowledge, and/or constructs are those most likely to guide perceptions and behavior (e.g. Bargh, Chen, & Burrows, 1996; Blair & Banaji, 1996; Dijksterhuis & van Knippenberg, 1998; Dovidio, Evans, & Tyler, 1986; Higgins, 1996; Srull & Wyer, 1979). For instance, first being exposed to the word *table* makes it more likely that one will complete the word fragment _ _ A I R with CHAIR than FLAIR. This is because *table* and *chair* are more often paired together in memory than are *table* and *flair*. Thus, seeing the word *table* makes concepts associated with table (i.e., chair) more accessible than concepts less associated with table (i.e., flair). Priming effects have been widely studied with a significant amount of this work examining how priming stereotypes or social categories leads to stereotype-consistent responses (for reviews, see Dijksterhuis & Bargh, 2001; Wheeler & Petty, 2001). Consider the seminal paper by Bargh et al. (1996). These researchers found that young college students walked *more slowly* down a hallway after being primed with traits stereotypic of the elderly compared to students who were not primed with these traits. This manipulation was based upon the idea that the elderly are stereotypically associated with walking slowly. Hence, stereotype priming led young college students to respond in a stereotype-consistent way because traits associated with the elderly were accessible to these students at that particular time.

Differentiating Theories

Both stereotype threat and stereotype priming effects rely on stereotype activation. As a consequence, this has led some researchers to view the priming of negative stereotypic traits as sufficient for creating a stereotype threat situation. This is because a stereotype threat situation is likewise a situation in which stereotype activation leads directly to stereotype-consistent behaviors (Ambady, Paik, Steele, Owen-Smith, & Mitchell, 2004; Dijksterhuis & Corneille, 2004; Dijksterhuis & van Knippenberg, 1998; Gladwell, 2005; Oswald & Harvey, 2000; Shih, Ambady, & Pittinsky, 1999; Wheeler, Jarvis, & Petty, 2001). This is problematic because viewing these two effects as interchangeable leads to a murky understanding of both. A lack of theoretical precision also makes it difficult to pinpoint the specific attributes and boundary conditions of each effect. This, of course, complicates theory development. Furthermore, it makes development of interventions tricky due to the lack of clarity regarding what process is at work. Hence, differentiating between the two theories seems important from both a theoretical and practical perspective.

Social Identity and Stereotype-relevance

Although priming effects typically rely on perception-to-behavior effects that refer to relatively global, nonspecific links between activation and behavior (see e.g., Wheeler et al., 2007, for a somewhat similar perspective), stereotype threat relies on perception-to-behavior effects that are more specific. That is, stereotype priming can affect "anyone," whereas stereotype threat, by definition, only occurs for those individuals who are *targeted* by the relevant stereotype. It is how individuals "view" the stereotype that helps distinguish between these two effects. For stereotype priming effects, it *does not* matter who you are—stereotype activation leads to stereotype-consistent behavior. But for stereotype threat effects, it *does* matter who you are—stereotype activation only leads to stereotype-consistent behavior when the stereotype is self-relevant.

One's social identity is a key piece of the stereotype threat experience. Recent research by Marx, Stapel, and Muller (2005) supports this line of reasoning. These researchers demonstrated that stereotype threat situations are especially likely to increase the accessibility of the social identity that is most relevant to the stereotype. Specifically, they found that female participants' gender identity (relative to other social identities, such as their student and family member identities) was more accessible in a math stereotype threat situation compared to a control situation. After all, it makes sense that one would be focused on the very identity that is being directly "threatened" in the immediate situation relative to an identity that is not being directly threatened—that is, an identity for which the stereotype does not apply (cf. Rydell, McConnell, & Beilock, 2009).[3]

Although Marx and Stapel were not the first to discuss the role of social identity and stereotype threat, they were the first to demonstrate how one's social identity can be used to help distinguish stereotype threat from priming effects. That is, with few exceptions, priming research, particularly as it relates to stereotype threat, failed to include the very group, or at least, systematically examine the group to which the stereotype applies. It is also important to note that because much of the research exploring the impact of stereotypic traits on performance had not included *both* targets and nontargets of the stereotype (see e.g., Ambady et al., 2004; Wheeler et al., 2001; but see, Shih et al., 2002 for work on positive trait priming), it was difficult to determine whether everyone would "feel" the same way to the primed content. Nevertheless, it seems clear that if the stereotype is relevant, then concerns about confirming the stereotype will be increased.

Threat-based Concerns and Stereotype Threat

Because the outcomes of stereotype threat and stereotype priming effects are generally identical, we argue that, in order to determine which effect is at work, it is necessary to include some type of measure that captures the concern that stereotyped targets have when in a stereotype threat situation. According to Marx, Brown, and Steele (1999), targets' poor test performance is due to the "situational pressure posed by the prospect of being seen or treated through the lens of a negative group stereotype" (p. 493). This situational pressure, in turn, increases targets' worry about being judged in terms of the stereotype if they underperform (e.g., Steele, 1997; Steele, Spencer, & Aronson, 2002). Over the years, many researchers have attempted to capture this concern using a variety of measures (e.g., self-reported anxiety, word-fragment completions, physiological measures). One additional measure that has proven useful is Marx and Stapel's measure of threat-based concerns (Marx & Stapel, 2006b; also see, Marx & Goff, 2005; Marx, Ko, & Friedman, 2009). This measure shows whether targets link their performance to their stereotyped social identity and, as result, feel concern about confirming this link. This measure is quite straightforward in this regard. It consists of three items that focus explicitly on the concern that targets have about confirming the self- and/or group-relevant stereotype if they perform poorly in the situation (e.g., "I worry that my ability to perform well on math tests is affected by my gender/race").

Surprisingly, no measure of participants' threat-based concerns has been included in past research using priming procedures as a way to activate stereotype threat.

This lack of a threat appraisal measure only helped fuel the misperception that typical stereotype priming procedures could elicit stereotype threat. Indeed, the applicable research to date has focused primarily on performance and not on participants' self-related, threat-based concerns (Ambady et al., 2004; Shih et al., 1999; Shih et al., 2002; Wheeler et al., 2001); thus, this research merely claimed, rather than empirically demonstrated, that typical priming procedures could elicit stereotype threat. Because of this, we argued that, by including a measure of threat appraisals, it should be possible to show that despite similar performance outcomes, stereotype priming can have very different effects on participants' threat appraisals—high concern = stereotype threat, low or no concern = priming.

In sum, although stereotype knowledge is sufficient for stereotype activation to result in general behavioral priming effects, such knowledge is not enough for stereotype threat effects. For stereotype threat, both *knowing* and *being* are necessary (see also Marx et al., 2005; Steele, 1997; Steele et al., 2002). In other words, in stereotype threat situations, targets' performance is affected because they *know* the stereotype about their group (e.g., "women are bad at math") and because they *are* members of the group that is targeted by the stereotype ("I am a woman"). Priming effects, on the other hand, can occur for anyone because no such link is necessary. When distinguishing between these two processes, it is critical, then, to include these key factors in the research design: targets and nonstereotyped targets, stereotype threat and control conditions, and a measure of threat-based concerns. By doing so, researchers should be able to pinpoint which process is at work. In the following section, we detail the research that has been conducted to differentiate stereotype threat from stereotype priming effects. This research not only added to the clarity of the research on stereotype-based performance effects, it also sharpened the theoretical distinction between stereotype threat and priming effects.

■ RESEARCH ON DIFFERENTIATING STEREOTYPE THREAT FROM STEREOTYPE PRIMING EFFECTS

To examine our knowing and being account of stereotype threat, we conducted a series of experiments that included what we view as the critical factors to distinguish stereotype threat from priming effects. The first two experiments pitted the effects of priming against stereotype threat on participants' math (Experiment 1) and emotion (Experiment 2) test performance and threat-based concerns. A third experiment was conducted to examine how merely heightening the accessibility of one's general sense of "groupness" (that is, when one is thinking in generalized "we" terms) can cause targets, but not nontargets, to have lower test performance and higher threat-based concerns. In other words, we tested the notion that an increased sense of groupness in combination with situational cues can create a stereotype threat effect, even when the test description does not purposefully activate a negative stereotype associated with targets' threatened social identity.

Experiment 1: Women and Math

For this first experiment (Marx & Stapel, 2006b), we used a commonly studied ability-based stereotype in the stereotype threat literature; namely, the stereotype that women are bad at math (Spencer, Steele, & Quinn, 1999). Accordingly, male and female participants took a difficult math test under stereotype threat or control conditions. In addition to the test description manipulation, half the participants were primed with the negative trait "dumb" and its semantic associates (e.g., unintelligent) before they took the test, while the other half were not primed. To prime participants, we used a procedure widely used in priming research. Specifically, participants were asked to unscramble four to five words into a grammatically correct sentence (e.g., Bargh et al., 1996). Of the 20 scrambled sentences, 12 were related to the negative trait "dumb," and eight were neutral in content. We chose this trait because it was fairly general and could apply to both men and women, hence activation of this trait should theoretically affect men and women equally. After the priming procedure, participants were given the math test and a measure of threat-based concerns.

Overall, we found strong support for our knowing-and-being account of stereotype threat (see Table 8.1). Of particular importance was the finding that women underperformed relative to men in the stereotype threat conditions, regardless of whether they were additionally primed. This effect both reflects the typical stereotype threat pattern and also demonstrates that our priming manipulation did not alter this pattern. Also of importance was the finding that, in the control conditions, both men and women performed poorly after being primed, relative to when they were not primed. And this priming effect was not qualified by the participant's gender. Hence, the typical priming effect occurred for both stereotyped (women) and nonstereotyped targets (men).

For participants' threat-based concerns, we also found consistent support for our reasoning. As expected, the prime had no meaningful influence on

TABLE 8.1 *Mean (SD) math test performance and threat-based concerns as a function of stereotype prime, test description, and participant gender*

| | Stereotype Prime | | | |
| | Not Primed | | Primed | |
Test Description	Threat	Control	Threat	Control
Math Test Performance				
Female Participant	10.67 (1.97)$_a$	12.29 (1.57)$_b$	9.27 (1.79)$_d$	10.63 (1.54)$_a$
Male Participant	13.50 (1.45)$_c$	12.25 (0.87)$_b$	12.50 (1.45)$_b$	10.86 (1.17)$_a$
Threat-Based Concerns				
Female Participant	3.03 (0.58)$_b$	2.08 (0.53)$_a$	2.87 (0.63)$_b$	2.02 (0.66)$_a$
Male Participant	2.31 (0.56)$_a$	1.92 (0.38)$_a$	1.78 (0.64)$_a$	2.21 (0.61)$_a$

From Marx, D. M., & Stapel, D. A. (2006). Distinguishing stereotype threat from priming effects: On the role of the social self and threat-based concerns. *Journal of Personality and Social Psychology, 91,* 243–254, with permission of the publisher, American Psychological Association.

All means that do not share a common subscript differ at *p* <.05

participants' threat-based concerns: Women had higher threat-based concerns in the stereotype threat conditions compared to the control conditions. Women also had higher threat-based concerns than did men in the stereotype threat conditions, but the magnitude of these differences remained the same in both the primed and not primed conditions.

This first experiment provided compelling evidence for the distinction between stereotype threat and priming effects, but it could have been argued that our knowing-and-being account only applied to women and math stereotype threat. Because of this we conducted a follow-up experiment, so that it would be possible to generalize our reasoning to another group and stereotype—namely, to men and the stereotype that they are emotionally insensitive (see also Leyens, Desert, Croizet, & Darcis, 2000; Marx & Stapel, 2006a). An additional benefit of this experiment was that we could apply our reasoning to a domain other than academics.

Experiment 2: Men and Emotional Insensitivity

The procedures for this second experiment were similar to the first experiment except that participants took an emotion test and were primed with the trait "emotional insensitivity" and its semantic associates (e.g., inconsiderate). Note that because we used the negative stereotypic trait "emotional insensitivity," men, instead of women, are the negatively stereotyped group. As before, our findings were strongly in support of our reasoning (see Table 8.2). We found that men (targets in this experiment) underperformed on the emotion test relative to women (nontargets), but only in the stereotype threat condition. We further found that men and women performed equally as poorly in the prime compared to the control condition. Results for participants' threat-based concerns again showed that priming did not increase concerns beyond the threat manipulation. Moreover, only those participants' targeted by the negative stereotype showed elevated concerns.

TABLE 8.2 *Mean (SD) emotion test performance and threat-based concerns as a function of stereotype prime, test description, and participant gender*

	Stereotype Prime			
	Not Primed		Primed	
Test Description	Threat	Control	Threat	Control
Emotion Test Performance				
Female Participant	8.92 (1.00)$_a$	6.64 (1.21)$_b$	6.92 (1.38)$_b$	5.28 (1.07)$_c$
Male Participant	5.08 (1.38)$_c$	7.17 (0.94)$_b$	4.07 (1.86)$_{dc}$	4.83 (1.03)$_c$
Threat-Based Concerns				
Female Participant	1.56 (0.62)$_a$	1.64 (1.04)$_a$	1.90 (1.37)$_a$	1.78 (1.12)$_a$
Male Participant	2.67 (0.84)$_b$	1.39 (0.49)$_a$	3.31 (0.81)$_b$	1.72 (1.05)$_a$

From Marx, D. M., & Stapel, D. A. (2006). Distinguishing stereotype threat from priming effects: On the role of the social self and threat-based concerns. *Journal of Personality and Social Psychology, 91*, 243–254, with permission of the publisher, American Psychological Association.

All means that do not share a common subscript differ at *p* <.05

As a whole, the results from these two experiments provide important insight into how stereotype threat and priming effects differ. Indeed, activation of a negative stereotypic trait is not enough for stereotype threat to occur. For stereotype threat to occur, targets need to make the connection between the stereotype and how well they perform in the current testing situation; consequently, they need to link what they know about the stereotype to who they are. And if the stereotype does not favor their group, then they may become concerned about confirming this stereotype if they perform poorly.

Experiment 3: Examining Situational Cues and One's General Sense of "Groupness"

To nail down the role of social identity in stereotype threat situations, we conducted one more experiment that looked at the relationship between the accessibility of one's stereotyped identity and situational cues. That is, we were interested in the question of whether putting participants into a group-based mindset (when they are focused on their groupness) just prior to taking a "nonthreatening" test would create a stereotype threat experience for targets, but not for nontargets (Marx & Stapel, 2006b). This question was based on our prior work (Marx et al., 2005) showing that stereotype threat increased the salience of the social identity most associated with the situation and corresponding stereotype (e.g., in a math stereotype threat situation, women indicated feeling closer to their gender identity than to other important social identities). Thus, we argued that it should be possible to cause poor performance among targets, not only by using a typical and well-established stereotype threat manipulation (i.e., test diagnosticity), but also by making targets' "groupness" salient before they take a nonthreatening test. Activating a general sense of groupness may make many social identities accessible, but once the context is factored in (e.g., "I am a person taking a math test") then the social identity (gender) that is most relevant to the situation (taking a math test) should become the most accessible (e.g., Major & O'Brien, 2005; Onorato & Turner, 2004; Turner, Hogg, Oakes, Reicher, & Wetherell, 1987; but see Rydell et al., 2009). And, if this identity is linked to a negative stereotype, then one's threat appraisals may also be affected.

To test this line of reasoning regarding the interaction of one's groupness and the situation, participants took a math test under one of four conditions. In the first condition, we activated participants' general groupness by having them read a short story detailing a trip to the city. While reading, participants were asked to circle all of the pronouns contained in the story. We constructed the story so that the pronouns were all group-based (e.g., we, us) and hence put participants into a general group-based mindset (Brewer & Gardener, 1996; Marx & Stapel, 2006c; Stapel & Koomen, 2001). After reading the story, participants took a nonthreatening math test. An interesting aspect of this approach was that we did not directly remind participants about their stereotyped identity (see Shih et al., 1999). Rather, we allowed for any identity to become accessible. This approach therefore permitted us to highlight the critical role of the situation and how situational cues may shape a general awareness of one's groupness into a specific awareness of a particular social identity, one most relevant to the task at hand (Marx et al., 2005, see also Rydell et al., 2009). In the second condition, as we had done in the first experiment, we primed participants with the negative trait *dumb* and its semantic associates, then gave them a nonthreatening test. In the third condition, the test was described as diagnostic of math ability, and in the fourth condition, participants simply took a nonthreatening test.

By including these four conditions, we were able to accomplish two things. One, we could replicate the effects from the first two experiments, and two, we could highlight how *knowing* the stereotype and *being* from the stereotyped group in combination with the situational cues that heighten accessibility of a particular social identity can lead to higher threat-based concerns and lower test performance among those participants who are targeted by a negative stereotype.

Results showed that men outperformed women in the stereotype threat condition, but men and women performed similarly in the control condition (see Table 8.3). These results are thus consistent with a typical stereotype threat effect. Critical to our reasoning about the salience of one's groupness and situational cues, we found that, in the groupness condition, women performed worse than men. Importantly, this result is identical to what we found in the stereotype threat condition: The accessibility of one's groupness led to the same effect as the test diagnosticity manipulation, because the situation helped shape a general awareness of groupness into a more specific awareness of the social identity (gender) that is relevant to the situation and associated stereotypes. Our final comparison again showed the typical priming effect, thus underscoring our point that when the group stereotype is not linked to how participants perform, stereotype priming has a similar effect on targets and nontargets' behavior.

For participants' threat-based concerns, we found the typical stereotype threat pattern evidenced in the first two experiments: Women had higher concerns in the stereotype threat condition relative to men, as well as relative to both men and

TABLE 8.3　*Mean (SD) math test performance and threat-based concerns as a function of condition type and participant gender*

	Condition Type			
	Threat	Control	Group-ness	Dumb Prime
Math Test Performance				
Female Participants	10.54 (0.97)$_a$	12.47 (1.64)$_b$	11.07 (1.90)$_a$	10.67 (1.76)$_a$
Male Participants	12.31 (1.97)$_b$	12.45 (0.82)$_b$	12.91 (0.70)$_b$	10.73 (1.42)$_a$
Threat-Based Concerns				
Female Participants	2.87 (0.52)$_b$	1.93 (0.47)$_a$	2.76 (0.76)$_b$	1.93 (0.63)$_a$
Male Participants	1.90 (0.53)$_a$	1.85 (0.31)$_a$	1.61 (0.47)$_{ac}$	2.06 (0.53)$_a$

From Marx, D. M., & Stapel, D. A. (2006). Distinguishing stereotype threat from priming effects: On the role of the social self and threat-based concerns. *Journal of Personality and Social Psychology, 91*, 243–254, with permission of the publisher, American Psychological Association.

All means that do not share a common subscript differ at *p* <.05

women in the control condition. Importantly, we also found that this same pattern occurred in the groupness condition. This last result provided the critical support for our notion that when a stereotype is relevant to a person's performance, regardless of how it is made relevant, it will increase their threat-based concerns.

In sum, these three experiments provided compelling evidence that stereotype threat and stereotype priming effects are, in fact, distinct. Stereotype priming is a general effect, whereby anyone can show the influence of the primed content; stereotype threat is a specific effect, whereby only those for whom the stereotype is directly relevant to their social identity will experience stereotype threat and the corresponding threat-based concerns.

Policy Box

As is self-evident from the chapters in this book, stereotype threat is a broad-ranging process that has serious implications for those who experience stereotype threat. Hence, clarifying the processes underlying the adverse effects of stereotypes on performance and behavior is paramount to developing workable and useful public policy. Moreover, without the clarity of process that is inherent in empirical, lab-based research, policy makers are left with a somewhat blurry picture of what may be contributing to the performance and academic achievement gap among many groups in society. From this perspective, we see that government assistance and funding priorities should be geared toward lab-based research that focuses on more "social" issues. Indeed, lab-based work can provide the needed theoretical and psychological insight for developing interventions geared toward altering those factors that impede the performance of individuals targeted by negative stereotypes. That being said, it is also the onus of researchers to facilitate this process by conducting translational studies that carry the basic lab findings to the field and/or by "spreading the word" about those lab findings that have a direct bearing on educational attainment and opportunities of students targeted by negative stereotypes. A more open line of communication among scholars, policy makers, and governmental agencies, will therefore allow for the best chance to understand the contextual factors and boundary conditions that contribute to poor performance, and thus help achieve the goal of equal opportunity for all without the burden of a threat in the air.

■ STEREOTYPE PRIMING AND SOCIAL IDENTITY

At this point, we would like to take a step back from our discussion of differentiating theories and touch on some additional issues regarding priming. As we stated earlier, priming effects generally rely on knowledge structures that guide behavior in ways consistent with the activated knowledge. And, for the most part, this may be an accurate portrayal of the typical priming effect. Yet, how would these effects differ when one's identity is salient? For instance, how would the students in the Bargh et al. (1996) study—discussed earlier—respond to the elderly primes if they were concurrently aware of their identity as young college students?

Examining how individuals relate to primed information when their social identity is salient would certainly add to our understanding of the "social" component of "social cognition."

Recently, researchers have begun examining how awareness of one's social identity may influence how one interprets and responds to primed information (e.g., Fazio, Dunton, Jackson, & Williams, 1995; Levy, 1996; Marx & Stapel, 2006a, 2006b; Schubert & Häfner, 2003; Shih et al., 2002; Spears, Gordijn, Dijksterhuis, & Stapel, 2004, see also Wheeler et al., 2007, for a discussion of priming and the active self-concept). For instance, in one experiment, Spears et al. (2004) demonstrated that when participants were focused on their student identity, the influence of an elderly prime worked differently from the usual prime-to-behavior sequence in which behavior is consistent with the primed information. Specifically, when focused on their student identity, these young college students distanced themselves from the activated stereotypes of the elderly (e.g., forgetful) because this stereotypical information was clearly irrelevant to this social identity: In this case, participants were slower to respond to words stereotypic of the elderly than were participants who were less aware of their student identity. Note, however, that this situation was not stereotyped in the sense that one's behavior would not serve to confirm or refute a stereotype linked to their social identity. That is, it would matter little how they responded in the situation because others could not use their responses as evidence for a stereotype associated with their social identity. What, then, would be the differences if the situation were stereotyped in nature, such as when one's behavior could be used as evidence for a stereotyped associated with one's social identity (i.e., a stereotype threat situation)?

Priming a Social Identity in Stereotyped Situations

Although we have made a strong claim regarding the differences between stereotype threat and stereotype priming, we are not making the claim that typical priming procedures cannot elicit stereotype threat. On the contrary, the key is what the priming procedure is intending to prime. That is, does it make one's stereotyped social *identity* accessible? Or, does it simply make a particular *stereotypic trait* accessible, which may or may not be associated with one's social identity? From our perspective, these are very different outcomes. It is one thing to prime a stereotypic trait such as "dumb" or "unintelligent," which can impact anyone's behavior regardless of who they are; it is an entirely different thing to prime one's social identity (e.g., Shih et al., 1999; 2002, see also Shih, Pittinsky, & Ho, 2011, Chapter 9, this volume), which then may elicit the very stereotypes associated with that identity. And, if those stereotypes are detrimental in the immediate situation, then it may harm performance; whereas if those stereotypes are beneficial, then it may enhance performance (see Brown & Josephs, 1999). However, as discussed above, if one's social identity is salient and the domain is not stereotypic (as is the case of the Spears et al. research), then priming one's social identity will most likely lead to behavioral contrast. Identity priming and the situation clearly play a critical role in determining how one will behave.

Although no research has explicitly examined this issue, a number of experiments provide support for the idea that certain priming procedures may elicit stereotype threat (Marx & Stapel, 2006a; Shih et al., 2002; see also Wheeler et al., 2001, for a somewhat related argument). For example, Marx and Stapel (2006) conducted an experiment that examined the effects of identity priming and perspective taking on the emotion test performance of men and women. Results showed that when participants wrote about a stereotyped target (a man named Paul) from a first-person perspective ("I am Paul"), both men and women performed poorly on an emotion test that was described as diagnostic of emotional sensitivity. Women performed poorly because writing from a first-person perspective made the stereotype about men and emotional insensitivity relevant for them in the immediate situation. They temporarily adopted a male identity and thus the concerns about confirming this stereotype applied to them as well as to men. Importantly, when participants wrote about Paul from a third-person perspective, only men underperformed and felt increased threat-based concerns because the stereotype was already relevant to them by virtue of their social identity.

Additional support for the idea that certain priming procedures can elicit a stereotype threat–like effect comes from DeMarree et al. (2005) and their work on the *active self-account*. According to these researchers, one reason why identity priming may have worked for female participants in the Marx and Stapel (2006a) research is that the activated prime content was linked to or included in these participants' self-concept. That is, at some level, female participants may have seen themselves as "emotionally insensitive," thus the identity prime worked because of the increased accessibility of the linkage between the prime and their active self-concept.

In other research looking at identity priming and performance, Shih and her colleagues (Shih et al., 1999, 2002; Shih et al., 2011, Chapter 9, this volume) have repeatedly shown that when priming manipulations activate a social identity that is either negatively (e.g., reminding a female participant about her female identity before taking a math test) or positively stereotyped in the situation (e.g., reminding an Asian participant about their Asian identity before taking a math test), they can harm or boost performance relative to when that specific social identity is not as salient. What is particularly intriguing about these results is the fact that subtle priming procedures (e.g., asking participants "to list three reasons why they would prefer a single-sex [dormitory] floor") were effective in triggering awareness of a particular social identity (gender), which then led to a stereotype-threat effect. So, just as the Marx and Stapel's (2006c) research showed, it may be the case that subtle priming procedures can create both a stereotype-threat or stereotype boost effect as long as the primes increase accessibility of a particular social identity. Indeed, as the Shih et al. work demonstrates, social identity need not be explicitly activated (i.e., indicating one's gender on the cover of a test) to have an effect on performance—subtle activation may be just as effective (see also McGlone & Aronson, 2006, for further research on identity priming and stereotype threat). As a whole, this work underscores the inextricable link between social identities and the corresponding stereotypes (see also e.g., Inzlicht & Ben-Zeev, 2000).

■ CONCLUSION

Why do we behave the way we do? Do outside forces influence our behavior? What bearing do our social identities have on the way we behave, think, and feel? Indeed, these are just some of fundamental questions that social psychologists ask. Although an answer to these questions may not be simple, or even complete, research on stereotype threat and stereotype priming have provided some insight into these fundamental questions, particularly as they pertain to the stereotypes that beset us. Focusing on these issues has great utility because it provides further insight into the effects of stereotypes on behavior; it helps distinguish between the many types of stereotyped-based effects that may look similar on the surface, but below the surface, are in fact distinct. Knowing what effect is at work can also clarify whether the stereotyped behavior is something that has only minor consequences or more far-reaching consequences for those individuals targeted by negative stereotypes. For example, does the effect of the stereotype impede an individual's career choice, or does it merely influence his behavior on a mundane laboratory task? In the first case, developing an intervention seems quite beneficial because it may allow stereotyped targets to overcome the barriers imposed by the stereotype and continue to pursue their chosen career. In the second case, developing an intervention seems less critical because behavior on a laboratory task does not have any far-reaching consequences for an individual's future. We are not arguing that understanding priming effects has no practical importance; indeed, understanding priming effects has considerable importance for theory development and expanded insight into social cognitive processes. What we are arguing is that, in the case of stereotype threat, there is a clear need for developing an intervention, whereas in the case of stereotype priming, an intervention seems less necessary.

In sum, whereas previous research has been somewhat elusive about the relationship between stereotype threat and priming effects (e.g., Wheeler et al., 2001), the theory and research detailed in this chapter makes it quite clear how these effects differ: Stereotype threat and priming effects both rely on stereotype activation, but once one's social identity and threat-based concerns are factored into the process, the paths to poor performance diverge (Major & O'Brien, 2005; Marx et al., 2005).

■ ENDNOTES

1. Portions of this chapter are based on Marx, D. M., & Stapel, D. A. (2006). Distinguishing stereotype threat from priming effects: On the role of the social self and threat-based concerns. *Journal of Personality and Social Psychology, 91,* 243–254; and Marx, D. M. (2009).

On the role of group membership in stereotype-based performance effects. *Social and Personality Psychology Compass, 3,* 77–93.

2. We would like to thank Chris Cole, Aly Monroe, Emily Shaffer, and Brad Weisz for their helpful comments on earlier versions of this chapter.

3. Research by Rydell et al. (2009) shows that when female participants are provided with reminders about their other social identities that are positively stereotyped in the situation (e.g., focusing on their student identity when taking a math test), these female participants will focus on this positive social identity rather than on a negative social identity (e.g., their gender identity). The logic behind these effects is that people have a need to feel positively about the self; thus, when possible, they will focus on their positive social identities (Tajfel & Turner, 1986). This research thus points to the importance of activating positive social identities in stereotype threat situations as way to combat the adverse effects of stereotypes on performance.

References

Ambady, N., Paik, S. K., Steele, J., Owen-Smith, A., & Mitchell, J. P. (2004). Deflecting negative self-relevant stereotype activation: The effects of individuation. *Journal of Experimental Social Psychology, 40,* 401–408.

Bargh, J. A., Chen, M., & Burrows, L. (1996). Automaticity of social behavior: Direct effects of trait construct and stereotype activation on action. *Journal of Personality and Social Psychology, 71,* 230–244.

Blair, I. V., & Banaji, M. R. (1996). Automatic and controlled processes in stereotype priming. *Journal of Personality and Social Psychology, 70,* 1142–1163.

Brewer, M. B., & Gardner, W. (1996). Who is this "we"? Levels of collective identity and self-representations. *Journal of Personality and Social Psychology, 71,* 83–93.

Brown, R. P., & Josephs, R. A. (1999). A burden of proof: Stereotype relevance and gender differences in math performance. *Journal of Personality and Social Psychology, 76,* 246–257.

Cesario, J., Plaks, J., & Higgins, E. (2006). Automatic social behavior as motivated preparation to interact. *Journal of Personality and Social Psychology, 90,* 893–910.

Chasteen, A. L., Kang, S. K., & Remedios, J. D. (2011). Aging and stereotype threat: Development, process, and interventions. In M. Inzlicht, & T. Schmader (Eds.), *Stereotype threat: Theory, process, and application.* New York: Oxford University Press.

Croizet, J. C., & Millet, M. (2011). Social class and test Performance: From stereotype threat to symbolic violence and vice versa. In M. Inzlicht, & T. Schmader (Eds.), *Stereotype threat: Theory, process, and application.* New York: Oxford University Press.

DeMarree, K. G., Wheeler, S. C., & Petty, R. E. (2005). Priming a new identity: Self-monitoring moderates the effects of non-self primes on self-judgments and behavior. *Journal of Personality and Social Psychology, 89,* 657–671.

Dijksterhuis, A., & Bargh, J. A. (2001). The perception-behavior expressway: Automatic effects of social perception on social behavior. *Advances in Experimental Social Psychology, 33,* 1–40.

Dijksterhuis, A., & Corneille, O. (2004). *On the relations between stereotype activation and intellectual underperformance.* Unpublished manuscript, University of Amsterdam, The Netherlands.

Dijksterhuis, A., & van Knippenberg, A. (1998). The relation between perception and behavior, or how to win a game of Trivial Pursuit. *Journal of Personality and Social Psychology, 74*(4), 865–877.

Dovidio, J. F., Evans, N., & Tyler, R. B. (1986). Racial stereotypes: The contents of their cognitive representations. *Journal of Experimental Social Psychology, 22,* 22–37.

Fazio, R. H., Jackson, J. R., Dunton, B. C., & Williams, C. J. (1995). Variability in automatic activation as an unobtrusive measure of racial attitudes: A bona fide pipeline? *Journal of Personality and Social Psychology, 69,* 1013-1027.

Gladwell, M. (2005). *Blink: the power of thinking without thinking.* New York: Little, Brown, and Co.

Herr, P. M. (1986). Consequences of priming: Judgment and behavior. *Journal of Personality and Social Psychology, 51,* 1106–1115.

Higgins, E. T. (1989). Knowledge accessibility and activation: Subjectivity and suffering from unconscious sources. In J. S. Uleman, & J. A. Bargh (Eds.), *Unintended thought* (pp. 75–123). New York: Guilford Press.

Higgins, E. T. (1996). Knowledge activation: Accessibility, applicability, and salience. In E. T. Higgins, & A. W. Kruglanski (Eds.), *Social psychology: Handbook of basic principles* (pp. 133–168). New York: Guilford.

Inzlicht, M., & Ben-Zeev, T. (2000). A threatening intellectual environment: Why females are susceptible to experiencing problem-solving deficits in the presence of males. *Psychological Science, 11,* 365–371.

James, W. (1890/1950). *The principles of psychology.* New York: Dover Publications. (Original work published 1890).

Levy, B. (1996). Improving memory in old age through implicit self-stereotyping. *Journal of Personality and Social Psychology, 71,* 1092–1107.

Leyens, J. P., Desert, M., Croizet, J. -C., & Darcis, C. (2000). Stereotype threat: Are lower status and history of stigmatization preconditions of stereotype threat? *Personality and Social Psychology Bulletin, 26,* 1189–1199.

Major, B., & O'Brien, L. T. (2005). The social psychology of stigma. *Annual Review of Psychology, 56,* 393–421.

Marx, D. M. (2009). On the role of group membership in stereotype-based performance effects. *Social and Personality Psychology Compass, 3,* 77–93.

Marx, D. M., Brown, J. L., & Steele, C. M. (1999). Allport's legacy and the situational press of stereotypes. *Journal of Social Issues, 55,* 491–502.

Marx, D. M., & Goff, P. A. (2005). Clearing the air: The effect of experimenter race on targets' test performance and subjective experience. *British Journal of Social Psychology, 44,* 645–657.

Marx, D. M., Ko, S. J., & Friedman, R. A. (2009). The "Obama Effect": How a salient role model reduces race-based performance differences. *Journal of Experimental Social Psychology, 45,* 953–956.

Marx, D. M., & Roman, J. S. (2002). Female role models: Protecting female students' math test performance. *Personality and Social Psychology Bulletin, 28,* 1185–1197.

Marx, D. M., & Stapel, D. A. (2006a). It depends on your perspective: The role of self-relevance in stereotype-based underperformance. *Journal of Experimental Social Psychology, 42,* 768–775.

Marx, D. M., & Stapel, D. A. (2006b). Distinguishing stereotype threat from priming effects: On the role of the social self and threat-based concerns. *Journal of Personality and Social Psychology, 91,* 243–254.

Marx, D. M., & Stapel, D. A. (2006c). Understanding stereotype lift: On the role of the social self. *Social Cognition, 24,* 776–791.

Marx, D. M., Stapel, D. A., & Muller, D. (2005). We can do it: The interplay of construal orientation and social comparisons under threat. *Journal of Personality and Social Psychology, 88*, 432–446.

McGlone, M. S., & Aronson, J. (2006). Stereotype threat, identity salience, and spatial reasoning. *Journal of Applied Developmental Psychology, 27*, 486–493.

Onorato, R. S., & Turner. J. C. (2004). Fluidity in the self-concept: The shift from personal to social identity. *European Journal of Social Psychology, 34*, 257–278.

Oswald, D. L., & Harvey, R. D. (2000). Hostile environments, stereotype threat, and math performance among undergraduate women. *Current Psychology: Developmental, Learning, Personality, Social, 19*, 338–356.

Rydell, R. J., McConnell, A. R., & Beilock, S. L. (2009). Multiple social identities and stereotype threat: Imbalance, accessibility, and working memory. *Journal of Personality and Social Psychology, 96*, 949–966.

Schubert, T. W., & Häfner, M. (2003). Contrast from social stereotypes in automatic behavior. *Journal of Experimental Social Psychology, 39*, 577–584.

Shapiro, J. R. (2011). Types of threats: From stereotype threat to stereotype threats. In M. Inzlicht, & T. Schmader (Eds.), *Stereotype threat: Theory, process, and application.* New York: Oxford University Press.

Shih, M., Ambady, N., Richeson, J. A., Fujita, K., & Gray, H. M. (2002). Stereotype performance boosts: The impact of self-relevance and the manner of stereotype activation. *Journal of Personality and Social Psychology, 83*, 638–647.

Shih, M., Ambady, N., & Pittinsky, T. (1999). Stereotype susceptibility: Identity salience and shifts in quantitative performance. *Psychological Science, 10*, 80–83.

Shih, M., Pittinsky, T., & Ho, G. C. (2011). Stereotype boost: Positive outcomes from the activation of positive stereotypes. In M. Inzlicht, & T. Schmader (Eds.), *Stereotype threat: Theory, process, and application.* New York: Oxford University Press.

Spears, R., Gordijn, E., Dijksterhuis, A., & Stapel, D. A. (2004). Reaction in action: Intergroup contrast in automatic behavior. *Personality and Social Psychology Bulletin, 30*, 605–616.

Spencer, S. J., Steele, C. M., & Quinn, D. (1999). Stereotype threat and women's math performance. *Journal of Experimental Social Psychology, 35*, 4–28.

Srull, T. K., & Wyer, R. S., Jr. (1979). The role of category accessibility in the interpretation of information about persons: Some determinants and implications. *Journal of Personality and Social Psychology, 37*, 1660–1672.

Stapel, D. A., & Koomen, W. (2001). I, we, and the effects of others on me: How self-construal level moderates social comparison effects. *Journal of Personality and Social Psychology, 80*, 766–781.

Steele, C. M. (1997). A threat in the air: How stereotypes shape intellectual identity and performance. *American Psychologist, 52*, 613–629.

Steele, C. M., & Aronson, J. (1995). Stereotype vulnerability and the intellectual test performance of African Americans. *Journal of Personality and Social Psychology, 69*, 797–811.

Steele, C. M., Spencer, S. J., & Aronson, J. (2002). Contending with group image: The psychology of stereotype and social identity threat. In M. Zanna (Ed.), *Advances in experimental social psychology* Vol. 34 (pp. 379–440). San Diego: Academic Press.

Stone, J., Chalabaev, A., & Harrison, C. K. (2011). The impact of stereotype threat on performance in sports. In M. Inzlicht, & T. Schmader (Eds.), *Stereotype threat: Theory, process, and application.* New York: Oxford University Press.

Tajfel, H., & Turner, J. C. (1986). The social identity theory of intergroup behavior. In S. Wordhel, & W. G. Austin (Eds.), *The social psychology of intergroup relations* (pp. 7–24). Chicago: Nelson-Hall.

Turner, J. C., Hogg, M. A., Oakes, P. J., Reicher, S. D., & Wetherell, M. S. (1987). *Rediscovering the social group: A self-categorization theory*. Oxford, UK: Blackwell.

Wheeler, S. C., DeMarree, K., & Petty R. E. (2007). Understanding the role of the self in prime-to-behavior effects: The active-self account. *Personality and Social Psychology Review, 11,* 234–261.

Wheeler, S. C., Jarvis, B. G., & Petty, R. E. (2001). Think unto others: The self-destructive impact of negative racial stereotypes. *Journal of Experimental Social Psychology, 37,* 173–180.

Wheeler, S. C., & Petty, R. E. (2001). The effects of stereotype activation on behavior: A review of possible mechanisms. *Psychological Bulletin, 127,* 797–826.

9 Stereotype Boost

*Positive Outcomes from the Activation
of Positive Stereotypes*

■ MARGARET J. SHIH,
TODD L. PITTINSKY,
AND GEOFFREY C. HO

Stereotype boost theory (SBT) runs in parallel to stereotype threat theory (STT). Although the primary concern of STT is the pernicious effects of negative stereotypes on performance, SBT examines how positive stereotypes can improve performance. In this chapter, we review the research on stereotype boosts conducted to date. Specifically, we review the evidence for stereotype boost, and clarify the distinctions between stereotype boost and stereotype lift. Stereotype performance boosts result from exposure to positive stereotypes, whereas stereotype lift results from exposure to negative stereotypes about another group. We also outline the conditions under which the activation of positive stereotypes can boost performance. We examine the role that the method of stereotype activation and the characteristics of the individual play in determining whether or not activating a positive stereotype will lead to a performance boost. Finally, we investigate the potential mechanisms that could cause positive stereotypes to boost performance. We find evidence for many potential mechanisms that may underlie stereotype performance boosts, including reducing anxiety, increasing efficiency in neural processing, and activating ideomotor processes. It is possible that many of these mechanisms may be working together to boost performance. Finally, in reviewing the research, we find that although some findings from stereotype threat research can be applied or generalized to stereotype boosts, many of the findings from stereotype threat cannot be applied or generalized to stereotype boosts. This suggests that stereotype boost is a separate phenomenon from stereotype threat that may involve different underlying processes.

Keywords: Stereotype threat, stereotype boost, positive stereotypes, model minority

Over the last decade, an explosion of research has examined the relationship between stereotypes and performance. The most notable work in this area is the research on stereotype threat that finds that negative stereotypes undermine the academic performance of the stereotyped individual (Steele & Aronson, 1995). In 1995, Steele and Aronson found that the stereotype "African American students have low academic ability" hurt the performance of African American students on academic tests. The stereotype threat effect has been characterized as "a psychological predicament in which individuals are inhibited from performing to their potential by the recognition that possible failure could confirm a negative stereotype that applies to their ingroup and, by extension, to themselves" (Schmader, 2002, p. 194). This effect has also been replicated many times in other groups such as Hispanic Americans (Aronson, Quinn, & Spencer, 1998), individuals from lower socioeconomic status (Croizet & Claire, 1998; Croizet & Millet, 2011, Chapter 12, this volume), women (Spencer, Steele, & Quinn, 1999; Logel, Peach & Spencer, 2011, Chapter 10, this volume) and the elderly (Chasteen, Kang, & Remedios, 2011, Chapter 13, this volume). Stereotype threat has also been documented in other performance domains, such as athletic tasks (Stone, Lynch, Sjomeling, & Darley, 1999) and memory tasks (Levy, 1996). Clearly, the activation of negative stereotypes about a group can impair the performance of individual group members.

Considering the harm that stereotype threat can cause, it is no wonder that research on stereotypes and performance has focused on the effects of negative stereotypes. But those effects are by no means the whole picture, and attention is turning to the effects of positive stereotypes on performance. Indeed, just as stereotype threat theory predicts that negative stereotypes can hurt performance, *stereotype boost theory* (SBT) predicts that positive stereotypes can boost performance (Dijksterhuis et al., 1998; Kray, Thompson, & Galinsky, 2001; Levy, 1996; Shih, Pittinsky, & Ambady, 1999). In this chapter, we elucidate SBT by reviewing the evidence for the stereotype boost, clarifying the distinctions between stereotype boost and stereotype lift, outlining the conditions under which the activation of positive stereotypes can boost performance, and investigating the potential mechanisms that can cause positive stereotypes to boost performance.

■ EVIDENCE OF STEREOTYPE BOOST

A growing body of work shows that, under certain conditions, activating positive stereotypes can boost performance. For instance, in the United States, women are stereotyped to have inferior quantitative skills (Benbow, 1995; Hedges & Nowell, 1995) but superior verbal skills (Shih, Pittinsky & Trahan, 2006), whereas Asians are stereotyped to have superior quantitative skills (Steen, 1987) but inferior verbal skills (Shih et al., 2006). Shih and her colleagues (1999) found that Asian American women performed better on a math test when their Asian identity was primed, but worse when their female identity was primed, when compared to a control condition, for which no particular social identity was primed. In addition, Shih, Pittinsky, and Trahan (2006) found that Asian American women performed better on a verbal test when their female identity was primed but worse when their Asian identity was primed. Together, these results suggest that it was the positive stereotypes associated with each of these identities, rather than the salience of the identities themselves, that improved performance.

■ STEREOTYPE BOOST VERSUS STEREOTYPE LIFT

Researchers have recently identified a different process by which stereotypes can improve performance, called the *stereotype lift* (Walton & Cohen, 2003). Specifically, stereotype lift occurs when individuals exposed to negative stereotypes about another group show improved performance (Mendoza-Denton, Kah, & Chan, 2008; Smith & Johnson, 2006; Walton & Cohen, 2003). The authors propose that the opportunity to look down on another group for being inferior with respect to a task at hand increased the subjects' self-efficacy and decreased their self-doubt, both of which led to improved performance (Walton & Cohen, 2003). Stereotype lift is similar to stereotype boost in that an activated stereotype leads to a performance boost. However, stereotype lift results—at least initially—from the activation of a *negative* stereotype about an outgroup, whereas stereotype boost results from the activation of *positive* stereotypes about one's ingroup. We write "at least initially" because it is conceivable that as a negative outgroup stereotype is induced, a positive ingroup stereotype is concurrently induced. What is central to the theory, however, is the initial activation of the negative stereotype. Also, although stereotype lift is an interesting phenomenon to study and understand, it is important to note that stereotype lift creates improved performance by relying on negative stereotypes about members of another group.

■ BOUNDARY CONDITIONS OF STEREOTYPE PERFORMANCE BOOSTS

Stereotype performance boosts occur under specific conditions. When these conditions are not met, the activation of positive stereotypes will not boost performance and, in some cases, may even hurt performance (Cheryan & Bodenhausen, 2000, discussed below). Although much research remains to be done on the boundary conditions under which the stereotype boost operates, the available research already shows the moderators clustering into two general groups: the method by which stereotype is activated, and the characteristics of the individual.

Method of Stereotype Activation

Any given stereotype can be made salient to an individual in a number of different ways. Research on stereotype boost is finding that some of the different ways that the stereotype is activated (i.e., made salient) can play a crucial role in determining the performance outcome. Two factors to consider when examining the stereotype activation of positive stereotypes are the activation process, and how the task is framed.

Activation Process

Stereotype threat and stereotype boost research studies have handled the activation of stereotypes in multiple ways that lead to different effects. One dimension of the activation process that has led to different outcomes in stereotype boost studies is the degree of subtlety with which positive stereotypes are activated.

Some researchers have made stereotypes implicitly salient through subtle methods such as subliminal priming (e.g., Bargh, Chen, & Burrows, 1996; Devine, 1989) and identity salience manipulations (e.g., Shih et al., 1999). Other researchers have made stereotypes explicitly salient by telling the research participants directly about them (e.g., Spencer et al., 1999; Aronson et al., 1998). Studies have found that the implicit activation of stereotypes tends to elicit assimilation effects (i.e., performance that falls in line with the stereotype) whereas explicit activation can generate contrast effects (i.e., performance turns out to be the opposite of what is predicted by the stereotype) (Kray et al., 2001). For example, Shih et al. (2002) observed positive stereotypes leading to a performance boost when introduced subtly, but leading to choking under pressure when introduced blatantly. Similarly, Cheryan and Bodenhausen (2000) found that positive stereotypes introduced using a blatant method of identity activation resulted in significantly lower performance relative to the control condition.

These different methods of activation may play a crucial role in determining performance outcomes because introducing positive stereotypes in different ways may alter the meaning of the situation for the individual. For instance, subtle introduction of a stereotype allows individuals to navigate their social environment without being aware that they are being stereotyped. Thus, an individual who is not explicitly aware of being positively stereotyped may not feel the added pressure of having to live up to social expectations and represent his or her group. On the other hand, introducing a positive stereotype blatantly makes it very salient to the individual that he or she is being stereotyped. An individual consciously aware of being positively stereotyped may feel the pressure associated with having to live to up to social expectations and represent his or her group. Introducing the added pressure introduces additional worry and anxiety that may be threatening. Schmader and Beilock (2011, Chapter 3, this volume) discuss in greater depth the effects of anxiety and worry on performance.

The level of subtlety with which a positive stereotype is introduced can also be a factor in the stereotype boost for individuals who are not targets of stereotypes. Studies have found that people who are not targets of the stereotype require stronger positive stereotype primes to elicit a stereotype boost than do targets of the stereotypes require to elicit stereotype boosts. Shih et al. (2002) found that non-Asian participants did not show performance boosts on a math test when they were subliminally exposed to words suggesting stereotypes about Asians, but did show performance boosts on a math test when they were explicitly exposed to those words. This effect may reflect the possibility that people are often less sensitive to information that is not self-relevant, and thus, stronger primes are needed to elicit stereotype boosts for individuals who are not the targets of positive stereotypes (see Marx, 2011, Chapter 8, this volume, for an extended discussion of the distinction between self-relevant and non–self-relevant stereotype priming).

The degree to which the activation process elicits social comparison processes also seems to matter. In fact, although positive stereotypes can boost the performance of the members of the stereotyped group, they can *hurt* the performance of nontargets of the stereotype when they are introduced in ways that elicit social comparison processes. Aronson and his colleagues (1999) asked a cohort of white study participants, who were about to take a math test, to read an article about how Asian Americans were *outperforming* white students in math. This was a strong social comparison manipulation. In contrast, a low social comparison manipulation might involve asking the study participants to read an article about how Asian Americans are good at math, without direct reference to their outperforming white students. As a result, this manipulation introduced positive stereotypes about Asian Americans and math performance in a way that elicited social comparison processes among the white participants, who, as a result, exhibited decreased math performance. Similarly, Dijksterhuis and his colleagues (1998) examined the effects of introducing the positive stereotype about the intelligence of college professors on the test performance of college students. They found that positive stereotypes (i.e., intelligence) introduced as categories (i.e., college professors) improved performance, but stereotypes introduced as exemplars (i.e., Albert Einstein) hurt performance. They propose that exposure to exemplars elicited social comparison processes, leading to upward social comparisons (i.e., "I am not as intelligent as Albert Einstein"), which in turn led to lower performance.

In sum, although SBT predicts, in general, enhanced performance, the different ways that the stereotype is activated (i.e., made salient) can play a crucial role in determining the performance outcome. The manner in which a stereotype is introduced into the social context could drastically change the meaning of the situation for the individual.

Framing the Task

Another way to introduce stereotypes is not to focus on changing perceptions of the individual's stereotyped abilities, but rather to focus on changing perceptions of the task. Framing tasks in different ways can also trigger performance boosts. Shih and Ho (2010a) found that changing the framing of a task could affect the leadership behaviors of men and women. With the stereotypes that "men are good at building" and "women are good at arts and crafts" in mind, male–female pairs worked together to build a box. When the task was called a "building task," the male team member showed greater leadership behavior, being the first to make a suggestion and the first to contradict a partner. However, this pattern of behavior was reversed when the task was called an "arts and crafts" task. When the task was called an "arts and crafts" task, the female team member was more often the first to make a suggestion and the first to contradict a partner.

Similarly, Wraga et al. (2006a) asked female participants to complete an imagined self-rotation task testing visual-spatial ability. Participants who were told that the task was a perspective-taking task and that women were expected to excel at such tasks performed significantly better than those who were told that the task was a spatial task and that women were not expected to excel at such tasks. Thus, changing the description of a task rather than the individual can also lead to positive stereotype performance boosts.

Summary

In sum, although SBT predicts, in general, enhanced performance, the specific way that the stereotype is activated is critical. With regard to the stereotype activation process (i.e., the way the stereotype is made salient), implicit stereotype activation of a positive stereotype seems to lead to enhanced performance, whereas explicit activation of a positive stereotypes can lead to depressed performance. With regard to social comparisons, when a positive stereotype is made salient in the context of a downward social comparison (a comparison in which another, inferior individual or group is salient), positive stereotypes lead to performance boosts. But when a positive stereotype is made salient in the context of an upward social comparison (a comparison in which another superior individual or group is made salient), positive stereotypes can lead to depressed performance. Finally, with regard to the framing of the task, SBT research finds that even for the same task, subtle changes in task framing—changes that highlight the task as one in which there are positive stereotypes—can lead to enhanced performance. On the other hand, subtle task framing changes in the opposite direction—that is, framing a task as one for which there are no positive stereotypes—can eliminate this boost, even when the task remains the same.

Characteristics of the Individual

A second critical area in stereotype boost processes relates to individuals. Not all individuals are equally likely to exhibit stereotype boost effects. In the following section, we review some characteristics of the individual that may affect or moderate stereotype boost effects. Three factors to consider with regard to how characteristics of the individual might affect stereotype performance boosts are whether the individual is a target or not a target of the stereotype, the individual's implicit theory about ability, and the individual's level of identification with the task domain.

Stereotype Target vs. Nontarget

Positive stereotypes can enhance the performance of people who are the subject of the stereotypes (i.e., targets) and people who are not (i.e., nontargets). Targets of the stereotypes show improved performance when positive stereotypes are activated subtly enough so that the targets are not consciously aware of the stereotype (e.g., Shih et al., 2002; Shih et al., 1999). This finding has been documented across a variety of performance domains. For instance, women performed better on a verbal test when their female identity was made salient prior to taking the test (Shih et al., 2006). Similarly, men performed better on a negotiations task when positive masculine stereotypes such as assertiveness and rationality were implicitly activated (Kray et al., 2001). Women exposed to positive stereotypes of women as better than men at perspective-taking performed better on a spatial reasoning task (Wraga et al., 2006a,). Female students reminded that they were students at an elite private college performed better on a mental rotation task testing visual-spatial ability (McGlone & Aronson, 2006). Also, elderly study participants primed with positive stereotypes of the elderly exhibited increased performance on a memory test (Levy, 1996).

Positive stereotypes have also been documented to improve the performance of individuals who are not targets of the stereotype when introduced blatantly and in a way that does not elicit social comparison processes. Dijksterhuis and van Knippenberg (1998), for instance, asked college students in a series of studies to think about traits typically associated with professors or soccer hooligans. They found that the students primed with the professor stereotypes performed better on a general-knowledge test relative to a control group, whereas those primed to think about soccer hooligan stereotypes performed worse relative to control groups. More recently, Ortner and Sieverding (2008) found that female study participants primed with general male stereotypes showed increased performance on a spatial task (see Marx, 2011, Chapter 8, this volume for a discussion of how priming effects can lead to negative performance).

Implicit Theories of Ability

A second characteristic of the individual that may impact the likelihood that she or he would show stereotype performance boosts is the individual's implicit theories of ability. Studies have discovered a relationship between people's implicit theories of intelligence and their academic performance. People with *entity theories* believe that their intellectual abilities are innate and immutable, whereas people with *incremental theories* believe that their intellectual abilities are malleable and can be developed (Dweck, 1999). Research finds that entity theorists are more likely than incremental theorists to disidentify with their academic studies following negative feedback (Dweck & Sorich, 1999). Entity theorists are more vulnerable to negative stereotypes because they don't believe their intellectual abilities can change (Dweck, 1999).

Although entity theorists are more vulnerable to negative stereotypes, they may also be more susceptible to positive stereotypes. For instance, Mendoza-Denton et al. (2008) examined the math performance of Asians and men. They found that participants primed with positive stereotypes and entity theories showed a greater boost in performance than did participants primed with positive stereotypes and incremental theories. Thus, implicit theories may moderate the effects of activating positive stereotypes.

Domain Identification

Researchers have also proposed that domain identification may be a moderating factor in stereotype boosts. Work on stereotype threat has found that individuals are more susceptible to the effects of stereotype threat when they are more highly identified in the domain of the negative stereotype (e.g., Aronson et al., 1999). Similarly, Walton and Cohen (2003) found tentative evidence in their meta-analysis that individuals most identified with the performance domain were most likely to be affected by stereotype lift.

Therefore, drawing from the findings of the relationship between domain identification and susceptibility stereotype threat, one might reason that domain identification might also be a moderating influence for stereotype boosts. Specifically, one might predict that the more highly an individual identifies with the domain in which he or she is positively stereotyped, the greater the likelihood the individual should be to experience a stereotype boost. Although this hypothesis is theoretically plausible, to our knowledge, there is no extant empirical support for it. In fact, Smith and Johnson (2006) failed to find an expected math performance boost in males highly identified with the math domain when comparing men in an implicit positive stereotype condition and a nullified stereotype condition. These conflicting results underscore the need to understand the processes contributing to stereotype performance boosts separately from stereotype threat. Research findings that illuminate the factors affecting stereotype threat may not automatically generalize to stereotype performance boosts. Thus, although much is known about the effects of domain identification and stereotype threat, more research is needed to understand the relationship between domain identification and stereotype performance boosts.

Summary

Although much knowledge is accumulating about the moderators of stereotype boosts—when performance increments are likely to occur and whether the increments will be weak or strong—there is much more to learn. Some moderators will be shared with stereotype threat theory, while others will be unique to SBT.

Policy Box

Stereotype boost theory runs in parallel to stereotype threat theory. Although the primary concern of stereotype threat theory is the pernicious effects of negative stereotypes on performance, stereotype boost theory (SBT) examines how positive stereotypes can improve performance. In this chapter, we review the research on stereotype boosts conducted to date. In this review, we find that, under some conditions, the activation of positive stereotypes can not only buffer negatively stereotyped individuals from poor performance, but it can also improve performance. These findings may have implications for policy makers who are concerned about the harmful effects that stereotypes may have on the performance of negatively stereotyped individuals. When creating policies to address performance gaps across groups, policy makers might not only focus on addressing negative stereotypes and outcomes, but could also complement that approach by focusing on identities that emphasize positive stereotypes.

■ MECHANISMS OF STEREOTYPE BOOSTS

There is much puzzling over the mechanisms set in motion by stereotype boosts. Why does the salience of positive stereotypes about one's group lead to performance boosts? Like the moderators of stereotype boost, the mechanisms of stereotype boost are likely to include some that are shared with stereotype threat and others that are not. And, just as there are different types of stereotype threat (Shapiro & Neuberg, 2007; Shapiro, 2011, Chapter 5, this volume), there will likely prove to be different types of stereotype boosts. It is also possible that multiple mechanisms could be at work when performance is boosted. Although we organize the following discussion into discrete categories, the processes discussed in this section are likely not to be mutually exclusive and may in fact, work together.

Anxiety

One might speculate that the activation of positive stereotypes boosts performance through mechanisms that are the reverse of stereotype threat mechanisms, such as anxiety. Wout et al. (2008) find that, in test-taking situations, negatively stereotyped individuals may experience increased anxiety when they are placed in a situation in which they perceive that they might be negatively stereotyped. Kray, Thompson, and Galinsky (2001) describe stereotype threat as the "concern and anxiety over confirming, as a self-characteristic, a negative stereotype about one's group" (p. 943). This anxiety siphons cognitive and emotional resources away from the task. It is possible that positive stereotypes boost performance by reversing that process, decreasing anxiety and allowing greater cognitive and emotional resources to be devoted to the task. In this book, Schmader and Beilock (2011, Chapter 3) discuss the effects of worry in depleting executive resources and, ultimately, hurting performance.

Increased Expectations

There is evidence that introducing positive stereotypes may improve test performance through increased expectations. Shih et al. (2010) found that increased expectations mediated stereotype boosts for nontargets of the stereotype but did not do so for targets of the stereotype. Specifically, they found that among nontargets of the stereotype (a) participants who were primed with stereotypical words expected themselves to do better on a math test relative to participants who were primed with neutral words, and (b) these increased expectations mediated the participants' performance boost.

Ideomotor Effects

Much evidence shows that positive stereotypes may improve performance through the *perceptual-behavioral expressway* (Dijksterhuis & Bargh, 2001). This model posits that human perception and behavior are directly linked through shared mental representation systems and overlapping neurophysiological connections, such that the perception of a behavior automatically sets up the corresponding behavioral representation, which in turn triggers action tendencies to produce the same behavior. For instance, in support of this theory, Fadiga, Fogassi, Pavesi, and Rizzolatti (1995) found that watching an experimenter grasp an object leads to muscular responses similar to those observed when participants are asked to grasp the object themselves. Furthermore, participants exposed to primes about rudeness will behave more rudely, whereas participants exposed to primes about the elderly will walk more slowly (Bargh, Chen, & Burrows, 1996). Researchers have also found evidence that the perceptual-behavioral expressway can be applied to complex behaviors such as test performance (Dijksterhuis & van Knippenberg, 1998; Dijksterhuis, Bargh, & Miedema, 2000).

Not surprisingly, ideomotor effects have been argued to mediate the stereotype boost effects in both targets and nontargets (Shih, Ambady, Richeson, Fujita, & Gray, 2002). Specifically, the introduction of a stereotype may activate the mental representation of the associated traits and behaviors of the stereotype that in turn activate the motor programs that instigate the corresponding behaviors (Dijksterhuis & Bargh, 2001). For instance, activating the stereotype of a professor may lead to the activation of trait representations such as "intelligent" (Dijksterhuis & van Knippenberg, 1998) and behavioral representations such as "think" and "concentrate" (Dijksterhuis & Marchand, 2000), which may in turn lead to increased performance on general knowledge tests (Dijksterhuis & van Knippenberg, 1998). Marx (2011, Chapter 8, this volume) provide a detailed discussion on the effects of priming on performance.

Increased Efficiency in Neural Processing

There is evidence that activating positive stereotypes may improve performance by increasing the efficiency of neural processing. Wraga and her colleagues (2006b) conducted functional magnetic resonance imaging (fMRI) scans on women performing a spatial-rotation task. When the task was framed as a spatial task and the subjects had been primed with a stereotype that men are better than women at spatial tasks, the fMRI scans showed increased activation in brain areas associated with emotional load. This suggests that individuals in the negative stereotype condition were burdened with an increased focus on self-conscious and negative emotional processing that may have decreased their capacity to perform, as supported by the fact that the women in this condition performed worse than the control group. However, when the task was framed as perspective-taking and the subjects had been primed with a stereotype that women are better than men at perspective-taking, the fMRI scans showed increased activation in brain areas associated with visual processing and complex memory processing. These regions of activation, in conjunction with the absence of emotional load brain region activity, suggest that individuals in the positive stereotype condition experienced greater neural processing efficiency in the spatial-rotation, task which was supported by the fact that the women in this condition exhibited increased performance relative to the control group.

Social Comparison

Downward social comparisons can improve performance, as the work on stereotype lift has shown (Walton & Cohen, 2003). Similarly, Dijksterhuis et al. (1998) examined the effects of priming negative stereotypes about supermodels and intelligence on the test performance of college students. They found that college students asked to think about a particular supermodel (e.g., Claudia Schiffer) showed an improvement in their performance because they were able to make downward social comparisons (e.g., "I am smarter than Claudia Schiffer"), whereas students asked to think about supermodels as a category showed decreased performance because they were not able to make social comparisons. It is possible that positive stereotypes might lead to improved performance through downward social comparisons. For example, Asians who are stereotyped to be good at math might show improved performance because they come out ahead on the social comparisons process (e.g., "Asians are better at math than other groups"). These social comparisons in turn could potentially improve performance by relieving individuals' anxieties associated with having to prove themselves.

This would be a mechanism shared with stereotype threat, as research has shown that upward social comparisons can produce stereotype threat and hurt performance. For example, white men who were explicitly told that Asian American students were outperforming white students on math tests showed lower performance than did white men who were not told that (Aronson et al., 1999).

Similarly, it may also be a mechanism shared with stereotype lift. However, the basis on which these comparisons are being made in the case of stereotype boost and stereotype lift would differ. In the case of stereotype lift, the individuals are comparing themselves to a negative stereotype about another group, whereas in the case of stereotype boosts, the individuals are using positive stereotypes about their own group in their comparisons. In both cases, the direction—downward— of the social comparison would be the same (i.e., the individual is better than the other group).

It is important to note that, when considering positive stereotypes, the social comparison mechanism would only boost performance for individuals who are the targets of the stereotypes. Individuals who are not the targets of positive stereotypes would be making upward comparisons (i.e., their group is worse because they are not positively stereotyped). This situation would lead to stereotype threat (Aronson et al., 1999).

Persistence

Persistence may prove to be an important mediator of stereotype boost effects. Specifically, individuals exposed to positive stereotypes may work longer.

Their sheer refusal to give up may improve their overall performance. However, the evidence thus far is inconclusive. Some performance-boost research that has looked at persistence (e.g., Shih et al., 1999) did not find evidence that it mediates performance boost, but that research used only a very blunt measure of persistence—the number of questions answered. It is possible that while the overall number of questions answered did not differ, the amount of time spent on each item did. That is, although students may not have attempted more questions, they may have worked longer on each one.

Regulatory Focus

Regulatory focus has been proposed as a mediator in the relationship between stereotypes and performance (Seibt & Forster, 2004). Regulatory focus theory describes goal-directed behavior as regulated by distinct motivational systems: promotion focus and prevention focus (Higgins 1997, 1999). *Promotion focus* is a motivational state of eagerness concerned with accomplishment and attainment, whereas *prevention focus* is a motivational state of vigilance concerned with safety and responsibilities. With this in mind, Seibt and Forster (2004) demonstrated that the activation of a positive self-stereotype increased risky and explorative processing styles (i.e., promotion focus), which manifested through enhanced speed and creativity in tests and decreased analytic thinking. On the other hand, activating a negative self-stereotype increased vigilant, risk-averse processing (prevention focus), which led to increased performance accuracy and analytic thinking, but diminished creativity and speed. Hence, they suggest that positive and negative stereotypes activate differential regulatory foci, which affect performance as a function of the type of task.

Summary of Mechanisms Underlying Stereotype Boosts

As discussed in the preceding section, many potential mechanism underlie stereotype performance boosts. These potential mechanisms may work together in any given situation to boost performance when positive stereotypes are made salient. For instance, individuals who are positively stereotyped may show less anxiety in doing a task, which in turn may increase efficiency in neural processing and lead to higher performance.

■ CONCLUSION

Stereotype threat research awakened us to the very real possibility that stereotypes "in the air" may undermine people's performance (Steele, 1997). Stereotype boost research seeks to complement stereotype threat research by examining another way in which stereotypes may affect performance—this time, for the better. Stereotype boost theory suggests that in some situations, positive stereotypes may also improve performance.

Positive stereotypes might be used to counteract the potential harmful effects of negative stereotypes. Rydell and his colleagues showed that by making positive stereotypes associated with an alternate social identity more accessible, individuals from negatively stereotyped groups could be buffered from stereotype threat (Rydell, McConnell, & Beilock, 2009). The research discussed in this chapter finds that positive stereotypes could not only buffer people from harmful effects of negative stereotypes, but could also improve performance. These findings may have implications for policy makers who are concerned about the harmful effects that stereotypes may have on the performance of negatively stereotyped individuals. When creating policies to address performance gaps across groups, policy makers might not only focus on addressing negative stereotypes and outcomes, but could also complement that approach by focusing on identities that emphasize positive stereotypes.

We are not, of course, recommending that stereotype boosts be exploited in the real world. It would be premature to try to do so because the subject is still so little understood and because stereotypes themselves—even positive ones—may be troubling in that they result in focusing on expectations of others, based on their actual, group memberships, or merely the group membership that perceivers ascribe to them. But we do believe that positive stereotypes and their effects fully deserve research and theorizing in order to complete our clearly deficient picture of how stereotypes and performance come together and to know more fully how individual behavior is shaped by social influences. The sooner we can get on with knowing more about stereotype boost and how it might be helpful to people in the real world, the better.

References

Aronson, J., Quinn, D. M., & Spencer, S. J. (1998). Stereotype threat and the academic underperformance of minorities and women. In J. K. Swim & C. Stangor (Eds.), *Prejudice: The target's perspective* (pp. 83–103). San Diego, CA: Academic Press.

Aronson, J., Lustina, M. J., Good, C., Keough, K., Steele, C. M., & Brown, J. (1999). When white men can't do math: Necessary and sufficient factors in stereotype threat. *Journal of Experimental Social Psychology, 3,* 29–46.

Bargh, J. A., Chen, M., & Burrows, L. (1996). Automaticity of social behavior: Direct effects of trait construct and stereotype activation on action. *Journal of Personality and Social Psychology, 71,* 230–244.

Benbow, C. P. (1995). Sex differences in mathematical reasoning ability in intellectually talented preadolescents: Their nature, effects, and possible causes. *Behavioral and Brain Sciences, 11,* 169–232.

Chasteen, A. L., Kang, S. K., & Remedios, J. D. (2011). Aging and stereotype threat: Development, process and interventions. In M. Inzlicht & T. Schmader. (Eds.), *Stereotype Threat: Theory, process, and application.* Oxford University Press.

Cheryan, S., & Bodenhausen, G. V. (2000). When positive stereotypes threaten intellectual performance: The psychological hazards of model minority status. *Psychological Science, 11,* 399–402.

Croizet, J., & Claire, T. (1998). Extending the concept of stereotype threat to social class: The intellectual underperformance of students from low socioeconomic backgrounds. *Personality and Social Psychology Bulletin, 24*, 588–594.

Croizet, J. -C., & Millet, M. (2011). Social class and test performance: From stereotype threat to symbolic violence. In M. Inzlicht & T. Schmader (Eds.), *Stereotype threat: Theory, process, and application*. New York: Oxford University Press.

Devine, P. G. (1989). Stereotypes and prejudice: Their automatic and controlled components. *Journal of Personality and Social Psychology, 56*, 5–18.

Dijksterhuis, A., & Bargh, J. A. (2001). The perception-behavior expressway: Automatic effects of social perception on social behavior. *Advances in Experimental Social Psychology, 33*, 1–40

Dijksterhuis, A., Bargh, J. A., & Miedema, J. (2000). Of men and mackerels: Attention and automatic behavior. In H. Bless & J. P. Forgas (Eds.), *Subjective experience in social cognition and behavior*, 36–51. Philadelphia: Psychology Press.

Dijksterhuis, A., & Marchand, M. (2000). The route from stereotype activation to overt behavior. Unpublished Manuscript.

Dijksterhuis, A., Spears, R., Postmes, T., Stapel, D. A., Koomen, W., van Knippenberg, A., & Scheepers, D. (1998). Seeing one thing and doing another: Contrast effects in automatic behavior. *Journal of Personality and Social Psychology, 75*, 862–871.

Dijksterhuis, A., & van Knippenberg, A. (1998). The relation between perception and behavior, or how to win a game of Trivial Pursuit. *Journal of Personality and Social Psychology, 74*, 865–877.

Dweck, C. S. (1999). *Self-Theories: Their role in motivation, personality, and development*. Philadelphia: Taylor & Francis.

Dweck, C. S., & Sorich, L. (1999). Mastery-oriented thinking. In C. R. Snyder (Ed.), Coping: The psychology of what works (pp. 232–251). New York: Oxford University Press.

Fadiga, L., Fogassi, L., Pavesi, G., Rizzolatti, G. (1995). Motor facilitation during action observation: A magnetic stimulation study. *Journal of Neurophysiology, 73*(6), 2608–2611.

Hedges, L. V., & Nowell, A. (1995). Sex differences in mental test scores, variability, and numbers of high-scoring individuals. *Science, 269*, 41–45.

Higgins, E. T. (1997). Beyond pleasure and pain. *American Psychologist, 52*, 1280–1300.

Higgins, E. T. (1999). Promotion and prevention as a motivational duality: Implications for evaluative processes. In S. Chaiken & Y. Trope (Eds.), *Dual-process theories in social psychology* (pp. 503–525). New York: Guilford Press.

Kray, L. J., Thompson, L., & Galinsky, A. (2001). Battle of the sexes: Gender stereotype confirmation and reactance in negotiations. *Journal of Personality and Social Psychology, 80*(6), 942–958.

Levy, B. (1996). Improving memory in old age through implicit self-stereotyping. *Journal of Personality and Social Psychology, 71*, 1092–1107.

Logel, C., Peach, J., & Spencer, S. J. (2011). Threatening gender and race: Different manifestations of stereotype threat. In M. Inzlicht & T. Schmader (Eds.), *Stereotype Threat: Theory, process, and application*. New York: Oxford University Press.

Marx, D. M. (2011). Differentiating theories: A comparison of stereotype threat and stereotype priming effects. In M. Inzlicht & T. Schmader (Eds.), *Stereotype Threat: Theory, process, and application*. New York: Oxford University Press.

McGlone, M. S., & Aronson, J. (2006). Stereotype threat, identity salience, and spatial, reasoning. *Journal of Applied Developmental Psychology, 27*, 486–493.

Mendoza-Denton, R., Kahn, K., & Chan, W. (2008). Can fixed views of ability boost performance in the context of favorable stereotypes? *Journal of Experimental Social Psychology, 44*, 1187–1193.

Ortner, T. M., & Sieverding, M. (2008). Where are the gender differences? Male priming boosts spatial skills in women. *Sex Roles, 59*, 274–281.

Rydell, R. J., McConnell, A. R., & Beilock, S. L. (2009). Multiple social identities and stereotype threat: Imbalance, accessibility and working memory. *Journal of Personality and Social Psychology, 96*, 949–966.

Schmader, T. (2002). Gender identification moderates stereotype threat effects on women's math performance. *Journal of Experimental Social Psychology, 38*, 194–201.

Schmader, T., & Beilock, S. (2011). An Integration of Processes that Underlie Stereotype Threat. In M. Inzlicht & T. Schmader (Eds.), *Stereotype Threat: Theory, process, and application.* New York: Oxford University Press.

Seibt, B., & Forster, J. (2004). Stereotype threat and performance: How self-stereotypes influence processing by inducing regulatory foci. *Journal of Personality and Social Psychology, 87*, 38–56.

Shapiro, J. (2011). Types of threats: From stereotype threat to stereotype threats. In M. Inzlicht & T. Schmader (Eds.), *Stereotype Threat: Theory, process, and application.* New York: Oxford University Press.

Shapiro, J. R., & Neuberg, S. L. (2007). From stereotype threat to stereotype threats: Implications of a multi-threat framework for causes, moderators, mediators, consequences, and interventions. *Personality and Social Psychology Review, 11*, 107–130.

Shih, M., Pittinsky, T. L., & Ambady, N. (1999). Stereotype susceptibility: Identity salience and shifts in quantitative performance. *Psychological Science, 10*, 80–83

Shih, M., Ambady, N., Richeson, J. A., Fujita, K., & Gray, H. M. (2002). Stereotype performance boosts: The impact of self-relevance and the manner of stereotype activation. *Journal of Personality and Social Psychology, 83*, 638–647.

Shih, M., Pittinsky, T. L., & Trahan, A. (2006). Domain-specific effects of Stereotypes on Performance. *Self and Identity, 5*, 1–14.

Shih, M., & Ho G. (2010a). Effects of implicit stereotypes on task behavior. *Manuscript in preparation.*

Shih, M., & Ho, G. (2010b). Differential effects of positive stereotype activation in targets and non-targets of a stereotype. Manuscript in preparation.

Smith, J. L., & Johnson, C. S. (2006). A stereotype boost or choking under pressure? Positive gender stereotypes and men who are low in domain identification. *Basic and Applied Social Psychology, 28*, 51–63.

Spencer, S. J., Steele, C. M., & Quinn, D. M. (1999). Stereotype threat and women's math performance. *Journal of Experimental Social Psychology, 35*, 4–28.

Steele, C. M. (1997). A threat in the air: How stereotypes shape intellectual identity and performance. *American Psychologist, 52*, 613–629.

Steele, C. M., & Aronson, J. (1995). Stereotype threat and the intellectual test performance of African Americans. *Journal of Personality and Social Psychology, 69*, 797–811.

Steen, L. A. (1987). Mathematics education: A predictor of scientific competitiveness. *Science, 237*, 251–253.

Stone, J., Lynch, C. I., Sjomeling, M., & Darley, I. M. (1999). Stereotype threat effects on Black and White athletic performance. *Journal of Personality and Social Psychology, 77*, 1213–1227.

Walton, G. M., & Cohen, G. L. (2003). Stereotype lift. *Journal of Experimental Social Psychology, 39*, 456–467.

Wout, D., Danso, H., Jackson, J., & Spencer, S. (2008). The many faces of stereotype threat: Group- and self-threat. *Journal of Experimental Social Psychology, 44*, 792–799.

Wraga, M., Duncan, L., Jacobs, E. C., Helt, M., & Church, J. (2006a). Stereotype susceptibility narrows the gender gap in imagined self-rotation performance. *Psychonomic Bulletin & Review, 13*, 813–819.

Wraga, M., Helt, M., Jacobs, E., & Sullivan, K. (2006b). Neural basis of stereotype-induced shifts in women's mental rotation performance. *Social Cognitive and Affective Neuroscience, 2*, 12–19.

PART THREE

Manifestations of Stereotype Threat

10 Threatening Gender and Race

Different Manifestations of Stereotype Threat

■ CHRISTINE LOGEL, JENNIFER PEACH, AND STEVEN J. SPENCER

We propose that there might be important differences in people's experience of stereotype threat depending on the group to which they belong, and on the nature of the stereotypes that apply to their group. In this chapter, we describe similarities and differences in the experience of threat that arises from two of the most commonly investigated stereotypes: those about gender and those about race. Although little research has examined women and racial minorities simultaneously, we draw on evidence from separate studies to make divergent predictions about the experience of stereotype threat among women and among non-Asian racial minorities. Proposing a modern version of W.E.B. Du Bois' "double consciousness," we suggest that the experience of stereotype threat may differ depending on how motivated group members are to avoid the stereotype, and how vigilant they are for signs that they may be judged in light of a negative stereotype.

Keywords: Stereotype threat, race, gender, double consciousness, motivation, vigilance

I have frequently been questioned, especially by women, of how I could reconcile family life with a scientific career. Well, it has not been easy.
MARIE CURIE, Nobel Prize Winner, 1867–1934

People are taking it for granted that [the Negro] ought not to work with his head.
PAUL LAURENCE DUNBAR, Poet, 1872–1906

Much of stereotype threat research has focused on the common experiences of stereotype threat—its triggers, mechanisms, and consequences. This has helped to advance a general theory that can be applied to many different stereotypes about different groups. But a reading of the social psychological literature—and of history, as illustrated in the quotes above—suggests that there might be important differences in people's experience of stereotype threat depending on the group to which they belong and the nature of the stereotypes that apply to their group. Marie Curie had to contend with the stereotype that women's skills and nurturance suited them primarily for work within the home, and that women lacked men's natural quantitative ability. Paul Laurence Dunbar faced a more general stereotype that blacks lacked whites' intelligence. Understanding how such differences shape experiences hones our understanding of stereotype threat and allows interventions to more effectively target the unique situations of particular groups.

■ STEREOTYPE THREAT BASED ON GENDER AND RACE

We suggest that many of the differences between gender- and race-based stereotype threat can be captured within the experience of "double consciousness." At the turn of the century, black scholar and activist W. E. B. Du Bois used this term to describe blacks' experience of viewing themselves through their own eyes and also through the disdainful eyes of whites, and of identifying themselves as Americans but also knowing that Americans saw them as inferior (Du Bois, 1903). Although whites' attitudes toward blacks have shifted in the years since Du Bois first made these observations, prejudice remains (e.g., Dovidio, Kawakami, & Gaertner, 2002; Jackson, Brown, Brown, & Marks, 2001), sometimes in subtler forms (Correll, Park, Judd, & Wittenbrink, 2002; Eberhardt, 2005). Blacks in Western culture still have reason to be wary about how they are viewed by whites.

Steele, Spencer, and Aronson (2002) drew on W. E. B. Du Bois' ideas to compare the experience of stereotype threat to that of a modern double consciousness: being motivated to avoid the negative implications of a stereotype and at the same time needing to be vigilant for signs that the stereotype could be applied to the self. That is, the double consciousness of stereotype threat includes both avoidance of, and vigilance for, the application of negative stereotypes.

In this chapter, we organize our discussion of gender and racial differences in the experience of stereotype threat around the idea of double consciousness. First, we discuss gender and race differences in how, and when, members of stereotyped groups attempt to avoid the negative implications of stereotype threat. Avoidance, which can be behavioral or psychological, may vary depending on the negativity of the stereotype. The stereotype's negativity may further play a role in the degree to which it is endorsed by group members. Although endorsement is not required for stereotype threat, it may affect the way it is experienced.

Second, we discuss predictions of gender and race differences in vigilance for signs that one may be judged in light of a negative stereotype. The degree to which members of stereotyped groups are vigilant for such signs may depend on the degree to which they are consciously aware of the stereotype, and whether the stereotype is domain-specific or involves multiple domains.

Our discussion will tend to compare women and racial minorities as though they are separate social categories. Of course, a person may be both, and women of color may face even more complex challenges than do white women or minority men. Although little research has examined the intersection between gender and racial stereotypes (cf. Walton & Cohen, 2007; Gonzales, Blanton, & Williams, 2002), we provide some preliminary theoretical analysis about being doubly stereotyped.

■ RACE, GENDER, AND AVOIDANCE

The experience of stereotype threat may differ depending on how motivated group members are to avoid the stereotype, and how that avoidance is manifested. Although people are motivated to confront and disconfirm stereotypes (Nussbaum, Logel, & Steele, 2011), they will rarely attempt to do so unless the situation is stereotype-safe. If they are at risk of confirming the stereotype instead of disproving it, they will be motivated to try to escape this potential negative outcome (Steele, 1997; Steele et al., 2002).

We expect avoidance to play out differently for gender than for racial stereotypes. Because of differences in the scope of the stereotype, women and non-Asian minorities have different options for avoidance. Avoidance can be behavioral: People experiencing stereotype threat may attempt to physically avoid domains in which their group is stereotyped. Most laboratory demonstrations of behavioral avoidance have involved female participants. For example, women who are exposed to stereotypic commercials claim less career interest in math and science than in the humanities (Davies, Spencer, Quinn, & Gerhardstein, 2002). Similarly, women who view a video of a gender-imbalanced quantitative conference report less desire to participate in the conference than do men or than do women who view a balanced gender ratio (Murphy, Steele, & Gross, 2007). Real-world examples of avoidance include both women and minorities—avoidance is thought to be one of the reasons why women are under-represented in the maths and sciences, and it has been argued that the higher school drop-out rate for black students than for white students reflects, in part, black students' attempt to avoid being judged by the stereotype derogating their academic ability (Osborne & Walker, 2006; Steele, 1997).

Avoidance can also be psychological. Targets may psychologically avoid stereotype threat by distancing themselves from stereotypic traits: Black participants expecting to take a high-threat test avoid describing themselves as lazy and belligerent and report less enjoyment of rap music and basketball than do black participants who are not under stereotype threat (Steele & Aronson, 1995). Targets may simply also avoid the stereotypes by trying not to think about them: Women beginning a high-threat math test suppress thoughts of the stereotype (Logel, Iserman, et al., 2009).

Over time, psychological avoidance may also take the form of disidentification, a reconceptualising of the self such that the stereotyped domain is no longer self-relevant (Steele, 1997). Demonstrating disidentification, black students disengage their self-esteem from performance feedback more than do European Americans, especially when racial bias is primed (Major, Spencer, Schmader, Wolfe, & Crocker, 1998). In addition, in a nationally representative sample, the correlation between school grades and self-esteem decreases among black students, especially black boys (Osborne, 1997).

Homogeneity of Valence of the Stereotype

People may be less motivated to avoid being judged by the negative aspects of a stereotype if they can also benefit from its positive aspects. The traditional female stereotype has both negative and positive aspects. Traditional women (i.e., housewives) are perceived as incompetence but also warm (Fiske, Cuddy, Glick, & Xu, 2002). This affective positivity, paired with derogation of women's competence, is also characteristic of benevolent sexism (Glick & Fiske, 1996).

In contrast, stereotypes about non-Asian minorities are more homogeneously negative: Not only are blacks, Hispanics, Muslims, and Native Americans seen as less competent than whites, but they are also rated as less warm. Given this overwhelming negativity, non-Asian minorities may attempt to avoid negative racial stereotypes whenever possible, perhaps more so than women.

Given the positive aspects of stereotypes about women relative to stereotypes about non-Asian minorities, it is perhaps not surprising that some women seem to endorse these stereotypes. Women tend to apply stereotypic traits to their gender, such as emotional, talkative, and unintelligent (Jackman, 1994). In one sample, 41% of undergraduate women believed that math and spatial ability stereotypes about women are somewhat true (Blanton, Christie, & Dye, 2002). In another sample, 24% of female math majors believed that there is some truth to the stereotype that men are better at math than are women (Schmader, Johns, & Barquissau, 2004). Furthermore, when gender is made salient, women report seeing themselves consistently with stereotypes—with stronger verbal than math ability (Sinclair, Hardin, & Lowery, 2006). In some cases, women may respond to stereotype threat with increased endorsement—women under stereotype threat make more internal attributions for failure at a computer task than do men (Koch & Muller, 2008). In contrast, blacks do not apply stereotypic traits to their group (Jackman, 1994). Even when race is made salient, black participants do not self-stereotype (Sinclair et al., 2006), and among blacks, stereotype endorsement is associated with especially negative effects of stereotype threat.

Given the low rate of endorsement among non-Asian minorities, it is not surprising that research on stereotype endorsement has examined women but not minorities. The more girls endorse negative stereotypes about women's athletic ability, the worse they perform in gym class (Chalabaev, Sarrazin, & Fontayne, 2009). The more women endorse gender stereotypes about math performance, the less they identify with math and the worse they perform under stereotype threat (Schmader et al., 2004). From a multithreat framework (Shapiro, 2011, Chapter 10, this volume), women's willingness to endorse the stereotype may make them more vulnerable than non-Asian minorities to self-concept threat (i.e., "I might prove the stereotype right to myself") or group concept threat (i.e., "I might prove the stereotype right to my group"; Shapiro & Neuberg, 2007). Stereotype endorsement may be difficult to reduce because, for women, it may be rewarding: One study found that women's self-esteem is buffered from math failure when they are given the opportunity to endorse the math gender stereotype (Burkley & Blanton, 2008). Given group differences in stereotype endorsement, these processes are less likely to affect racial minorities.

The positive aspects of gender stereotypes may also help perpetuate and legitimize them. Benevolent sexist attitudes serve to justify men's dominance by positing that women are not fully competent adults and thus need to be taken care of (protective paternalism) and that women lack traits that are required for working outside the home (complementary gender differentiation). Women give mildly positive ratings to men high in benevolent sexism, in contrast to the negative ratings they give to men high in hostile sexism (Kilianski & Rudman, 1998).

The positive aspects of stereotypes about women also make their negative effects more pernicious. For example, in one of our own studies, we trained a male confederate to act like a sexist man in one condition, by showing dominance in a conversation, sitting close to his female colleague, and displaying an open posture, and to act like an egalitarian man in the other condition, by not displaying these subtle behaviors. Female engineering students who interacted with the confederate when he behaved like a sexist man liked him more and found him more attractive, but they also underperformed on an engineering test, relative to women exposed to egalitarian behavior (Logel, Walton, et al., 2009).

Implications of Avoidance

We have argued that stereotypes about non-Asian minorities are more uniformly negative than are stereotypes about gender and that blacks, at least, endorse them less than do women. If this is the case, blacks and other non-Asian minorities may be more avoidant of the stereotype. What implications does avoidance have for racial minorities?

Behavioral avoidance allows stereotyped individuals to escape (temporarily) the risk of being viewed stereotypically. In doing so, however, they may miss opportunities to disprove the stereotype (Nussbaum et al., 2011). Because stereotypes about the academic ability of blacks and Hispanics target a domain that is essential for a broad range of careers, behaviorally avoiding the stereotype by skipping a test, enrolling in easy rather than challenging classes, or, at the extreme, dropping out of school, may contribute to poverty and poor life outcomes. In contrast, women can avoid quantitative fields without entirely giving up their education, thus allowing them to have rewarding careers in fields in which their identity is not stereotyped. Evidence suggests that they do just that. Women threatened with the negative quantitative stereotype direct their career plans away from quantitative fields but toward fields in which they are not stereotyped (Davies et al., 2002, Logel & Blatz, 2008).

Psychological avoidance is effective as an identity-protection mechanism. Disengaging self-esteem from academic achievement does appear to protect black students' self-esteem (Crocker & Major, 1989; Osborne, 1997, Osborne & Walker, 2006). But psychological avoidance can also have negative consequences, which have been demonstrated for both women and racial minorities. Avoidance through suppressing thoughts of the stereotype contributes to performance decrements under stereotype threat (Logel, Iserman, et al., 2009; Schmader, Johns, & Forbes, 2008). Disidentification is associated with lower grade point average (Major & Schmader, 1998). And although disengaging self-esteem from intellectual performance when racial bias is suspected prevents targets from experiencing a decrease in self-esteem after failure, it also prevents them from experiencing an increase in self-esteem after success (Crocker, Voelkl, Testa, & Major, 1991) and from learning from critical feedback (Aronson & Inzlicht, 2004; Cohen, Steele, & Ross, 1999).

■ VIGILANCE

Women and non-Asian minorities may also differ in how vigilant they are for signs that they may be judged in light of a negative stereotype. Vigilance plays an important role in theorizing about social identity threat, as it is thought to be individuals' first response after realizing they are at risk of being judged by a negative stereotype (Steele et al., 2002). Some of the earliest evidence for vigilance shows that women respond to stereotype threat in ways that suggest arousal—they perform better on easy tests but worse on difficult ones, and they no longer underperform when given a misattribution (Ben-Zeev, Fein, & Inzlicht, 2005; O'Brien & Crandall, 2003). Recent evidence, however, has measured vigilance directly. Women who watched a video of a gender-imbalanced quantitative conference displayed both cognitive vigilance (remembering more details about the video and the lab room in which they watched it) and physiological vigilance (sympathetic activation of the cardiovascular system) than did women who view a gender-balanced video (Murphy et al., 2007). There can also be individual differences in vigilance among women—stigma-conscious women are especially vigilant for rejection cues (Inzlicht, Kaiser, & Major, 2008).

There is also evidence that racial minorities are vigilant to cues of threat. Steele and Aronson (1995) found that simply labelling a test as diagnostic of a stereotyped ability is enough to activate concepts related to the black stereotype. In addition, subtle cues conveying to black students that they do not belong in an academic arena are sufficient to activate race-related thoughts and to cause students to discourage a same-race peer from pursuing that field (Walton & Cohen, 2007). Neurocognitive evidence shows that minority students who value academics are especially vigilant to their errors on a high-threat test (Forbes, Schmader, & Allen, 2008).

Stereotypes That Cross Multiple Domains

When stereotypes cross multiple domains, targets are likely to spend more time in a vigilant state, because there are fewer safe situations in which they can let their guard down. Non-Asian minorities, who are negatively stereotyped across the academic spectrum and in their social behavior (e.g., aggressive) and general motivation (e.g., lazy) may thus need to be vigilant more often than women, who are primarily negatively stereotyped in competence, particularly quantitative ability.

The domain-specificity of the gender stereotype may also lead women to be vigilant to different kinds of threats than are racial minorities. Walton and Cohen (2007) found that black and Latino participants, but not women, were affected by a threat to social belonging in computer science. Women, unlike racial minorities, are positively stereotyped in the social domain (e.g., as warm), so they do not need to be vigilant to threats to their social skills.

Conscious Awareness of Stereotype Threat

One important difference between women' and racial minorities' experience may be the degree to which they are explicitly (consciously and deliberately) or implicitly (automatically and not necessarily consciously) vigilant for signs that they might be stereotyped. The degree to which vigilance is explicit or implicit is likely to depend on whether stereotype threat is experienced explicitly or implicitly. Although stereotype threat can certainly be experienced outside of consciousness (see Spencer, Logel, & Davies, in press, for a review of studies that fail to capture self-reports consistent with awareness and those that succeed), evidence suggests that non-Asian minorities tend to be more aware of the experience than are women.

After reading a threatening corporate brochure, black professionals readily report a concern about being devalued due to their racial identity in open-ended responses (Purdie-Vaughns, Steele, Davies, & Ditlmann, 2008). In another study, black students who had just taken an intelligence test administered by a white experimenter reported fears of being judged in light of stereotypes on a paper-and-pencil scale (Marx & Goff, 2005). Similar results were obtained in the one study we know of that directly compared gender and ethnicity: Latino men who took a high-threat test reported experiencing stereotype threat on paper-and-pencil measures. Latino women also reported experiencing stereotype threat but white women did not (even though their performance, too, suffered under stereotype threat). The results suggest that perhaps women are not consciously aware of experiencing stereotype threat unless they are sensitized to it by race-based threat (Gonzales et al., 2002).

Additional research supports the possibility that women may not be consciously aware of their experience of stereotype threat. Whereas black participants' self-reported probability of being stereotyped mediates performance decrements, women's does not (Wout, Shih, Jackson, & Sellers, 2009). By contrast, more implicit measures, such as activation or suppression of stereotypes on lexical-decision tasks, mediate stereotype threat effects among women (Davies et al., 2002; Logel, Iserman, et al., 2009). Further evidence that women may not be fully aware of their stereotype threat experience comes from findings on stigma consciousness (or, how much one worries about being judged by group stereotypes). Women score lower on stigma consciousness than do even men—the only tested group to be lower on stigma consciousness than the nonstigmatized group (Pinel, 1999).

These differing levels of awareness may help explain some interesting meta-analysis findings. Nguyen and Ryan (2008) found that minority test takers under-performed to a greater degree following moderate or blatant stereotype cues (such as instructions that a test produces race differences) than following subtle stereotype threat cues (such as instructions that a test is diagnostic of a stereotyped ability). In contrast, women performed *worse* when cues were subtle than when they were moderate or blatant. It may be that cues trigger the most stereotype threat when they occur at the same level as targets' vigilance for the threat. Racial minorities, who are likely to be more consciously vigilant, would thus be more vulnerable to explicit cues, whereas women, who are less consciously vigilant, would be more vulnerable to subtle cues.

Interestingly, the opposite pattern may be required for creating stereotype safety. Minorities performed better following subtle stereotype threat removal strategies (such as instructions that the test is nondiagnostic) than following moderate or blatant strategies (such as instructions that the test does not produce group differences), whereas women's performance was more improved by explicit stereotype threat removal strategies than by subtle ones. Stereotype threat may be so explicit for racial minorities that subtle threat removal strategies are more effective at getting below their defensive radar. For women, stereotype threat is less well-articulated, so bringing the threat into awareness and delegitimizing it removes the need for them to suppress their concerns, thus restoring working memory and allowing them to perform better.

Implications of Vigilance

Vigilance is mentally taxing. Mentally taxing activities use up self-control, which is a limited resource (Baumeister, Heatherton, & Tice, 1994). Thus, the effort of monitoring situations for signs that one could be judged by a negative stereotype uses up self-control that could be applied to other important areas of one's life. Both black students and women show impaired performance on self-control tasks under stereotype threat (Inzlicht, McKay, & Aronson, 2006; also see Inzlicht, Tullett, & Gutsell, 2011, Chapter 7, this volume). And the more sensitive black students are to stigma—and thus the more vigilant they likely are—the less self-control they report having in their day-to-day lives (Inzlicht et al., 2006).

These findings suggest that racial minorities, who must be vigilant across multiple domains, will be more depleted than women, who can let down their guard in nonstereotyped domains. If racial minorities are indeed more consciously aware of the risk of being viewed through a stereotyped lens, and thus enact a more conscious form of vigilance than women do, this may also lead to more depletion. We suspect that conscious vigilance may take up even more working memory than less conscious vigilance—automatic, implicit tasks are more efficient than conscious, deliberately controlled tasks. If so, racial minorities' vigilance may impact their intellectual performance more than it does women's.

Not only will this vigilance take a toll on minorities' self-control, it may even harm their health. Black students writing a high-threat test exhibit larger increases in mean arterial blood pressure than do white students (Blascovich, Spencer, Quinn, & Steele, 2001), suggesting that vigilance could be associated with vulnerability to hypertension (see also Inzlicht et al., 2011, Chapter 7, this volume).

The consequences of conscious awareness of stereotype threat, and thus the implications for intervention, seem to depend on the situation. Among racial minorities, conscious awareness of stereotype threat seems to be associated with negative outcomes. Black students who are stereotype vulnerable—that is, who expect to be perceived in light of stereotypes—have more unstable academic self-efficacy, less academic self-knowledge, and underperform more under stereotype threat (Aronson & Inzlicht, 2004). For women, however, bringing the stereotype into awareness may help them overcome its deleterious effects. Women who are taught about stereotype threat before writing a math test attribute their anxiety to stereotype threat and perform equally to men (Johns, Schmader, & Martens, 2005). It is unclear whether such an intervention would restore racial minorities' performance. Given that many minorities are already consciously aware of stereotype threat, a further manipulation may be required to change their perception of it (Cohen, Garcia, Apfel, & Master, 2006; Cohen, Garcia, Purdie-Vaughns, Apfel, & Brzustoski, 2009; Walton & Cohen, 2007).

Policy Box

The findings and theory reviewed in this chapter may suggest that a "one-size-fits-all" approach to supporting under-represented groups may not target assistance where it is needed most. Women may need support staying in quantitative fields in which they are under-represented, when alternative career paths, in which they do not have to worry about being judged by negative stereotypes, are so salient. They may also need encouragement from mentors as they attempt to reconcile the negative parts of the stereotype, which they may want to avoid or disprove, with the positive parts, which they may want to endorse. Stereotypes about non-Asian minorities are so negative and pervasive that these individuals may need support coping with the resulting stress and vigilance in a way that does not drive them to disidentification or erode their quality of life. More research is needed to help inform policy makers about how best to foster the success of specific groups of negatively stereotyped and under-represented individuals.

■ CONCLUSION

This chapter sought to go beyond the common experiences of stereotype threat to discuss how women and non-Asian minorities might have unique experiences because of the different stereotypes they face. We presented these differences as part of the "double consciousness" of stereotype threat: the experience of being motivated to avoid the negative implications of the stereotype, together with the necessity of remaining vigilant to the possibility of being judged by it.

Because racial stereotypes tend to be more uniformly negative than gender stereotypes, we predict that minorities may be more likely than women to avoid them. The need for avoidance is likely to undermine minorities' career aspirations, academic engagement, and achievement. However, the positive aspects of the traditional female stereotype is not a panacea for women. Their higher levels of endorsement of the stereotype may be especially detrimental to their performance under stereotype threat, and the positivity of the stereotype may help legitimize and perpetuate it.

Because racial stereotypes cross multiple domains, we expect minorities to be vigilant more often than women. This perpetual need for vigilance is likely to deplete minorities' cognitive resources. The domain-specificity of gender stereotypes allows women to avoid the stereotyped quantitative domain and still achieve in nonstereotyped domains, an option that is relatively less available to racial minorities. Minorities' more conscious awareness of stereotype threat may make their vigilance more deliberate, using up more working memory than women's less conscious, more automatic vigilance. Minorities may also be more vulnerable to blatant threat cues, whereas women are more vulnerable to subtle ones.

What are the experiences of ethnic minority women? The one study that has investigated stereotype threat among women and minorities together finds a double minority effect. Latina women show greater underperformance than Latino men, who show the standard high-threat underperformance effect, and than white women, who in this study did not underperform (Gonzales et al., 2002). The authors conclude that being a racial minority may sensitize people to gender stigmatization. More research is needed to understand double minority effects, especially given that white women in this sample did not show stereotype threat effects on performance.

From the hypotheses presented in this chapter, it might appear that women who are immersed in a high-threat environment would have a similar experience of stereotype threat to that of racial minorities. Female math majors, for example, might experience stereotype threat more often, and thus be more conscious of it, and may perceive it as more negative, because it is in an important domain. Hence, we might expect female math majors to be as vigilant and avoidant of the stereotype as racial minorities.

Implications for Intervention

Interventions are discussed elsewhere in this volume (Cohen, Purdie-Vaughns, & Garcia, 2011, Chapter 18, this volume), so we constrain our discussion to the unique issues of gender- and race-based stereotype threats. After a period of sustained vigilance, the reprieve provided by avoidance must seem like a welcome respite. Avoidance is an understandable and practical (in the short term) way of handling a difficult situation. But avoidance has long-term consequences that are likely to be especially pernicious for non-Asian minorities, who do not have nonstereotyped intellectual domains to turn to. Before developing interventions to prevent avoidance, the testing, learning, and working environment must be made stereotype-safe (Walton, Spencer, & Erman, 2011). Otherwise, even if women and minorities enter those fields in larger numbers, stereotype threat will make it difficult for them to perform according to their true ability.

For women in quantitative fields, removing references to the traditionally male "geek" culture (Cheryan, Plaut, Davies, & Steele, 2009) may reduce the level of threat. Interactions with nonsexist men may also help (Logel, Walton, et al., 2009). For racial minorities, models that encourage collaboration rather than competition, such as the jigsaw classroom, appear to be successful (Aronson & Patnoe, 1997). A professional culture that encourages diversity rather than a color-blind ideology can also be effective (Purdie-Vaughns et al., 2008). We also suspect that it may be important to decrease the salience of an institution's exclusive history and increase the salience of a diverse future. This can be as simple as avoiding holding tests in rooms surrounded by pictures of white male former department heads, and instead ensuring that classrooms feature pictures of female and minority role models.

Clearly, more research is needed to understand the best ways to eliminate threat in the environment. In the meantime, social psychological interventions (e.g. Cohen et al., 2011, Chapter 18, this volume) provide tools that can be used when a threat is present, or can change women and minorities' construal of the threat itself (Cohen et al., 2006, 2009; Walton & Cohen, 2007).

Once the risk of being judged in light of the stereotype is reduced, efforts must be made to let members of stereotyped groups know that the environment is safe. If these efforts are made, educators and employers may receive a higher proportion of female and minority applicants than might be expected from base rates: People are motivated to approach safe situations in order to disprove stereotypes (Nussbaum et al., 2011), and they do not avoid stereotype-relevant situations if they are made aware that they are stereotype-safe (Cheryan et al., 2009; Davies et al., 2002; Murphy et al., 2007; Purdie-Vaughns et al., 2008). As more women and racial minorities enter fields in which they have traditionally been under-represented, their very presence will further reduce avoidance and underperformance for others (Murphy et al., 2007).

References

Aronson, E. & Patnoe, S. (1997). *The jigsaw classroom: Building cooperation in the classroom* (2nd ed.) New York: Addison Wesley Longman.

Aronson, J., & Inzlicht, M. (2004). The ups and downs of attributional ambiguity: Stereotype vulnerability and the academic self-knowledge of African American college students. *Psychological Science, 15*, 829–836.

Baumeister, R. F., Heatherton, T. F., & Tice, D. (1994). *Losing control: How and why people fail at self-regulation.* San Diego: Academic Press.

Ben-Zeev, T., Fein, S., & Inzlicht, M. (2005). Arousal and stereotype threat. *Journal of Experimental Social Psychology, 41*, 174–181.

Blanton, H., Christie, C., & Dye, M. (2002). Social identity versus reference frame comparisons: The moderating role of stereotype endorsement. *Journal of Experimental Social Psychology, 38*, 253–267.

Blascovich J., Spencer, S. J., Quinn, D, & Steele, C. (2001). African Americans and high blood pressure: The role of stereotype threat. *Psychological Science, 12*, 225–229.

Burkley, M., & Blanton, H. (2008). Endorsing a negative in-group stereotype as a self-protective strategy: Sacrificing the group to save the self. *Journal of Experimental Social Psychology, 44*, 37–49.

Chalabaev, A., Sarrazin, P., & Fontayne, P. (2009). Stereotype endorsement and perceived ability as mediators of the girls' gender orientation-soccer performance relationship. *Psychology of Sport and Exercise, 10,* 297–299.

Cheryan, S., Plaut, V. C., Davies, P. G., & Steele, C. M. (2009). Ambient belonging: How stereotypical cues impact gender participation in computer science. *Journal of Personality and Social Psychology, 97,* 1045–1060.

Cohen, G. L., Garcia, J., Apfel, N., & Master, A. (2006). Reducing the racial achievement gap: A social-psychological intervention. *Science, 313,* 1307–1310.

Cohen, G. L., Garcia, J., Purdie-Vaughns, V., Apfel, N., & Brzustoski, P. (2009). Recursive processes in self-affirmation: Intervening to close the minority achievement gap. *Science, 324,* 400–403.

Cohen, G. L., Purdie-Vaughns, V., & Garcia, J. (2011). An identity threat perspective on intervention. In M. Inzlicht & T. Schmader (Eds.), *Stereotype threat: Theory, process, and application.* New York: Oxford University Press.

Cohen, G. L., Steele, C. M., & Ross, L. D. (1999). The mentor's dilemma: Providing critical feedback across the racial divide. *Personality and Social Psychology Bulletin, 25,* 1302–1318.

Correll, J., Park, B., Judd, C. M., & Wittenbrink, B. (2002). The police officer's dilemma: Using ethnicity to disambiguate potentially threatening individuals. *Journal of Personality and Social Psychology, 83,* 1314–1329.

Crocker, J., & Major, B. (1989). Social stigma and self-esteem: The self-protective properties of stigma. *Psychological Review, 96,* 608–630.

Crocker, J., Voelkl, K., Testa, M., & Major, B. (1991). Social stigma: The affective consequences of attributional ambiguity. *Journal of Personality and Social Psychology, 60,* 218–228.

Davies, P. G., Spencer, S. J., Quinn, D. M., & Gerhardstein, R. (2002). Consuming images: How television commercials that elicit stereotype threat can restrain women academically and professionally. *Personality and Social Psychology Bulletin, 28,* 1615–1628.

Dovidio, J. F., Kawakami, K., & Gaertner, S. L. (2002). Implicit and explicit prejudice and interracial interaction. *Journal of Personality and Social Psychology, 82,* 62–68.

Du Bois, W. E. B. (1903). *The souls of black folk.* New York: Bantam, 1989.

Eberhardt, J. L. (2005). Imaging race. *American Psychologist, 60,* 181–190.

Fiske, S. T., Cuddy, A. J. C., Glick, P., & Xu, J. (2002). A model of (often mixed) stereotype content: Competence and warmth respectively follow from perceived status and competition. *Journal of Personality and Social Psychology, 82,* 878–902.

Forbes, C. E., Schmader, T., & Allen, J. J. B. (2008). The role of devaluing and discounting in performance monitoring: A neurophysiological study of minorities under threat. *Social Cognitive and Affective Neuroscience, 3,* 253–261.

Glick, P., & Fiske, S. T. (1996). The ambivalent sexism inventory: Differentiating hostile and benevolent sexism. *Journal of Personality and Social Psychology, 70,* 491–512.

Gonzales, P. M., Blanton, H., & Williams, K. J. (2002). The effects of stereotype threat and double-minority status on the test performance of Latino women. *Personality and Social Psychology Bulletin, 28,* 659–670.

Inzlicht, M., Kaiser, C. R., & Major, B. (2008). The face of chauvinism: How prejudice expectations shape perceptions of racial affect. *Journal of Experimental Social Psychology, 44,* 758–766.

Inzlicht, M., McKay, L., & Aronson, J. (2006). Stigma as ego depletion: How being the target of prejudice affects self-control. *Psychological Science, 17,* 262–269.

Inzlicht, M., Tullett, A. M., & Gutsell, J. N. (2011). Stereotype threat spillover: The short-term and long-term effects of coping with threats to social identity. In M. Inzlicht, & T. Schmader (Eds.), *Stereotype threat: Theory, process, and application.* New York: Oxford University Press.

Jackman, M. R. (1994). *The velvet glove: Paternalism and conflict in gender, class, and race relations.* Berkeley: University of California Press.

Jackson, J. S., Brown, K. T., Brown, T. N., & Marks, B. (2001). Contemporary immigration policy orientations among dominant-group members in Western Europe. *Journal of Social Issues, 57,* 431–456.

Johns, M., Schmader, T., & Martens, A. (2005). Knowing is half the battle: Teaching stereotype threat as a means of improving women's math performance. *Psychological Science, 16,* 175–179.

Kilianski, S. E., & Rudman, L. A. (1998). Wanting it both ways: Do women approve of benevolent sexism? *Sex Roles, 39,* 333–352.

Koch, S., & Muller, S. (2008). Women and computers. Effects of stereotype threat on attribution of failure. *Computers & Education, 51,* 1795–1803.

Logel, C., & Blatz, C. W. (2008, June). *The negative impact of public figures' sexist comments: The Larry Summers effect.* Poster presented at the 7th Biennial SPSSI Convention, Chicago, Illinois.

Logel, C., Iserman, E. C., Davies, P. G., Quinn, D. M., & Spencer, S. J. (2009). The perils of double consciousness: The role of thought suppression in stereotype threat. *Journal of Experimental Social Psychology, 45,* 299–312.

Logel, C., Walton, G. M., Spencer, S. J., Iserman, E. C., von Hippel, W., & Bell, A. E. (2009). Interacting with sexist men triggers social identity threat among female engineers. *Journal of Personality and Social Psychology, 96,* 1089–1103.

Major, B., & Schmader, T. (1998). Coping with stigma through psychological disengagement. In J. Swim & C. Stangor (Eds.), *Prejudice: The target's perspective* (pp. 219–241). San Diego: Academic Press.

Major, B., Spencer, S., Schmader, T., Wolfe, C., & Crocker, J. (1998). Coping with negative stereotypes about intellectual performance: The role of psychological disengagement. *Personality and Social Psychology Bulletin, 24,* 34–50.

Marx, D. M., & Goff, P. A. (2005). Clearing the air: The effect of experimenter race on targets' test performance and subjective experience. *British Journal of Social Psychology, 44,* 645–657.

Murphy, M. C., Steele, C. M., & Gross, J. J. (2007). Signaling threat: How situational cues affect women in math, science, and engineering settings. *Psychological Science, 18,* 879–885.

Nguyen, H. D., & Ryan, A. M. (2008). Does stereotype threat affect test performance of minorities and women? A meta-analysis of experimental evidence. *Journal of Applied Psychology, 93,* 1314–1334.

Nussbaum, D., Logel, C., & Steele, C. M. (2011). *Confronting stereotype threat: The motivation to disprove and avoid confirming stereotypes.* Manuscript Under Review, University of Chicago.

O'Brien, L. T., & Crandall, C. S. (2003). Stereotype threat and arousal: Effects on women's math performance. *Personality and Social Psychology Bulletin, 29,* 782–789.

Osborne, J. W. (1997). Race and academic disidentification. *Journal of Educational Psychology, 89,* 728–735.

Osborne, J. W., & Walker, C. (2006). Stereotype threat, identification with academics, and withdrawal from school: Why the most successful students of colour might be most likely to withdraw. *Educational Psychology, 26,* 563–577.

Pinel, E. C. (1999). Stigma consciousness: The psychological legacy of social stereotypes. *Journal of Personality and Social Psychology, 76,* 114–128.

Purdie-Vaughns, V., Steele, C. M., Davies, P. G., & Ditlmann, R. (2008). Social identity contingencies: How diversity cues signal threat or safety for African Americans in mainstream institutions. *Journal of Personality and Social Psychology, 94,* 615–630.

Schmader, T., Johns, M., & Barquissau, M. (2004). The costs of accepting gender differences: The role of stereotype endorsement in women's experience in the math domain. *Sex Roles, 50,* 835–850.

Schmader, T., Johns, M., & Forbes, C. (2008). An integrated process model of stereotype threat effects on performance. *Psychological Review, 115,* 336–356.

Shapiro, J. R. (2011). Types of threats: From stereotype threat to stereotype threats. In M. Inzlicht, & T. Schmader (Eds.), *Stereotype threat: Theory, process, and application.* New York: Oxford University Press.

Shapiro, J. R., & Neuberg, S. L. (2007). From stereotype threat to stereotype threats: Implications of a multi-threat framework for causes, moderators, mediators, consequences, and interventions. *Personality and Social Psychology Review, 11,* 107–130.

Sinclair, S., Hardin, C. D., & Lowery, B. S. (2006). Self-stereotyping in the context of multiple social identities. *Journal of Personality and Social Psychology, 90,* 529–542.

Spencer, S. J., Logel, C., & Davies, P. G. (in press). Stereotype threat. *Annual Review of Psychology.*

Steele, C. M. (1997). A threat in the air: How stereotypes shape intellectual identity and performance. *American Psychologist, 52,* 613–629.

Steele, C. M., & Aronson, J. (1995). Stereotype threat and the intellectual test performance of African Americans. *Journal of Personality and Social Psychology, 69,* 797–811.

Steele, C. M., Spencer, S. J., & Aronson, J. (2002). Contending with group image: The psychology of stereotype and social identity threat. In M. P. Zanna (Ed.), *Advances in Experimental Social Psychology* Vol. 34 (pp. 379–440). San Diego: Academic Press.

Walton, G. M., & Cohen, G. L. (2007). A question of belonging: Race, social fit, and achievement. *Journal of Personality and Social Psychology, 92,* 82–96.

Walton, G., Spencer, S. J., & Erman, S. (2011). *Affirmative meritocracy.* Manuscript under review.

Wout, D. A., Shih, M. J., Jackson, J. S., & Sellers, R. M. (2009). Targets as perceivers: How people determine when they will be negatively stereotyped. *Journal of Personality and Social Psychology, 96,* 349–362.

11 Stereotype Threat in Organizations

An Examination of Its Scope, Triggers, and Possible Interventions

■ LAURA J. KRAY AND AIWA SHIRAKO

This chapter explores stereotype threat in organizational contexts. Building on the understanding that stereotype threat involves concerns about confirming a negative stereotype about one's group, we begin by elucidating the scope of potential stereotype threat effects in organizations. We first examine the ubiquity of evaluations in organizations, which are at the heart of stereotype threat. Next, we specify the potential psychological consequences of stereotype threat on targeted individuals within organizations, including weakening domain identification and engagement, reducing aspirations, increasing self-handicapping, and reducing openness to feedback. In the next section, we focus on specific performance consequences of stereotype threat in four domains: leadership, negotiations, entrepreneurship, and competitiveness. We follow by identifying the likely triggers of stereotype threat within organizations, including task difficulty, organizational structure, minority representation, and organizational culture. Finally, we identify three categories of strategies that organizations can implement to reduce stereotype threat: stereotype management, which includes acknowledging stereotypes, emphasizing positive stereotypes, and de-emphasizing negative stereotypes; hiring and training, which includes increasing minority representation and job training; and organizational culture, including both fostering identity safety and valuing effort.

Keywords: Stereotype threat, business, management, leadership, negotiations, workplace

The workplace is a breeding ground for stereotype threat. Whether receiving annual performance evaluations by bosses or periodic informal feedback from mentors, organizations are evaluation-intensive environments. As such, individuals from negatively stereotyped groups are often exposed to situations in which negative expectations may undermine performance. Although the bulk of stereotype threat research over the past 15 years has centered on academic contexts, in this chapter, we explore its implications in organizational settings.

Given that the workplace is inextricably linked with individuals' financial liveli-hood and lifetime achievement, understanding how stereotype threat affects work experiences is essential. Elucidating how stereotype threat is likely to creep into commonplace experiences on the job may provide organizations with fruitful direc-tions for expanding diversity management training programs, which typically focus on bias from the perspective of the observer. Entire units of organizations are designed to monitor the fairness of evaluation processes, yet little systematic train-ing is provided to employees to buffer them against the damaging effects of stereo-type-based expectations. Because stereotype threat arises within the target of negatively stereotyped groups, understanding how the workplace is experienced by traditionally disadvantaged groups will enable organizations to manage diversity more completely, incorporating threats arising from multiple sources.

Another reason to examine closely stereotype threat in organizations is that huge racial and gender disparities in pay and advancement persist in virtually every indus-try in the United States. The statistics are staggering. Although women make up 46% of the U.S. labor force, they comprise just 3% of *Fortune 500* CEOs and only 15.2% of *Fortune 500* board seats (Catalyst, 2009). Likewise, African Americans, Asian Americans, and Latinos make up fewer than 3% of *Fortune 500* CEOs (Cole, 2008). Understanding how stereotype threat may contribute to these disparities is essential.

We organize this chapter into three sections. First, we define the potential scope of stereotype threat in organizations by exploring the ubiquity of evaluations. Second, we examine psychological and performance consequences of stereotype threat. Finally, we identify contextual factors likely to exacerbate versus mitigate stereotype threat within organizations.

■ THE SCOPE OF STEREOTYPE THREAT IN ORGANIZATIONS

The Ubiquity of Evaluations

Given that stereotype threat arises from concerns about confirming negative stereo-types, it is relevant in contexts in which individuals are evaluated, either by others or the self (Inzlicht & Ben-Zeev, 2003). Stereotypes derive their potency by anticipat-ing the performance of individuals based on their membership in social groups. Steele and Aronson's (1995) original demonstration of stereotype threat relied on a diagnosticity manipulation purporting to measure and evaluate core abilities. Diagnostic conditions coupled with low expectations can trigger a variety of intra-psychic processes characterizing stereotype threat (Schmader, Johns, & Forbes, 2008), including physiological stress, excessive performance monitoring, and suppression of negative thoughts and emotions. Because organizations frequently measure and evaluate performance, they are fertile grounds for stereotype threat.

In contrast to academic settings that emphasize learning as a valued outcome, many profit-oriented organizations focus on bottom line performance as the sole metric of success. Accordingly, organizations are particularly focused on evaluating employees. Whether submitting job applications or being considered for promotion, inferences and evaluations are made regarding individuals' abilities. Stereotype threat can steer targeted individuals away from seeking challenging jobs; for those who do apply and gain employment, stereotype threat can produce under-performance. Finally, stereotype threat can affect whether individuals persevere down a career path versus opt out of the workforce entirely. With the potential for stereotype threat to impact each successive career stage, its harm is potentially far-reaching.

Psychological Effects of Stereotype Threat in Organizations

Stereotype threat affects how much targeted group members care about excelling in stereotype-relevant domains. Somewhat ironically, high identification with a stereo-typed domain can trigger stereotype threat (Steele, 1997; Steele, Spencer, & Aronson, 2002), and yet stereotype threat can reduce domain identification via a process of disengagement (Crocker, Major, & Steele, 1998; Major & Schmader, 1998). Disengagement, a psychological defense designed to insulate the self from evaluations, allows negatively stereotyped group members to avoid the possibility of confirming the stereotype (Steele et al., 2002). Low domain identification may ultimately depress career and performance goals.

An environment riddled with negative stereotypes may threaten targeted group members' aspirations as future leaders. For example, exposure to television com-mercials depicting women in traditional roles led women to emphasize homemaking roles over achievement in describing their future lives (Geis, Brown, Jennings, & Porter, 1984). Similarly, Davies, Spencer, and Steele (2005) observed that women who viewed gender stereotypic television commercials were less likely to choose a leadership role in a subsequent task. Related to women's relatively weak leadership aspirations, women report weaker entrepreneurial intentions than do men, particu-larly when masculine traits are subtly associated with leadership activities (Gupta, Turban, & Bhawe, 2008). Whether it be starting up new businesses or leading exist-ing ones, women's aspirations and intentions are weaker than those of their male counterparts, partly as a result of stereotype threat.

The pernicious effect of stereotype threat on aspirations extends more generally to women's willingness to embrace challenges with uncertain success, an essential element of leadership in competitive business contexts. Niederle and Yestrumskas (2009) found that women and men who initially performed comparably on a cogni-tive task diverged in their subsequent preferences for engaging in a difficult version of the task that provided opportunities for greater rewards. Women's aversion for risk and greater uncertainty about their ability led them to forgo challenges, thereby adopting lower aspirations.

Stereotype threat may also reduce aspirations via self-handicapping (Steele & Aronson, 1995). Rather than put forth effort and risk defeat, negatively stereotyped individuals may instigate alternate explanations for poor performance (Keller, 2002). Although *self-handicapping* is typically characterized as a defensive reaction to negative stereotypes, it can also occur in the face of positive stereotypes, such as when men are expected to perform well in competitive tasks (Self, 1990). Regardless of the valence of the threatening stereotype, its very existence can lead targeted group members to introduce psychological excuses for their lack of success.

Stereotype threat can influence employees' willingness to seek feedback and, when unavoidable, their openness to it (Roberson, Deitch, Brief, & Block, 2003). Among African American managers, stereotype threat predicted indirect feedback seeking, or reliance on ambiguous cues to gauge performance. It can also lead to feedback discounting, whereby the accuracy of feedback and the motives of feedback providers is questioned. Individuals seek indirect feedback when the perceived costs of direct feedback are high (Ashford & Northcraft, 1992; Morrison & Bies, 1991). Because seeking and utilizing direct feedback is essential for improving work performance (Ashford & Tsui, 1991), avoiding this vulnerability-producing behavior may limit achievement over time.

Finally, stereotype threat may influence the degree of trust experienced by employees toward potential and actual employers. In one of the few studies examining stereotype threat among African Americans in organizational settings, Purdie-Vaughns, Steele, Davies, Ditlmann, and Crosby (2008) observed that advocating a color-blind policy (as opposed to explicitly valuing diversity) in a context in which minority visibility was low led African American managers to experience heightened distrust and discomfort with the organization. By creating bogus company brochures for display at a job fair, the researchers determined that the message organizations send concerning their views on diversity, including both subtle and blatant messages contained in websites and recruitment materials, may activate stereotype threat.

Eliminating gender- and race-based discrepancies in identification with leadership and its correlates is vital if leadership diversity in organizations is to be increased. Stereotype threat likely impacts both whether potential employees apply for jobs and whether existing employees fulfill their potential. Organizations frequently encourage employees to strive for excellence, and yet stereotype threat may lead negatively stereotyped groups to fail to see themselves as having "the right stuff." In organizations that revere the innate talent of their employees, individuals faced with increasingly complex and novel challenges as they move up the career ladder may fail to see themselves as having leadership potential, reduce career aspirations, and self-handicap as ways to reduce the threat of failure.

Performance Effects of Stereotype Threat in Organizations

Here, we examine the potential downstream consequences of stereotype threat on performance on organizational tasks. Because stereotype threat is relevant for any task in which certain social groups are believed to be more naturally adept than others, each of these domains has the potential for cultivating stereotype-based group differences.

We note up front that examinations of performance effects to date have been limited to studying the impact of gender stereotypes. Consistent with role congruity theory (Eagly & Karau, 2002), the communal aspect of the female stereotype is incompatible with the agentic behaviors associated with performance in many organizational tasks, thus setting the stage for stereotype threat to emerge. Whether it be leading or negotiating, stereotypically masculine traits such as assertiveness and rationality are commonly associated with high performers (Kray, Thompson, & Galinsky, 2001). Stereotypes suggesting men are more comfortable taking risks also gives them an advantage over women when it comes to entrepreneurial efforts to innovate and create new businesses (Baron, Markman, & Hirsa, 2001). Finally, stereotypical expectations that women be relationally oriented may affect how they approach competition in general.

Perhaps the broadest individual performance domain relevant to organizations concerns leadership effectiveness. Common metrics of CEO leadership effectiveness include gains in market share and stock price, yet these measures are far removed from any specific behaviors of individual leaders and virtually impossible to study in the laboratory, where much of stereotype threat research occurs. As described above, stereotype threat researchers have primarily examined leadership efficacy and leadership intentions, which gauge individuals' willingness and desire to assume leadership roles.

A notable exception to the study of leadership simply in terms of intentions and aspirations is work examining the moderating role of leadership efficacy, or self-assessed ability to lead (Bandura, 1997; Murphy, 1992). High leadership efficacy buffers women against stereotype threat (Hoyt, 2005). After hearing that effective leaders are masculine, women who were initially high in leadership efficacy actually strengthened their identification with the leadership domain; in contrast, women who initially reported low leadership efficacy reduced their identification with the leadership domain. Subsequently, Hoyt and Blascovich (2007) showed that the increased domain identification for high self-efficacy women translated into better performance, as measured by the effectiveness of advising and motivating employees on a simulated hiring committee.

Another performance domain in which stereotype threat occurs is negotiations. Negotiating is a decision-making process over the division of scarce resources between two or more interdependent parties. Effective leaders must be skilled negotiators (Kray & Haselhuhn, 2008), and studying negotiation in the laboratory has the advantage of being easily quantified, thus rendering clear measures of relative performance. To demonstrate that gender stereotypes can produce stereotype threat in negotiations, Kray and colleagues adapted Steele and Aronson's (1995) manipulation of task diagnosticity prior to having mixed-sex negotiating dyads complete a buyer–seller simulation. Consistent with stereotype threat, women in the diagnostic condition achieved significantly worse outcomes than did their male counterparts; in the nondiagnostic condition, men and women performed comparably. Negotiators' financial aspirations appear to be one mechanism driving this effect (Kray, Galinsky, & Thompson, 2002). Disidentification with the negotiation domain may also be a mechanism that reduces women's propensity to initiate negotiations (Babcock, Gelfand, Small, & Stayn, 2006).

Although negotiations have an inherently competitive component that can clearly produce stereotype threat, the interdependent nature of negotiations makes it more difficult to determine whether women's performance is affected only by activated stereotypes versus an effect driven by their counterparts or even by a dyadic-level phenomenon. To address this concern, we consider related research examining the debilitating effect of competitive payoff structures on women's performance on individual cognitive tasks. Specifically, Gneezy, Niederle, and Rustichini (2003) had participants work on computerized mazes for pay under competitive versus noncompetitive payoff structures. In the noncompetitive condition, participants were paid a fixed amount for each maze they completed within the allotted time. In the competitive condition, only the top performer was compensated. Whereas no gender differences in performance were observed with the noncompetitive payment scheme, the competitive payment structure led women's performance to drop significantly relative to men's performance, which remained constant regardless of the level of competitiveness. In subsequent research, participants were given a choice of payment scheme (Niederle & Vesterlund, 2007). Not surprisingly, men were significantly more likely to select competitive payments than women, despite the lack of a priori performance differences. To the degree that competitive environments are inherently threatening to women due to negative stereotypes about their ability to "hold their own," women may reap fewer rewards than men.

In conclusion, the literature examining stereotype threat's quantifiable effect on performance on organizational tasks is sparse. Virtually all of the existing research has examined gender as the social categorization triggering stereotype threat. The vast majority of work in this domain examines competitive performance interdependent decision-making tasks (i.e., negotiations) or individual-based cognitive tasks (i.e., mazes). All of the research reported above took place in laboratory settings with students rather than with employees of actual organizations. As a result of these limitations, stereotype threat's impact on a wide array of organizational work is poorly understood, including sales and marketing effectiveness, accuracy in accounting and technical tasks, financial investing skill, and labor output. More generally, our understanding of how chronic exposure to stereotype threat impacts promotion rates and turnover within organizations is currently limited. Although the implications of stereotype threat for organizations are abundant and relatively straightforward, more empirical demonstrations of the multiple ways in which this phenomenon affects organizations is needed. As such, the next generation of stereotype threat research should take seriously the call to hold up a microscope to organizational settings with as much vigor as has already been applied to academic settings.

■ THE ORGANIZATIONAL CONTEXT: SITUATIONAL TRIGGERS OF STEREOTYPE THREAT

Whereas the previous section considered stereotype threat's wide-ranging effects on individuals, in this section we identify and describe four situational characteristics that may create "threats in the air," including task difficulty, organizational structure, minority representation, and organizational culture.

Task Difficulty

The degree to which employees are adequately trained and prepared for the challenges they confront should predict whether stereotype threat occurs. Difficult tasks are both more likely to lead to stereotype threat, and are more affected by stereotype threat (Roberson & Kulik, 2007; Steele et al., 2002). Employees are expected and encouraged to take on complex tasks, especially as they climb the corporate ladder. As such, the connection between task difficulty and stereotype threat activation produces a challenge for organizations as negatively stereotyped group members assume greater responsibility.

Organizational Structure

Organizations vary in the degree to which clear status differences exist between individuals. We expect that rigid hierarchical structures may increase stereotype threat for individuals low on the "totem pole." Just as low-status nonhuman primates experience heightened anxiety and stress (Barkow, 1975; Sapolsky, 2005), low-status members of organizations may be in a perpetual state of negativity. Because anxiety has been linked to stereotype threat (Ben-Zeev, Fein, & Inzlicht, 2005; Bosson, Haymovitz, & Pinel, 2004; O'Brien & Crandall, 2003), hierarchies themselves may produce stereotype threat effects for low-status members. Along these lines, Galinsky, Shirako, and Kray (2011) observed that low-power negotiators (i.e., job candidate relative to job recruiter, or buyer relative to seller) experienced performance drops in a negotiation framed as diagnostic of their abilities. Thus, occupying a position lacking in power and status may trigger stereotype threat–consistent effects, even when a consensually shared negative stereotype is absent.

Minority Representation

Recently, Supreme Court Justice Ruth Bader Ginsberg commented on the lack of gender diversity on the Court: "It's almost like being back in law school in 1956, when there were nine of us in a class of over 500, so that meant most sections had just two women, and you felt that every eye was on you. Every time you went to answer a question, you were answering for your entire sex. It may not have been true, but certainly you felt that way. You were different and the object of curiosity" (Bazelon, 2009).

This quote captures many of the challenges inherent in being the sole minority member in a group context (Kanter, 1977). Low demographic diversity in organizations signals to negatively stereotyped individuals that the stereotype may be relevant and, in so doing, increases the perceived evaluation pressures on the individual. By heightening the salience of identity group membership, low demographic diversity can also trigger stereotype threat (Inzlicht & Ben-Zeev, 2000; Sekaquaptewa & Thompson, 2003). Stereotype threat can also be triggered when negatively stereotyped group members represent a small numerical proportion of a professional organization (Murphy, Steele, & Gross, 2007).

We also consider the macro-level impact of minority representation on stereotype threat. In a multinational study, Guiso, Monte, Sapienza, and Zingales (2008) observed a negative correlation between the gender gap in math scores and women's opportunities for advancement at the societal level. In other words, as women's representation in political, educational, and economic activities of a given society increases, girls' underperformance on standardized tests decreases. Although the correlational nature of this research leaves open the question of directionality, one interpretation is that the degree to which minority groups are adequately represented in the power structure is a key driver of performance.

Organizational Culture

Another contextual factor that may trigger stereotype threat is an organization's culture. Broadly speaking, organizational culture is defined as "a system of shared values (defining what is important) and norms (defining appropriate attitudes and behaviors)" (Chatman & Cha, 2003, p. 21). Most research on stereotype threat in organizations has identified ways in which women experience its debilitating effects due to stereotypes suggesting women lack "the right stuff" to succeed in cut-throat industries. To this end, we would expect organizations and industries that cultivate rigid beliefs about innate talent underlying success would exacerbate stereotype threat. As expectations and evaluations become increasingly entwined, members of negatively stereotyped groups become more vulnerable to confirming negative expectations.

Along these lines, in a provocative *New Yorker* article, Gladwell (2002) argued that a pernicious "talent mindset" permeates American management orthodoxy. This mindset is characterized by a firmly held belief that putting the right people in place—defined by their impressive credentials and intellect—will guarantee an organization's effortless success. He argues that this mindset leads managers to evaluate their employees' performance on expectations rather than actual performance. Just like implicit beliefs suggesting individuals are born with a fixed set of abilities (Dweck & Leggett, 1988), organizations whose cultures are characterized by a fixed mindset may be particularly prone to eliciting stereotype threat.

Sexist Attitudes

The degree of sexism felt and expressed in organizations is another cultural characteristic that may promote stereotype threat. Dating at least as far back as the *Anne Hopkins v. Price Waterhouse Coopers* Supreme Court case, we have known that sexist attitudes can harm women's career advancement (Fiske, Bersoff, Borgida, Deaux, &

Heilman, 1991). We now know that sexism can adversely affect women by lowering their objective performance. In an examination of women engineer's problem-solving abilities, merely being in the presence of men who held sexist attitudes caused women's performance to suffer (Logel, Walton, Spencer, Iserman, von Hipple, & Bell, 2009). Specifically, because sexist men tend to exhibit subtle cues (i.e., increased dominance, sexual interest) revealing negative attitudes toward women, women who interacted with sexist men performed worse on a standardized assessment of engineering ability. The sexism raised women's risk of being devalued and judged according to a negative stereotype. Attempting to suppress the negative stereotype taxed women's limited cognitive resources, thus producing stereotype threat. In addition, sexism can undermine women's performance by increasing the salience of other potentially threatening behavior (Kaiser, Vick, & Major, 2006).

Policy Box

Upon reviewing the literature on stereotype threat in organizations, several policy implications emerge. We note that stereotype threat is most likely to harm the career progress of the very same social groups whom organizational diversity programs typically devote large quantities of resources to recruit and retain. Very often, it is under-represented minorities for whom negative stereotypes are most salient, thus setting into motion a vicious cycle in which performance shortcomings thwart diversity goals. With this realization, a more comprehensive approach to managing stereotypes is needed. We propose the development and implementation of stereotype management programs, which involve: (a) communicating the power of stereotypes and developing employees' capacity to actively manage responses to stereotype activation in threatening performance domains, and (b) developing organizational programs designed to reduce the potential for stereotype threat activation. For the threatened individual, this process could involve consciousness-raising about the activation of stereotypes and training about deliberate self-focused techniques aimed at reducing the potential for stereotype threat to become triggered (such as emphasizing positive stereotypes and de-emphasizing negative stereotypes). Organizations could further minimize the prevalence of stereotype threat by reframing potentially threatening tasks and reducing emphasis on threatening social identities, focusing instead on shared identities such as membership in the organization. Organizations may also provide additional mentoring to those employees most vulnerable to stereotype threat and train managers and human resource specialists to monitor the organizational environment for the presence of "threats in the air."

▪ ORGANIZATIONAL INTERVENTIONS TO MITIGATE STEREOTYPE THREAT EFFECTS

We now consider the various steps that organizations can take to reduce stereotype threat. Each intervention aims to reduce the potency of negative stereotypes on targeted group members' performance on organizational tasks.

Stereotype Management

- *Acknowledging stereotypes.* By teaching stereotype threat and specifying how it may become activated, organizations can work to reduce its harmful effects (Johns, Schmader, & Martens, 2005). When negative stereotypes about one's social group are confronted directly, one counterintuitive response is *stereotype reactance,* or a pattern of behavior inconsistent with a negative stereotype. This performance-boosting response has been demonstrated both within the negotiations (Kray et al., 2001) and the entrepreneurship domains (Gupta et al., 2008) by women typically thought to be most vulnerable to stereotype threat. Presumably, directly acknowledging stereotypes helps individuals to question their validity, to understand better why they might experience anxiety or discomfort in certain situations, and possibly to increase the motivation to disprove them. Rather than demonstrating behavior assimilating the stereotype, explicitly activating the stereotype may produce contrast effects. Organizations may carefully consider ways of confronting stereotypes directly, setting the stage for stereotype reactance rather than stereotype threat.

- *Emphasizing positive stereotypes.* One mechanism for mitigating negative stereotypes' harmful effects is by raising awareness about positive stereotypes that may be relevant to a given task (Kray et al., 2002; Rydell, McConnell, & Beilock, 2009). For example, Kray and colleagues demonstrated that explicitly valuing stereotypically feminine traits, such as empathy and verbal communicativeness, led female negotiators to claim more of the bargaining pie than male negotiators. This pattern emerged under conditions typically designed to elicit stereotype threat—a negotiation framed as highly diagnostic of one's underlying abilities. Organizational leaders may reduce stereotype threat by actively managing and shaping the message employees hear about what personal characteristics contribute to task success. Additionally, training in stereotype management may include teaching specific techniques proven to reduce stereotype threat's impact. By teaching negatively stereotyped employees how to engage in self-affirmation, in which valued attributes about the self are actively considered, stereotype threat may be avoided (Martens, Johns, Greenberg, & Schimel, 2006.

- *De-emphasizing negative stereotypes.* Another tool for eliminating stereotype threat is to reduce the power of negative stereotypes by focusing on characteristics that transcend stereotype-relevant social identities. Just as cooperative behavior between groups is promoted via commonly shared identities or goals (Kramer & Brewer, 1984; Sherif, 1966), stereotypes lose their power to drive performance when shared identities are valued. Kray et al. (2001) completely eliminated gender differences in negotiation performance in a diagnostic negotiation after highlighting the power of career aspirations, education, and work experience in predicting negotiating success. Because these characteristics transcend gender, negotiators presumably entered the negotiation without gender being a salient factor. In addition to eliminating differences in how men and women divided the pie, this approach also helped negotiators to create more joint resources. More recently, Rosenthal and Crisp (2006) demonstrated that, by emphasizing overlapping identities between the sexes, women's career preferences become less stereotypically feminine, suggesting this approach may help women to achieve greater presence in the top echelon of organizations. Finally, disavowing personal characteristics strongly associated with negative stereotypes can insulate against stereotype threat (Pronin, Steele & Ross, 2004).

Hiring and Training

- *Increasing minority representation.* Organizations would also be wise to pay careful attention to the representation of minorities within the workplace. By explicitly stating that individuals from a diverse set of backgrounds are welcomed and valued, stereotype threat can be mitigated (Purdie-Vaughns et al., 2008). The availability of role models from under-represented groups who provide examples of success can also reduce stereotype threat (Marx & Roman, 2002; Marx, Stapel, & Muller, 2005; McIntyre et al., 2005). One way for organizations to simultaneously increase minority representation and reduce stereotype threat is to adopt policies advancing diversity, as opposed to simple color-blindness (Purdie-Vaughns et al., 2008). By prioritizing diversity, organizations are poised to increase minority representation and ensure that existing and potential minority group members are less vulnerable to stereotype threat.
- *Job training.* Given that a key moderator of stereotype threat is task difficulty, it seems logical that one way to mitigate its harmful effects is to provide proper training to employees for the challenges they face. In so doing, heightened self-efficacy in the relevant domain may counteract the negative effects of stereotype threat (Hoyt, 2005). By investing in employees' skills via comprehensive training programs, negatively stereotyped group members may feel more capable of exploring alternative career paths within an organization. At least in the context of negotiations, the availability of alternatives inoculates women negotiators against stereotype threat (Kray, Reb, Galinsky, & Thompson, 2004).

Organizational Culture

- *Fostering identity safety.* Simply providing assurances that one's social identity will not be a determining factor for success on a task typically deemed to be stereotype-relevant may reduce stereotype threat. Davies and colleagues (2005) eradicated the notion that gender is relevant to leadership by explicitly assuring their participants that researchers have not observed gender differences in leadership ability. Even in the face of threatening images depicting women in traditional roles, women high in identity safety strongly identified with the leadership domain.

- *Valuing effort.* An effective means of reducing stereotype threat may be to increase the emphasis placed on social identity-neutral traits, such as hard work and perseverance. Aronson, Fried, and Good (2002) demonstrated that endorsing incremental mindsets, which emphasize the connection between hard work and success, reduces stereotype threat relative to entity mindsets, which emphasize innate characteristics (such as gender or race) as predictors of success. Along similar lines, incremental mindsets improve negotiation performance relative to entity mindsets (Kray & Haselhuhn, 2007) and even provide a buffer against negative stereotypes about women's negotiating effectiveness (Kray, Locke, & Haselhuhn, 2009).

■ CONCLUSION

In this chapter, we have reviewed and organized the literature examining stereotype threat in organizations. Upon reflection, we conclude that myriad opportunities exist for stereotype threat to exert pernicious effects on targeted individuals within organizations. Given the sheer ubiquity of evaluations within organizations focused on bottom-line performance, efforts to reduce stereotype threat will hinge on active efforts to manage stereotypes, diversify workforces, provide proper training to employees, and shape organizational cultures in ways that cultivate adaptive beliefs.

References

Aronson, J., Fried, C. B., & Good, C. (2002). Reducing the effects of stereotype threat on African American college students by shaping theories of intelligence. *Journal of Experimental Social Psychology, 38,* 113–125.

Ashford, S. J., & Northcraft, G. B. (1992). Conveying more (or less) than we realize: The role of impression-management in feedback-seeking. *Organizational Behavior and Human Decision Processes, 32,* 370–398.

Ashford, S. J., & Tsui, A. S. (1991). Self-regulation for managerial effectiveness: The role of active feedback seeking. *Academy of Management Journal, 34,* 251–280.

Babcock, L., Gelfand, M., Small, D., & Stayn, H. (2006). Gender differences in the propensity to initiate negotiations. In D. De Cremer, M. Zeelenberg, & K. Murnighan (Eds.), *Social psychology and economics* (pp. 239–259). Mahwah, NJ: Lawrence Erlbaum.

Bandura, A. (1997). *Self-efficacy: The exercise of control.* New York: Freeman.

Barkow, J. H. (1975). Prestige and culture - Biosocial interpretation. *Current Anthropology, 16,* 553–572.

Baron, R. A., Markman, G. D., & Hirsa, A. (2001). Perceptions of women and men as entrepreneurs: Evidence for differential effects of attributional augmenting. *Journal of Applied Psychology, 86,* 923–929.

Bazelon, E. (2009, July 7). The place of women on the court. *The New York Times,* p. MM22.

Ben-Zeev, T., Fein, S., & Inzlicht, M. (2005). Arousal and stereotype threat. *Journal of Experimental Social Psychology, 41,* 174–181.

Bosson, J. K., Haymovitz, E. L., & Pinel, E. C. (2004). When saying and doing diverge: The effects of stereotype threat on self-reported versus nonverbal anxiety. *Journal of Experimental Social Psychology, 40*, 247–255.

Catalyst. (2009). *U.S. women in business.* Retrieved August 15, 2009, from http://www.catalyst.org/publication/132/us-women-in-business

Chatman, J. A., & Cha, S. E. (2003). Leading by leveraging culture. *California Management Review, 45*, 20–34.

Cole, Y. (2008). *Why are so few CEOs people of color and women?* Retrieved August 15th, 2009, from www.diversityinc.com/public/2696print.cfm

Crocker, J., Major, B., & Steele, C. (1998). Social stigma. In D. T. Gilbert, & S. T. Fiske (Eds.), *The handbook of social psychology* Vol. 2 (4th ed., pp. 504–553). Boston: McGraw-Hill.

Davies, P. G., Spencer, S. J., & Steele, C. M. (2005). Clearing the air: Identity safety moderates the effects of stereotype threat on women's leadership aspirations. *Journal of Personality and Social Psychology, 88*, 276–287.

Dweck, C. S., & Leggett, E. L. (1988). A social-cognitive approach to motivation and personality. *Psychological Review, 95*, 256–273.

Eagly, A. H., & Karau, S. J. (2002). Role congruity theory of prejudice toward female leaders. *Psychological Review, 109*, 573–598.

Fiske, S. T., Bersoff, D. N., Borgida, E., Deaux, K., & Heilman, M. E. (1991). Social science research on trial: The use of sex stereotyping research in *Price Waterhouse v. Hopkins. American Psychologist, 46*, 1049–1060. (Reprinted in E. Mertz [Ed.], *The role of social science in law.* Hants, UK: Ashgate Publishing, International Library of Essays in Law and Society, 2008).

Galinsky, A. D., Shirako, A., & Kray, L. J. (2011). *The minimal stereotype threat effect: Power differences drive performance decrements when the pressure is on.* Unpublished manuscript, Northwestern University, Chicago, IL.

Geis, F. L., Brown, V., Jennings (Walstedt), J., & Porter, N. (1984). TV commercials and achievement scripts for women. *Sex Roles, 10*, 513–525.

Gladwell, M. (2002, July 22). The talent myth: Are smart people overrated? *The New Yorker, 78*, 28–33.

Gneezy, U., Niederle, M., & Rustichini, A. (2003). Performance in competitive environments: Gender differences. *Quarterly Journal of Economics, CXVIII*, 1049–1074.

Guiso, L., Monte, F., Sapienza, P., & Zingales, L. (2008). Culture, gender, and math. *Science, 320*, 1164–1165.

Gupta, V. K., Turban, D. B., & Bhawe, N. M. (2008). The effect of gender stereotype activation on entrepreneurial intentions. *Journal of Applied Psychology, 93*, 1953–1061.

Hoyt, C. L. (2005). The role of leadership efficacy and stereotype activation in women's identification with leadership. *Journal of Leadership and Organizational Studies, 11*, 2–14.

Hoyt, C. L., & Blascovich, J. (2007). Leadership efficacy and women leaders' responses to stereotype activation. *Group Processes and Intergroup Relations, 10*, 595–616.

Inzlicht, M., & Ben-Zeev, T. (2000). A threatening intellectual environment: Why females are susceptible to experiencing problem-solving deficits in the presence of males. *Psychological Science, 11*, 365–371.

Inzlicht, M., & Ben-Zeev, T. (2003). Do high-achieving female students underperform in private? The implications of threatening environments on intellectual processing. *Journal of Educational Psychology, 95*, 796–805.

Johns, M., Schmader, T., & Martens, A. (2005). Knowing is half the battle: Teaching stereotype threat as a means of improving women's math performance. *Psychological Science, 16,* 175–179.

Kaiser, C. B., Vick, S. B., & Major, B. (2006). Prejudice expectations moderate preconscious attention to cues that are threatening to social identity. *Psychological Science, 17,* 332–338.

Kanter, R. M. (1977). *Men and women of the organization.* New York: Basic Books.

Keller, J. (2002). Blatant stereotype threat and women's math performance: Self-handicapping as a strategic means to cope with obtrusive negative performance expectations. *Sex Roles, 47,* 193–198.

Kramer, R. M., & Brewer, M. D. (1984). Effects of group identity on resource use in a simulated commons dilemma. *Journal of Personality and Social Psychology, 46,* 1044–1057.

Kray, L. J., Galinsky, A. D., & Thompson, L. (2002). Reversing the gender gap in negotiations: An exploration of stereotype regeneration. *Organizational Behavior and Human Decision Processes, 87,* 386–410.

Kray, L. J., & Haselhuhn, M. (2008). Implicit negotiation beliefs and performance: Longitudinal and experimental evidence. *Journal of Personality and Social Psychology, 93,* 49–64.

Kray, L. J., Locke, C., & Haselhuhn, M. (2009). In the words of Larry Summers: Gender stereotypes and implicit beliefs in negotiations. In A. A. Stanton, M. Day, & I. M. Welpe (Eds.), *Neuroeconomics and the firm.* Cheltenham, UK: Edward Elgar Publishing.

Kray, L. J., Reb, J., Galinsky, A., & Thompson, L. (2004). Stereotype reactance at the bargaining table: The effect of stereotype activation and power on claiming and creating value. *Personality and Social Psychology Bulletin, 30,* 399–411.

Kray, L. J., Thompson, L., & Galinsky, A. (2001). Battle of the sexes: Gender stereotype confirmation and reactance in negotiations. *Journal of Personality and Social Psychology, 80,* 942–958.

Logel, C., Walton, G. M., Spencer, S. J., Iserman, E. C., von Hippel, W., & Bell, A. E. (2009). Interacting with sexist men triggers social identity threat among female engineers. *Journal of Personality and Social Psychology, 96,* 1089–1103.

Major, B., & Schmader, T. (1998). Coping with stigma through psychological disengagement. In J. K. Swim & C. Stangor (Eds.), *Prejudice: The target's perspective* (pp. 219–241). San Diego: Academic Press.

Martens, A., Johns, M., Greenberg, J., & Schimel, J. (2006). Combating stereotype threat: The effect of self-affirmation on women's intellectual performance. *Journal of Experimental Social Psychology, 42,* 236–243.

Marx, D. M., & Roman, J. S. (2002). Female role models: Protecting women's math test performance. *Personality and Social Psychology Bulletin, 28,* 1183–1193.

Marx, D. M., Stapel, D. A., & Muller, D. (2005). We can do it: The interplay of construal orientation and social comparisons under threat. *Journal of Personality and Social Psychology, 88,* 432–446.

McIntyre, R. B., Lord, C. G., Gresky, D. M., Ten Eyck L. L., Frye, G. D. J., & Bond, C. F., Jr. (2005). A social impact trend in the effects of role models on alleviating women's mathematics stereotype threat. *Current Research in Social Psychology, 10,* 116–136.

Morrison, E. W., & Bies, R. J. (1991). Impression management in the feedback seeking process: A literature review and research agenda. *Academy of Management Review, 16,* 522–541.

Murphy, S. E. (1992). *The contribution of leadership experience and self-efficacy to group performance under evaluation apprehension.* Unpublished doctoral dissertation, University of Washington, Seattle.

Murphy, M. C., Steele, C. M., & Gross, J. J. (2007). Signaling threat: How situational cues affect women in math, science, and engineering settings. *Psychological Science, 8,* 879–885.

Niederle, M., & Vesterlund, L. (2007). Do women shy away from competition? Do men compete too much? *Quarterly Journal of Economics, 122,* 1067–1101.

Niederle, M., & Yestrumskas, A. H. (2009). *Gender differences in seeking challenges: The role of institutions.* Unpublished manuscript, Stanford University, Stanford, CA.

O'Brien, L. T., & Crandall, C. S. (2003). Stereotype threat and arousal: Effects on women's math performance. *Personality and Social Psychology Bulletin, 29,* 782–789.

Purdie-Vaughns, V., Steele, C. M., Davies, P. G., Ditlmann, R., & Crosby, J. R. (2008). Social identity contingencies: How diversity cues signal threat or safety for African Americans in mainstream institutions. *Journal of Personality and Social Psychology, 94,* 615–630.

Pronin, E., Steele, C. M., & Ross, L. (2004). Identity bifurcation in response to stereotype threat: Women and mathematics. *Journal of Experimental Social Psychology, 40,* 152–168.

Roberson, L., Deitch, E. A., Brief, A. P., & Block, C. J. (2003). Stereotype threat and feedback seeking in the workplace. *Journal of Vocational Behavior, 62,* 176–188.

Roberson, L., & Kulik, C. (2007). Stereotype threat at work. *Academy of Management Perspectives, 21,* 24–40.

Rosenthal, H. E. S., & Crisp, R. J. (2006). Reducing stereotype threat by blurring intergroup boundaries. *Personality and Social Psychology Bulletin, 32,* 501–511.

Rydell, R. J., McConnell, A. R., & Beilock, S. L. (2009). Multiple social identities and stereotype threat: Imbalance, accessibility, and working memory. *Journal of Personality and Social Psychology, 96,* 949–966.

Sapolsky, R. M. (2005). The influence of social hierarchy on primate health. *Science, 29,* 648–652.

Schmader, T., Johns, M., & Forbes, C. (2008). An integrated process model of stereotype threat effects on performance. *Psychological Review, 115,* 336–356.

Sekaquaptewa, D., & Thompson, M. (2003). Solo status, stereotype threat, and performance expectancies: Their effects on women's performance. *Journal of Experimental Social Psychology, 39,* 68–74.

Self, E. A. (1990). Situational influences on self-handicapping. In R. L. Higgins (Ed.), *Self-handicapping: The paradox that isn't. The Plenum series in social/clinical psychology* (pp. 37–68). New York: Plenum Press.

Sherif, M. (1966). *In common predicament: Social psychology of intergroup conflict and cooperation.* Boston: Houghton Mifflin.

Steele, C. M. (1997). A threat in the air: How stereotypes shape intellectual identity and performance. *American Psychologist, 52,* 613–629.

Steele, C. M., & Aronson, J. (1995). Stereotype threat and the intellectual test performance of African Americans. *Journal of Personality and Social Psychology, 85,* 440–452.

Steele, C. M., Spencer, S. J., & Aronson, J. (2002). Contending with group image: The psychology of stereotype and social identity threat. *Advances in Experimental Social Psychology, 34,* 379–440.

12 Social Class and Test Performance

From Stereotype Threat to Symbolic Violence and Vice Versa

■ JEAN-CLAUDE CROIZET AND
MATHIAS MILLET

Each year, the profile report issued by the College Board systematically reveals that Scholastic Assessment Test (SAT) scores are strongly related to parental annual income (College Entrance Examination Board, 2009). The very rich get the best scores, the very poor the lowest. This chapter focuses on the ways in which stereotypes that portray the poor as not intelligent impact test achievement. Compared to other literatures on gender or race, research on stereotype threat associated to social class remains largely underdeveloped, albeit consistent. First, we present research on the attitudes and stereotypes that people hold toward those who are poor. Poor people are the victims of a contemptuous stereotype that portray them as unintelligent and lazy. We then review the work that has studied the impact of such negative stereotypes on both achievement and ability testing. Borrowing from work on intersectionality and social reproduction (Bourdieu & Passeron, 1970), we next advocate for conceptualizing socioeconomic status, not as a personal variable, but more as a social process involving power asymmetry in the social structure. We then propose that stereotype threat is the psychological manifestation of a symbolic violence embedded in evaluative settings. We finally suggest that future research should investigate how ideology (stereotypes), institutional practices (evaluative settings), and behavior (performance) work together to recycle power and privilege into individual differences in intellectual merit.

Keywords: Stereotype threat, socioeconomic status, poverty, intelligence, power, symbolic violence

Rich people are not only rich; they are also more intelligent.[1] Research in psychometrics reveals that on average, people who are better off have higher IQs than do the poor (Sirin, 2005; White, 1982). This is old news. Soon after developing the first intelligence test in 1905, Binet discovered that children from affluent neighborhoods had a superior intelligence than their peers living in the poor suburbs of Paris (Binet, 1911). Since then, this fact has been repeatedly and consistently observed. This is perhaps the only aspect of this literature that is not controversial.

The relationship between socioeconomic status (SES) and Scholastic Assessment Test (SAT) scores for example is particularly illustrative. For a long time, the College Board has claimed that the SAT measures academic skills and not intelligence. Yet, available research indicates that the SAT, in accordance with the spirit of its inventor, still measures "IQ" or intelligence to a large extent (Frey & Detterman, 2004). Figure 12.1 plots the 2009 distribution of SAT scores according to parental income (College Entrance Examination Board, 2009). The graph shows a gradual increase of 10–70 points in SAT scores with each extra $20,000 in parental annual income. This association is strong enough so that a student's score could actually be guessed based on the car his or her parents drive, something referred to as the "Volvo effect" (Sacks, 1999).

Many explanations have been proposed to account for the fact that the poor have, on average, lower IQs than the rich. Some stress that IQ is the cause of social class. According to the hereditarian view incarnated by Hernnstein and Murray's *Bell Curve* (1994), individual and group differences in IQ are mainly a matter of heredity. Rich kids have higher IQs because they inherit smart genes from smarter parents. Opposed to this view, some advocate that IQ is the consequence rather than the cause of social class. Poor kids have a lower IQ because they grow up in environments characterized by strong material deprivation and substandard schooling, which prevents the normal development of their cognitive abilities (Duncan & Brooks-Gunn, 1999). The opposition of these two camps has focused most of the attention on the debate about the social class gap in intelligence. The vividness

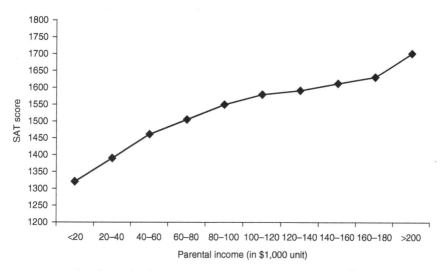

Figure 12.1 The relationship between parental income and SAT score (i.e., the "Volvo effect," adapted from College Entrance Examination Board, 2009).

of the confrontation has nevertheless overshadowed an implicit, but important, agreement of views between the two positions: Test scores measure intelligence.

In opposition to this postulate, some researchers have argued that test scores are not a valid reflection of individual endowment in intelligence (Davis & Havighurst, 1948). Thus, the relationship between social class and IQ may be more informative of the property of the test itself rather than of the attributes of the test takers. For example, test items can be biased in their content, and being able to identify the Milo's Venus statue (e.g., The Kaufman Assessment Battery for Children K-ABC, Kaufman & Kaufman, 1983) is more indicative of a child's familiarity with the white upper middle-class culture than of her intelligence. According to this approach, IQ would predict important outcomes not because it identifies cognitive ability but more simply because it measures acculturation with white middle-class values, which are fundamental to succeed in a white middle-class society. Removing content bias should not only offer a more valid measure of competency, it could also eliminate the gap between the rich and the poor (Eells, Davis, Havighurst, Herrich & Tyler, 1951). Adding to the skepticism about the significance of the class gap in test scores, some research has proposed that the gap could reflect the situational impact of social stereotypes that target people from low socioeconomic backgrounds.

Testing situations are explicitly designed to be "neutral." Their function is to locate variations in performance only at the individual level. They apparently constitute a perfect implementation of Kelley's (1967) covariation principle for dispositional attribution: sameness of circumstances—the test situation is the same for all takers, and sameness of stimuli—the test is the same for all and is not biased against certain groups. Literature on stereotype threat, however, reveals a different picture. Indeed, a standard testing situation is saturated with undermining and enhancing ideologies (Adams, Biernat, Branscombe, Crandall, & Wrightsman, 2008) that selectively affect the performance of the poor and the rich and contribute to the test score gap. In this chapter, our goal is to review this literature. We will first present the research that documents the existence of social class stereotypes. Second, we will review the evidence of stereotype threat effects related to social class. We will finally discuss several theoretical issues for future research.

■ STEREOTYPES ABOUT SOCIAL CLASS

Although research on attitudes, prejudice, and stereotypes constitute by far the most productive area of social psychology, psychologists have shown surprisingly little interest in the attitudes and stereotypes toward the poor. Yet, social class is a fundamental determinant of any individual's life course, and poverty is a pervasive problem in many industrialized countries. In 2008, in the United States, for example, 39.8 million people lived below the federal poverty level (13.2% of the population). Despite this situation, and the fact that poverty has been at the heart of the political debate for decades (welfare, health care, education, etc.; see Bullock, 1995), the literature on prejudice and discrimination against the poor remains marginal (Lott, 2002).

When it is taken into account, class is often just an additional variable in the study of prejudice and discrimination that target other groups (Spencer & Castano, 2007). Until recently, most of the research on the perception of social class had focused almost exclusively on the kind of attributions people make to explain why some are poor (Bullock, 1995; Kluegel & Smith, 1986). Findings consistently reveal that the American Dream is still alive: Individuals believe that social status is earned and that people are responsible for their social standing in society. Research on the attitudes toward the poor is scarce, but available evidence indicates that people expect those who are poor to have lower intellectual ability (Baron, Albright, & Malloy, 1995; Darley & Gross; 1983; Désert, Préaut, & Jung, 2009; Miller, McLaughlin, Haddon, & Chansky 1968; Régner, Huguet, & Monteil, 2002). It is only recently that scholars have systematically investigated the attitudes that young white Americans hold about social class (Cozarelli, Wilkinson, & Tagler, 2001). These researchers showed stereotypes about the poor were largely negative; people from low SES groups were portrayed as being unintelligent, uneducated, unmotivated, and irresponsible. Out of the 39 personality traits used to describe the groups, 38 yielded significant differences unfavorable to the working class. This fact has been captured by research on the stereotype content model, which has demonstrated that the poor form one of the few social groups targeted by a clearly negative (i.e., nonambivalent) stereotype (Fiske, Cuddy, Glick, & Xu, 2002). They are disliked and disrespected, and this attitude is widely spread across cultures (Fiske et al., 2002), even among educated liberals (Brantlinger, 2003). In other words, the poor are the victims of a "contemptuous" prejudice (see Fiske et al., 2002) that portrays them as unintelligent and lazy.

■ STEREOTYPE THREAT AND SOCIAL CLASS

Since the classic research of Steele and Aronson (1995), an important literature has yielded support for the hypothesis that, in standard testing situations, stereotypes of intellectual inferiority can affect intellectual achievement. Once again, although the number of studies examining how social stereotypes undermine performance has skyrocketed, research on stereotype threat and social class is largely underdeveloped.

The first study revealing stereotype threat effect related to social class was conducted in France. Croizet and Claire (1998) asked undergraduates to take a difficult test adapted from the verbal section of the Graduate Record Examination (GRE). Class was determined by parental occupation and education. Students were selected as low SES if their parents never finished high school and were unskilled workers. Students of high SES had parents who had college degrees and held professional occupations. Because there were some concerns about the possibility that the stereotype may not be salient enough, the researchers asked half of the participants before they took the test to indicate the level of their parents' education. Surprisingly, this salience manipulation had absolutely no impact on intellectual achievement. When participants were informed that the test was a measure of their cognitive ability, students from low socioeconomic backgrounds performed lower than their high SES peers. Yet, when the test was introduced as a simple laboratory exercise, nondiagnostic of ability, the low SES students performed as well as the others. Interestingly and congruent with the literature on stereotype threat, high SES benefitted from the diagnostic condition (i.e., a lift effect, see Croizet & Claire, 1998; Croizet & Dutrévis, 2004, 2010; Walton & Cohen, 2003).

Surprisingly, some doubts were raised about the generality of this finding. The argument coined even at the editorial stage was that the social class stereotype threat effect was a "French" effect because of the classist structure of the French society. The implicit assumption was that this finding would not be observed in the United States, where stereotypes about social class are less prevalent. It took several years for this issue to be settled. Harrison, Stevens, Monty, and Coakley (2006) had white and non-white college students take difficult math and verbal tests (SAT). Participants were from lower ($39,000 and under per year), middle ($40,000—$79,999 per year), or upper classes (over $75,000 per year). For one half of the participants, the test was framed to minimize stereotype threat: A study of the cognitive processes underlying performance. The other participants were informed that they were about to take a valid measure of math and verbal abilities to investigate the reasons for the underachievement of the poor in college. Consistent with previous research, this study demonstrated a stereotype threat effect related to social class on both verbal and math performance. Students of lower income performed worse on the task when it was presented as a valid test of their abilities than they did when it was characterized in a nonthreatening way. Whereas middle-class college students were unaffected by the manipulation, those from upper-class backgrounds performed better under the diagnostic condition than they did under the nondiagnostic. Almost at the same time, B. Spencer and Casteno (2007) confirmed both stereotype threat and stereotype lift related to class with another American sample. Importantly and contrary to Croizet and Claire's initial finding, these researchers showed that the mere salience of SES was enough to disrupt performance among the poor when the task was nondiagnostic, suggesting that there might be some cultural differences about the situational prevalence of class stereotypes in educational contexts.

Research has also documented the psychological cost of stereotype threat beyond performance disruption. Indeed, lower -income participants exposed to stereotype threat report higher test anxiety, lower confidence in their ability to perform, and lower identification with academic domains (Harrison et al., 2006; Spencer & Castano, 2007). The literature has also established the generalizability of the phenomenon across several tasks: From verbal, math, and English GRE-like tasks (e.g., Croizet & Claire, 1998; Harrison et al., 2006) to psychometric tests (Croizet & Dutrévis, 2004; Désert & al., 2009). Probably one of the most disturbing findings concerning stereotype threat related to social class is the fact that it affects performance on nonverbal IQ tests that were specially developed to limit language bias in psychometric assessment. Raven's progressive matrices test (Raven, Raven, & Court, 1988), for example, is often considered as one of the purest measures of intelligence (i.e., "g," see Herrnstein & Murray, 1994, p. 273; Snow, Kyllonen & Marshalek,

1984). Yet, research has demonstrated that achievement on such tests is sensitive to stereotype threat that targets the poor (Croizet & Dutrévis, 2004). For example, Désert et al. (2009) showed that children from a low socioeconomic background performed worse on Raven's test when it was introduced using the standard instructions rather than when it was described as a game. Importantly, this finding was observed among children who were only 6 years old and replicated among 7- to 9-year-old students, suggesting that stereotype threat can affect achievement and therefore students' life very early on.

■ INTERSECTIONALITY AND STEREOTYPE THREAT

Even though research has cleverly demonstrated that even dominant groups can experience stereotype threat, social settings are framed in a way that most of the groups experiencing this predicament are from the bottom of the social hierarchy: blacks, Latinos, the poor, women. Those are the groups targeted by a stereotype of lower intelligence (Fiske et al., 2002). So far, the existence of stereotype threat has been established by focusing on separate identities defined in terms of race, gender, or class. But this approach is limiting because it ignores the fact that individuals usually belong to several categories that overlap and depend on one another.

The concept of *intersectionality*, initially developed by feminist and critical race theorists (e.g., Crenshaw, 1993), explicitly refers to the reality that groups hold multiple statuses in society. Although theoretically neglected, intersectionality may explain certain findings in the stereotype threat literature, like the fact that the debilitating effect of stereotype threat occurs for only certain combinations of identities. For example, in one study, stereotype threat disrupted women's math performance but only for Mexican American females not white women, something referred to as the "double minority effect" (Gonzales, Blanton, & Williams, 2002). In the same vein, Andreoletti and Lachman (2004) investigated how age stereotypes that depict the elderly as having poor memory affects recall performance. Their results showed that older participants (aged 60 or higher) performed less well when a memory test was characterized as revealing age differences (stereotype condition) than when it was described as a test showing no age difference (counter stereotype condition) or when no reference to the stereotype was made (standard condition). Interestingly, the elderly with higher education (more than a 4-year college degree) were the only ones showing this standard stereotype threat effect. Participants with low education showed memory deficit in both the stereotype and the counterstereotype conditions as compared to the standard condition. The authors' conclusion was that "education may be a more important factor than age with regard to susceptibility and resilience to memory aging stereotypes" (Andreoletti & Lachman, 2004, p. 145).

Here, we argue that these findings point to the necessity to consider intersectionality. Cumulative lack of power and control may make one more sensitive to the undermining effect of stereotypes in the same way that accumulation of power may make one more sensitive to the enhancing effect of stereotypes. Therefore, one could predict that some African Americans may experience stereotype threat related to race at a lower level of situational threat when they also happen to be poor and female.

The intersectionality framework has a lot to offer at this level because it questions the implicit but often powerful understanding of identity as a simple demographic individual attribute. It forces theoretical refinement of the predicament associated to social identities (American Psychological Association, Task Force on Socioeconomic Status, 2007). Cole (2009) recently proposed that a systemic consideration of intersectionality would lead researchers to do three things: question the definition of their categories (e.g., who are the elderly in the sample, what gender, what race, what class?); examine the role played by inequality (i.e., power and resources asymmetry); and identify the commonalities between groups (e.g., most groups experiencing stereotype threat have lower status and are excluded from the educational system, whereas those experiencing stereotype lift are the beneficiaries of it). In other words, this approach advocates conceptualizing identity not as a personal variable but more as a social process involving groups' position in the social structure.

A study carried out by a group of sociologists yielded evidence suggesting that such a shift may have heuristic value. Lovaglia, Lukas, Houser, Thye, and Markowsky (1998) experimentally assigned participants to either a low- or high-status position. Status was randomly determined by left- or right-handedness, which was predicted to be positively or negatively related to the ability required for an upcoming task. This relationship was further justified by a biological rationale invoking the right or left parts of the brain. Participants were informed that they would also later be assigned to different occupations and pay level, based on their status and aptitude score (i.e., supervisors $17 per hour; analysts $8; menials $4.5). Assignment rules were clearly favorable for high-achieving high-status individuals and unfavorable for low-achieving low-status individuals. Participants then took the Raven Progressive Matrices test. Results from three studies revealed that participants' scores were influenced by their status. Participants who had a higher status (i.e., expectation of higher ability and advantaged by the system) obtained a higher IQ (e.g., 120, Experiment 2) than did those who were randomly assigned to a low status (i.e., who had a reputation of low ability and disadvantaged by the system; IQ = 112). In other words, Lovaglia et al. (1998) revealed that creating a social hierarchy with different status and privilege was enough to induce stereotype threat effects on IQ scores.

The reasons why stereotype threat effects are limited to or magnified by certain combinations of identities (e.g., ethnicity and gender, age and class) therefore deserves further attention. The answer is unlikely to involve the inclusion of more demographic variables. Rather, research on intersectionality proposes a shift in our understanding of the concept of social categories and identities. Instead of informing about the individuals within the groups, social categories define the structural relations that shape individual, social, and institutional practices (Cole, 2009; Markus & Moya, 2010; Zuberi & Bonilla Silva, 2008).

Policy Box

The persistence of the achievement gap between the rich and the poor constitutes one of the biggest challenges for a democratic society committed to equal opportunity. Education serves the important function of selecting individuals based on their sole merit, but research on stereotype threat and social class suggests that the implementation of equality in educational settings is problematic. Testing situations are usually considered to be neutral, but they are actually differently experienced by the rich and the poor. They contribute substantially to the class gap in test scores. Test scores should therefore be considered less an indicator of individual cognitive potential but more as the by-product of educational and social situations. One positive consequence of this finding is that the power of educational situations on performance is more important than usually thought. Research shows that subtle situational changes, notably minimizing the belief that level of achievement reflects intellectual value, generate positive educational outcomes in terms of performance, motivation, and sense of belonging. Because immediate situations are under the control of teachers, such interventions are easy to implement. On the more negative side, this literature questions our commitment to meritocracy because test scores systematically measure something other than individual merit. Therefore, using them to determine who gets ahead in education becomes problematic. Finally, research points out that the process driving these effects is beyond the level of the classroom or the school. Although this should in no way be a reason for inaction, we should also avoid "educationalizing" social problems, looking to the classroom for the key to an issue that is deeply rooted in the wider society.

■ FROM STEREOTYPE THREAT TO SYMBOLIC VIOLENCE

The move from the person to the situation has been a signature of stereotype threat research from the very discovery of the phenomenon. Early on, stereotype threat was defined as a "threat in the air," something in the situation, not within the individual (Steele, 1997). According to the initial formulation of the theory, stereotype threat is not a motivational trait of stigmatized individuals; it is a predicament brought into the testing situation by the stereotype. It can be alleviated with subtle situational changes, like altering the presentation of a test. Groups that usually enjoy high status can also experience stereotype threat whenever they are placed in a situation that puts their ability into question (e.g., see Aronson et al. 1999; Leyens, Désert, Croizet, & Darcis, 2000). Yet, such situations are far less frequent in the real world that those encountered by disadvantaged groups.

Indeed, in a given society, situations are not randomly arranged and distributed in space. They are organized across institutions. They are nested with ideology, shaped by history and culture, and enacted daily through institutional practices. In other words, they constitute "intentional worlds" (Adams, 2010; Shweder, 1990). Research has revealed that ideologies that depict certain groups as inferior constitute a crucial element of individuals' reality in testing situations. But evaluative situations by themselves should not be considered as just a "neutral" environment permeable to negative stereotypes. Testing situations should also be conceptualized as a social process, historically and culturally situated, that actively contributes to group domination (Croizet, in press). Research on stereotype threat and stereotype lift has consistently demonstrated that evaluative situations reproduce the status quo. People from high-status groups outperform, while those from low-status groups underperform. We believe that this commonality has been overlooked and should be investigated further (see Cole, 2009). Understanding how situations shape individual construal of reality and performance is essential, but decrypting the social logic of inequality embedded and enacted in evaluative situations appears now unavoidable.

Long-term relations of domination that define class, race, and gender relations are characterized by two important features (Jackman, 1994). They rely heavily on symbolic domination, and they are institutionalized. As pointed out by Max Weber (1914/1978), power relations are also symbolic relations. Throughout history, dominant groups have sought to justify their power by manufacturing ideologies that depict them as superior and entitled to control the dominated groups (Zelditch, 2001). Some authors argued that the notions of "aptitude" and "intelligence" have served to rationalize the domination of the haves over the have-nots (Bisseret, 1974; Bourdieu & Passeron, 1964). For example, the meaning of aptitude evolved during the 19th century from an unstable predisposition totally dependent on the environment to an immutable and inherited trait (Bisseret, 1974). At that time, the French bourgeoisie, who had accessed power after the revolution, was in need of justification for its power over the working class that it had earlier mobilized to overthrow the monarchy in the name of freedom, equality, and brotherhood. It was also an era in which slavery and colonialism had to be made compatible with democracies founded on the idea of equality of men. It is at that time that the concept of intelligence made its appearance to justify the superiority of rich white men (Carson, 2007). Group stereotypes have also played a crucial role in system justification (Jost & Banaji, 2004; Tajfel, 1981). We argue that the idea of intelligence as a stable and individually owned characteristic was also manufactured for that purpose (Croizet, in press).

Yet, domination would not be efficient without some degree of institutionalization. Institutionalization of domination relieves group members who enjoy high status for having to act individually to benefit from their privilege. Bourdieu and Passeron (1970) proposed that education is an institution that actively contributes to reproduction of the social class structure of society. First, it achieves this function by negating the cultural arbitrariness of educational material and practices that favor certain groups of students (i.e., a group culture is imposed as the only legitimate culture); second, it locates performance not as the outcome of social inequalities and power differentials but as the product of individual differences in talent and merit. Through these two processes, education perpetrates a form of *symbolic violence* that locates the cause of failure of lower-class students on their personal limitations and the success of the upper middle class, not on privilege and power, but on their individual superiority (Bourdieu & Passeron, 1970).

We propose that an important function of evaluative situations is to perpetrate this symbolic violence.

Research on stereotype threat has brought ample evidence documenting the psychological impact of this symbolic violence (Schmader, Johns, & Forbes, 2008). In standard testing situations, low-status group members face symbolic disqualification (Millet & Thin, 2004); they struggle with a suspicion of intellectual inadequacy that creates an imbalance among their self-concept, their group identity, and the intellectual domain. This disqualification triggers emotions, drains cognitive resources, and disrupts performance (Johns, Inzlicht, & Schmader, 2008).

Like intersectionality, the notion of symbolic violence suggests that stereotype threat and lift phenomena related to social class can be conceptualized as the behavioral outcome of power dynamics embedded in the exam situation. Under the cover of explicit equality of treatment (i.e., sameness of exam and time), test situations allow the confrontation of social and structural inequality in a confined environment that "essentializes" or transforms privilege and power into individual merit and talent (Croizet & Guinier, 2010). By perpetrating this symbolic violence on a daily basis, tests and exams play a key role in legitimating and reproducing the current social order. Such issues have a long history in sociology. Stereotype threat research suggests that they are opened to sociopsychological scrutiny as well.

■ CONCLUSION

In 1911, Alfred Binet was confronted with the fact that the poor scored lower than the rich on his test. After a careful analysis of the available evidence, he concluded that the superiority of the young "bourgeois" was likely due to the language spoken in wealthy families, which, according to him, advantaged them on the test. Almost a century later, the question of why people from low socioeconomic backgrounds underachieve on intellectual tests remains a hotly debated issue. Some recent research scrutinizes prefrontal regions of the brain (Kishiyama, Boyce, Jiminez, Perry, & Knight, 2009), brain size (Rushton & Ankney, 2009), or genes (Posthuma & de Geus, 2006) to identify the cause of lower intelligence. The literature on stereotype threat suggests that part of the answer may reside not within the individual but outside, in the testing situation and in a pervasive cultural ideology that portrays the poor as intellectually inadequate. In this chapter, we have documented this evidence. We have argued that research on stereotype threat and social class would benefit from questioning the so-called neutrality of testing situations a step further. Borrowing from work on intersectionality and social reproduction, we have advocated for conceptualizing SES, not as an individual attribute, but as a social process involving power relations in a social hierarchy. According to this approach, evaluative settings contribute to group domination by perpetrating symbolic violence that organizes the disqualification of low SES people's sense of self-worth. Stereotype threat research has widely documented how suspicions of inferiority and superiority affect test performance. Still more effort is required to understand how ideology (stereotypes), institutional practices (evaluative settings), and behavior (performance) work together to transform power and privilege into individual differences in intellectual merit.

▓ ENDNOTE

1. Throughout this text, the word "intelligence" refers to psychometric intelligence.

References

Adams, G. (2010, March 17–19). *"Intentional worlds" of injustice: A cultural-psychological analysis of racist oppression.* Paper presented at the Society for the Psychological Study of Social Issues/European Association of Social Psychology meeting on "Forgotten Alternatives," New York.

Adams, G., Biernat, M., Branscombe, N. R., Crandall, C. S., & Wrightsman, L. S. (2008). Beyond prejudice: Toward a sociocultural psychology of racism and oppression. In G. Adams, M. Biernat, N. R. Branscombe, C. S. Crandall, & L. S. Wrightsman (Eds.), *Commemorating Brown: The social psychology of racism and discrimination* (pp. 215–246). Washington, DC: American Psychological Association.

American Psychological Association, Task Force on Socioeconomic Status. (2007). *Report of the APA Task Force on Socioeconomic Status.* Washington, DC: American Psychological Association.

Andreoletti, C., & Lachman, M. E. (2004). Susceptibility and resilience to memory aging stereotypes: Education matters more than age. *Experimental Aging Research, 30,* 129–148.

Aronson, J., Lustina, M. J., Good, C., Keough, K., Steele, C. M., & Brown, J. (1999). When white men can't do math: Necessary and sufficient factors in stereotype threat. *Journal of Experimental Social Psychology, 35,* 29–46.

Baron, R. M., Albright, L., & Malloy, T. E. (1995). Effects of behavioral and social class information on social judgment. *Personality and Social Psychological Bulletin, 21,* 308–315.

Binet, A. (1911). Nouvelles recherches sur la mesure du niveau intellectuel chez les enfants d'école [New studies on the measurement of the intellectual level among pupils]. *L'Année Psychologique, 19,* 145–201.

Bisseret, N. (1974). *Les inégaux ou la sélection universitaire* [Unequals or college selection]. Paris: Presses Universitaires de France.

Bourdieu, P., & Passeron, J.-C. (1964). *Les héritiers* [The heirs]. Paris: Editions de Minuit.

Bourdieu, P., & Passeron, J.-C. (1970). *La reproduction.* Paris: Editions de Minuit. (English translation, *Reproduction in education, society and culture.* London: Sage, 1977).

Brantlinger, E. (2003). *Dividing classes: How the middle class negotiates and rationalizes school advantage.* New York: RoutledgeFalmer.

Bullock, H. E. (1995). Class acts: Middle-class responses to the poor. In B. Lott, & D. Maluso (Eds.), *The social psychology of interpersonal discrimination* (pp. 118–159). New York: Guilford.

Carson, J. (2007). *The measure of merit: Talents, intelligence, and inequality in the French and American republics, 1750–1940.* Princeton: Princeton University Press.

Cole, E. R. (2009). Intersectionality and research in psychology. *American Psychologist, 64,* 170–180.

College Entrance Examination Board. (2009). *College-board seniors national report: A profile of SAT program test-takers.* Retrieved on January 6, 2010 from http://professionals. collegeboard.com/profdownload/cbs-2009-national-TOTAL-GROUP.pdf

Cozarelli, C., Wilkinson, A. V., & Tagler, M. J. (2001). Attitudes toward the poor and attributions for poverty. *Journal of Social Issues, 57,* 207–227.

Crenshaw, K. (1993). Demarginalizing the intersection of race and sex: A Black feminist critique of antidiscrimination doctrine, feminist theory and antiracist politics. In D. K. Weisbert (Ed.), *Feminist legal theory: Foundations* (pp. 383–395). Philadelphia: Temple University Press. (Original work published 1989).

Croizet, J. C. (in press) The racism of intelligence: How mental testing practices have constituted an institutionalized form of group domination. In H. L. Gates, Jr. (Ed.), *Handbook of African American citizenship.* Oxford: Oxford University Press.

Croizet, J. -C., & Claire, T. (1998). Extending the concept of stereotype threat to social class: The intellectual underperformance of students from low socioeconomic backgrounds. *Personality and Social Psychology Bulletin, 24,* 588–594.

Croizet, J. -C., & Dutrévis, M. (2004). Why test scores do not equal merit. *Journal of Poverty, 8,* 91–107.

Croizet, J. -C., & Dutrévis, M. (2010). *Alleviating stereotype threat through affirming one's stereotyped identity.* University of Poitiers, France.

Croizet, J. -C., & Guinier, L. (2010). *Now you see it, now you don't: Race, wealth and the magic trick of merit.* Center for the Advanced Study in the Behavioral Sciences, Stanford University.

Darley, J. M., & Gross, P. H. (1983). A hypothesis-confirming bias in labeling effects. *Journal of Personality and Social Psychology, 44,* 20–33.

Davis, W. A., & Havighurst, R. J. (1948). The measurement of mental systems (can intelligence be measured?). *Scientific Monthly, 65,* 301–316.

Désert, M., Préaut, M., & Jung, R. (2009). So young and already victims of stereotype threat: Socio-economic status and performance of 6 to 9 years old children on Raven's progressive matrices. *European Journal of Psychology of Education, 24,* 207–218.

Duncan, G. J., & Brooks-Gunn, J. (Eds.). (1999). *The consequences of growing up poor.* New York: Russell Sage Foundation.

Eells, K., Davis, W. A., Havighurst, R. J., Herrick, V. E., & Tyler, R. W. (1951). *Intelligence and cultural differences: A study of cultural learning and Problem-solving.* Chicago: University of Chicago Press.

Fiske, S. T., Cuddy, A. J. C., Glick, P., & Xu, J. (2002). A model of (often mixed) stereotype content: Competence and warmth respectively follow from perceived status and competition. *Journal of Personality and Social Psychology, 82,* 878–902.

Frey, M. C., & Detterman, D. K. (2004). Scholastic assessment org? The relationship between the Scholastic Assessment Test and general cognitive ability. *Psychological Science, 15,* 373–378.

Gonzales, P. M., Blanton, H., & Williams, K. J. (2002). The effect of stereotype threat and double-minority status on the test performance of Latino women. *Personality and Social Psychology Bulletin, 28,* 659–670.

Harrison, L. A., Stevens, C. M., Monty, A. N., & Coakley, C. A. (2006). The consequences of stereotype threat on the academic performance of White and non-White lower income college students. *Social Psychology of Education, 9,* 341–357.

Herrnstein, R. J., & Murray, C. (1994). *The bell curve: Intelligence and class structure in American life.* New York: Free Press.

Jackman, M. R. (1994). *The velvet glove: Paternalism and conflict in gender, class, and race relations*. Berkeley: University of California Press.

Johns, M. J., Inzlicht, M., & Schmader, T. (2008). Stereotype threat and executive resource depletion: Examining the influence of emotion regulation. *Journal of Experimental Psychology: General, 137*, 691–705.

Jost, J. T., & Banaji, M. R. (1994). The role of stereotyping in system-justification and the production of false consciousness. *British Journal of Social Psychology, 3*, 1–27.

Kelley, H. H. (1967). Attribution theory in social psychology. In D. Levine (Ed.), *Nebraska symposium on motivation* Vol. 15 (pp. 192–238). Lincoln: University of Nebraska Press.

Kaufman, A. S., & Kaufman, N. L. (1983). *Kaufman assessment battery for children*. Circle Pines, MN: American Guidance Service.

Kishiyama, M. M., Boyle W. T., Jimenez, A. M., Perry, L. M., & Knight, R. T. (2009). Socioeconomic disparities affect prefrontal function in children. *Journal of Cognitive Neuroscience, 21*, 1106–1115.

Kluegel, J. R., & Smith, E. R. (1986). *Beliefs about inequality: American's views of what is and what ought to be*. New York: Aldine de Gruyter.

Leyens, J. -Ph., Désert, M., Croizet, J. -C., & Darcis, C. (2000). Stereotype threat: Are lower status and history of stigmatization preconditions of stereotype threat. *Personality and Social Psychology Bulletin, 26*, 1189–1199.

Lott, B. (2002). Cognitive and behavioral distancing from the poor. *American Psychologist, 57*, 100–110.

Lovaglia, M. J., Lucas, J. W., Houser, J. W., Thye, S. R., & Markovsky, B. (1998). Status processes and mental ability test scores. *American Journal of Sociology, 104*, 195–228.

Markus, H. R., & Moya, P. M. L. (Eds.). (2010). *Doing race: 21 essays for the 21st century*. New York: Norton.

Miller, C. M., McLaughlin, J. A., Haddon, J., & Chansky, N. M. (1968). Socioeconomic class and teacher bias. *Psychological Reports, 23*, 806.

Millet, M., & Thin, D. (2004). La déscolarisation comme parcours de disqualification symbolique [School dropout as a path of symbolic disqualification]. In D. Glasman, & F. Oeuvrard (Eds.), *La déscolarisation*. Paris: La Dispute.

Posthuma, D., & de Geus, J. C. (2006). Progress in the molecular-genetic study of intelligence. *Current Directions in Psychological Science, 15*, 151–155.

Raven, J. C, Raven, J., & Court, J. H. (1998). *A manual for Raven's progressive matrices and vocabulary scales*. London: H. K. Lewis.

Régner, L., Huguet, P., & Monteil, J. -M. (2002). Effects of socioeconomic status information on cognitive ability inferences: When low-SES students make use of a self-threatening stereotype. *Social Psychology of Education, 5*, 253–269.

Rushton, J. P., & Ankney, C. D. (2009). Whole brain size and general mental ability: A review. *International Journal of Neuroscience, 119*, 691–731.

Sacks, P. (1999). *Standardized minds: The high price of America's testing culture and what I can do to change it*. Cambridge, MA: Perseus Books.

Schmader, T., Johns, M., & Forbes, C. (2008). An integrated process model of stereotype threat effects on performance. *Psychological Review, 115*, 336–356.

Shweder, R. A. (1990). Cultural psychology: What is it? In J. Stigler, & R. Shweder, & G. Herdt (Eds.), *Cultural psychology: Essays on comparative human development*. Cambridge, UK: Cambridge University Press.

Sirin, S. R. (2005). Socioeconomic status and academic achievement: A Meta-analytic review of research 1990–2000. *Review of Educational Research, 75*, 417–453.

Snow, R. E., Kyllonen, P. C., & Marshalek, B. (1984). The topography of ability and learning correlations. In R. J. Sternberg (Ed.), *Advances in the psychology of human intelligence* (Vol. 2, pp. 47–103). Hillsdale: Erlbaum.

Spencer, B., & Castano, E. (2007). Social class is dead. Long live social class! Stereotype threat among low socioeconomic status individuals. *Social Justice Research, 20*, 418–432.

Steele, C. M. (1997). A threat in the air: How stereotypes shape the intellectual identities and performance of women and African Americans. *American Psychologist, 52*, 613–629.

Steele, C. M., & Aronson, J. (1995). Stereotype threat and the intellectual test performance of African Americans. *Journal of Personality and Social Psychology, 69*, 797–811.

Tajfel, H. (1981). *Human groups and social categories.* Cambridge: Cambridge University Press.

Walton, G. M., & Cohen, G. L. (2003). Stereotype lift. *Journal of Experimental Social Psychology, 39*, 456–467.

Weber, M. (1914/1978). *Economy and society.* Berkeley: University of California Press.

White, K. R. (1982). The relation between socioeconomic status and academic achievement. *Psychological Bulletin, 91*, 461–481.

Zelditch, M., Jr. (2001). Theories of legitimacy. In J. Jost, & B. Major (Eds.), *The psychology of legitimacy: Emerging perspectives on ideology, justice, and intergroup relations* (pp. 33–53). Cambridge, UK: Cambridge University Press.

Zuberi, T., & Bonilla-Silva, E. (Eds.). (2008). *White logic, white methods: Racism and methodology.* New York: Rowman & Littlefield Publishers.

13 Aging and Stereotype Threat

Development, Process, and Interventions

■ ALISON L. CHASTEEN,
SONIA K. KANG, AND
JESSICA D. REMEDIOS

Age stereotypes are widespread and, although they contain some positive elements, they are primarily negative. It is likely that age stereotypes become internalized at an early age, only to negatively impact individuals when they themselves grow old. Negative views of aging can operate either explicitly or implicitly, affecting both physical and cognitive health. Thus, it is not surprising that older adults, like many other negatively stereotyped groups, experience stereotype threat. In the case of age-related stereotype threat, consequences have been observed primarily in the domain of memory. Similar to stereotype threat effects among other groups, domain and group identification moderate age-based stereotype threat effects. In addition, task demands, memory self-efficacy, and age (young-old vs. old-old) also determine who is most affected by stereotype threat. In terms of mediators, a unique set of mechanisms including lowered performance expectations and disrupted strategy use help explain how stereotype threat decreases memory performance in older adults. Initial work on interventions to combat the negative effects of aging stereotypes has shown some promising results with respect to intergenerational contact and exposure to positive aspects of aging. Although we have learned much about the effects of negative aging stereotypes on older adults, further research is required to determine the breadth of stereotype threat effects across domains, pinpoint which mechanisms best account for these effects, and test the efficacy of a wider variety of interventions.

Keywords: Stereotype threat, elderly, aging, memory, cognitive decline

> Of all the self-fulfilling prophecies in our culture, the assumption that aging means decline and poor health is probably the deadliest.
> MARILYN FERGUSON, *The Aquarian Conspiracy*, 1980

Negative views of aging can be particularly damaging, as they not only influence today's older adults, but can also affect the outlook of younger generations as they age. Indeed, the fact that most individuals will one day be old themselves makes understanding the impact of age stereotypes particularly important. In the United States, the proportion of the population aged 65 and over is expected to increase from 13% in 2010 to 20% by 2050 (United States Census Bureau, 2008). A similar trend is projected for Canada, where an increase of people aged 65 and older from 13% in 2006 to 23% in 2031 is expected (Statistics Canada, 2006). In addition to the projection that the number of older adults will double over the next 30 to 40 years in both countries, it is also expected that the number of older workers will rise (Statistics Canada, 2006). The increasing numbers of older adults who are working beyond the traditional retirement age are vulnerable to the deleterious effects of negative aging stereotypes in the workplace as well as in other spheres of life (e.g., health care). Thus, learning more about how age stereotypes affect today's seniors in a variety of settings is imperative for improving conditions for them as well as for future generations of elderly people. In this chapter, we will examine the influence of age stereotypes on older adults, particularly with respect to physical and cognitive health. We draw on literature from both the fields of social psychology and gerontology to better understand the content of aging stereotypes and how exposure to these stereotypes affects seniors' function in everyday life.

■ THE CONTENT OF AGE STEREOTYPES

Compared to stereotypes about other groups, one unique aspect of age stereotypes is the relatively normative and institutionalized existence of negative attitudes toward aging and older adults in general (for reviews see Pasupathi & Lockenhoff, 2002; Wilkinson & Ferraro, 2002). Although racism and sexism are widely considered unacceptable, ageism is ubiquitous and readily accepted by young and old individuals alike. Indeed, ageism can be found within our language and literature (Coupland & Coupland, 1993; Ryan, Hamilton, & Kwong See, 1994), humor (Dillon & Jones, 1981), music (Cohen & Kruschwitz, 1990), and television and advertising (Robinson & Skill, 1995). Unlike members of other devalued groups, furthermore, older adults are as likely to endorse age stereotypes as are younger age groups (Levy, 2003).

According to the Stereotype Content Model (SCM; Fiske, Cuddy, Glick, & Xu, 2002), a stereotyped group may be described as either warm or cold, and either competent or incompetent. Research on the perception of older adults reveals that aging stereotypes are mixed, describing older adults as warm but incompetent, reflecting the simultaneous existence of both positive and negative perceptions (Cuddy, Norton, & Fiske, 2005; Fiske et al., 2002; Hummert, Garstka, Shaner, & Strahm, 1994).

Kite and her colleagues conducted a meta-analytic review of North American research on attitudes toward younger and older adults (Kite, Stockdale, Whitley, & Johnson, 2005; for an earlier review, see Kite & Johnson, 1988). Across 232 effect sizes from 131 articles, the review analyzed how older adults are evaluated differently from younger adults in five categories: age stereotype (e.g., old-fashioned, talks a lot about the past), attractiveness (e.g., pretty, wrinkled), competence (e.g., intelligent, good memory), behavior (e.g., willingness to interact with, make a phone call to), and evaluation (e.g., generous, friendly). Across all of these categories, older adults were consistently judged more negatively than younger adults. Thus, a great deal of evidence shows the pervasive nature of negative perceptions of seniors, often including potentially damaging views of their cognitive abilities. It is not surprising, then, that adults of all ages expect memory to decline with age (e.g., Lineweaver & Hertzog, 1998; Lineweaver, Berger, & Hertzog, 2009; Ryan, 1992; Ryan & Kwong See, 1993), and that these negative expectations may act as self-fulfilling prophecies for cognitive performance. Future examinations of ethnic and cultural variability in the content and experience of age-based stereotypes are necessary to gain an understanding of these phenomena across cultures and ethnic groups.

In the following sections, we discuss how age stereotypes influence older adults in terms of their physical and cognitive function. We focus on how older adults are affected by their own views of aging, as well as how stereotype threat regarding aging and memory influences seniors' cognitive performance. Finally, we examine the efficacy of different techniques that have been used to help older adults combat the effects of negative aging stereotypes.

■ AGE STEREOTYPES AS INTERNALIZED VIEWS OF AGING

As noted earlier, age stereotypes are distinct from stereotypes applied to other groups. For example, unlike race and gender stereotypes, individuals acquire generalized beliefs about aging long before they join the older adult group. This notion is critical to understanding why age stereotypes affect seniors differently from how stereotypes affect members of other devalued groups. Some people, like women and racial minorities, live their entire lives as members of stigmatized groups and, unlike older adults, possess a lifetime of experience challenging the stereotypes by which they are targeted. During youth, however, all individuals are exposed to elderly stereotypes that do not currently apply to them and, as a result, tend to accept these stereotypes as valid. Furthermore, individuals continue to accept the truth of these stereotypes as they age (Levy, Slade, Kunkel, & Kasl, 2002). Researchers have argued, therefore, that stereotypes about aging affect the self through a process of *internalization*, in which older adults endorse stereotypical views of aging (e.g., beliefs about health and function in old age; Levy, 2003). As a result, older adults may experience stereotype threat very differently than do women and racial minorities. Whereas gender- and race-based stereotype threat involves worrying about confirming stereotypes that targets recognize as false, targets of age-based stereotype threat worry about confirming stereotypes that they believe to be true, making them particularly vulnerable to self-concept threats (see Shapiro, 2011, Chapter 5, this volume). According to Shapiro and Neuberg (2007), self-concept threat affects individuals who worry that their behavior will confirm that the negative group stereotypes are true of the self. Subsequently, a large portion of the aging stereotypes literature has been devoted to understanding how internalized views of aging affect older adults.

How Are Older Adults Affected by Internalized Negative Age Stereotypes?

Levy and her colleagues have examined this question extensively by exposing older adults to words related to aging stereotypes (see Levy, 1996). Older adults subliminally primed with negative age stereotypes have shown elevated cardiovascular responses to stress (Levy, Hausdorff, Hencke, & Wei, 2000; Levy et al., 2008), impaired physical balance (Levy & Leifheit-Limson, 2009), decrements in memory performance (Levy, 1996; Levy & Leifheit-Limson, 2009), and shaky, sloppy handwriting (Levy, 2000). In another study, Levy, Slade, and Gill (2006a) measured explicit age stereotypes by asking elderly individuals what words or phrases they associate with older adults in general. Elderly people who held mostly negative stereotypic views about aging experienced more hearing decline than others in their age group. Thus, across a variety of outcomes, both physical and cognitive, researchers have found that exposure to negative aging stereotypes, whether implicit or explicit, has a detrimental impact on older adults.

■ STEREOTYPE THREAT AND AGING

Given the insidious effects of aging stereotypes for older adults who are subliminally exposed to them, it is likely that other situations that activate aging stereotypes might also impact elderly people. One specific way in which targets of stereotypes can be negatively affected by stereotyping is through stereotype threat (Steele & Aronson, 1995). Stereotype threat occurs when concerns about fulfilling a negative stereotype about one's group disrupt performance on tasks related to the stereotype, and it has been shown to affect members of a variety of stereotyped groups, including older adults (e.g., Chasteen, Bhattacharyya, Horhota, Tam, & Hasher, 2005; Hess, Auman, Colcombe, & Rahhal, 2003; Rahhal, Hasher, & Colcombe, 2001). To date, all of the work examining stereotype threat among older adults has focussed on consequences for memory or other cognitive processes. For example, poor memory performance has been found among older adults exposed to instructions emphasizing the memory component of a task compared to those for whom memory is not emphasized (Chasteen et al., 2005; Rahhal et al., 2001). Similarly, older adults exposed to an article discussing the finding that older adults' memory skills are worse than those of young adults performed worse on a recall memory task than did older adults exposed to an article espousing more positive views about aging and memory (Hess et al., 2003). In what follows, we discuss a variety of variables that help to explain the negative consequences of stereotype threat for older adults' cognitive performance.

How Does Stereotype Threat Interfere with Older Adults' Cognitive Performance?

Researchers have examined a number of different variables as possible mediators of age-based stereotype threat effects. Thus far, three mediators have been identified: the degree to which an individual perceives stereotype threat, disruptions in strategy use, and memory performance expectations.

Given that experiencing stereotype threat leads to cognitive decrements, the effects should be most pronounced for those who perceive threat most strongly. Indeed, the degree to which individuals perceive stereotype threat mediates the relationship between age and performance on both recall and recognition memory tasks (Chasteen et al., 2005). Older adults tend to perceive more age-related stereotype threat than do younger adults, and this explains their comparatively poor performance on memory tasks. A recently developed scale, the Age-Based Rejection Sensitivity Questionnaire, shows promise in identifying older adults who will be most likely to perceive stereotype threat (Kang & Chasteen, 2009a). Rejection sensitivity describes the degree to which individuals anxiously expect, readily perceive, and intensely react to situations in which stigma-based rejection is possible (e.g., Downey & Feldman, 1996; Mendoza-Denton, Downey, Purdie, Davis, & Pietrzak, 2002). Those identified by the scale as sensitive to rejection should be most likely to perceive, and therefore be affected by, stereotype threat in a given situation. In this way, perceived threat can both mediate and moderate the stereotype threat effect. More specifically, those who are more prone to perceive threat are more likely to be susceptible to its effects and, further, the attentional and emotional consequences of perceiving threat go on to contribute to the mechanisms underlying stereotype threat (see Schmader & Beilock, 2011, Chapter 3, this volume).

In addition to perceived stereotype threat, disrupted strategy use has been proposed as a mechanism underlying age-based stereotype threat effects. In one study (Hess et al., 2003), young and old participants completed a memory task under varying levels of stereotype threat. As expected, younger adults outperformed older adults on a 30-word free-recall task. Interestingly, the researchers also examined the degree to which semantically related words were recalled together, a strategy referred to as *clustering*. Analyses revealed that 58% of the variance associated with stereotype threat–related decline in recall was explained by decreases in clustering among those who experienced stereotype threat. These results are supported by another study showing that middle-aged and older adults who perceived greater control over their cognitive functioning were more likely to use the clustering strategy and therefore showed better performance on the recall task (Lachman & Andreoletti, 2006). Although this latter study did not measure the effects of stereotype threat, per se, it provides additional evidence that memory decrements among older adults may be explained, at least in part, by decreased use of a clustering or similar strategy during cognitive tasks.

Finally, researchers have identified performance expectations as a mechanism underlying age-related stereotype threat effects. Previous research has shown that older adults expect to perform worse than young adults on cognitive tasks (Berry & West, 1993; Cavanaugh, 1996), and researchers hypothesized that these low performance expectations might explain older adults' reduced cognitive performance under threat. For example, one study asked young and old participants to evaluate how they expected to perform on each of three memory tests (Desrichard & Köpetz, 2005, Study 2). Among older participants, emphasizing the memory-related aspects of the task led to performance decrements. This deficit was mediated by lowered task performance expectations. Essentially, when older adults were faced with task instructions emphasizing memory performance, their performance expectations decreased, thereby decreasing their actual performance on the memory task. Performance expectations were also found to explain the relationship between stereotype threat and decreased memory performance among older adults in an examination of a variety of possible mediators and moderators of the effect (Hess, Hinson, & Hodges, 2009).

It is important to note commonalities and distinctions between age-related stereotype threat and other types of stereotype threat in terms of mediators. For example, lowered performance expectations have also been found to mediate gender-related stereotype threat among women completing tasks involving spatial perception (Stangor, Carr, & Kiang, 1998) and negotiation (Kray, Galinsky, & Thompson, 2002). Although strategy use has not been examined directly with other groups, research has implicated reduced effort (less time spent practicing, for example) as an underlying cause of race-based stereotype threat (Stone, 2002; but see also Jamieson & Harkins, 2007 and Oswald & Harvey, 2000–2001). Practicing, of course, is an excellent strategy for anyone looking to improve their performance in a particular domain, so it is perhaps not surprising that this mechanism may be shared across groups who are targeted by stereotype threat.

On the other hand, age-related stereotype threat also seems to differ from race- or gender-based stereotype threat with regard to mediation by negative affect or working memory. Evidence from examinations of other types of stereotype threat points to decreased working memory capacity (e.g., Beilock, Rydell, & McConnell, 2007; Schmader & Johns, 2003; Schmader, Johns, & Forbes, 2008) and negative affect (e.g., Cadinu, Maass, Rosabianca, & Kiesner, 2005; Keller & Dauenheimer, 2003; Krendl, Richeson, Kelley, & Heatherton, 2008) as mechanisms of the effect. In contrast, a recent examination testing mediation by negative affect and working memory suggests that the same mechanisms do not seem to play a role in age-based stereotype threat (Hess et al., 2009), instead implicating performance expectations as a main mediating factor. Although further examinations are necessary to clarify this effect (it is of course unlikely that negative affect and working memory have *no* contribution to age-based stereotype threat), this preliminary evidence highlights the importance of expectations for the experience of age-based stigma. Given that age stereotypes seem to be more internalized than other types of stereotypes, expectations regarding aging and cognitive and physical performance in old age are likely to have an especially strong effect. Further examinations of the mediation of age-based stereotype threat should focus on identifying situations in which emotions and working memory may play a role.

Who Is Most Susceptible to Age-Based Stereotype-Threat?

Researchers examining age-based stereotype threat have also investigated risk factors that can increase one's vulnerability to threat effects. For example, researchers have shown that older adults can be differentially affected by stereotype threat based on the degree to which they value the memory domain (e.g., Hess et al., 2003). Intuitively, it seems reasonable that negative stereotypes would only affect an individual if that individual cares about the stereotyped domain, or, at least cares about being viewed as incompetent in that domain. Hess and his colleagues show that stereotype threat in the domain of memory is more disruptive for older adults who value their memory ability more highly than for those who do not value memory achievement as much.

Other research has shown that stereotype threat effects can be moderated by identification with the stereotyped group. Similar to research on gender-related stereotype threat (e.g., Pronin, Steele, & Ross, 2004; Schmader, 2002), older adults who are more identified with the older adult group as a whole are more affected by negatives stereotypes about older adults and memory ability (Kang & Chasteen, 2009b). This same study (Kang & Chasteen, 2009b) also showed moderation by state (situational) and trait (dispositional) perceived stereotype threat, such that those who perceived greater levels of stereotype threat in the current experimental situation and in general were more negatively affected by stereotype threat. Of course, those who perceive stereotype threat in a situation likely do so because stereotypes have become activated in their minds (Steele & Aronson, 1995). Others have treated stereotype activation as a moderator and have found that it moderates age-related stereotype threat effects (Hess et al., 2003).

Another interesting moderator of age-based stereotype threat is age itself. Stereotype threat appears to exert stronger effects among "young-old" (age 60–70 years) compared to "old-old" (age 71–82 years) adults (Hess, Hinson, & Hodges, 2009), presumably because old-old adults have had more time to transition to the older adult category and are no longer as threatened by comparisons to middle-aged or young adults. Also of note, middle-aged adults (~40–60 years old) have been shown to perform *better* when reminded about stereotypes linking old age with decreased memory ability (Hess & Hinson, 2006). This stereotype lift effect (Walton & Cohen, 2003) is thought to occur due to middle-aged adults making downward social comparisons to older adults, thereby enabling them to enjoy the associated performance benefits.

Finally, memory self-efficacy (Desrichard & Köpetz, 2005, Study 1) and task demands (Hess, Emery, & Queen, 2009) have been shown to moderate age-related stereotype threat effects. The moderation by memory self-efficacy is such that those with low memory self-efficacy are more negatively impacted by stereotype threat, presumably because these individuals have lower performance expectations (Desrichard & Köpetz, 2005, Study 2).

Thus far, the moderators we have discussed have been situated within the individual; task demands represent a moderator situated outside of the individual. An examination of task demands shows that older adults are negatively impacted by stereotype threat only when task demands are high, but not when task demands are low (Hess, Emery, & Queen, 2009). Specifically, when forced to respond to a recognition memory test within a certain time frame (high task demand), older adults in a threat condition performed worse than those in a nonthreat condition; this same threat-based underperformance effect was not found when responses did not have to be made within a limited time frame (low task demand). Thus, as with other types of stereotype threat, a number of factors have been identified that help us to predict who will be more or less vulnerable to the consequences of exposure to negative age stereotypes.

Policy Box

It is expected that the number of people aged 65 and older in North America will double over the next few decades. With such a dramatic change in age distribution forthcoming, it is imperative to begin work on finding ways to improve the cognitive and physical function of both today's and tomorrow's seniors. Research has already begun to determine how negative aging stereotypes affect older adults, with many studies demonstrating that exposure to negative aging stereotypes decreases both cognitive and physical health. In particular, research on the effects of stereotype threat has found that older adults experience a decline in a variety of types of memory when in threatening situations. Given the prevalence of negative aging stereotypes in North America, developing interventions to assist older adults with combating the consequences of these negative stereotypes is particularly important. Teaching seniors about stereotype threat, for example, could prove effective. It is equally important to find ways to prevent the internalization of negative aging stereotypes in younger generations, so that they are less vulnerable to these stereotypes when they themselves grow old. Positive intergenerational contact may help to challenge negative aging stereotypes and thus inoculate younger age groups against these stereotypes, as well as reduce anxiety in older people. By testing the efficacy of different intervention techniques, policies can be developed to help ensure that current and future generations of older adults maintain active, independent, and healthy lifestyles for as long as possible.

■ INTERVENTIONS: REDUCING THE EFFECTS OF NEGATIVE AGE STEREOTYPES ON OLDER ADULTS

As the mechanisms and moderators of stereotype threat among older adults become better understood, researchers will likely turn their attention toward developing interventions to reduce the impact of negative age stereotypes for this group. Abrams and his colleagues (Abrams, Eller, & Bryant, 2006; Abrams et al., 2008) are at the forefront of this movement, and have identified positive intergenerational contact as one possible intervention to inoculate older adults against stereotype threat effects. Promisingly, positive intergenerational contact reduces vulnerability to stereotype threat, whether this contact is real (Abrams et al., 2006; Abrams et al., 2008, Study 1) or imagined (Abrams et al., 2008, Study 2). The inoculating effects of intergenerational contact appear to be mediated by reduced anxiety, suggesting that future intervention attempts aimed at reducing performance-related anxiety should also be successful.

Earlier in the chapter, we discussed the ubiquity of aging stereotypes on television and in advertising. This fact can be particularly harmful for older adults, who often use television as a replacement for reduced social contact (Graney, 1974; Rubin, 1986). Indeed, older adults with more lifetime television exposure report the highest level of negative age stereotypes (Donlon, Ashman, & Levy, 2005). To make older adults more aware of the negative and infrequent portrayal of elders on television programming, an intervention study instructed older adults to keep a viewing diary outlining how older characters were presented on television each day of the week (Donlon et al., 2005). The results of this study show that keeping a viewing diary increased both the awareness of infrequent and negative portrayals of older adults on television and the intention to decrease future television viewing. Increasing individuals' awareness of domains in which their group is negatively stereotyped allows (and apparently motivates) individuals to avoid these domains in the future, likely decreasing the impact of these negative stereotypes and, consequently, stereotype threat.

Finding ways to help seniors focus on more positive aspects of aging may be another promising route to improving their physical and cognitive health. Research has shown that, just as negative stereotypes operate to the detriment of older adults' health and functioning, positive aging stereotypes beneficially impact the behaviors and self-concepts of the elderly. Older adults primed with positive age stereotypes show reduced cardiovascular responses to stress (Levy et al., 2000, 2008), improved balance (Levy & Leifheit-Limson, 2009), and superior memory performance (Levy, 1996; Levy & Leifheit-Limson, 2009). Research has also shown that, compared to individuals with more negative self-stereotypes, older adults with positive self-stereotypes and self-perceptions of aging demonstrate faster recovery following a life-threatening event (Levy, Slade, May, & Caracciolo, 2006b), better functional health (Levy, Slade, & Kasl, 2002a), and an increased tendency to engage in preventive health behaviors (Levy & Myers, 2004). Incredibly, other studies have revealed that older adults who viewed their own aging in a positive light lived, on average, 7.5 years longer (Levy et al., 2002b) and were less likely to die of respiratory causes (Levy & Myers, 2005) than did individuals with negative self-views. The power of positive aging expectations is particularly impressive when compared to the longevity increases afforded by exercise (3.5 years; Franco et al., 2005), a more commonly recognized and encouraged health behavior. These data provide compelling evidence that helping older adults embrace a more positive view of aging can have tremendously beneficial results.

■ CONCLUSION

Age stereotypes are widespread, and although they contain some positive elements, they are primarily negative. Because adults of all ages apply these stereotypes, it is likely that age stereotypes become internalized at an early age, only to negatively impact individuals when they themselves grow old. These negative views of aging can operate either explicitly or implicitly, affecting both physical and cognitive health. Thus, it is not surprising that, like many other negatively stereotyped groups, older adults also experience stereotype threat. In the case of older adults, stereotype threat effects have mostly been observed in the domain of memory. However, a set of mechanisms that is different from those identified with other groups has been found regarding stereotype threat, aging, and memory. Both decreased performance expectations and disrupted strategy use help account for how stereotype threat decreases memory performance in older adults. Similar to stereotype threat with other groups, however, both domain identification and group identification moderate those effects. In addition, task demands, memory self-efficacy, and age (young-old vs. old-old) also determine who is most affected by stereotype threat. Last, some initial work on interventions to combat the effects of negative aging stereotypes has shown some promising results with respect to intergenerational contact and exposure to positive aspects of aging.

■ FUTURE DIRECTIONS

Despite this initial work examining the effects of negative aging stereotypes on older adults, many issues remain unexplored. First, more research is needed to examine the breadth of stereotype threat effects in older adults. Although it has been well established that exposing older adults to negative age stereotypes affects a variety of physical and cognitive health indicators, only the domain of memory has received a great deal of attention in examinations of stereotype threat and aging. An obvious course for future research is to determine in what other domains we would observe stereotype threat effects in older adults. For example, paralleling the work by Levy and colleagues, might we see consequences in the domain of physical health, such as performance on a vision or hearing test? These types of tests have important implications for older adults, such as for keeping a driver's license. Similarly, would stereotype threat regarding aging and physical frailty lead older adults to be less willing to exercise or do weight training, both of which have been shown to be beneficial to physical and cognitive health (Hillman, Erickson, & Kramer, 2008)?

As well, much more work needs to be done to understand *how* stereotype threat affects older adults. Shapiro (2011, Chapter 5, this volume) has indicated a number of conditions that will or will not elicit threat effects, and many of those parameters need to be tested with seniors. Other potential mediators also require further testing, such as affect and working memory, to more fully determine whether mechanisms observed with other groups operate with older adults.

Last, a variety of interventions have been examined to determine their efficacy in reducing or preventing stereotype threat in other groups (Cohen, Purdie-Vaughns, & Garcia, 2011, Chapter 18, this volume). At present it remains to be seen whether those techniques would be effective in older adults. This last step is particularly crucial, with the proportion of adults aged 65 or older projected to double over the next few decades in North America. More must be done now to help ensure that our current and future older adults function to the best of their abilities, free from the negative effects of age stereotypes.

References

Abrams, D., Crisp, R. J., Marques, S., Fagg, E., Bedford, L., & Provias, D. (2008). Threat inoculation: Experienced and imagined intergenerational contact prevent stereotype threat effects on older people's math performance. *Psychology and Aging, 23,* 934–939.

Abrams, D., Eller, A., & Bryant, J. (2006). An age apart: The effects of intergenerational contact and stereotype threat on performance and intergroup bias. *Psychology and Aging, 21,* 691–702.

Beilock, S. L., Rydell, R. J., & McConnell, A. R. (2007). Stereotype threat and working memory: Mechanisms, alleviations, and spillover. *Journal of Experimental Psychology: General, 136,* 256–276.

Berry, J. M., & West, R. L. (1993). Cognitive self-efficacy in relation to personal mastery and goal setting across the life span. In E. M. Lachman (Ed.), *Planning and control processes across the life span* (pp. 351–379). London: Lawrence Erlbaum Associates.

Cadinu, M., Maass, A., Rosabianca, A., & Kiesner, J. (2005). Why do women underperform under stereotype threat? *Psychological Science, 16,* 572–578.

Cavanaugh, J. C. (1996). Memory self-efficacy as a moderator of memory change. In F. Blanchard-Fields, & T. M. Hess (Eds.), *Perspectives on cognitive change in adulthood and aging* (pp. 488–507). New York: McGraw-Hill.

Chasteen, A. L., Bhattacharyya, S., Horhota, M., Tam, R., & Hasher, L. (2005). How feelings of stereotype threat influence older adults' memory performance. *Experimental Aging Research, 31,* 235–260.

Cohen, E. S., & Kruschwitz, A. (1990). Old age in America represented in 19th and 20th century sheet music. *The Gerontologist, 30,* 345–354.

Cohen, G. L., Purdie-Vaughns, V., & Garcia, J. (2011). An identity threat perspective on intervention. In M. Inzlicht, & T. Schmader (Eds.), *Stereotype threat: Theory, process, and application.* New York: Oxford University Press.

Coupland, M., & Coupland, J. (1993). Discourses of ageism and anti-ageism. *Journal of Aging Studies, 7,* 279–301.

Cuddy, A. J. C., Norton, M. I., & Fiske, S. T. (2005). This old stereotype: The pervasiveness and persistence of the elderly stereotype. *Journal of Social Issues, 61,* 267–285.

Desrichard, O., & Köpetz, C. (2005). A threat in the elder: The impact of task-instructions, self-efficacy and performance expectations on memory performance in the elderly. *European Journal of Social Psychology, 35*(4), 537–552.

Dillon, K., & Jones, R. (1981). Attitudes toward aging portrayed by birthday cards. *International Journal of Aging and Human Development, 13,* 79–84.

Donlon, M. M., Ashman, O., & Levy, B. R. (2005). Re-vision of older television characters: A stereotype-awareness intervention. *Journal of Social Issues, 61*, 307–319.

Downey, G., & Feldman, S. (1996). Implications of rejection sensitivity for intimate relationships. *Journal of Personality and Social Psychology, 70*, 1327–1343.

Ferguson, M. (1980). *The Aquarian conspiracy: Personal and social transformation in the 1980s.* Los Angeles: J. P. Tarcher.

Fiske, S. T., Cuddy, A. C., Glick, P., & Xu, J. (2002). A model of (often mixed) stereotype content: Competence and warmth respectively follow from status and competition. *Journal of Personality and Social Psychology, 82*, 878–902.

Franco, O. H., de Laet, C., Peeters, A., Jonker, J., Mackenbach, J., & Nusselder, W. (2005). Effects of physical activity on life expectancy with cardiovascular disease. *Archives of Internal Medicine, 165*, 2355–2360.

Graney, M. J. (1974). Media use as a substitute activity in old age. *Journal of Gerontology, 29*, 322–324.

Hess, T. M., Auman, C., Colcombe, S. J., & Rahhal, T. A. (2003). The impact of stereotype threat on age differences in memory performance. *Journals of Gerontology: Series B: Psychological Sciences & Social Sciences, 58B*, 3–11.

Hess, T. M., Emery, L. J., & Queen, T. L. (2009). Task demands moderate stereotype threat effects on memory performance. *Journal of Gerontology Series B: Psychological Sciences, 64*, 482–486.

Hess, T. M., & Hinson, J. (2006). Age-related variation in the influences of aging stereotypes on memory in adulthood. *Psychology and Aging, 21*, 621–625.

Hess, T. M., Hinson, J., & Hodges, E. (2009). Moderators of and mechanisms underlying stereotype threat effects on older adults' memory performance. *Experimental Aging Research, 35*, 153–177.

Hillman, C. H., Erickson, K., & Kramer, A. F. (2008). Be smart, exercise your heart: Exercise effects on brain and cognition. *Nature Reviews Neuroscience, 9*, 58–65.

Hummert, M. L., Garstka, T. A., Shaner, J. L., & Strahm, S. (1994). Stereotypes of the elderly held by young, middle-aged and elderly adults. *Journal of Gerontology: Psychological Sciences, 49*, 240–249.

Jamieson, J. P., & Harkins, S. G. (2007). Mere effort and stereotype threat performance effects. *Journal of Personality and Social Psychology, 93*, 544–564.

Kang, S. K., & Chasteen, A. L. (2009a). The development and validation of the age-based rejection sensitivity questionnaire. *The Gerontologist, 49*, 303–316.

Kang, S. K., & Chasteen, A. L. (2009b). The moderating role of age-group identification and perceived threat on stereotype threat among older adults. *International Journal of Aging and Human Development, 69*, 201–220.

Keller, J., & Dauenheimer, D. (2003). Stereotype threat in the classroom: Dejection mediates the disrupting threat effect on women's math performance. *Personality and Social Psychology Bulletin, 29*, 371–381.

Kite, M. E., & Johnson, B. T. (1988). Attitudes toward older and younger adults: A meta-analysis. *Psychology and Aging, 3*, 233–244.

Kite, M. E., Stockdale, G. D., Whitley, B. E., & Johnson, B. T. (2005). Attitudes toward younger and older adults: An updated meta-analytic review. *Journal of Social Issues, 61*, 241–266.

Kray, L. J., Galinsky, A. D., & Thompson, L. (2002). Reversing the gender gap in negotiations: An exploration of stereotype regeneration. *Organizational Behavior and Human Decision Processes, 87*, 386–409.

Krendl, A. C., Richeson, J. A., Kelley, W. M., & Heatherton, T. F. (2008). The negative consequences of threat: A functional magnetic resonance imaging investigation of the neural mechanisms underlying women's underperformance in math. *Psychological Science, 19,* 168–175.

Lachman, M. E., & Andreoletti, C. (2006). Strategy use mediates the relationship between control beliefs and memory performance for middle-aged and older adults. *Journals of Gerontology Series B: Psychological Sciences and Social Sciences, 61,* 88–94.

Levy, B. (2000). Handwriting as a reflection of aging self-stereotypes. *Journal of Geriatric Psychiatry, 33,* 81–94.

Levy, B. R. (1996). Improving memory in old age by implicit self-stereotyping. *Journal of Personality and Social Psychology, 71,* 1092–1107.

Levy, B. R. (2003). Mind matters: Cognitive and physical effects of aging self-stereotypes. *Journal of Gerontology: Psychological Sciences, 58B,* 203–211.

Levy, B. R., Hausdorff, J. M., Hencke, R., & Wei, J. Y. (2000). Reducing cardiovascular stress with positive self-stereotypes of aging. *Journals of Gerontology: Psychological Sciences, 55,* 205–213.

Levy, B. R., & Leifheit-Limson, E. (2009). The stereotype-matching effect: Greater influence on functioning when age stereotypes correspond to outcomes. *Psychology and Aging, 24,* 230–233.

Levy, B. R., & Myers, L. (2004). Preventive health behaviors influenced by self-perceptions of aging. *Preventive Medicine, 39,* 625–629.

Levy, B. R., & Myers, L. (2005). Relationship between respiratory mortality and self-perceptions of aging. *Psychology & Health, 20,* 553–564.

Levy, B. R., Ryall, A. L., Pilver, C. E., Sheridan, P. L., Wei, J. Y., & Hausdorff, J. M. (2008). Influence of African American elders' age stereotypes on their cardiovascular response to stress. *Anxiety, Stress, and Coping, 21,* 85–93.

Levy, B. R., Slade, M. D., & Gill, T. M. (2006a). Hearing decline predicted by elders' stereotypes. *Journals of Gerontology: Psychological Sciences, 61,* 82–87.

Levy, B. R., Slade, M. D., May, J., & Caracciolo, E. A. (2006b). Physical recovery after acute myocardial infarction: Positive age self-stereotypes as a resource. *The International Journal of Aging and Human Development, 62,* 285–301.

Levy, B. R., Slade, M. D., & Kasl, S. (2002a). Longitudinal benefit of positive self-perceptions of aging on functional health. *Journals of Gerontology Series B: Psychological Sciences and Social Sciences, 57,* 409–417.

Levy, B. R., Slade, M. D., Kunkel, S. R., & Kasl, S. V. (2002b). Longevity increased by positive self-perceptions of aging. *Journal of Personality and Social Psychology, 83,* 261–270.

Lineweaver, T. T., Berger, A. K., & Hertzog, C. (2009). Expectations about memory change are impacted by aging stereotypes. *Psychology and Aging, 24,* 169–176.

Lineweaver, T. T., & Hertzog, C. (1998). Adults' efficacy and control beliefs regarding memory and aging: Separating general from personal beliefs. *Aging, Neuropsychology, and Cognition, 5,* 264–296.

Mendoza-Denton, R., Downey, G., Purdie, V. J., Davis, A., & Pietrzak, J. (2002). Sensitivity to status-based rejection: Implications for African American students' college experience. *Journal of Experimental Social Psychology, 83,* 896–918.

Oswald, D. L., & Harvey, R. D. (2000–2001). Hostile environments, stereotype threat, and math performance among undergraduate women. *Current Psychology: Developmental, Learning, Personality, Social, 19,* 338–356.

Pasupathi, M., & Lockenhoff, C. (2002). Ageist behavior. In T. D. Nelson (Ed.), *Ageism: Stereotyping and prejudice against older persons* (pp. 201–246). Cambridge, MA: MIT Press.

Pronin, E., Steele, C. M., & Ross, L. (2004). Identity bifurcation in response to stereotype threat: Women and mathematics. *Journal of Experimental Social Psychology, 40,* 152–168.

Rahhal, T. A., Hasher, L., & Colcombe, S. J. (2001). Instructional manipulations and age differences in memory: Now you see them; now you don't. *Psychology and Aging, 16,* 697–706.

Robinson, J., & Skill, T. (1995). The invisible generation: Portrayals of the elderly on prime-time television. *Communication Reports, 8,* 111–119.

Rubin, A. M. (1986). Television, aging, and information seeking. *Language & Communication, 6,* 125–137.

Ryan, E. B. (1992). Beliefs about memory changes across the adult lifespan. *Journals of Gerontology, Series B: Psychological and Social Sciences, 47,* P41–P46.

Ryan, E. B., Hamilton, J. M., & Kwong See, S. (1994). Patronizing the old: How do younger and older adults respond to baby talk in the nursing home? *International Journal of Aging and Human Development, 39,* 21–32.

Ryan, E. B., & Kwong See, S. (1993). Age-based beliefs about memory changes for self and others across adulthood. *Journals of Gerontology, Series B: Psychological and Social Sciences, 48,* P199–P201.

Schmader, T. (2002). Gender identification moderates stereotype threat effects on women's math performance. *Journal of Experimental Social Psychology, 38,* 194–201.

Schmader, T., & Beilock, S. (2011). An integration of processes that underlie stereotype threat. In M. Inzlicht, & T. Schmader (Eds.), *Stereotype threat: Theory, process, and application.* New York: Oxford University Press.

Schmader, T., & Johns, M. (2003). Converging evidence that stereotype threat reduces working memory capacity. *Journal of Personality and Social Psychology, 85,* 440–452.

Schmader, T., Johns, M., & Forbes, C. (2008). An integrated process model of stereotype threat effects on performance. *Psychological Review, 115,* 336–356.

Shapiro, J. (2011). Types of threats: From stereotype threat to stereotype threats. In M. Inzlicht, & T. Schmader (Eds.), *Stereotype threat: Theory, process, and application.* New York: Oxford University Press.

Shapiro, J. R., & Neuberg, S. L. (2007). From stereotype threat to stereotype threats: Implications of a multi-threat framework for causes, moderators, mediators, consequences, and interventions. *Personality and Social Psychology Review, 11,* 107–130.

Stangor, C., Carr, C., & Kiang, L. (1998). Activating stereotypes undermines task performance expectations. *Journal of Personality and Social Psychology, 75,* 1191–1197.

Statistics Canada. (2006). *Projected population by age group and sex according to a medium growth scenario for 1006, 2011, 2016, 2021, 2026, and 2031.* Retrieved August 19, 2009 from http://www40.statcan.ca/101/cst01/demo23c-eng.htm

Steele, C. M., & Aronson, J. (1995). Stereotype threat and the intellectual test performance of African Americans. *Journal of Personality and Social Psychology, 69,* 797–811.

Stone, J. (2002). Battling doubt by avoiding practice: The effect of stereotype threat on self-handicapping in white athletes. *Personality and Social Psychology Bulletin, 28,* 1667–1678.

U.S. Census Bureau, Population Division. (2008, August 14). *Table 3. Percent distribution of the projected population by selected age groups and sex for the United States: 2010 to 2050* (NP2008-T3). Washington, DC: Author. Retrieved August 18, 2009, from http://www.census.gov/population/www/projections/2008projections.html

Walton, G. M., & Cohen, G. L. (2003). Stereotype lift. *Journal of Experimental Social Psychology, 39,* 456–467.

Wilkinson, J. A., & Ferraro, K. F. (2002). Thirty years of ageism research. In T. D. Nelson (Ed.), *Ageism: Stereotyping and prejudice against older persons* (pp. 338–358). Cambridge, MA: MIT Press.

14 The Impact of Stereotype Threat on Performance in Sports

■ JEFF STONE, AINA CHALABAEV, AND C. KEITH HARRISON

This chapter examines the role of stereotype threat in creating racial and gender differences in sports performance. During the last decade, scholars, journalists, and athletes relied on bioevolutionary or sociological factors to explain racial and gender differences in athletic competition. The contemporary research in this review shows that negative stereotypes tied to race and gender can also produce differences in the way athletes prepare for and perform in sports. Carefully controlled studies reveal that people hold both positive and negative racial and gender stereotypes about athletes, and that when the negative stereotypes are brought to mind in a sports performance context, they create the burden of stereotype threat that robs athletes of their potential. Both blatant and subtle reminders of a negative stereotype can sabotage athletic performance, and ironically, the athletes most susceptible to the negative impact of stereotype threat are those who are the most psychologically invested in their sport. The available evidence suggests that the threat of confirming a negative stereotype in a sports context causes athletes to focus on avoiding failure, which weakens performance because it interrupts proceduralized sensorimotor responses and impairs working memory capacity. Finally, whereas in the long run it may be possible to reduce the prevalence of stereotyping in the institution of sport, the most effective short-term solution is to inoculate athletes against the debilitating influence of stereotype threat when it is brought to mind in a sports performance context.

Keywords: Stereotype threat, athletics, sports, race, gender, self-handicapping

The research on stereotype threat indicates that negative stereotypes can adversely affect the thoughts, feelings, and actions of individual group members in a wide variety of settings. Can stereotype threat also impair performance in sports? Consider this observation from Warren Moon, the first African American quarterback inducted into the National Football League Hall of Fame, about his experience playing professional football (2009):

A lot has been said about me as being the first African American quarterback into the Pro Football Hall of Fame. It's a subject that I'm very uncomfortable about sometimes only because I've always wanted to be judged as just a quarterback . . . . I only played this game not for just myself, not just for my teammates, but I always had that extra burden when I went on that field that I had a responsibility to play the game for my people. That extra burden I probably didn't need to go out on the field with, because I probably would have been a much better player if I didn't have that burden. But you know what, I carried that burden proudly.

The "burden" that Moon refers to is remarkably similar to the description of stereotype threat that echoes throughout this volume. The purpose of this chapter is to present evidence that, as implied by Moon's experience, athletic performance can be weakened by the "burden" of stereotype threat. To describe the impact of stereotype threat on athletes, we begin by reviewing the debate over racial and gender differences in sport that parallels the debate over similar group differences in academic standardized testing. We turn next to the evidence for the cultural, racial, and gender stereotypes about athletes that permeate the "air" of sport. We then present the evidence that, when brought to mind during a sports competition, negative stereotypes induce threat processes that inhibit how athletes prepare and perform. The chapter finishes with a discussion of the potential psychological mechanisms underlying threat effects in sports and how these processes can be mitigated.

■ RACIAL DIFFERENCES IN SPORTS

Differences in the sports performance of black and white athletes are well established. For example, according to the Racial and Gender Report Card (Lapchick, 2009), in 2007–2008 the National Basketball Association was made up of 20% white and 76% black athletes, the National Football League was 31% white and 66% black athletes, and Major League Baseball was 60% white and 8.2% black athletes. The Olympic games also produce racial differences in sport; for example, between 1976 and 2000, all 32 finalists in the 100-meter races were of West African descent, whereas very few athletes of African descent have ever won a medal in swimming (Entine, 2000). Historically, black athletes are over-represented at the elite levels of basketball, football, and track and field, but under-represented in baseball, golf, and tennis, compared to whites.

Like the disparities known to exist in academic testing, scholars debate the cause of racial differences in sport. The nature side of the debate focuses on biological differences that correspond with race or ethnic distinctions. Considerable evidence shows that people of African ancestry possess a distinct musculoskeletal system, metabolic structure, and other physical characteristics (e.g., Bejan, Jones & Charles, 2010; Jordan, 1969; Metheny, 1939). The critical question is how much the physical differences account for racial differences in sports performance. In one recent review, Entine (2000) concludes that black athletes have a phenotypic advantage over white athletes that creates a larger pool of potential athletes and a higher likelihood that black athletes will dominate in sports.

On the nurture side of the debate, sport sociologists argue that the racial differences in athletics are due to differences in socioeconomic status, socialization, and institutionalized discrimination (Edwards, 1972). In this view, society encourages and provides access for whites to pursue careers in multiple professional domains, whereas blacks are channeled toward sport and entertainment to achieve financial success. In impoverished black communities, playing sports is portrayed as one of the few alternatives to the violence and criminal activity that disproportionately affects those living in poverty (Edwards, 1973). Moreover, blacks have limited access to the "country club" sports like tennis, golf, and swimming, and have greater access to public facility or "playground" sports like basketball and football. Consequently, from an early age, blacks hone their skills in the sports to which they have access, and this creates the respective over- and under-representation of black athletes across sports (Coakley, 2001; Sailes, 1987).

We offer a third explanation for racial differences in sport: stereotypes and stereotype threat. Specifically, the debate over racial differences in sport has created cultural stereotypes about the attributes of black and white athletes. These beliefs help observers explain differences in the representation and performance of black and white athletes in specific sports. But the cultural stereotypes also directly impact the performance of athletes when they are communicated directly or indirectly in the performance context, such as through verbal comments and nonverbal actions made by coaches, managers, administrators, sports writers, fans, or other athletes. When linked to performance, the negative stereotypes become an extra burden that ironically, can *create* the racial differences often seen in sports.

■ RACIAL STEREOTYPES ABOUT ATHLETES

Survey and experimental research indicates that, in North America, people hold both positive and negative stereotypes about black and white athletes. People generally believe that white athletes possess low natural athletic ability but make up for their lack of athletic ability through their high intelligence and work ethic. In contrast, people generally view blacks as naturally gifted athletes who do not possess high intelligence and do not need to work hard to succeed (Sailes, 1996;). Similarly, Harrison and Lawrence (2004, 2008) report that college students attribute black athletic superiority to genetic and biological factors and white athletic inferiority to cultural factors. Thus, the stereotypes tend to reflect the public discourse regarding the nature and nurture explanations for why differences persist.

Stereotyped beliefs can also determine how people interpret athletic performance. In one study, Stone, Perry, and Darley (1997) had participants listen to a radio broadcast of a basketball game and focus on evaluating the performance of one player, described as a black male or a white male. Participants who thought that the target player was black rated him higher in athletic ability and basketball skill, but lower in intelligence and "hustle" during the game, compared to participants who thought the player was white. This and other studies indicate that people rely on their racial and gender stereotypes about athletes to interpret and evaluate athletic performance (e.g., Biernat & Vescio, 2002; Knight & Guiliano, 2001; Tuggle & Owen, 1999).

Like cultural stereotypes about the intellectual or academic abilities of blacks and the mathematical or leadership abilities of women, people hold negative stereotypes about the athletic abilities of black and white athletes. This suggests that when the negative stereotypes are brought to mind in a sports performance context, they can induce the stereotype threat processes known to impair the performance of stigmatized individuals in other domains.

▪ STEREOTYPE THREAT CAN PRODUCE RACIAL DIFFERENCES IN SPORT

The first study on the role of stereotype threat in sports examined if linking athletic performance to the negative stereotype about black athletes (i.e., low sports intelligence) and white athletes (i.e., low natural athletic ability) would cause each group to perform more poorly, compared to when positive stereotypes or neutral attributes were linked to the sports task. Stone, Lynch, Sjomeling, and Darley (1999) had black and white former high school athletes complete a golf putting task that was described as a standardized measure of sports aptitude. To manipulate stereotype threat, some participants were told that the test measured their sports intelligence (e.g., "Your ability to think strategically while playing a sport"), while others were told that the test measured their natural athletic ability. Participants in one control condition were told that the test measured "sports psychology," a stereotype-irrelevant attribute. Participants in another control condition were also told that the test measured sports psychology, but in addition, their racial identity was primed by completing a demographic measure.

The putting task was designed to resemble a 10-hole golf course. To measure their accuracy in putting, there was also a hole-apparatus with three holes that varied from large to small. Participants were told that their goal on each "hole" was to use the fewest number of strokes to stop the ball in the smallest of the three holes. The primary dependent measure was the total number of strokes participants required, and the accuracy they exhibited, over the entire task.

In support of the stereotype threat hypothesis, the results showed that (a) both black and white participants performed equally well on the putting task when it was said to measure "sports psychology," (b) white participants performed significantly worse than black participants when performance was said to measure "natural athletic ability," and (c) black participants performed significantly worse than white participants, and worse than blacks in the control condition, when performance was said to measure "sports intelligence." Thus, framing the "test" in terms of the negative racial stereotype about each group decreased their performance on the sports task.

In addition, blacks performed worse than whites, and worse than blacks in the control conditions, when their race was primed but the putting task was framed as measuring sports psychology. Similar to the findings of Steele and Aronson (1995, Experiment 4), priming race in the context of performing a "standardized test of athletic aptitude" based on a sport in which blacks are historically under-represented was sufficient to activate stereotype threat among black participants.

A second experiment extended the findings of the first in two directions. First, if anxiety over confirming the negative stereotype about their athletic ability mediated performance on the putting task, Stone and colleagues (1999) reasoned that providing white athletes with another explanation for their discomfort should reduce the impact of the negative stereotype on their performance. Thus, in the second study, some participants were told that the laboratory lights and ventilation might cause them to feel uncomfortable during the golf putting task.

Second, based on Steele's (1997) "vanguard" hypothesis, Stone and colleagues (1999) proposed that stereotype threat should primarily impact the performance of those for whom sport represents a significant measure of their self-worth. People who do not maintain their self-worth through performance in sports, in contrast, should not be threatened by the prospect of confirming a negative stereotype about their racial group. Thus, white athletes for whom sports performance is a significant aspect of their self-worth (i.e., "engaged" individuals) were compared under stereotype threat to white athletes for whom sports performance is not important to their self-worth (i.e., "disengaged" individuals).

After they completed the same golf putting task used in the first experiment, the results showed that framing the golf task as a measure of their natural athletic ability caused engaged white athletes to perform worse compared to disengaged white athletes, and compared to engaged white athletes in the neutral control condition. However, when exposed to the misattribution cue, engaged white athletes performed better than engaged white athletes not exposed to the cue in the threat condition. As predicted, the threat of confirming the negative stereotype about white athleticism inhibited the performance of those most psychologically invested in sports unless they were provided with an external explanation for their performance anxiety during the test.

These initial findings raise two important questions about the experience of stereotype threat in sports: When negative stereotypes are salient, at what point do athletes begin to worry about the implications? And, how do they then attempt to cope? Stone (2002) proposed that the anticipation of being negatively stereotyped in a sport could engage defensive responses as athletes practice or prepare for an important competition. Some coping responses may facilitate performance, but others, like self-handicapping, are self-defeating. To examine if stereotype threat causes athletes to self-handicap, engaged and disengaged white athletes were told that a putting task measured either their natural athletic ability (threat) or sports psychology (control). They were then told they could practice on the first hole of the course for as long as they wanted before the test began. The results showed that when natural athletic ability was linked to their performance, engaged white athletes self-handicapped by practicing less compared to engaged white athletes in the control condition. These results show that threat processes can start to impair athletic performance well before a competition begins.

Together, these studies provide a new explanation for racial differences in sport. They suggest that when negative racial stereotypes are salient in a sporting context, even athletes who are physically and socially predisposed to perform well can reduce

their preparatory effort before a competition or succumb to the pressure of disconfirming the negative stereotype during the competition itself. Such may be the case
for white athletes in sports like football, basketball, and track, or black athletes in
sports like golf or tennis, when cues in the context link an important tryout, match,
or game to the negative stereotypes about why their group does not perform well in
these sports. As a result, white and black athletes perform more poorly in certain
sports because, psychologically, the burden of stereotype threat interferes with their
ability to perform up to their physical and socialized potential.

■ STEREOTYPES THREAT PRODUCES GENDER DIFFERENCES IN SPORT

Stereotype threat also provides new insight into the parallel debate about gender
differences in sports. In this case, physical differences between males and females are
well documented and accepted (e.g., Thomas & French, 1985), and as a result, men
and women rarely compete against each other in most types and levels of sport.

Nevertheless, the gender segregation of sports reflects more than just physical
differences between men and women. Specifically, "poor athletic ability" is a widely
held negative stereotype about female athletes (Biernat & Vescio, 2002; Knight &
Guiliano, 2000). Several sociocultural sources contribute to the belief that women
are less athletic than men. For example, in the United States, women's sports received
less funding and support than men's sports until Title IX legislation was passed in
1972. Nevertheless, women still occupy fewer administrative, management, and
training positions than do men, implying that, off the field, men are more qualified
to run the show (Roper, 2002). The media also convey that women are less athletic
than men when they devote less attention to women's than men's sports at the
high school, college, and professional level (Tuggle & Owen, 1999). People who
participate in sports often transmit negative stereotypes about female athleticism,
such as when a coach admonishes a young player to "stop throwing like a girl"
(Fredrickson & Harrison, 2005) or when a teacher underestimates girls' performance in physical education classes compared to boys (Chalabaev, Sarrazin,
Trouilloud, & Jussim, 2009).

If these various sources contribute to culturally held beliefs that females are less
athletic than males, then linking athletic ability to a sports performance could cause
stereotype threat for female athletes. To test this hypothesis, Stone and McWhinnie
(2008) had white females complete a golf putting task. To explicitly induce stereotype threat, participants were told that the test measures gender differences in
athletic ability. Participants in the control conditions were told that the test measures racial differences in athletic ability or sports psychology. In addition, to create
an implicit cue for threat, a male or female experimenter ran the testing session. The
results showed that the female athletes required significantly more strokes to finish
the course when the task was explicitly framed as measuring gender differences in
athletic ability compared to when it was framed as measuring racial differences or
sports psychology.

In addition, women tended to stop the ball in a larger hole, suggesting less accuracy on their final putt, when run by a male compared to a female experimenter. Thus, both explicit (e.g., the test frame) and implicit (i.e., experimenter gender) reminders of the negative stereotype about female athleticism impaired different aspects of the performance of females on the golf putting task.

The cultural nature of stereotypes suggests that there may be negative beliefs about female athletes that are specific to certain regions. For example, Chalabaev, Sarrazin, Stone, and Cury (2008) propose that, in Western Europe, female soccer players are viewed as having poor "technical abilities" compared to males. To test if this negative cultural stereotype could influence their soccer performance, Chalabaev and colleagues had female club soccer players perform a soccer dribbling task as fast as possible. To manipulate the type of stereotype threat, the test was either framed as measuring technical ability in soccer (the cultural stereotype), natural athletic ability (the broader negative stereotype about female athletes), or sports psychology (the neutral control). Replicating the results of Stone and McWhinnie (2008), participants were not able to match their baseline score if the dribbling task was explicitly framed as measuring their natural athletic ability compared to when it was framed as measuring sports psychology. Explicitly framing the task as measuring "technical ability" also hampered their performance, suggesting that the performance of female athletes can be influenced by threat processes linked to specific cultural beliefs about their abilities in a sport.

The study by Chalabaev and colleagues suggests that elite-level athletes are not immune to the salience of negative stereotypes in a sports context. Beilock, Jellison, Rydell, McConnell, and Carr (2006) provide direct evidence for this possibility in studies showing that the salience of negative gender stereotypes can impact the performance of expert male golfers. The expert golfers in these studies had two or more years of high school or college varsity experience or a Professional Golfers' Association (PGA) handicap of at least eight. After a baseline round of putting, the expert golfers in the stereotype threat condition were informed that the putting accuracy task showed an advantage for female over male golfers; those in a control condition were told that the test measured individual differences in putting style. The results showed that experts in the stereotype threat condition were significantly less accurate during the second round than in the control condition. Thus, as implied by Warren Moon's quote that opened this chapter, negative stereotypes can cause threat processes that impair the performance of athletes even at the highest level of a sport.

The role of stereotype threat for creating gender differences in sports also extends to playing competitive board games. In an intriguing study on how stereotype threat impacts women who play the game of chess, Maass and colleagues (2008) had females compete against males and females in an online chess tournament. To induce stereotype threat, some were told that their performance was a measure of gender differences in chess; those in a control condition received the standard instructions for playing chess. The results showed that women under stereotype threat lost more matches to men compared to when they played women or when they played men in the control condition.

Finally, there is evidence that bringing to mind negative stereotypes about the *other* gender can improve or "lift" performance on a physical activity (Walton & Cohen, 2003). Chalabaev, Stone, Sarrazin, and Croizet (2008) told males and females that either males or females have a poor sense of balance, and then had them stand on an unbalanced platform and try to balance their weight for as long as possible. The results showed that when men were told that women have poor balance, and women were told that men have poor balance, each group's performance on the balance task was "lifted" or improved above a no-information control condition. Thus, in this case, reference to negative stereotypes about the outgroup caused ingroup members to perform better on a physical activity that relates to sports.

The evidence showing that stereotype threat produces gender differences in sports goes beyond simply providing another explanation for why women are not as athletic as men. It suggests that when negative gender stereotypes are linked to sports performance, they add a psychological burden to the sports task that can diminish any physical advantage that men might otherwise have over women. Together with the research on racial differences in sport, the research on stereotype threat suggests that many of the well-documented group differences in sport may stem not from biological or sociological differences that athletes bring with them to a sports competition, but rather from psychological differences that are "in the air" before and during a competitive performance.

■ THE PSYCHOLOGICAL MECHANISMS THAT MAKE THE DIFFERENCE(S)

Stereotype threat influences a variety of sports-related activities ranging from those that rely primarily on the cognitive processes associated with planning and problem solving (e.g., playing chess; how long to practice) to those that rely primarily on sensorimotor responses (e.g., balance, golf putting, soccer dribbling). Whereas stereotype threat may impact most sports-related responses through one causal mechanism, contemporary theory and research suggests that it may involve more than one pathway (see Schmader & Beilock, 2011, Chapter 3, this volume).

One view is that, whereas performance in most sports requires both efficient cognitive processing and the successful execution of well-honed sensorimotor skills, different mechanisms govern these two aspects of performance (e.g., Schmader, Johns, & Forbes, 2008). Specifically, successful execution of controlled processing tasks depend heavily on working memory, and stereotype threat harms performance on these tasks by increasing cognitive load (Stone et al., 1999) and by directly compromising the working memory system (Schmader & Johns, 2003). This suggests that when stereotype threat impacts the successful execution of cognitive processes in sport, like those used to strategize before or during a competition, it does so by impairing the working memory processes that facilitate the recall and application of sport-related knowledge.

In contrast, Beilock and colleagues (2006; see Beilock & McConnell, 2004) propose that for skilled athletes, execution of critical sensorimotor skills become so proceduralized that they run off automatically with minimal intervention from working memory. As a result, impaired working memory should not mediate the effect of stereotype threat on automated responses in sports. Indeed, Beilock and colleagues (2006) showed that stereotype threat reduces the automatic execution of a proceduralized behavior by inducing explicit monitoring of the sensorimotor response, which interrupts its efficiency and execution. Beilock and colleagues (2006) conclude that stereotype threat exerts independent effects on working memory that depend on the degree to which competitive responses rely on proceduralized or controlled cognitive skills.

Schmader and colleagues' (2008) propose that stereotype threat effects on controlled and proceduralized responses in sport do not differ as much as they appear, because both rely on monitoring processes (i.e., vigilance to performance cues, internal states, and social feedback). Specifically, monitoring processes like vigilance *indirectly* impairs controlled processing responses by reducing working memory, and *directly* impairs automatic processing responses by inducing conscious attention to execution of the task. This suggests that although stereotype threat processes can differ according to the nature of the task, some mechanisms will be similar across tasks.

There is reason to suspect that stereotype threat enhances vigilance because when a negative stereotype is salient in a sports performance context, athletes become focused on avoiding failure (e.g., Brodish & Devine, 2009; Seibt & Forster, 2004). For example, in the study by Chalabaev and colleagues (2008), expert female soccer players performed more poorly and more strongly endorsed a performance-avoidance goal—defined as the desire to avoid performing worse than others on a particular task—when their performance was linked to gender differences in athletic ability compared to the control condition. The study on self-handicapping by Stone (2002) also supports this assumption by showing that white participants under stereotype threat generated more self-doubts about poor athleticism compared to control participants. Taken together, these studies suggest that some stereotype threat mechanisms are similar across tasks (i.e., motivation to avoid failure, monitoring processes, self-doubts), and that working memory is likely to be the primary mechanism that differs according to the nature of the task.

However, the research by Stone and McWhinnie (2008) suggests that the mechanism might also depend on how the negative stereotype is conveyed in a sports performance context. When threat cues are blatant (e.g., the task is explicitly framed as measuring a negative stereotype), they induce a motivation to avoid failure, which negatively affects automatic processing responses, such as the number of strokes needed to complete a round of golf. In contrast, subtle stereotype threat cues cause targets to focus on reducing uncertainty about the presence of bias. By reducing working memory capacity, subtle cues impact those aspects of performance that require effortful processing, like strategizing about how to accurately execute a golf putt. Consistent with a "dual process" model, the results in Stone and McWhinnie (2008) show that whereas the gender of the experimenter reduced accuracy on the final putt on each hole of the course, framing the golf putting task as a measure of gender differences increased the number of strokes required to complete the overall course. Thus, working memory may account for stereotype threat effects in sports when activation of the stereotype is subtle rather than blatant, and when competitive performance requires controlled attention.

In summary, whereas it appears clear that the salience of a negative stereotype can impair the performance of athletes in sport, it is presently less clear what mechanisms account for all of the performance decrements. An important direction for future research is the development of a comprehensive model that can predict the mechanism, or set of mechanisms, that most directly impact how athletes prepare for and execute the various skills and responses that contribute to their achievement in sports.

Policy Box

The negative racial and gender stereotypes that permeate the global institution of sport can have dire consequences for athletes. The research shows that not only do the stereotypes bias the way that people evaluate athletic potential and performance, but when the negative stereotypes are brought to mind in a sports performance context, they create the psychological burden of stereotype threat that drains the cognitive and emotional resources that athletes need to compete. An effective way to reduce the pernicious effect of threat on performance is to eliminate the structural and social cues in sport that convey racial and gender disadvantage. However, while we wait for the institution of sport to become race and gender neutral, we can ameliorate the effects of stereotype threat by teaching athletes about the threat process, exposing them to positive counterstereotypic role models, and emphasizing the malleability of their athletic skills. Inoculating them against the distraction and doubt caused by stereotype threat should help them compete on a more even playing field.

■ HOW TO REDUCE THE IMPACT OF STEREOTYPE THREAT IN SPORTS

One consequence of repeated exposure to stereotype threat in a performance domain is that targets may need to psychologically disengage their self-worth from the poor outcomes they continue to acquire (Major, Spencer, Schmader, Wolfe, & Crocker, 1998). Eventually, when the burden of battling the stereotype overwhelms their coping responses, individuals must abandon participating in the domain altogether (Steele, 1997). In sport, the process of disengagement and disidentification may not only cause some talented individuals to quit playing a sport, but also avoid future participation in recreational sport, which has important consequences for their health. It is therefore critical to understand how the institution of sport can reduce the negative impact that stereotype threat has on people who participate in athletics.

One solution can be found in most studies on stereotype threat: When stigmatized targets perform a task under stereotype-irrelevant or neutral conditions, group differences significantly attenuate or disappear. This implies that coaching and administrative personnel can reduce stereotype threat by emphasizing the racial or gender neutrality of the performance situation. However, we recognize that this may be difficult to accomplish in an institution like sport that has such a long history of measuring, debating, and to a large extent, accepting and making provisions for racial and gender differences in performance. It might be difficult for the institution of sport to frame itself as race or gender neutral until female tennis players play five sets instead of three, female golfers hit from the same tees as men, more white males excel in basketball and the 100 meter dash, more blacks win Olympic gold in swimming, and are hired as coaches and administrators at the highest levels of sport (Harrison, 2008). A more practical solution may be to provide athletes with coping responses when the threat of confirming a negative stereotype becomes salient when they compete.

Research suggests that if athletes can learn to view stereotyped dimensions like athletic ability or sports intelligence as a malleable attribute that can improve with practice, they may be less likely to engage the threat processes that impair performance (e.g., Aronson, Fried, & Good, 2002). Their sense of efficacy to overcome the negative group characterization may also strengthen by exposing them to ingroup role models who exhibit strong counterstereotypic attributes (Marx & Roman, 2002; McIntyre, Paulson, & Lord, 2003). Finally, we can teach athletes to recognize when threat is having an effect on them. Johns, Schmader, and Martens (2005) instructed women about the negative effects of stereotype threat and then had them complete a test of math ability. Results showed that the women performed significantly better on the math test after learning about stereotype threat compared to a control condition in which the process of threat was not explained. This suggests that teaching athletes to recognize the causes and consequences of stereotype threat may empower them to avoid its detrimental effects when they prepare for and perform in their sport (see also, Cohen, Purdie-Vaughns, & Garcia, 2011, Chapter 18, this volume).

■ CONCLUSION

Decades of research in sport focuses on bioevolutionary or sociological explanations for racial and gender differences in athletic competition. We propose that stereotype threat offers a new perspective on what causes racial and gender differences in sports performance. A growing number of carefully controlled laboratory and field experiments show that when negative stereotypes are brought to mind in a sports performance context, either through blatant statements about the link between group membership and performance, or through subtle reminders of racial and gender differences, they create a burden that robs athletes of their potential. Importantly, being highly skilled, prepared, and invested in sport makes athletes more, not less, susceptible to stereotype threat. Competitive performance suffers because the threat of confirming the negative stereotype causes athletes to focus on avoiding failure, which interrupts proceduralized sensorimotor responses and impairs working memory capacity. The long-term solution to reducing the influence of stereotype threat from athletic performance is to eliminate the prevalence of stereotyping in the global institution of sport. Until then, we believe that the most effective short-term solution is to inoculate athletes against the debilitating influence of stereotype threat when it is brought to mind in a sports performance context.

References

Aronson, J., Fried, C. B., & Good, C. (2002). Reducing the effects of stereotype threat on African-American college students by reshaping theories of intelligence. *Journal of Experimental Social Psychology, 38,* 113–125.

Beilock, S. L., Jellison, W. A., Rydell, R. J., McConnell, A. R., & Carr, T. H. (2006). On the causal mechanisms of stereotype threat: Can skills that don't rely heavily on working memory still be threatened? *Personality and Social Psychology Bulletin, 32,* 1059–1071.

Beilock, S. L., & McConnell, A. R. (2004). Stereotype threat and sport: Can athletic performance be threatened? *Journal of Sport and Exercise Psychology, 26,* 597–609.

Bejan, A., Jones, E. C., & Jordan, C. (2010). The evolution of speed in athletics: Why the fastest runners are black and swimmers white. *International Journal of Design and Nature, 5,* 1–13.

Biernat, M., & Vescio, T. K. (2002). She swings, she hits, she's great, she's benched: Implications for gender based shifting standards for judgment and behavior. *Personality and Social Psychology Bulletin, 28,* 66–77.

Brodish, A. B., & Devine, P. G. (2009). The role of performance-avoidance goals and worry in mediating the relationship between stereotype threat and performance. *Journal of Experimental Social Psychology, 45,* 180–185.

Chalabaev, A., Sarrazin, P., Stone, J., & Cury, F. (2008). Do achievement goals mediate stereotype threat? An investigation on females' soccer performance. *Journal of Sport & Exercise Psychology, 30,* 143–158.

Chalabaev, A., Sarrazin, P., Trouilloud, D., & Jussim, L. (2009). Can sex-undifferentiated teacher expectations mask an influence of sex stereotypes? Alternative forms of stereotype inaccuracies. *Journal of Applied Social Psychology, 39,* 2469–2498.

Chalabaev, A., Stone, J., Sarrazin, P., & Croizet, J. C. (2008). Investigating physiological and self-reported mediators of stereotype lift effects on a motor task. *Basic and Applied Social Psychology, 30,* 18–26.

Coakley, J. (2001). *Sport in society.* Boston: McGraw-Hill.

Cohen, G. L., Purdie-Vaughns, V., & Garcia, J. (2011). An identity threat perspective on intervention. In M. Inzlicht, & T. Schmader (Eds.), *Stereotype threat: Theory, process, and application.* New York: Oxford University Press.

Edwards, H. (1972). The myth of the racially superior athlete. *Intellectual Digest, 2,* 58–60.

Edwards, H. (1973). *Sociology of sport.* Homewood, IL.: The Dorsey Press.

Entine, J. (2000). *Taboo: Why black athletes dominate sports and why we're afraid to talk about it.* New York: Public Affairs.

Fredrickson, B. L., & Harrison, K. (2005). Throwing like a girl: Self-objectification predicts adolescent girls' motor performance. *Journal of Sport & Social Issues, 29,* 79–101.

Harrison, C. K. (2008). African American coaches, the NFL and popular culture: Change is the only constant. In T. Boyd (Ed.), *African Americans and popular culture: Volume 2 Sports* (pp. 149–165). Westport, CT: Praeger Publishers.

Harrison, C. K., & Lawrence, S. M. (2004). College students' perceptions, myths, and stereotypes about African American athleticism: A qualitative investigation. *Sport, Education and Society, 9*(1), 33–52.

Johns, M., Schmader, T., & Martens, A. (2005). Knowing is half the battle: Teaching stereotype threat as a means of improving women's math performance. *Psychological Science, 16,* 175–179.

Jordan, J. (1969). Physiological and anthropometrical comparisons of Negroes and Whites. *Journal of Health, Physical Education, and Recreation, November/December,* 93–99.

Knight, J. L., & Guiliano, T. A. (2001). He's a Laker; she's a "looker": The consequences of gender-stereotyped portrayals of male and female athletes by the print media. *Sex Roles, 45,* 217–229.

Lapchick, R. E. (2009). *2009 racial and gender report card.* Orlando: The Institute for Diversity and Ethics in Sport, University of Central Florida.

Maass, A., D'Ettole, C., & Cadinu, M. (2008). Checkmate? The role of gender stereotypes in the ultimate intellectual sport. *European Journal of Social Psychology, 38,* 231–245.

Major, B., Spencer, S., Schmader, T., Wolfe, C., & Crocker, J. (1998). Coping with negative stereotypes about intellectual performance: The role of psychological disengagement. *Personality and Social Psychology Bulletin, 24,* 34–50.

Marx, D. M., & Roman, J. S. (2002). Female role models: protecting women's math test performance. *Personality and Social Psychology Bulletin, 28,* 1183–1193.

Metheny, E. (1939). Some differences in bodily proportions in American Negro and White male college athletes as related to athletic performance. *Research Quarterly, 10,* 40–53.

McIntyre, R. B., Paulson, R. M., & Lord, C. G. (2003). Alleviating women's mathematics stereotype threat through salience of group achievements. *Journal of Experimental Social Psychology, 39,* 83–90.

Moon, W. (2006). Enshrinement speech transcript, August 5, 2006. Pro Football Hall of Fame. Accessed October 10, 2009, from www.profootballhof.com

Roper, E. A. (2002). Women working in the applied domain: Examining the gender bias in applied sport psychology. *Journal of Applied Sport Psychology, 14,* 53–66.

Sailes, G. (1987). A socioeconomic explanation of Black sports participation. *Western Journal of Black Studies, 11*(4), 164–167.

Sailes, G. (1996). An investigation of campus stereotypes: The myth of Black athletic superiority and the dumb jock stereotype. In R. E. Lapchick (Ed.), *Sport in society: Equal opportunity or business as usual?* (pp. 193–202). Thousand Oaks, CA: Sage.

Schmader, T., & Beilock, S. (2011). An integration of processes that underlie stereotype threat. In M. Inzlicht, & T. Schmader (Eds.), *Stereotype threat: Theory, process, and application.* New York: Oxford University Press.

Schmader, T., & Johns, M. (2003). Converging evidence that stereotype threat reduces working memory capacity. *Journal of Personality and Social Psychology, 85,* 440–452.

Schmader, T., Johns, M., & Forbes, C. (2008). An integrated process model of stereotype threat effects on performance. *Psychological Review, 115,* 336–356.

Seibt, B., & Forster, J. (2004). Stereotype threat and performance: How self-stereotypes influence processing by inducing regulatory foci. *Journal of Personality and Social Psychology, 87,* 38–56.

Steele, C. M. (1997). A threat in the air: how stereotypes shape intellectual identity and performance. *American Psychologist, 52,* 613–629.

Steele, C. M., & Aronson, J. (1995). Stereotype threat and the intellectual test performance of African Americans. *Journal of Personality and Social Psychology, 69*(5), 797–811.

Stone, J. (2002). Battling doubt by avoiding practice: The effects of stereotype threat on self-handicapping in White athletes. *Personality and Social Psychology Bulletin, 28,* 1667–1678.

Stone, J., Lynch, C. K., Sjomeling, M., & Darley, J. M. (1999). Stereotype threat effects on Black and White athletic performance. *Journal of Personality and Social Psychology, 77*(6), 1213–1227.

Stone, J., & McWhinnie, C. (2008). Evidence that blatant versus subtle stereotype threat cues impact performance through dual processes. *Journal of Experimental Social Psychology, 44,* 445–452.

Stone, J., Perry, Z., & Darley, J. (1997). "White Men Can't Jump": Evidence for the perceptual confirmation of racial stereotypes following a basketball game. *Basic and Applied Social Psychology, 19,* 291–306.

Thomas, J. R., & French, K. E. (1985). Gender differences across age in motor performance: A meta analysis. *Psychological Bulletin, 98,* 260–282.

Tuggle, C. A., & Owen, A. (1999). A descriptive analysis of NBC's coverage of the centennial Olympics. *Journal of Sport and Social Issues, 23,* 171–182.

Walton, G. M., & Cohen, G. L. (2003). Stereotype lift. *Journal of Experimental Social Psychology, 39,* 456–467.

15 Stereotype Threat in Interracial Interactions

■ JENNIFER A. RICHESON AND
J. NICOLE SHELTON

This chapter adopts a stereotype threat perspective to examine dynamics of interracial interactions. We first review relevant literature suggesting that both white and racial minority individuals are likely to experience stereotype threat during interracial interactions. We focus on the threat of being perceived as stereotypical of one's racial/ethnic group as the primary trigger of such threat reactions. Next, we examine the cognitive consequences of harboring such prejudice concerns during interracial interactions and consider the relation between these outcomes and those found in work specifically designed to examine the cognitive component processes of stereotype threat. Later, we consider the potential consequences of stereotype threat during interracial interactions for individuals' experiences during those interactions, as well as the experiences had by their interaction partners. We close the chapter with a brief discussion of the potential theoretical and practical implications of these dynamics.

Keywords: Stereotype threat, interracial interactions, fear of appearing racist, perceiver, target

Intergroup interactions may provide fertile ground for the experience of stereotype threat and, more broadly, social identity threat.[1] Members of traditionally dominant, high-status groups and members of traditionally stigmatized, low-status groups often experience heightened concerns about the integrity and value of their social identities during intergroup interactions (see Shelton, Richeson, & Vorauer, 2006, for a review). The goal of this chapter is to review the research that has accumulated to date on the experience and consequences of such concerns during interracial interactions.[2] We begin with evidence suggesting that stereotype threat is indeed a relevant lens through which to examine the dynamics of interracial interactions. Specifically, we review research on cognitive dynamics of interracial interactions and consider the relation of these dynamics to parallel work in the stereotype threat tradition. After, we identify the ways that individuals are likely to respond affectively and behaviorally to such threats during the interaction and consider the consequences of these responses for interpersonal outcomes of the interaction; namely, how "threatened" participants' interaction partners are likely to experience the interaction.

We end the chapter with a discussion of the implications of this work for theory and research on both stereotype threat and interracial contact as well as the broader implications for our understanding of intergroup relations.

■ INTERRACIAL INTERACTIONS: A CONTEXT FOR STEREOTYPE THREAT

Several facets of interracial interactions make them ripe for stereotype threat. First, individuals' racial/ethnic group memberships are likely to be salient (at least initially) during the interaction. As is required for stereotype threat to manifest, furthermore, interracial interactions often lead individuals to realize that there is potential for them to be judged according to negative group stereotypes (Steele, Spencer, & Aronson, 2002). Recent theoretical perspectives on stereotype threat argue that this combination of identity salience and the realization that one is in a context in which one is likely to be evaluated by negative group stereotypes triggers cognitive vigilance and preoccupation with cues that bear on these negative evaluations (Schmader, Johns, & Forbes, 2008). Consistent with this perspective, research has shown that individuals are often preoccupied with how they are being perceived and evaluated by outgroup members during interracial interactions (Shelton & Richeson, 2006; Vorauer, 2006). In other words, although the interpersonal context has not been a popular domain for the study of stereotype threat, research suggests that it is a site in which stereotype threat does indeed occur.

In addition to examining a relatively understudied context for stereotype threat, research on interracial interactions has differed from the larger stereotype threat tradition by focusing on both the experiences of members of high-status sociocultural groups and those of members of low-status groups. That is, although the majority of research in the stereotype threat tradition has focused on the experiences of members of groups that have relatively low status and are associated with negative stereotypes in their particular sociocultural context, work in the domain of interracial interactions suggests that members of both low- and high-status groups are susceptible to threat during the interaction, and, perhaps, equally so. Specifically, whites tend to be concerned about appearing prejudiced, and racial minorities tend to be concerned about confirming negative (and sometimes positive) group stereotypes during interracial interactions (e.g., Shelton, 2003).

The context of an interracial interaction can be threatening, therefore, because individuals often expect outgroup interaction partners to judge them negatively. In the sections that follow, we summarize research on the cognitive, affective, and behavioral consequences of interracial interactions, much of which is consistent with a stereotype threat perspective. Although not much research on the dynamics of interracial interactions has adopted a stereotype threat framework for its investigation, many of the findings are consistent with the processes observed in studies that are distinctly designed to examine stereotype threat. In other words, research suggests that concerns about appearing prejudiced or being judged according to group stereotypes during interracial interpersonal interactions instigate a cascade of cognitive, affective, and behavioral responses similar to those found in other stereotype threat domains.

■ COGNITIVE DYNAMICS OF INTERRACIAL INTERACTIONS

Stereotype threat triggers cognitive vigilance and preoccupation with cues pertaining to the potential for negative evaluation (Schmader et al., 2008). In this section, we examine the evidence for these cognitive processes during interracial interactions. Specifically, we examine three cognitive consequences of interracial contact: the activation of prejudice-related concepts, vigilance for and attentional bias to prejudice-related cues, and the recruitment of central executive resources.

Stereotype Activation

Similar to one effect of stereotype threat, research has shown that individuals are often preoccupied with how they are being perceived and evaluated by outgroup members during interracial interactions (Vorauer, 2006). For instance, Vorauer, Hunter, Main, and Roy (2000) conducted a study in which white Canadians were shown a videotape of another student responding to a series of questions. The student in the video was either also white or a First Nations (i.e., Native Canadian) individual, and participants were led to believe that they would either be having an interaction with the other student or that they would only be watching the video. After watching the video, participants completed a lexical decision-making task that assessed the extent to which concepts that are related to the stereotype that outgroup members often hold about whites (i.e., "meta-stereotypes" such as racist, bigoted) had been activated. Results revealed that these meta-stereotypes were more likely to be activated when white Canadians anticipated having an interaction with a First Nations Canadian compared with simple exposure to a First Nations Canadian, or to expected interaction with or exposure to another white Canadian. That is, the stereotype that whites are racist was activated for whites who expected to interact with an outgroup member, but not for those who expected to interact with an ingroup member. In addition, meta-stereotype activation and preoccupation with negative evaluation more broadly are quite common events for most participants, both of high- and low- sociocultural status, during interracial interactions (Vorauer, 2006).

Vigilance and Attentional Bias

In addition to the activation of relevant stereotypes, research suggests that whites and racial minorities often vigilantly monitor their environments for cues that are consistent with their respective prejudice concerns—that is, about appearing prejudiced and being the target of prejudice—during interracial interactions (Murphy, Steele, & Gross, 2007). Indeed, a number of studies have shown that both members of low-status groups (e.g., Inzlicht, Kaiser, & Major, 2008) and members of high-status groups (e.g., Richeson & Trawalter, 2008) tune their attention toward "threat-relevant" cues. Specifically, Inzlicht et al. (2008) found that women high in stigma consciousness are slow to detect the offset of contempt—an emotional expression related to rejection—in the faces of male, but not female, targets. Similarly, Richeson and Trawalter (2008) found that white Americans who are high in external motivation to appear nonprejudiced against blacks (EMS) reveal race-based patterns of selective attention. That is, black male faces initially capture these high-EMS individuals' attention, but are subsequently selectively avoided. Interestingly, this race-based pattern of selective attention is not observed if the black (and white) male faces are smiling; thereby, reducing their perceived threat. Taken together, these studies reveal patterns of vigilance and visual attention to salient prejudice concerns that are consistent with those found among individuals under stereotype threat.

Recruitment of Executive Resources

The extant research on stereotype threat has also found that individuals' worries and concerns about confirming stereotypes, once activated, recruit important resources of the central executive (e.g., working memory resources, Schmader & Beilock, 2011, Chapter 3, this volume). Studies investigating cognitive effects of interracial interactions have uncovered similar processes. For instance, we demonstrated that interracial interactions prompt white Americans to monitor and attempt to regulate their thoughts, feelings, and behaviors in order to avoid being perceived as prejudiced (see Richeson & Shelton, 2007). This line of work tested and found that the monitoring and regulation of such thoughts, feelings, and behavior is cognitively demanding, recruiting resources of the central executive.

Initial evidence for the potential role of executive resources in shaping cognitive experiences during interracial interactions was garnered from a functional magnetic resonance imaging (fMRI) study in which white participants were shown facial photographs of black and white males (Richeson et al., 2003). Although the task involved little executive attentional demand, several brain regions thought to be involved in the inhibition of habitual or dominant responses (e.g., the dorsolateral prefrontal cortex [DLPFC]) were more active during exposure to black faces than to white faces. What was most intriguing, however, was that the level of neural activity in response to black faces in one region of right DLPFC predicted the extent to which individuals were impaired on the Stroop color naming task—a measure of the ability to engage in response inhibition—after an interracial interaction that had occurred more than 2 weeks prior. In other words, when exposed to black male faces, those individuals who revealed the greatest activity in a brain region known to be involved in executive attentional control were most likely to be impaired on an executive control task (i.e., the Stroop) after an actual interracial interaction. Consequently, these results provide evidence for the possibility that individuals recruit executive resources in order to navigate interracial interactions.

To test this possibility further, we drew upon Baumeister, Vohs, and Tice's (2007) strength model of self-regulation, which states that one act of self-regulation leaves individuals either less willing or able to engage in subsequent self-regulatory acts— a phenomenon often referred to as *cognitive depletion*. Our fMRI data coupled with Baumeister's strength model suggests, therefore, that not only do many individuals recruit executive control resources during interracial interactions, more so than during same-race interactions, but that such differential recruitment can be observed through these individuals' impaired performance on the Stroop task after an interracial, compared with same-race, interaction. Indeed, consistent with this prediction, research has found that both white and black individuals perform significantly worse on the Stroop task after interracial, compared with same-race, interactions (Richeson & Shelton, 2003; Richeson, Trawalter, & Shelton, 2005). Taken together, this research suggests that interracial interactions seem to engage cognitive component processes similar to those that have been observed in other threatening environments (Inzlicht, McKay, & Aronson, 2006).

So, why do individuals recruit these executive control resources during interracial interactions more than during same-race interactions? We have suggested that one primary trigger of such engagement is the activation of prejudice concerns (Richeson & Shelton, 2007). Specifically, we argued that for white Americans, it is essentially the threat of appearing prejudiced that activates these cognitive processes. In one test of this idea, Richeson and Trawalter (2005) heightened (Experiment 1) or allayed (Experiment 2) the prejudice concerns of white Americans prior to an interaction that involved discussing a race-related topic (e.g., racial profiling) with either a white or black partner. To heighten prejudice concerns, participants were provided with false feedback regarding their performance on a measure of automatic racial bias. Participants were told, "most people are more prejudiced than they think they are." Control condition participants, by contrast, were provided with negative performance feedback that was not explicitly linked to prejudice. To allay prejudice concerns in the second study, participants were provided with scripted comments regarding racial profiling that they were told they should use to formulate their own responses during the interaction. Hence, any potentially discriminatory remarks that these participants made during the interaction could be attributed to the script rather than to their personal opinions, thereby reducing their concern about appearing prejudiced. Control participants were not provided with such scripted remarks.

Next, participants in both studies engaged in either the same-race or interracial interaction and then completed the Stroop task. Consistent with a stereotype threat perspective, results revealed that participants who received the prejudice feedback (i.e., prejudice concerns were heightened) performed significantly worse on the Stroop task after interracial contact than did participants who received the general performance feedback. In addition, participants who received the scripted comments performed significantly better on the Stroop task after interracial contact than did participants who did not receive the script. Neither the performance feedback nor the script condition influenced participants' Stroop performance after same-race interactions. Taken together, these findings are strikingly consistent with a stereotype threat framework, suggesting that individuals recruit the resources of the central executive in response to the threat of appearing prejudiced during interracial interactions.

Summary of Cognitive Outcomes

These results provide evidence for the role of prejudice concerns in shaping individuals' cognitive experiences during interracial interactions. Specifically, prejudice concerns can be manifest in the activation of relevant stereotypes that, in turn, result in increased vigilance to and preoccupation with prejudice-relevant cues in the environment. Heightened vigilance and mental preoccupation, furthermore, consume cognitive resources, resulting in their depletion after interracial interactions. Taken together, prejudice concerns and stereotype threat during interracial interactions are likely to leave individuals cognitively exhausted after the interaction. In the next section, we consider the effects of stereotype threat during interracial interactions on the affective and behavioral experiences of the threatened participant, as well as on the experiences had by participants' interaction partners.

■ AFFECTIVE AND BEHAVIORAL DYNAMICS OF INTERRACIAL INTERACTIONS

As argued in previous sections, interracial interactions often trigger concerns about confirming negative group stereotypes for both whites and racial minorities. Nevertheless, the work on interracial interactions suggest that some of the outcomes of stereotype threat, when elicited in the context of interracial interactions, may differ from those associated with the threats elicited in the performance contexts more commonly studied. Specifically, although stereotype threat experienced during interracial interactions typically results in negative affective consequences for "threatened" participants, it does not always result in poor behavior—the relevant "performance marker" in interaction contexts. In fact, research suggests that stereotype threat can engender positive behavior during interracial interactions. In the sections that follow, we first review research on how concerns about prejudice shape individuals' affective experiences during interracial interactions. We then consider the implications of stereotype threat for individuals' behavior during the interaction as well as for interpersonal interaction outcomes.

Affective Outcomes

Members of both high- and low-status groups often experience anxiety during intergroup interactions because they are concerned about behaving in prejudiced ways or being the target of prejudice, respectively (e.g., Bosson, Haymovitz, & Pinel, 2004; Page-Gould, Mendoza-Denton, & Tropp, 2008; Plant, 2004; Trawalter, Richeson, & Shelton, 2009). Page-Gould et al. (2008), for example, found that the higher in race-based rejection sensitivity Latino individuals are, the more anxiety they experience during interpersonal interactions with white, but not with other Latino, partners. Similarly, individuals who are motivated to behave in nonprejudiced ways because of external pressures (such as the fear of social disapproval) are especially likely to feel anxious about interracial interactions (Plant, 2004). In other words, interracial interactions that are experienced as threatening due to the activation of prejudice concerns are often anxiety-provoking and/or physiologically arousing, much like the experience of stereotype threat in other contexts (see Mendes & Jamieson, 2011, Chapter 4, this volume, for review).

Negative Behavioral and Interpersonal Outcomes

Given the other chapters in this volume, it should come as no surprise that the threat activated during interracial interactions can result in negative behavioral outcomes. Such negative behavioral responses, in turn, can result in negative interpersonal outcomes more generally—i.e., lead threatened participants' interaction partners also to have negative experiences in the encounter. Indeed, members of low-status, stigmatized groups can respond quite negatively when they anticipate interacting, or actually engage in interactions, with members of nonstigmatized groups who they expect to be prejudiced against them. For instance, Pinel (2002) led women who were dispositionally high in concern about being the target of sexism (i.e., high stigma conscious women) to believe (erroneously) that they were interacting with a sexist male. In response to this information, these high stigma conscious women acted critically toward their male interaction partners, which, in turn, resulted in actually being evaluated negatively by their male partners in return. In other words, these women's expectation that they would be treated negatively became a self-fulfilling prophecy.

In addition to this type of self-fulfilling prophecy mechanism, the cognitive load that results from concerns about being the target of prejudice and/or stereotypes (including the stereotype that one is prejudiced) can result in negative behavior during interactions. Recall that prejudice concerns often lead individuals to become preoccupied with prejudice-relevant thoughts and to vigilantly monitor their environments for cues that are consistent with their concerns (e.g., Murphy et al., 2007). Moreover, heightened vigilance consumes individuals' cognitive resources, which, in turn, can disrupt their ability to engage in positive interaction behaviors. Research by Vorauer and Turpie (2004) suggests, for instance, that when individuals are unsure about both how they are viewed by outgroup interaction partners, as well as how to behave to achieve their desired self-image, the uncertainty may disrupt normal scripts for appropriate behavior during interactions, resulting in suboptimal interaction outcomes. Specifically, the cognitive load associated with individuals' monitoring of their own actions can result in hesitation, self-censorship, and second-guessing, thereby preventing individuals from doing what comes naturally. The result of this type of cognitive load is particularly disruptive for low-prejudice white individuals. That is, under identity threat, low-prejudice whites' automatic positive responses to outgroup members are disrupted, resulting in behavior that is more rigid and less warm and friendly than it would be in a nonthreatening context.[3]

Taken together, this research suggests that prejudice concerns, once activated, can contribute to negative interaction dynamics because individuals' increased vigilance to and preoccupation with prejudice cues (a) increases the extent to which their partners' ambiguous behaviors will be attributed to prejudice, perhaps, erroneously, and (b) reduces the extent to which individuals can behave in positive, affiliative ways during the interaction.

Positive Behavioral and Interpersonal Outcomes

Stereotype threat may result in positive behavior on the part of threatened participants and thus result in positive experiences for their interaction partners. Shelton (2003), for instance, examined the perceptions that racial minorities had of white interaction partners who were either concerned about appearing prejudiced or were not concerned. Specifically, white and black Americans engaged in a "get-to-know-you" interaction with one another during which they discussed four neutral and four racially sensitive topics. Prior to the interaction, half of the white participants were explicitly told to try not to be prejudiced and half were given no instruction. Participants then engaged in a 15-minute interaction with a different-race partner and later indicated how much they liked their partner. Results revealed that black participants liked white partners who were instructed to try not to be prejudiced (i.e., participants in the prejudice concern condition) more than they liked white partners who were not given this instruction.

Similar to whites' self-regulatory efforts as a means of coping with a threatened self-image, racial minorities' responses to social identity threat can also have positive consequences for their interaction partners. In one study revealing this effect, Shelton et al. (2005a) primed racial minority participants to be concerned about racial prejudice by having them read a newspaper article that focused on the high incidence of racial bias. After reading the article, participants had an interaction with a white participant. Results revealed that racial minorities who were led to be concerned about being the target of prejudice displayed more socially engaging behaviors during the interaction compared with participants who did not have this concern. Moreover, although these concerned (i.e., threatened) participants had more negative affective experiences during the interactions compared with their unconcerned counterparts, their white partners had a more pleasant experience during the interaction than did the white interaction partners of unconcerned racial minorities. Specifically, white Americans who interacted with a racial minority individual who had been primed to be concerned about racial prejudice liked their partner more, experienced less negative affect, and enjoyed the interaction more than did white Americans who interacted with a racial minority who was not primed to be concerned about racial prejudice. In similar research, Shelton (2003) found that white Americans who were paired with black partners who had been primed with the potential for racial prejudice experienced less anxiety and enjoyed the interaction more than did white Americans who were paired with black partners who had not been primed with prejudice concerns.

Why did the black participants like white partners whose prejudice concerns were activated more than white partners whose prejudice concerns were not activated (Shelton, 2003)? And, why did white participants enjoy interactions with racial minority partners who were concerned about being the target of prejudice more than with racial minority partners who were not so concerned (e.g., Shelton et al., 2005a)? Both these results are consistent with research on the use of compensatory strategies, such as behaving especially positively, in the face of potential bias (Miller, Rothblum, Felicio, & Brand, 1995). Specifically, Miller et al. (1995) found that obese women who thought that they were visible to normal weight interaction partners (and, thus, vulnerable to antifat prejudice) behaved in a more socially skillful manner than did obese women who thought that they were not visible. Similarly, in the study by Shelton et al. (2005a), racial minority participants who were primed to be concerned about racial prejudice behaved in a more socially engaging manner, such as smiling more, during interactions with white American partners, compared with racial minority participants who were not primed with this prejudice concern. These compensatory efforts, of course, were successful; the white partners of racial minority participants who were primed to expect prejudice had more positive encounters than did the white partners of racial minority participants who were not primed in this way.

This research reveals one of the ways in which individuals attempt to distance themselves from the stereotype and/or negative evaluation that is expected to follow in the interracial dyadic context. These processes are certainly consistent with basic stereotype threat research. For instance, Steele and Aronson's (1995) original stereotype threat work found that African American students in the threatening position of anticipating taking a test that was described as diagnostic of intellectual ability dissociated themselves from activities linked to stereotypes of African Americans, such as listening to rap music. Moreover, Jamieson and Harkins (2007) argue that one consequence of stereotype threat is an increased motivation to perform well in order to refute the stereotype, which can result in individuals performing better under threat compared with when not under threat. Consistent with this hypothesis, Kray, Thompson, and Galinsky (2001) revealed evidence of such striving under threat among women involved in a negotiation task. Specifically, female participants who were told that men perform better than women on the task (i.e., strong stereotype condition) outperformed their male counterparts who were given a similar instruction. In other words, even outside of the interpersonal interaction context, stereotype threat can serve to improve performance rather than undermine it.

In sum, the threat of appearing prejudiced or being the target of prejudice during interracial interactions can result in compensatory behavior designed to thwart those outcomes. These efforts can be successful insofar as they lead to positive outcomes for threatened participants' interaction partners. Nevertheless, these compensatory efforts often come with a price to participants themselves in the form of negative affect and, as reviewed previously, cognitive depletion.

Summary of Affective and Behavioral Outcomes

Although stereotype threat is almost uniformly associated with negative affective experiences for individuals, its effects on behavior during interactions can vary. Concerns about activated group stereotypes can lead individuals to behave in negative ways during interracial interactions and thus result in negative interpersonal outcomes. Specifically, prejudice concerns have been found to lead individuals to behave anxiously, to disrupt individuals' positive behavioral intentions, and, sometimes, to preemptively reject outgroup interaction partners, among other negative behavioral outcomes. Needless to say, these behaviors are apt to result in negative experiences for participants' interaction partners.

The work on threat during interracial contact, however, also suggests that prejudice concerns can result in positive behavior on the part of "threatened" individuals and, thus, positive interpersonal outcomes. This work suggests that participants under threat are often motivated to behave in ways that create their desired self-image or avoid an undesired self-image. Specifically, research has found that individuals often engage in compensatory strategies to create a positive interaction with outgroup members and/or work to distance themselves from activated group stereotypes during interracial interactions. Engaging in self-regulation (e.g., monitoring behavior, deploying compensatory strategies) to foster positive interactions can be extremely successful and yield positive outcomes for interaction partners. The same processes, however, are likely to lead "threatened" individuals to be cognitively depleted and may also bolster their experience of negative affect.

▪ DIVERGENT EXPERIENCES

The research reviewed thus far suggests that the consequences of stereotype threat during interracial interactions are primarily negative for the self (i.e., individuals' affective and cognitive outcomes) and can either be negative or positive for one's partner (i.e., the interpersonal outcomes). Hence, the research on stereotype threat in interracial interactions is distinctive in that divergent self- and partner-outcomes are prevalent (see Richeson & Shelton, 2007; Shelton & Richeson, 2006, for reviews). Specifically, participants' efforts to manage their reactions to stereotype threat can lead to cognitive and affective experiences that diverge between themselves and their interaction partners. Moreover, the positive *inter*personal outcomes of interracial interactions may often come at the expense of the very self-regulatory efforts that give rise to the negative *intra*personal outcomes. Consequently, although stereotype threat experienced during interracial interactions may on some occasions result in positive interpersonal outcomes, the psychological costs to individuals may be experienced as too severe, and thus the experience of stereotype threat may lead them to attempt to avoid interracial interactions all together.

Policy Box

Since the civil rights struggles of the 1960s, efforts to create a more harmonious, yet racially integrated, society have largely been directed toward developing and enforcing laws and policies that serve to reduce blatant racial bias. The logic was, of course, that racially biased individuals are the source of negative interracial interactions. As revealed in this chapter, however, bias is only one factor that can create problems during interracial interactions. This chapter outlines the ways in which both stigmatized and nonstigmatized groups members' concerns about the value of their social identities—that is, their experiences of social identity threat—can also be problematic in interracial interactions. Given the number of important contexts in which interpersonal interactions are key (e.g., interactions between doctors and patients, teachers and students, bosses and employees), this chapter suggests a myriad of ways in which negative interracial contact experiences could be quite consequential. Research has found, for instance, that concerns about appearing prejudiced can undermine teacher effectiveness during interactions with racial minority students. More broadly speaking, the negative affective and cognitive outcomes that often stem from stereotype threat during interracial interactions may lead individuals to attempt to avoid them. Given the documented positive effects of intergroup contact on racial attitudes, this possibility is particularly troubling. Hence, policy makers need to be cognizant of the role of individuals' social identity concerns as they seek to develop programs and interventions aimed at fostering more positive interracial encounters.

■ IMPLICATIONS AND FUTURE DIRECTIONS

The research reviewed here offers a number of important implications for intergroup relations. As we alluded to at the end of the previous section, for example, the negative affective and cognitive outcomes associated with stereotype threat during interracial interactions may lead individuals to attempt to avoid them. Given the documented positive effects of intergroup contact on racial attitudes (Pettigrew & Tropp, 2006), this possibility is particularly troubling. Indeed, it is imperative for future research to identify ways in which individuals can enjoy the benefits of interracial contact without the seemingly high costs. In addition, stereotype threat can also affect the dynamics of interracial interactions that take place in important sectors such as education and medicine. For instance, concerns about appearing prejudiced can undermine teacher effectiveness during interactions with racial minority students. Specifically, studies have found that whites often provide less critical, and, thus, less helpful, performance feedback to racial minority students in order to avoid providing negative feedback that could be perceived as stereotypical (Crosby & Monin, 2007; Harber, 1998). In other words, concerns about prejudice can disrupt the quality of work that would normally take place in any number of important interaction domains, perhaps, ironically, even contributing to the persistence of many racial inequities in health, wealth, and education.

In addition to these important practical implications, this review also suggests theoretical implications and directions for future research for both the extant work on interracial interactions and the body of work on stereotype threat. Adopting a stereotype threat perspective for interracial contact research, for instance, could generate new hypotheses regarding how to foster positive interaction experiences. For instance, the extant work on stereotype threat has established the role of self-affirmation in reducing the negative consequences of a threatened social identity (Cohen, Garcia, Apfel, & Master, 2006). Research on interracial interactions should consider this type of intervention. Similarly, the study of stereotype threat would be wise to consider the findings of recent research on interracial contact. Indeed, many of the "threat-inductions" employed in standard stereotype threat paradigms involve the presence of outgroup experimenters, teachers, and evaluators without much explicit consideration of the potential interaction dynamics that may be at play (but see Cohen, Steele, & Ross, 1999; Goff, Steele, & Davies, 2008). Of course, in reality, the so-called targets of stereotype threat are indeed active agents who participate in the dynamics of even threatening encounters. These types of interactive effects should, therefore, be considered more frequently in work on stereotype threat. Although we do not want to overstate the synergy between these two research streams, we think that the present review suggests that there is much that the intergroup interaction domain can learn from the extant research on stereotype threat and vice versa.

■ CONCLUSION

In this chapter, we applied a social identity threat framework to understand cognitive and affective experiences during interracial interactions. We discussed the role of prejudice concerns in shaping these experiences, arguing that a stereotype threat framework explains the patterns of results found quite well. Unlike research within the stereotype threat tradition, however, research on interracial interaction dynamics suggests that individuals' behavioral responses to identity threats can be either positive or negative. That is, research has found that both racial majority and minority individuals under threat can behave in ways that are more positive than their unthreatened counterparts and, as a result, create interactions with outgroup partners that are more positive than those created by individuals who were not so threatened. Again, we caution against an overinterpretation of these positive behavioral and interpersonal outcomes, noting that even these outcomes seem to be coupled with negative intrapersonal (cognitive and affective) outcomes for the threatened participants themselves.

Nevertheless, we believe that the examination of interracial contact through the lens of stereotype threat is likely to be useful. Many countries are becoming increasingly multiethnic/multiracial. Indeed, immigration is one of the most pressing societal issues for any number of countries. Consequently, opportunities for interethnic contact—and thus identity threat in many cases—are bound to rise. Given the compelling evidence that perceived threats to one's social identity are a primary source of intergroup hostility, it is important to develop a clear understanding of how interracial interactions may engender identity threat, and, more importantly, how to foster interactions that result in positive experiences for both individuals.

■ ENDNOTES

1. We use the terms *stereotype threat* and *social identity threat* interchangeably.

2. Although the focus of this chapter is on interracial interactions, where relevant, evidence from studies based on other intergroup divides (e.g., gender) will be included.

3. Interestingly, stereotype threat can sometimes result in behavior that is more positive for higher-prejudice whites. Because their baseline response to low-status outgroup members is more negative, the threat of appearing prejudiced and the monitoring of their subsequent thoughts and behavior serves to disrupt their normally negative behavior, resulting in more positive treatment of their outgroup interaction partners (Shelton et al., 2005b; Vorauer & Turpie, 2004).

References

Baumeister, R. F., Vohs, K. D., & Tice, D. M. (2007). The strength model of self-control. *Current Directions in Psychological Science, 16,* 396–403.

Bosson, J. K., Haymovitz, E. L., & Pinel, E. C. (2004). When saying and doing diverge: The effects of stereotype threat on self-reported versus non-verbal anxiety. *Journal of Experimental Social Psychology, 40,* 247–255.

Cohen, G. L., Garcia, J., Apfel, N., & Master, A. (2006). Reducing the racial achievement gap: A social-psychological intervention. *Science, 313,* 1307–1310.

Cohen, G. L., Steele, C. M., & Ross, L. D. (1999). The mentor's dilemma: Providing critical feedback across the racial divide. *Personality and Social Psychology Bulletin, 25,* 1302–1318.

Crosby, J. R., & Monin, B. (2007). Failure to warn: The effect of race on warnings of potential academic difficulty. *Journal of Experimental Social Psychology, 43,* 663–670.

Goff, P. A., Steele, C. M., & Davies, P. G. (2008). The space between us: Stereotype threat and distance in interracial contexts. *Journal of Personality and Social Psychology, 94,* 91–107.

Harber, K. D. (1998). Feedback to minorities: Evidence of a positive bias. *Journal of Personality and Social Psychology, 74,* 622–628.

Inzlicht, M., Kaiser, C. R., & Major, B. (2008). The face of chauvinism: How prejudice expectations shape perceptions of facial affect. *Journal of Experimental Social Psychology, 44,* 758–766.

Inzlicht, M., McKay, L., & Aronson, J. (2006). Stigma as ego depletion: How being the target of prejudice affects self-control. *Psychological Science, 17,* 262–269.

Jamieson, J. P., & Harkins, S. G. (2007). Mere effort and stereotype threat performance effects. *Journal of Personality and Social Psychology, 93,* 544–564.

Kray, L. J., Thompson, L., & Galinsky, A. (2001). Battle of the sexes: Gender stereotype confirmation and reactance in negotiations. *Journal of Personality and Social Psychology, 80,* 942–958.

Mendes, W. B., & Jamieson, J. P. (2011). Embodied stereotype threat: Exploring brain and body mechanisms underlying performance impairments. In M. Inzlicht, & T. Schmader (Eds.), *Stereotype threat: Theory, process, and application.* New York: Oxford University Press.

Miller, C., Rothblum, E., Felicio, D., & Brand, P. (1995). Compensating for stigma: Obese and nonobese women's reactions to being visible. *Personality and Social Psychology Bulletin, 21,* 1093–1106.

Murphy, M. C., Steele, C. M., & Gross, J. J. (2007). Signaling threat: How situational cues affect women in math, science, and engineering settings. *Psychological Science, 18*, 879–885.

Page-Gould, E., Mendoza-Denton, R., & Tropp, L. R. (2008). With a little help from my cross-group friend: Reducing anxiety in intergroup contexts through cross-group friendship. *Journal of Personality and Social Psychology, 95*, 1080–1094.

Pettigrew, T., & Tropp, L. (2006). A meta-analytic test of intergroup contact theory. *Journal of Personality and Social Psychology, 90*, 751–783.

Pinel, E. C. (2002). Stigma consciousness in intergroup contexts: The power of conviction. *Journal of Experimental Social Psychology, 38*, 178–185.

Plant, E. A. (2004). Responses to interracial interactions over time. *Personality and Social Psychology Bulletin, 30*, 1458–1471.

Richeson, J. A., Baird, A. A., Gordon, H. L., Heatherton, T. F., Wyland, C. L., Trawalter, S., & Shelton, J. N. (2003). An fMRI investigation of the impact of interracial contact on executive function. *Nature Neuroscience, 6*, 1323–1328.

Richeson, J. A., & Shelton, J. N. (2007). Negotiating interracial interactions: Costs, consequences, and possibilities. *Current Directions in Psychological Science, 16*, 316–320.

Richeson, J. A., & Shelton, J. N. (2003). When prejudice does not pay: Effects of interethnic contact on executive function. *Psychological Science, 14*, 287–290.

Richeson, J. A., & Trawalter, S. (2008). The threat of appearing prejudiced and race-based attentional biases. *Psychological Science, 19*, 98–102.

Richeson, J. A., & Trawalter, S. (2005). Why do interethnic interactions impair executive function? A resource depletion account. *Journal of Personality and Social Psychology, 88*, 934–947.

Richeson, J. A., Trawalter, S., & Shelton, J. N. (2005). African Americans' racial attitudes and the depletion of executive function after interracial interactions. *Social Cognition, 23*, 336–352.

Schmader, T., & Beilock, S. (2011). An integration of processes that underlie stereotype threat. In M. Inzlicht, & T. Schmader (Eds.), *Stereotype threat: Theory, process, and application.* New York: Oxford University Press.

Schmader, T., Johns, M., & Forbes, C. (2008). An integrated process model of stereotype threat effects on performance. *Psychological Review, 115*, 336–356.

Shelton, J. N. (2003). Interpersonal concerns in social encounters between majority and minority group members. *Group Processes and Intergroup Relations, 6*, 171–185.

Shelton, J. N., & Richeson, J. A. (2006). Interracial interactions: A relational approach. In M. P. Zanna (Ed.), *Advances in experimental social psychology* Vol. 38 (pp. 121–181). New York: Academic Press.

Shelton, J. N., Richeson, J. A., & Salvatore, J. (2005a). Expecting to be the target of prejudice. Implications for interethnic interactions. *Personality and Social Psychology Bulletin, 31*, 1189–1202.

Shelton, J. N., Richeson, J. A., Salvatore, J., & Trawalter, S. (2005b). Ironic effects of racial bias during interethnic interactions. *Psychological Science, 16*, 397–402.

Shelton, J. N., Richeson, J. A., & Vorauer, J. D. (2006). Threatened identities and interethnic interactions. *European Review of Social Psychology, 17*, 321–358.

Steele, C. M., & Aronson, J. (1995). Stereotype threat and the intellectual test performance of African-Americans. *Journal of Personality and Social Psychology, 69*, 797–811.

Steele, C. M., Spencer, S. J., & Aronson, J. (2002). Contending with group image: The psychology of stereotype and social identity threat. In M. P. Zanna (Ed.), *Advances in experimental social psychology* Vol. 34 (pp. 379–440). San Diego: Academic Press.

Trawalter, S., Richeson, J. A., & Shelton, J. N. (2009). Predicting behavior during interracial interactions: A stress and coping approach. *Personality and Social Psychology Review, 13,* 243–268.

Vorauer, J. D. (2006). An information search model of evaluative concerns in intergroup interaction. *Psychological Review, 113,* 862–886.

Vorauer, J. D., Hunter, A., Main, K., & Roy, S. (2000). Concerns with evaluation and meta-stereotype activation. *Journal of Personality and Social Psychology, 78,* 690–707.

Vorauer, J. D., & Turpie, C. (2004). Disruptive effects of vigilance on dominant group members' treatment of outgroup members: Choking versus shining under pressure. *Journal of Personality and Social Psychology, 87,* 384–399.

PART FOUR

Stereotype Threat and the Real World

16 Concerns About Generalizing Stereotype Threat Research Findings to Operational High-stakes Testing

■ PAUL R. SACKETT AND
ANN MARIE RYAN

The vast majority of stereotype threat research has been done in laboratory settings, and the focus of the chapter is on generalizing findings to the use of cognitive ability tests in high-stakes settings, such as personnel selection and admission for higher education. We first discuss some mischaracterization of the research findings on stereotype threat. Next, we discuss concerns regarding the generalizability of research findings to operational testing contexts, focusing on the degree to which boundary conditions for the experience of stereotype threat are met in high-stakes settings, and on the possibility of overcoming the inhibitory effects of experienced threat in high-stakes settings. We then review the limited existing research conducted in operational settings, including experimental, quasi-experimental, and observational studies. Our assessment is that research to date has not provided evidence of consistent and replicable threat effects in high-stakes settings, and that more research in operational testing settings is needed.

Keywords: Stereotype threat, academic performance, black–white test score gap, male–female science gap, intervention

This chapter focuses on the applied issue of the effects of stereotype threat on scores on psychological tests of developed abilities in high-stakes settings, such as postsecondary admissions and pre-employment screening. We write from the perspective of testing researchers with a long-standing interest in issues of fairness and bias. A major theme in the testing arena is the tension between two well-documented research findings. The first is that measures of developed abilities are very useful predictors of academic and job performance; the second is that mean differences are commonly found by race/ethnicity and gender in some specific domains (e.g., mathematics). As many educational institutions and employers value both high performance and diversity, the use of these tests is a potential route to one of these objectives and creates challenges in achieving the other

(Sackett, Borneman, & Connelly, 2008; Sackett, Schmitt, Ellingson, & Kabin, 2001; Sackett & Wilk, 1994).

Over the years, many proposed causes and potential remedies for the finding of mean differences have been put forward. Some view the existence of mean differences as primarily the result of an accumulation of life events that result in a lower mean level of the developed ability in question and focus on interventions aimed at life opportunities (e.g., reducing group differences in prenatal health care, childhood nutrition, educational resources, etc.; see Outtz & Newman, 2010, for a review). Others view the differences as primarily an artifact of the testing process and posit that changes in test content, format, or administration condition may reduce, if not eliminate, group differences. Sackett, Schmitt, Ellingson, and Kabin (2001) and Schmitt and Quinn (2010) review literature on strategies related to changing test content and context that have been proposed for reducing mean differences.

Stereotype threat straddles these two different positions as to causes of group differences. There is research that involves intervention studies aimed at true change in the construct of interest. For example, Good, Aronson, and Inzlicht (2003) describe an intervention occurring throughout the course of a school year investigating whether imparting a position that intelligence was malleable led to higher achievement among 7th graders. The argument is not that threat prevented students from demonstrating their ability when tested, but rather that threat interfered with learning throughout the year, and the intervention helped remove those barriers. Our interest in this chapter, though, is limited to studies in which the proposition is that threat has an artifactual effect on test scores (i.e., test takers do not demonstrate their true standing on the construct of interest due to threat).

As scientist-practitioners whose work focuses on testing in high-stakes settings and who monitor and evaluate various proposed strategies for reducing group differences, the issue of stereotype threat is of great interest. We approach this like any other proposed strategy, with hope that reducing stereotype threat may indeed prove effective in reducing mean differences while retaining, if not improving, the validity of the inferences drawn from test scores. At the same time, this hope is accompanied by a critical eye, as a number of strategies put forth in the past for reducing mean differences while retaining validity have proved ineffective once sufficient data have been amassed to evaluate the claim (e.g., using differential item functioning analysis to remove test items, or providing additional testing time (Sackett et al., 2001). That is, in the eagerness to find ways to resolve a major social concern regarding score gaps, some researchers have seized on simple solutions to what is a complex problem. Our aim in this chapter is to caution against a similar overeagerness with regard to the applicability of stereotype threat research to the problem of group differences on cognitive tests.

In this chapter, we first discuss some mischaracterization of the research findings on stereotype threat. Next, we discuss concerns regarding the generalizability of research findings to operational testing contexts. We then review existing research conducted in operational settings.

■ MISCHARACTERIZING THREAT AS FULLY EXPLAINING GROUP MEAN DIFFERENCES ON COGNITIVE TESTS

Sackett, Hardison, and Cullen (2004) observed that many summaries of the initial stereotype threat experiments by Steele and Aronson (1995) characterized the studies as showing that eliminating stereotype threat eliminated black–white differences. For example, the PBS show *Frontline* (1999) described stereotype threat research as follows: "blacks who believed the test was merely a research tool did the same as whites. But blacks who believed the test measured their abilities did half as well." However, *Frontline* failed to note that Steele and Aronson's work examined black and white students statistically equated on the basis of prior (SAT) scores. What Steele and Aronson report is not that actual test scores are the same for black and white students when threat is removed, but rather that after scores are statistically adjusted for differences in students' prior SAT performance, scores of both groups are the same. Thus, the findings actually show that, absent stereotype threat due to labeling, when the test is used as a measure of intelligence, the black and white students differ to about the degree that would be expected based on differences in prior SAT scores.

Note that in presenting Steele and Aronson's findings, an author can focus on within-group effects, between-group effects, or both. Sackett et al. found that discussions of threat research that focused on within-group effects were not prone to misinterpretation. Such presentations compare black student performance under threat and no threat conditions and properly note that the research clearly shows that the performance of black students differs under the two conditions. Presentations of threat research that focused on between-group effects (e.g., black vs. white) were prone to misinterpretation: Here, appropriate interpretation requires taking into account the fact that adjustments were made for existing SAT differences. Sackett et al. categorized accounts of between-subject effects in Steele and Aronson's findings. Accounts that specifically noted the adjustments for SAT differences were classified as correct. Accounts of the research that ignored the SAT adjustment and reported that, absent threat, the scores of the black and white groups were the same were classified as incorrect. Fourteen of 16 studies in the popular media, 10 of 11 studies in scientific journals, and 5 of 9 introductory textbooks were classified as incorrect.

We reiterate that nothing we report here is intended as criticism of Steele and Aronson's original research, or as a challenge to the concept of stereotype threat as a phenomenon with potential relevance to testing settings. The graphs in Steele and Aronson's research that document score differences consistently label them "adjusted by SAT score." Steele and Aronson do clearly show that imposing and eliminating stereotype threat can, in laboratory settings, affect the test performance of both black and white students, and other researchers have extended this to other groups (e.g., gender, age, etc.). This is important in that it highlights that fact that test scores can be influenced by factors other than the examinee's true level of skill and achievement. At one level, this is well known: The whole notion of standardized testing is based on controlling extraneous features of the testing environment. What is novel, though, is the demonstration that a standardized feature of test administration (e.g., the description of what the test measures) can have a differential effect on one group of examinees compared with another. Thus, continued attention to stereotype threat is certainly warranted, but the common misinterpretation of findings regarding between-group differences suggests the need for clearer communication regarding the implications of stereotype threat.

We also note that our critique of the misinterpretation of research that controls for a pretest does not imply that the presence or absence of a pretest is relevant per se to detecting stereotype threat effects. It is a critique of the interpretation of research results, rather than of research design.

■ ISSUES WITH ASSUMING GENERALIZABILITY OF LAB STUDIES TO OPERATIONAL TESTING SETTINGS

The initial Steele and Aronson (1995) studies offered an attractive and useful paradigm, and a great many studies have used some variant of it. The vast majority of studies examining the effects of threat on cognitive test performance have used student participants taking tests in a research context, as opposed to in a context in which test performance has long-term consequences, such as taking a high-stakes test in a personnel selection or college admissions setting. Nguyen and Ryan (2008) report a meta-analysis of 116 experimental studies of stereotype threat effects on cognitive test performance by race or gender. Of these studies, 103 used undergraduates, 12 used high school students, and one used a nonstudent sample, although not in an operational testing setting. In contrast, we are aware of only a handful of studies that attempt to examine threat effects in an operational high-stakes testing setting; these are reviewed later in this chapter.

Although this extensive body of laboratory research has resulted in a refined and nuanced understanding of threat effects, the generalizability of these effects to operational testing settings remains a relatively unexamined question. When thinking of "effects application research" in which the purpose is to produce parameter estimates of an effect for particular settings, such as determining the size of stereotype threat effects in high-stakes contexts, generalizability questions are of particular concern (Calder, Philips & Tybout, 1981, 1982). There are several plausible reasons why threat effects in the laboratory might not generalize. One is that threat may not be experienced in high-stakes settings; another is that threat may be experienced, but that test takers may be able to overcome the inhibitory influences of the stereotype threat effect.

Ryan and Sackett (in press) review the conditions posited as leading to the experience of threat and examine the degree to which they are likely to be met in high-stakes workplace settings. They conclude that, although almost all workplace assessment contexts meet some of the boundary conditions of the theory (e.g., a diagnostic task), there is likely considerable variability in whether others are met in a particular assessment context for various test takers (e.g., a highly difficult task, high domain identification). Lab studies are purposely designed to ensure the conditions to produce an effect are present—individuals can be made aware of a stereotype, and its relevance to the task can be pointed out to them directly. Individuals can be preselected for study participation based on their levels of domain identification, and tests can be selected that are highly difficult for that group. In workplace contexts, greater variability across contexts and persons in these theoretically required conditions is highly likely. Thus, Ryan and Sackett caution against assuming that stereotype threat automatically occurs when tests are administered for workplace decision making.

Regarding the possibility that test takers may experience threat, but be able to overcome the inhibitory influences of the stereotype threat effect, effort and cognitive focus may differ between research settings and high-stakes testing settings. There is research showing that student research participants perform worse than those with some incentive for taking tests (e.g., Tomporowski, Simpson, & Hager, 1993), that students simulating job applicants react differently to testing than do those in actual hiring contexts (Hausknecht, Day, & Thomas, 2004), and that self-reported motivation is typically high and restricted in range in studies with actual job applicants (e.g., Schmit & Ryan, 1997). Wheeler and Petty (2001), in reviewing research on stereotype activation, note that there are a number of strategies an individual might engage in when a stereotype is activated, and these may vary in their outcomes. They note "the same situation could be perceived as a threat or as a challenging opportunity . . . both positive and negative expectations for one's performance can lead to both performance improvements and performance decrements" (p. 819). In essence, Wheeler and Petty argue that there are multiple paths by which stereotype primes might affect behavior; this suggests the importance of considering key environmental variables (e.g., the stakes associated with testing outcomes) as potential influences on which paths are taken in real-world testing contexts.

Policy Box

The vast majority of stereotype threat research has been done in laboratory settings, and the focus of the chapter is on the extent to which findings generalize to the use of cognitive ability tests in high-stakes settings, such as personnel selection and admission for higher education. We offer concerns regarding the generalizability of research findings to operational testing contexts, such as the fact that boundary conditions for the experience of stereotype threat are not always met in high-stakes settings. Our assessment of the limited existing research conducted in operational settings is that, to date, it has not provided evidence of consistent and replicable threat effects in high-stakes settings, and that more research in operational testing settings is needed.

As such, we caution against blanket conclusions that tests are biased due to stereotype threat, absent specific information showing bias in the setting in which the test is to be used. Similarly, we caution against conclusions that test scores obtained by members of specific groups should be adjusted due to presumed effects of stereotype threat, absent evidence of the biasing effects of threat in the setting in question.

■ STUDIES OF STEREOTYPE THREAT IN OPERATIONAL TESTING SETTINGS

As motivational differences between participants in lab studies and operational testing settings may be important boundary conditions on generalizability of findings, a question of interest, then, is what the limited number of studies in operational testing settings tell us about threat effects in such settings. We examined three types of studies relevant to operational testing settings. The first type is experimental studies in laboratory settings that contrast test performance under threat and nonthreat conditions in the laboratory with performance on an operational test. The second involves experiments or quasi-experiments that either create or take advantage of naturally occurring differences in the context in which an operational test is taken. These studies use priming methods that have been shown to produce threat effects in laboratory settings: namely, varying whether examinees are asked to report race and gender prior to or after taking a test. The third involves nonexperimental studies that attempt to draw inferences about threat effects from patterns of operational testing data, absent an explicit manipulation of threat. We review each in turn.

Studies Comparing an Operational Test with a Test Given Under Experimental Threat Versus Nonthreat Conditions

Walton and Spencer (2009) presented a meta-analysis in which they reanalyzed 39 stereotype threat studies that also included an external measure, such as an SAT or ACT test taken as part of the admissions process. Walton and Spencer reconfigured the studies into a regression format in which the test taken under operational conditions was used to predict scores obtained in the threat experiment. They conceptualized the score obtained on the experimental test in nonthreat conditions as a measure of "latent ability," and asked whether tests taken under different conditions in the laboratory over- or underestimate operational test scores. They reported that, in nonthreat conditions, members of stereotyped groups obtained higher experimental test scores than did members of nonstereotyped groups with the same score on the operational test. These findings led them to conclude that the operational test underestimates latent ability by .17 to .18 standard deviations (SD).

However, there is a straightforward alternate explanation for the observed findings. As a general principle, latent ability is best estimated in conditions in which no other sources of construct-irrelevant variance are present. Any motivational, cognitive, or situational source of construct-irrelevant variance confounds ability estimates. Any feature that reduces test-taking motivation or interferes with cognitive processing (e.g., distractions) biases ability estimates downward. Note that all biases related to examinee behavior must be directional: They can reduce estimates of latent ability, but cannot increase them, as latent ability is definitionally a maximum performance construct.

Thus, it follows that since stereotyped students' scores in a nonthreat condition are higher than their scores in a threat condition, then nonthreat scores are a better approximation of latent ability than are threat scores for stereotyped students. However, Walton and Spencer did not apply the same logic to nonstereotyped students. They based their conclusion that tests are biased on a comparison of the relationship between operational test (e.g., SAT) scores and experimentally administered tests. To estimate latent ability for the stereotyped students, they used the experimental test in nonthreat conditions. To estimate latent ability for nonstereotyped students, they also used the experimental test in nonthreat conditions. On the surface, this sounds reasonable: Stereotyped and nonstereotyped students are being compared in the same condition. But the "catch" is that, for nonstereotyped students, performance in the nonthreat condition is a downwardly biased estimate of latent ability.

A prior meta-analysis by Walton and Cohen (2003) found evidence of "stereotype lift": Nonstereotyped students obtained higher scores in the threat condition than in the nonthreat condition. The fact that nonstereotyped students scored higher in threat conditions means that their performance in nonthreat conditions is not a measure of their latent ability. Walton and Cohen (2003) reported that they score on average .25 SD higher in the threat condition. So, if one views the condition in which higher scores are obtained as the condition producing better estimates of latent ability, one would choose the threat condition for the nonstereotyped students—a condition in which scores are .25 SDs higher than the condition chosen by Walton and Spencer (2009). Rather than showing that stereotyped students' latent ability scores are underestimated by .17–.18 SD, as they reported, that underestimation would disappear if the best estimate of latent ability were used for the nonstereotyped group.

Walton and Spencer's (2009) analyses fall under the rubric of "differential prediction," also labeled "predictive bias," in which regression lines are compared across subgroups. This is the established method for examining predictive bias in the Standards for Educational and Psychological Testing (American Educational Research Association/American Psychological Association/National Council on Measurement in Education [AERA, APA, NCME], 1999). Differences in slopes or intercepts by subgroup indicate predictive bias. The analysis assumes that that the criterion against which the operational predictor is being compared is itself unbiased (Linn & Werts, 1971).

Thus, for Walton and Spencer to draw conclusions about bias in operational tests based on comparisons with laboratory tests of latent ability, the latent ability measures must be unbiased for both groups. The authors focused on an argument that groups must be compared in comparable experimental treatment conditions (i.e., scores obtained in nonthreat conditions for both stereotyped and nonstereotyped groups), despite the evidence that scores of nonstereotyped group members in nonthreat conditions are biased (i.e., they are underestimates of latent ability). Thus, we are not persuaded by Walton and Spencer's argument that this analysis of the relationship between operational and experimental scores provides evidence that operational test scores are biased.

Nonexperimental Studies of Operational Tests Examining Predictions from the Theory of Stereotype Threat

There are significant obstacles to attempting a direct experimental test of stereotype threat theory in applied high-stakes testing settings. One concern is ethical. Imagine that it were possible to experimentally induce stereotype threat in one group of applicants and to completely remove stereotype threat in another. If results supported the theory and showed meaningful differences in test performance, then the educational or employment opportunities of those assigned to the threat condition would be harmed. Thus, the risk of harm to research participants would appear to limit such experimental research in high-stakes settings. Another concern is pragmatic. In the laboratory setting, it is feasible to present differing cover stories about the purpose of a test (e.g., to measure intelligence vs. to investigate a newly developed lab task) or about group differences. In high-stakes testing, the purpose of the testing is clear to the applicants, and it is doubtful that it would be believable—or ethical—to present information attempting to minimize threat by downplaying the importance of the test or by presenting factually untrue information suggesting no subgroup differences. Thus, most cues used to create stereotype threat groups in lab settings cannot be experimentally induced in high-stakes operational testing for ethical or pragmatic reasons.

Given the difficulties with direct experimentation, attempts have been made to turn to nonexperimental data collected in operational testing settings and to offer propositions regarding data patterns that would be expected if stereotype threat did affect scores. Data are then examined to see whether or not the patterns expected in the presence of threat effects are indeed observed. Two related studies taking this approach were undertaken by Cullen, Hardison, and Sackett (2004) and Cullen, Waters, and Sackett (2006), both examining threat effects by gender on the SAT Math (SATM) test. They obtained data on over 49,000 college students, including SAT Math and Verbal scores and subsequent college grades in math and English courses. They posited that stereotype threat theory results in a set of testable predictions about the expected pattern of regression lines relating test scores to criteria for different subgroups.

A key notion in stereotype threat theory is that threat affects individuals identified with the domain in question. Cullen, Waters, and Sackett (2006) used intended major as a measure of domain identification, reasoning that students intending to major in math were, on average, more strongly identified with the math domain than were students not intending to major in math. Thus, they contrasted these two groups, with the key analysis being whether the regression coefficient for intent to major in math differed for males and females. They reasoned that if math-identified female students obtained lowered SAT Math scores as a result of stereotype threat, then intent to major in math should capture the threat effect for females, but there would be no parallel effect for males. Thus, if threat were operating, the coefficient for math identification should be greater for females than for males. Contrary to this pattern—which would be expected under stereotype threat—the male and female coefficients for math identification did not differ.

Cullen, Hardison, and Sackett (2004) reported an additional set of analyses with a striking set of results. As Cullen et al. had both SAT Math and SAT Verbal, and both English and Math grades, it is possible to examine male and female regression lines for all combinations of SAT subtests and grade types. In an analysis pairing SAT Math with English grades, threat effects would be posited for the test but not the criterion. In contrast, for SAT Verbal paired with English grades, there is no reason to posit stereotype threat effects for either the test or the criterion. For SAT Math paired with Math grades, one would expect that if threat were operating, it would affect both test and criterion. And, finally, for SAT English paired with Math grades, threat would be posited on the criterion, but not on the test. A common pattern of findings across conditions would be counter to what would be expected if threat were affecting the test, the criterion, neither, or both. Yet a common pattern of findings does result.

Experimental and Quasi-experimental Studies in Operational Testing Settings

As noted earlier, there are obstacles to using the prototypical stereotype threat experimental paradigm in operational testing settings. However, there have been several studies that build on the finding that threat effects have been produced in laboratory settings by a manipulation as subtle as asking participants to self-report their race or gender prior to testing. Although many operational testing settings collect this self-report data, the point in the testing process when this has been collected varies across settings. In response to this finding, Stricker and Ward (2004) reported two experiments in which they manipulated the timing of collection of this demographic data. Study 1 examined an advanced placement (AP) calculus examination; 755 students reported demographic information after the test, and 897 reported the information before the test. Study 2 examined four computerized placement tests (CPT) in algebra, arithmetic, reading comprehension, and sentence skills; for each test, experimental and control groups ranged from 487 to 615. These tests are used to grant college credit for courses taken in high school in the case of AP calculus and to aid decisions about the appropriate community college or college course level for a student placement in the case of the four placement tests. Stricker and Ward examined differences by race (black vs. white) and gender and concluded that the specific manipulation of the timing of collection of race and gender information did not produce a discernible effect in these samples.

Danaher and Crandall (2008) revisited the Stricker and Ward findings and reported a significant condition-by-gender interaction for a number of derived scores for the AP calculus exam, and also reported a gender by condition interaction for reading comprehension on the CPT. For AP calculus, they made a number of projections about these effects. First, assuming that scores are normally distributed, they projected that changing the timing of the collection of demographic data leads to a 6% higher pass rate for females and a 4% lower rate for males. They projected this to the national population of test takers as of the time they wrote their article, and estimated that changing the timing of collection of demographic information would increase the number of female students receiving AP credit by 4,763. Stricker and Ward (2008) offered a rebuttal to Danaher and Crandall's reassessment.

We will examine this dispute in more detail, as Danaher and Crandall's reanalysis is emerging as a key response to concerns about generalizability of threat to non-laboratory settings. For example, in their prominent integrative article Schmader, Johns, and Forbes (2008) cite Danaher and Crandall's reanalysis of the AP Calculus data as their sole rebuttal to concerns about lack of generalizability. In particular, we feel that Danaher and Crandall's focusing on one effect vs. considering the full pattern of findings provides a misleading interpretation of the data.

We reframe the Stricker and Ward data in terms of effect sizes, specifically, as the standardized mean difference (d) between the test performance of a group of interest when demographic information is not collected prior to the test versus when it is collected prior to the test. On the AP calculus test, Stricker and Ward reported six scores, many of which reflect different ways of scoring the same test information (e.g., number correct vs. number correct/number attempted vs. number correct corrected for guessing), with correlations as high as .96 between the different scoring methods. Five of the six reflect differing ways of estimating performance in calculus; the sixth (number attempted) does not and shows the lowest correlations with the others. Thus, we set aside number attempted and focused on the other five. As there was no clear a priori reason to choose one of these five over another (prior threat research has used various scoring methods), we computed d values for each and averaged them to produce an estimate of the effects of condition on calculus performance. For the CPT tests, there was only one score metric—number right—and thus d could be computed directly.

Table 16.1 shows d values by race and gender for all five tests. We find computing separate d's for each subgroup useful. A minimum requirement for a threat effect, we believe, is that members of a group hypothesized to experience threat perform better in conditions posited as less threatening than do members of the same groups in conditions viewed as threatening. If no difference is found, there is no threat effect. If a difference is found, then one should also look at the nonstereotyped group. If testing condition affects *both* groups in the same way, then the effect cannot be attributed to threat. Only if there is differential performance in the direction predicted by threat theory can the findings be interpreted as evidence of threat.

Table 16.1 presents a number of interesting findings. First, consider female performance. Although information is available for five tests, three of them are in the math domain, in which a gender stereotype exists; the other two are in the reading/verbal domain, in which no negative stereotype exists about female performance. Thus, there are three tests where one might posit a threat effect. In these three, the

TABLE 16.1 *Standardized mean differences by race and gender in Stricker and Ward (2004)*

	Male d	Female d	White d	Black d
AP Calculus	−.125	.166	.016	.155
Algebra	−.231	−.152	−.103	.033
Arithmetic	−.110	.051	.087	.037
3-Test Mean	**−.155**	**.022**		
Reading Comprehension	−.099	.264	−.014	.061
Sentence Skill	−.033	.067	.00	.082
5-Test Mean			**−.003**	**.074**

results are varied. In AP calculus, the table shows the female mean is .166 SDs higher in the less-threatening condition (i.e., without a pretest inquiry as to gender). This is the finding that is the basis for Danaher and Crandall's projection of the increase in the number of women who would receive AP credit if the pretest gender inquiry were removed.

Note, though, that on the CPT algebra test, an effect of comparable magnitude is found, but in the opposite direction ($d = −.152$). One might point to this effect as evidence that the intervention of removing the pretest gender inquiry *harms* female test performance. The third relevant test, CPT arithmetic, shows a near-zero effect of .051. The mean across these three relevant tests is .022.

Note also that there is a d of .264 across conditions for females on the reading comprehension test, but there is no basis for positing a stereotype about women's performance on this test. There is no comparable effect for the other reading/verbal test, namely sentence skill. Thus, for the four CPT tests, there are two where gender effects are seen. One is on a test where threat effects could be hypothesized, but the effect is in the opposite direction. The other is on a test where threat effects would not be hypothesized.

Overall, across eight settings in which threat would be hypothesized (three tests for gender, five for race), the mean d for the stereotyped group is .043, and the mean d for the nonstereotyped group is −.037. There is considerable variability in findings, with some larger effects consistent with threat theory (e.g., the female d of .166 for AP calculus; the black female mean d of .265 across all five test) and some larger effects in the opposite direction from predictions from threat theory (e.g., the female d of −.152 for algebra; the black male mean d of −.149 across all five tests). If the pattern were one of some supporting effects and some null effects, one might make a case for interpreting this as supportive of one's theory. But this pattern of small effects in opposite directions is, as we see it, difficult to interpret as evidence that threat effects do generalize to operational testing settings.

We mention briefly a study by Kernan, Alfieri, Bragger, and Harris (2008), which, like Stricker and Ward (2004), also attempted to examine threat effects via varying the placement of demographic information. They examined a setting in which an employment test was administered for a number of years with applicant demographics collected prior to the test. The test was then modified and updated, and demographics were shifted to the end of the test. The authors noted that this is a weak design for drawing inferences about threat, as test difficulty might be different (in fact, all groups performed substantially better on the revised test), and the quality of applicant pools might change over time. They found small and inconsistent race and gender effects, and concluded that it was difficult to draw meaningful conclusions about threat effects from the study.

One additional true experiment in an operational setting that dealt with a specific prediction dealing with stereotype threat was reported by Walker and Bridgeman (2008). Beilock, Rydell, and McConnell (2007) have proposed a spillover hypothesis, such that threat effects in one domain (e.g., women in math) would affect subsequent test performance in other domains (e.g., verbal; see also Inzlicht, Tullett, & Gutsell, 2011, Chapter 7, this volume). Walker and Bridgeman took advantage of the fact that the SAT has multiple sections, administered in different orders. They examined whether scores on a critical reading subtest differed as a result of following a math, reading, or writing subtest, using a very large sample of 200,000 test-takers. Spillover effects were very small: The gender-by-subtest interaction accounted for less than one-tenth of 1% of the variance, which translates to differences of less than 1/20th of an SAT score point. Walker and Bridgeman concluded that there was no evidence of either stereotype threat or stereotype lift resulting from the type of test to which examinees were first exposed.

Also in the vein of attempting a conceptual replication of a laboratory finding in an operational setting is a quasi-experiment by Walters, Lee, and Trapani (2004) that examined the effects of test proctor race and gender on Graduate Record Examination (GRE) test performance. Walters, Shepperd, and Brown (2003) had found proctor race effects, and Marx and Roman (2002) found proctor gender effects in laboratory settings. Walters, Lee, and Trapani examined whether having a same or different race/ethnicity proctor ($N = 12,397$) or a same or different gender proctor ($N = 7,524$) affected operational GRE performance. Findings were not consistent with what would be expected if a different-race or different-gender proctor induced stereotype threat. Only a few significant differences were found, and those were small effects in the direction opposite to that expected (e.g., Hispanic test takers scored lower in the presence of a Hispanic proctor).

■ CONCLUSION

This chapter has several key messages. The first is that the results of the original stereotype threat experiments have frequently been wrongly interpreted as showing that black–white test score differences disappear when threat is removed. This misinterpretation is a result of failing to recognize that the studies controlled for prior SAT scores. Thus, the finding of no difference between groups in the nonthreat condition does not mean that the commonly observed mean difference has been eliminated, as the groups being compared have been statistically equated in terms of prior SAT scores.

The second is that there are concerns that the motivational differences between lab and operational settings limit the generalizability of lab findings. Varying the motivation of lab participants might yield insights into where the motivational boundary might be. Other boundary conditions might also be explored (e.g., manipulating threat by using cues that mirror operational setting cues, such as when demographics are reported).

The third is that there has been a very limited amount of investigation of stereotype threat effects on cognitive tests in operational testing settings. The body of work in laboratory settings is extensive, and a large number of studies have reported threat effects. It is common in these studies to note the potential relevance of the findings to applied settings. But the leap from potential relevance to actual evidence is a substantial one.

The fourth is that the limited set of studies that have examined threat effects in operational testing settings has been consistent in a lack of consistent patterns of support for threat effects. These studies include examinations of whether features found to produce threat effects in laboratory settings produce similar effects in operational settings. Features examined include race or gender priming by asking for self-reports of race or gender just prior to taking a test, the effects of taking a test in a domain posited as threatening (e.g., math for females) on subsequent test performance in a domain posited as nonthreatening (e.g., verbal), and the use of same versus different race or gender test proctors. As others have noted (e.g., Walker & Bridgeman, 2008) these findings do not prove that stereotype threat does not exist in operational testing settings. It is possible that, in high-stakes testing environments, examinees are already sufficiently worried about their test performance, and thus subtle features, such as being asked to provide demographic information, play no measurable incremental role.

This argument about the totality of the threatening nature of a high-stakes test setting versus the subtle effects of the types of manipulations discussed above highlights the value of the paradigm followed in the Cullen et al. (2004, 2006) investigations, in which the focus is not on a specific threat manipulation, but rather on seeking evidence for the relationship between test scores and subsequent performance that would be expected if test scores of members of stereotyped groups were systematically lowered as a result of threat. Cullen et al. examined test performance relationships in domains in which threat would be hypothesized on both test and outcome (e.g., both math tests and subsequent performance in math courses for females), on neither test and outcome (e.g., verbal tests and English course performance for females), and on test, but not outcome (and on outcome, but not test). The comparability of test–outcome relationships in these different settings is not consistent with patterns that would be expected if threat had systematic effects.

We reiterate our strong interest in mechanisms that might reduce the test score mean differences between groups. We endorse broad exploration of the full spectrum of potential strategies for reducing these differences. Although our evaluation is that evidence from operational test settings that stereotype threat removal might be such a strategy has not emerged, our message is that more work in applied settings is needed.

References

American Educational Research Association/American Psychological Association/National Council on Measurement in Education (AERA, APA, NCME). (1999). *Standards for educational and psychological testing.* Washington, DC: American Educational Research Association.

Beilock, S. L., Rydell, R. J., & McConnell, A. R. (2007). Stereotype threat and working memory: Mechanisms, alleviation, and spillover. *Journal of Experimental Psychology: General, 136,* 256–276.

Calder, B. J., Phillips, L. W., & Tybout, A. M. (1981). Designing research for application. *Journal of Consumer Research, 8,* 197–207.

Calder, B. J., Phillips, L. W., & Tybout, A. M. (1982). The concept of external validity. *Journal of Consumer Research, 9,* 240–244.

Cullen, M. J., Hardison, C. M., & Sackett, P. R. (2004). Using SAT-grade and ability-job performance relationships to test predictions derived from stereotype threat theory. *Journal of Applied Psychology, 89,* 220–230.

Cullen, M. J., Waters, S. D., & Sackett, P. R. (2006). Testing stereotype threat theory predictions for math majors and non-majors by gender. *Human Performance, 19,* 421–440.

Danaher, K., & Crandall, C. S. (2008). Stereotype threat in applied settings reexamined: A reply. *Journal of Applied Social Psychology, 34,* 1656–1663.

Good, C., Aronson, J., & Inzlicht, M. (2003). Improving adolescents' standardized test performance: An intervention to reduce the effects of stereotype threat. *Journal of Applied Developmental Psychology, 24,* 645–662.

Hausknecht, J. P., Day, D. V., Thomas St., C. (2004). Applicant reactions to selection procedures: An updated model and meta-analysis. *Personnel Psychology, 57,* 639–683.

Inzlicht, M., Tullett, A. M., & Gutsell, J. N. (2011). Threat spillover: The short-term and long-term effects of coping with threats to social identity. In M. Inzlicht, & T. Schmader (Eds.), *Stereotype threat: Theory, process, and application.* New York: Oxford University Press.

Kernan, J. P., Alfieri, J. A., Bragger, J. D., & Harris, R. S. (2009). An investigation of stereotype threat in employment tests. *Journal of Applied Social Psychology, 39,* 359–388.

Linn, R. L., & Werts, C. E. (1971). Considerations for studies of test bias. *Journal of Educational Measurement, 8*(1), 1–4.

Marx, D. M., & Roman, J. S. (2002). Female role models: Protecting women's math test performance. *Personality and Social Psychology Bulletin, 28,* 1183–1193.

Nguyen, H. D., & Ryan, A. M. (2008). Does stereotype threat affect test performance of minorities and women? A meta-analysis of experimental evidence. *Journal of Applied Psychology, 93,* 1314–1334.

Outtz, J. L., & Newman, D. A. (2010). A theory of adverse impact. In J. L. Outtz (Ed.), *Adverse impact: Implications for organizational staffing and high stakes selection* (pp. 53–94). New York: Routledge.

Ryan, A. M., & Sackett, P. R. (in press). Stereotype threat in workplace assessments. In K. Geisinger (Ed.), *APA handbook of testing and assessment in psychology.* Washington, DC: American Psychological Association.

Sackett, P. R., Borneman, M. J., & Connelly, B. S. (2008). High-stakes testing in higher education and employment: Appraising the evidence for validity and fairness. *American Psychologist, 63*, 215–227.

Sackett, P. R., Hardison, C. M., & Cullen, M. J. (2004). On interpreting stereotype threat as accounting for African American-White differences on cognitive tests. *American Psychologist, 59*, 7–13.

Sackett, P. R., Schmitt, N., Ellingson, J. E., & Kabin, M. B. (2001). High-stakes testing in employment, credentialing and higher education: Prospects in a post-affirmative action world. *American Psychologist, 56*, 302–318.

Sackett, P. R., & Wilk, S. L. (1994). Within-group norming and other forms of score adjustment in preemployment testing. *American Psychologist, 49*, 929–954.

Schmader, T., Johns, M., & Forbes, C. (2008). An integrated process model of stereotype threat effects on performance. *Psychological Review, 115*, 336–356.

Schmit, M. J., & Ryan, A. M. (1997). Applicant withdrawal: The role of test-taking attitudes and racial differences. *Personnel Psychology, 50*, 855–876.

Schmitt, N., & Quinn, A. (2010). Reduction in measured subgroup differences: What is possible? In J. L. Outtz (Ed.), *Adverse impact: Implications for organizational staffing and high stakes selection* (pp. 425–451). New York: Routledge.

Steele, C. M., & Aronson, J. (1995). Stereotype threat and the intellectual performance of African-Americans. *Journal of Personality and Social Psychology, 69*, 797–811.

Stricker, L. J., & Ward, W. C. (2004). Stereotype threat, inquiring about test takers'ethnicity and gender, and standardized test performance. *Journal of Applied Social Psychology, 34*, 665–693.

Stricker, L. J., & Ward, W. C. (2008). Stereotype threat in applied settings reexamined: A reply. *Journal of Applied Social Psychology, 34*, 1656–1663.

Tomporowski, P. D., Simpson, R. G., & Hager, L. (1993). Method of recruiting subjects and performance on cognitive tests. *American Journal of Psychology, 106*, 499–521.

Walker, M. E., & Bridgeman, B. (2008). *Stereotype threat spillover and SAT scores* (Research Report 2008–2). New York: The College Board.

Walters, A. M., Lee, S., & Trapani, C. (2004). *Stereotype threat, the test-center environment, and performance on the GRE general test.* (GRE Board Research Report No. 01–03R). Princeton, NJ: Educational Testing Service.

Walters, A. M., Shepperd, J. A., & Brown, L. M. (2003). *The effect of test administrator ethnicity on test performance.* Manuscript submitted for publication.

Walton, G. M., & Cohen, G. L. (2003). Stereotype lift. *Journal of Experimental Social Psychology, 39*, 456–467.

Walton, G. M., & Spencer, S. S. (2009). Latent ability: Grades and test scores systematically underestimate the intellectual ability of women and ethnic minority students. *Psychological Science, 20*, 1132–1139.

Wheeler, S. C., & Petty, R. E. (2001). The effects of stereotype activation on behavior: A review of possible mechanisms. *Psychological Bulletin, 127*, 797–826.

17 Stereotype Threat in the Real World

■ JOSHUA ARONSON AND
THOMAS DEE

Hundreds of laboratory experiments have shown that stereotype threat can undermine intellectual performance in the laboratory. But do the same processes demonstrated in the laboratory operate in the real world? And, can they help us explain and remediate achievement gaps between blacks and whites, well to do and poor, and women and men? In this chapter, we take up this question, reviewing the most pertinent evidence and the best-known critiques of stereotype threat. Specifically, we argue that the confluence of evidence from meta-analyses of experiments, longitudinal studies, field experiments, natural experiments, and field interventions points strongly to the conclusion that stereotype threat is a very useful construct for understanding and improving real-world achievement.

Keywords: Stereotype threat, academic performance, black–white test score gap, high-stakes testing, testing and measurement

A great many laboratory experiments have examined the effects of stereotype threat on intellectual performance. The general finding is that stereotype threat influences performance. If a negative stereotype is made relevant to a challenging task, people perform worse on it (Inzlicht & Ben-Zeev, 2000; Spencer, Steele, & Quinn, 1999; Steele & Aronson, 1995). If a positive stereotype is made relevant, performance generally improves (McGlone & Aronson, 2006; Shih, Pittinsky, & Ambady, 1999). Although this is the general finding, the chapters in this volume reveal the many specifics to consider if one wants to make predictions about how and how much a given individual's performance will be affected by stereotype threat. In this chapter, we discuss the extensive literature on stereotype threat to consider its implications for "real-world" performance and achievement. We also consider criticisms of stereotype threat that suggest its real-world influence is negligible.

We think it is important to note that, even without considering how much stereotype threat matters in the real world, the laboratory findings are interesting and important in their own right; they reveal something profound about the dynamics of social identity and intellectual functioning. In a broad sense, that "something" is the mere fact that subtle situational cues—details easily overlooked—can meaningfully influence performance, depending on the way one's group is viewed by the larger culture. The first author of this chapter continues to marvel at this fact, even though it has been almost 20 years since he designed and conducted his first stereo-type threat experiments (Steele & Aronson, 1995). Clearly, he hasn't been alone in being struck by the fragility and malleability of human intellectual performance. Since the publication of the first stereotype threat experiments (Spencer, Steele, & Quinn, 1999; Steele & Aronson, 1995), over 300 experiments have confirmed, refined, and extended aspects of the theory, and the result of these experiments is a wealth of knowledge about the parameters of these effects—the range of behaviors and social identities subject to stereotype threat, the moderating influences on these effects, the mental processes that mediate the effects, and so on (see Aronson & McGlone, 2009; Schmader, Johns, & Forbes, 2008, for reviews).

■ THE REAL WORLD

Still, despite this impressive record of replication, it is reasonable to ask whether stereotype threat operates outside the controlled conditions of the laboratory and therefore, whether we can reasonably count it as a factor in the performance and achievement gaps that exist between blacks and whites, poor and well-to-do, Latinos and whites, Asians and whites, men and women, and so on (see, for example, Sackett & Ryan, 2011, Chapter 16, this volume). Some critics of the theory have bemoaned the fact that the laboratory experiments have not produced a clear sense of *how much* the black–white test score gap or the male–female engineering Ph.D. gap can be attributed to stereotype threat. For example, Wax (2009) points to the artificiality of the experiments, the specialized populations, and the use of analysis of covariance as all obscuring our ability to know how much we should care about the role of stereotype threat in mediating performance outside the laboratory (see Aronson, 2009, for a detailed rebuttal of this position).

The practical relevance of lab-based studies has become a source of lively debate among economists (e.g., Falk & Heckman 2009; Levitt & List 2007). Regarding stereotype threat, we believe this criticism reflects a profound misunderstanding about what laboratory experiments are for and why they are critical to understanding important psychological processes wherever they occur. A laboratory experiment—whether artificial or realistic, whether conducted with "college sophomores" or inner-city 3rd-graders, whether employing analysis of covariance or propensity scores—cannot definitively establish the degree to which a particular phenomenon matters in the real world. Experiments can be a powerful tool for testing if theories about the real world generalize to the laboratory, for examining human responses to stimuli in the laboratory, and for asking about what *can* happen in the laboratory and in the real world—all very important things. But experiments are not an appropriate tool for estimating the degree of importance or impact of variables in the real world. Criticizing experiments on stereotype threat for not providing estimates of its real-world impact is a bit like cursing at your toaster for not toasting an unsliced loaf; experiments are not designed to yield this information (e.g., Gilbert, 1998; Mook, 1983). However, it should also be noted that the distinctions made between laboratory and field experiments are not always crisp. In particular, according to the taxonomy introduced by Harrison and List (2004), many of the canonical stereo-type threat experiments would actually be categorized as "framed field experiments." This is both because the study population (i.e., students) is often the exact study population of interest and because the experimental task (i.e., test performance) is a field task of central interest. Furthermore, the unusual degree of scrutiny that characterizes laboratory experiments is also a feature of key field settings like classrooms or testing centers (see Schmader & Stone, 2008).

The stereotype threat laboratory experiments do bear importantly on an alternative theory about the nature of intellectual performance, one encapsulated in *the Bell Curve* (Herrnstein & Murray, 1994) and embraced by many. That theory goes like this: A person's intelligence test score is determined by native intelligence, preparation, and effort; little else matters (e.g., Murray, 2008). Although such experiments may tell us little about how much stereotype threat generalizes to the real world, they do tell us how well the *Bell Curve* theory generalizes to the laboratory: Not terribly well, it turns out. Experiment after experiment in this literature shows that social factors other than effort, intelligence, and preparation will boost or spoil performance, and thus, that, at least in the laboratory, the *Bell Curve* theory requires modification: It is simply not enough to know how smart or motivated a student is. If intellectual performance can be made to rise or fall in response to simple and subtle manipulations of the social context, then something else must be involved beyond intelligence and motivation.

So, what is known about the role of stereotype threat in real-world settings? A small but growing number of studies (e.g., Arbuthnot, 2009; Good, Aronson, & Harder, 2008; Keller & Dauenheimer, 2003; Kellow & Jones, 2007) have addressed this question using rigorous research designs (i.e., random assignment) that support causal inference, but doing so in the field settings of interest (i.e., in actual class-rooms). The number of field experimental studies is still quite small, but the evidence from these early studies is largely consistent with the much larger body of lab-based evidence and suggests the real-world relevance and utility of stereotype threat.

These early field experiments constitute an important new direction for exploring the relevance of stereotype threat for education-related policies and practices. This is particularly so because these studies do not focus narrowly on whether stereotype threat exists in field settings; instead, they focus on rigorously evaluating interventions designed to improve student performance by *buffering* students from the negative consequences stereotype threat. Although this group of studies is provocative, the nature of field experiments and the small number of studies currently available invite several caveats. For example, the "external validity" of a study is always an open question, if it is based on a small number of classrooms, involves only students for whom consent is provided, and so on.

Furthermore, although field experiments may have "mundane realism," they may lack "experimental realism" (Aronson & Carlsmith, 1968), and thus may fail to capture the quality of the real world that most distinguishes it from the laboratory—real consequences for performance. To provide a complete overview of the real-world implications of stereotype threat, we therefore need to consider multiple kinds of studies at the same time.

■ LABORATORY EXPERIMENTS

The first kind of data comes from the hundreds of laboratory demonstrations of how stereotypes influence performance in the laboratory. These experiments provide a sense of what *can* happen—what kind of manipulations can promote or impair performance, mediated by which mechanisms, and moderated by which individual differences or motives. The understanding that comes from such studies provides a solid basis for asking intelligent questions about the real world and making predictions about the situations likely to produce either boosts or declines in performance. Although not definitive all by themselves, such experiments represent a very important pillar in the foundation on which we may base an understanding of stereotype threat in real-world educational outcomes.

One approach to synthesizing the findings of these experiments is to conduct a meta-analysis that can provide summative evidence on the extent to which stereotype threat suppresses test scores and grades. For example, Gregory Walton and Steven Spencer (2009) conducted two meta-analyses involving nearly 19,000 students. The study compared participants' test performance in stereotype threat situations with those in threat-reduced situations and used prior test scores (e.g., Scholastic Assessment Test [SAT]) or grades—which most would agree qualify as real-world performances. Walton and Spencer found strong evidence that, for minorities and women, real-world scores and grades are systematically suppressed by stereotype threat. Specifically, on verbal tasks in laboratory settings under conditions that reduced stereotype threat, non-Asian minorities consistently performed better than their nonminority counterparts at the same level of prior grades and scores; women showed the identical pattern. Thus, with regard to the SAT, this analysis indicates that women's true math abilities—what they could score in a threat-reduced environment—is about 20 points higher than estimated by their official SAT score. Likewise, these results suggest that, in the absence of stereotype threat, the real-world SAT scores of black and Latino students' would increase by about 40 points.

This study is notable, not only because it reveals a systematic bias in standardized testing and grading, but also because it refutes perhaps the most trivializing interpretation of the stereotype threat phenomenon. As Paul Sackett and colleagues have argued:

> Specifically, absent stereotype threat, the African American–White difference is just what one would expect based on the African American–White difference in SAT scores, whereas in the presence of stereotype threat, the difference is larger than would be expected based on the difference in SAT scores. (Sackett, Hardison, & Cullen 2004, p. 9)

In other words, Sackett et al. believe the SAT to be a reliable, unbiased measure of ability; the gap it reveals between blacks and whites is the "true" ability gap, as God sees it, and although stereotype threat can widen the gap, reducing stereotype threat will not narrow it. It is important to stress what some critics (e.g., Wax, 2009) clearly missed: Sackett et al.'s critique is a theoretical speculation, not a conclusion based on empirical data. Walton and Spencer's review of the available data offer no support for the Sackett et al. critique.

A more engaging critique of the practical relevance of the lab-experimental evidence documenting stereotype threat effects focuses on whether such effects are likely to exist when there are genuinely high stakes for performance. For example, in a commentary on a set of studies (McFarland, Lev-Arey, & Ziegert, 2003; Nguyen, O'Neal, & Ryan, 2003; Ployhart, Ziegert, & McFarland, 2003) that failed to replicate the Steele and Aronson effects in mock employment-testing contexts, Sackett (2003) suggested that the inclusion of life-like elements wipes away the effects of stereotype threat. Namely, participants in these studies were asked to imagine that they were in an actual job search and were (in most of the studies) offered a financial incentive for superior performance ($10–$20). But do such procedures make these studies good approximations of the real world, where nontrivial stakes are attached to performance? It is not at all clear to us that the prospect of winning even $20 engages the same psychological mindset as the prospect of, say, not gaining admission to college. Moreover, incentives in these studies were offered to all participants (i.e., they were not a variable in these studies), so we cannot know if and how much such incentives contributed to the findings.

A subsequent laboratory study by Fryer, Levitt, and List (2008) addressed the incentive question more directly by varying stereotype threat and financial incentives for performance in a study of gender-based stereotype threat. They found that offering money for correct answers had only small effects on female test performance, and in the opposite direction predicted by Sackett; it *undermined* female performance. This result suggests that studies discussed by Sackett (2003) did not fail to find stereotype threat effects because threatened test takers were motivated to perform well. Indeed, a consistent finding in stereotype threat experiments is that conditions that produce stereotype threat also increase motivation, not effort withdrawal, as the Sackett critique (again, without data) implies. A more plausible explanation for these results is their other common feature: All the students were from nonelite college populations; they were, on average, students with lower abilities, aspirations, and work ethic, than those in the Steele-Aronson studies. In our view, asking relatively disengaged students to imagine that they are in a real job interview and offering a bit of cash for outperforming others is unlikely to dramatically change this low level of motivation. Still, this remains an empirical question well worthy of testing, and Sackett's summation of these studies is a provocative—and easily testable—hypothesis:

> Thus the argument is not that minority group participants may not experience ST [stereotype threat], but rather that those who do are able to effectively put concerns about stereotypes aside and strive for high test performance. Thus this is a hypothesis that stereotype threat does not affect test performance in applied testing settings in the same fashion, as it does in a decontextualized experimental setting. (2003, p. 301)

This makes crystal clear how Sackett's view of the phenomenon differs from ours. We believe that stereotype threat arises mainly when stereotype-eliciting cues are present and the stakes for performance are high. These stakes can be induced by internal considerations ("I care about how I perform on this test because I pride myself on my verbal abilities"), or more external contingencies ("if I don't do well, I may not get into a good graduate school"). This is precisely why, in most experiments, it is only the elite and "domain identified" students (who attach high stakes to no-stakes experimental tasks) who reliably show the stereotype threat effect (e.g., Aronson et al., 1999). Sackett, in contrast, argues that stereotype threat effects should occur only under low stakes and should evaporate when external stakes are raised.

In a recent experiment (Aronson & Salinas, 2010), we pitted these two explanations against each other by crossing a stereotype threat manipulation with a manipulation of high or low stakes in a sample of nonelite Latino students. In this case, the stakes were not trivial amounts of money or obtaining an imaginary job. Instead, the stakes were severe and immediate: Test takers in the high-stakes condition were told that if they tried hard they could win their freedom and leave the experiment after 20 minutes; but if their effort and performance were deemed insufficient, they would be kept for an additional 2 hours of testing. In the no-stakes condition, no such penalty or reward was offered; it was a simple replication of the Steele-Aronson paradigm. Were the students under high stakes able to "effectively put concerns about stereotypes aside and strive for high test performance"? Apparently not. Latino students who were both primed with a stereotype performed significantly *worse* under high stakes than low stakes. And, as predicted, when there were low stakes attached to performance, stereotype threat had little effect on the performance of these nonelite students.

Policy Box

In a broad sense, the potential for stereotype threat to pervade everyday life—virtually any time one person evaluates another along dimensions that are linked to stereotypes—means that we often do not see people as they are. Thus, we advocate a general mindfulness of the fact that people may be smarter than their test scores—or even their grades—seem to suggest.

The finding that tests like the Scholastic Assessment Test (SAT) systematically underestimate minority students' latent abilities has at least three important implications. First, test scores should be given less weight in the admissions or graduation process than many schools and colleges currently give them. Many colleges, wary of the meaning of test scores, have adopted SAT-optional policies or have done away with the test altogether. Our research suggests the wisdom of such policies. Second, "high-stakes testing" appears to have no advantages and a handful of troubling disadvantages. It tends to increase dropout rates, lower graduation rates, and confer no discernible benefits to the learning process. Third, the conditions of testing can be significantly improved through attention to the psychological climate, so that tests better reflect what students are capable of.

Finally, the research underscores the importance of conducting and rigorously evaluating performance-enhancing interventions of the sort we describe. Claims about the educational value of standardized testing or this or that method of teaching abound and often conflict with one another. Nothing clarifies such ambiguity more convincingly than a randomized trial that pits competing ideas against one another.

■ LONGITUDINAL RESEARCH

Another indicator of the role of stereotype threat in the real world comes from measuring individual-level predictors of stereotype threat. Such measures tap into both the awareness of social stereotypes and the respondent's concern about confirming them (e.g., "teachers expect poor achievement from people of my race"; "I worry that others think less of my abilities because of my race"). We refer to these as measures of "stereotype vulnerability" (see Aronson & Inzlicht, 2004; Aronson & Steele, 2005). A number of studies have used such measures to predict actual school and test performance, graduation rates, and so on. Although not nearly as abundant as the experiments, the findings of such studies have been quite consistent with the laboratory research: Higher stereotype vulnerability scores predict worse academic outcomes.

Douglas Massey and Mary Fischer (2005) conducted such a study involving 4,000 freshmen from different ethnic backgrounds attending over 28 American colleges. Students were surveyed at the beginning of their college careers, and their performance was monitored thereafter. Large differences in grade point average (GPA) were found between ethnic groups; Asians and whites outperformed blacks and Latinos, even when controlling for prior ability and preparation, family income, and other background factors. Consistent with the theory and with Walton and Spencer's (2009) meta-analysis, individual differences in stereotype vulnerability predicted between 9% and 10% of their variation in grades, and when added to a predictive model along with traditional background factors (e.g., family income, SAT scores, etc.) enabled Massey and Fisher to account for the entire black–white GPA gap.

In a briefer longitudinal diary study, Aronson and Inzlicht (2004) found that black college students who measured higher in stereotype vulnerability showed significantly more fluctuations in self-efficacy throughout the day. That is, they reported significantly more highs and lows in feeling smart and capable than did black students who measured lower in stereotype vulnerability and than all of the white students. Moreover, the high stereotype vulnerable students also exhibited inferior performance during laboratory testing and were less accurate in assessing these test performances. A longer-term longitudinal study conducted by Mendoza-Denton et al. (2002) found similar results; students in their study who were more concerned than their counterparts about being rejected on the basis of race earned significantly lower grades over a period of 2–3 years.

Longitudinal studies of high school students generally support the theory as well. For example, in one longitudinal study, Osborne and Walker (2006) found that high levels of caring about academics predicted higher GPA for all students, but there was a cost for caring a lot about doing well for students of color: higher degrees of stereotype threat (Aronson et al., 1999). Students of color who, during freshman year, reported caring a great deal about doing well in high school were significantly more likely to drop out of high school than were those who cared less. This rather counterintuitive finding makes sense if we consider that high identification increases stress, anxiety, and unpleasantness among stereotyped students. Thus, the same variable that predicts low performance among minority students in the laboratory predicts withdrawal from school in the real world.

■ RANDOM-ASSIGNMENT EVALUATIONS OF INTERVENTIONS IN THE FIELD

At least two experimental studies have attempted to replicate the body of laboratory evidence in high-stakes field settings. Specifically, working under the auspices of the Educational Testing Service, Stricker and Ward (2004) examined the effects of manipulating a stereotype threat prime on student performance on high-stakes tests. In one study, the test administration for an advanced placement (AP) calculus exam was modified so that one group of students was asked about race and gender prior to the test, whereas another group was not. In a second study of community-college students, the same manipulation of pretest questions about race and gender occurred prior to taking a computerized placement test (CPT). Stricker and Ward (2004) reported that these manipulations did not have statistically meaningful effects and conjectured that this nonreplication was due to student motivation to perform in a high-stakes setting. However, a reanalysis of these data by Danaher and Crandall (2008) found that moving the demographic questions to the end of these tests actually did significantly improve the performance of women. The differing interpretation of these data is due both to the Stricker and Ward's use of a highly conservative multiple-comparisons correction and to a decision rule that ignored smaller but policy-relevant effect sizes. Danaher and Crandall (2008) concluded that moving demographic questions to the end of the AP calculus AB exam would increase the number of women receiving credit by more than 4,700 annually. In our view, this is not a negligible effect, as Stricker and Ward argue.

Moreover, it is important to stress that the Stricker and Ward study was not designed to study whether or not stereotype threat suppresses real-world test performance. After all, the students were taking an important diagnostic test under many of the conditions shown to produce stereotype threat (testing occurred in heterogeneous groups, the test was presented as diagnostic of ability, and so on). In reality, what the study asks is whether removing one source of stereotype threat among many (the request for gender or race) improves the performance of black and female test takers. The fact that women improved when this element was removed from the testing situations, whereas blacks did not improve is an interesting finding, but there is simply no justification for concluding, as Stricker and Ward do, that stereotype threat does not influence performance for African Americans; such an inference would require a no-stereotype threat control condition, which the study did not include. We suspect that moving the request for race was simply not enough to unseat the already considerable levels of stereotype threat present in the situation, but this remains an open question.

A perhaps more convincing and practical way to see if a theory has value for understanding and remediating a problem is to use the theory to help solve that problem. If stereotype threat widens the performance gap in the real world, then manipulating those factors in the real world should either increase or reduce the gap accordingly. This has been the rationale of several targeted interventions.

Proceeding from the finding that self-affirmations reduce stereotype threat effects in the laboratory (Martens, Johns, Greenberg, & Schimel, 2006), Geoffrey Cohen and his colleagues (Cohen, Garcia, Apfel, & Master, 2006; Cohen, Purdie-Vaughns, & Garcia, 2011, Chapter 18, this volume) created an intervention wherein students wrote about their most important values a few times during the year. This affirmation was designed to buffer them from the experience of stereotype threat that minority students were presumed to be experiencing in their middle school classrooms. Remarkably, compared to students in the control conditions (who wrote about unimportant values), affirmed students earned markedly higher GPAs. This effect was durable; a follow-up study showed sustained improvements 2 years later. Because of the sensational nature of these findings, a number of replication attempts are under way by independent laboratories.

Stereotype threat is assumed to be accompanied by feelings that one does not belong in an academic setting (Steele, 1997), and this has been empirically validated among middle school girls in math class (Good, Dweck, & Rattan, 2008). Walton and Cohen (2007) designed an intervention for college students in which students were led to believe that it was perfectly normal during the transition to college to feel like an outsider and that such feelings diminish over time as part of a normal adjustment process. This simple intervention had immediate effects on the black students, but not the white students: It reduced their feelings of not belonging during periods of adversity, it increased their assessments of their academic potential, and it increased positive academic behaviors like studying. In the subsequent semester, black students in the intervention group earned significantly higher grades.

Aronson, Fried, and Good (2002) found similar results by teaching college students that intelligence is expandable with effort, an intervention designed to lessen the impact of stereotype threat. In the intervention, students wrote letters to fictitious middle school students, encouraging them to work hard in school. Some students had been presented with evidence that intelligence can be developed by hard work; others had been presented with evidence about multiple intelligences. Both groups were encouraged to include this information in their letters. Three months later, black students (and to a lesser degree white students) showed significantly higher grades. Black students also showed significant gains in their identification with academics and their enjoyment of college.

These results were also extended to a study of a middle school population of low-income Hispanic students (Good, Aronson, & Inzlicht, 2003). The expandability of intelligence intervention completely closed the gender gap on the statewide end-of-year exam, and significantly boosted the reading scores of Latino students. Although meditational analyses on these studies do not force the conclusion that stereotype threat alone suppressed the performance of these students, the consistent finding is that interventions theoretically designed to reduce threat reduce minority–white and male–female performance gaps. Given that stereotype threat predictions are borne out by the results, we have increased confidence that stereotype threat—or at least a process very similar to it—is in operation, suppressing the achievement of students in the real world.

■ INCIDENTAL FIELD TESTS OF STEREOTYPE THREAT

Every so often, an experiment or intervention tests a particular theory or intervention, and in so doing, it tests an important corollary of stereotype threat. For example, the well-known Tennessee Class Size Experiment randomly assigned students to either small or large classes and then followed students over time to see if class size affected learning. But class size was not the only variable in play. Because students and teachers were randomly assigned to classes of different sizes, they were also randomly assigned to each other. Among other things, this meant that whether students had same-race teachers was determined by random assignment, allowing the effects of having a same-race teacher to be evaluated. Dee (2004) found that assignment to a same-race teacher improved test performance. For example, black students earned lower test scores at the end of the year if they had been assigned to a white teacher, although smaller classes attenuated these results. The Project STAR class size experiment did not include enough male teachers to test for similar effects related to teacher gender. However, quasi-experimental evidence suggests that assignment to a same-sex teacher can also improve student performance (Dee, 2007). Although these findings do not constitute a direct test of stereotype threat in the field, the results are consistent with those of laboratory studies on stereotype threat and role models. Specifically, experiments have found that having a black "expert" administer the test eliminates the stereotype threat effect among black students and that having a female test administrator eliminates the gender effect on math tests (Marx & Goff, 2005; Marx & Roman, 2002). In an interesting wrinkle in the role model effect, Beilock et al. (2010) found that girls' math stereotype threat was higher as a function of their (female) teacher's math anxiety. Clearly, how a role model feels about a domain can have important effects on his or her students' experiences in the domain.

Quasi-experimental analyses of state high school exit exams have also generated results that are consistent with the presence of stereotype threat. Specifically, these high-stakes tests appear to increase drop-out rates but do so largely among racial minorities (e.g., Dee & Jacob, 2007). A recent study (Reardon, Atteberry, Arshan, & Kurlander, 2009) addresses this connection explicitly. Reardon et al. studied the effects of the new high school exit exam policy in California that requires students to pass a proficiency exam in order to graduate. In previous years, the same test had been used in California simply to gauge what students had learned in school. Thus, the data from prior years could be compared to how students performed after the policy change—a real-world test of high versus low stakes. The pattern of results was strikingly consistent with a stereotype threat analysis.

Specifically, the policy had little effect overall for whites, but significantly fewer girls passed the math portion of the test. Asian students fared worse under high stakes—not on mathematics, but in language arts. And blacks and Latinos scored significantly worse in all subjects under the new high-stakes regime. In all, some 24,000 students did not graduate because they failed a test they would have passed under low stakes. To be sure, despite the consistency between the high school data and stereotype threat predictions, we cannot be certain that stereotype threat was at work; only stakes were manipulated, stereotype threat was not measured, the policy change is confounded with the year of testing, and so on. But when considered alongside the laboratory studies (e.g., Aronson & Salinas, 2010), it is hard to make a compelling case that imposing high stakes on performance nullifies the effects of stereotype threat.

■ NONEXPERIMENTAL CRITIQUES OF STEREOTYPE THREAT

Some recent criticisms of the real-world relevance of stereotype threat have been based on interpretations of the evidence from "differential prediction" studies (e.g., Cullen, Hardison, & Sackett, 2004). Differential prediction refers to group differences in the fitted regression lines that indicate how performance on high-stakes tests (e.g., the SAT) predicts performance on a subsequent (and, ostensibly, objective) performance criterion (e.g., college GPA). For example, SAT scores "underpredict" the first-year GPA of women in that women tend to perform better in college than one would have expected based on comparisons to males with similar SAT scores (Young, 2001). When an admissions test consistently underpredicts how well a particular subgroup subsequently performs, a common (although controversial) inference is that the test is biased against the subgroup (e.g., American Educational Research Association; American Psychological Association; National Council on Measurement in Education, 1999; Millsap, 2007).

A consistent finding across dozens of race-based differential-prediction studies spanning over four decades (Young, 2001; Mattern et al., 2008) is that the SAT performance of black students "overpredicts" their first-year college GPA. In other words, black students perform less well in college than would have been predicted based on a comparison with white students who had similar SAT scores. Zwick (2002) notes that stereotype threat could actually explain this "overprediction mystery" if stereotype threat has more pronounced negative effects on college GPA performance than on SAT performance. This is actually a theoretically reasonable possibility, given that issues related to social identity could be particularly salient in a classroom. The classroom environment is an evaluative setting in which students repeatedly interact with teachers and peers whom they may reasonably expect to know for years. In contrast, although a high-stakes testing environment is uniquely evaluative too, it is also often a one-shot episode that involves the company of strangers. Which environment is more likely to trigger a social identity phenomenon like stereotype threat should, arguably, be viewed as an empirical question.

A study by Cullen, Hardison, and Sackett (2004) presented alternative differential-prediction evidence to advance a more forceful critique of the applied relevance of stereotype threat. Specifically, they argued that threat-induced reductions in SAT performance should be larger for high-performing students because those students have stronger baseline identification with the academic domain. This would then imply that the underprediction associated with SAT scores would be correspondingly pronounced for high-performing students. However, in their "purest test of stereotype threat," they found that the *degree* of gender-related underprediction is not significantly larger for students with higher SAT scores, and they thus concluded that stereotype threat has limited practical relevance for SAT performance.

Our view is that this correlational evidence provides at best a weak test of stereotype threat effects in applied settings (see also Wicherts & Millsap, 2009). Apart from concerns about the validity of college GPA as an objective criterion (Zwick, 2002), these results are also open to alternative interpretations related to plausible patterns in omitted variables. For example, suppose that stereotype threat does reduce female SAT scores, implying that such scores then underpredict female performance in English classes and that this underprediction is concentrated among higher-achieving female students. However, suppose that females—particularly lower-achieving females—outperform males with similar SAT scores in college English classes simply because they have comparatively higher levels of unobserved intellectual engagement with English as a subject. This simultaneous combination of underprediction determinants (i.e., one unique to high-achieving students and one unique to low-achieving students) could result in the exact patterns observed by Cullen, Hardison, and Sackett—female underprediction that is constant by SAT scores—even in the presence of stereotype threat.

This type of interpretative ambiguity is driven by the fact that the variables of interest in differential-prediction studies (i.e., SAT scores and college GPA) are also influenced by potentially confounding but unobserved variables. In sharp contrast, field experimental studies (and credibly specified quasi-experimental studies) can separate convincingly the effects of interest from the potentially contaminating influence of other unmeasured variables because they rely on random (or credibly independent) assignment. Such concerns about omitted variables have long been understood as a fundamental concern when interpreting models of differential prediction (e.g., Linn & Werts, 1971). A closely related problem with interpreting differential prediction results concerns the bias that may occur because of sample selection. For example, suppose that female students are subject to more stringent and informal admissions criteria that predict future performance (e.g., indicators of student engagement) than are male students with similar SAT scores. The results of this nonrandom selection would be that male students perform less well than would be predicted by their SAT scores but for reasons unrelated to stereotype threat. Such challenges to interpreting correlational evidence underscore our conviction that the best way to learn if stereotype threat matters in the real world or in the lab is to be found in experimental and quasi-experimental research designs that credibly support causal inference.

■ CONCLUSION

The performance consequences associated with stereotype threat have been repli-cated in hundreds of studies with diverse social identities and tasks, in studies with strong experimental, quasi-experimental, and longitudinal designs. Still, there is always room for doubt about the role of stereotype threat in real-world settings. Several provocative new studies suggest the promise of interventions to establish the importance of stereotype threat by reducing its effects on student achievement. These developments are important and exciting not only because they show remark-able concurrence between the laboratory and the real world, and because the inter-ventions are cost-effective and scalable, but also because they demonstrate how social scientists can do good research and do good at the same time.

References

American Educational Research Association, American Psychological Association, & National Council on Measurement in Education. (1999). *Standards for educational and psychological testing.* Washington, DC: American Educational Research Association.

Arbuthnot, K. (2009). The effects of stereotype threat on standardized mathematics test performance and cognitive processing. *Harvard Educational Review, 79*(3), 448–472.

Aronson, E., & Carlsmith, J. M. (1968). Experimentation in social psychology. In G. Lindzey, & E. Aronson (Eds.), *The handbook of social psychology* Vol. 2 (2nd ed., pp. 1–79). Reading, MA: Addison-Wesley.

Aronson, J. (2009). Low numbers: Stereotype threat and the under-representation of women in math and science careers. In C. Hoff Summers (Ed.), *The science of women in science* (pp. 104–131). Washington DC: American Enterprise Institute.

Aronson, J., Fried, C., & Good, C. (2002). Reducing the effects of stereotype threat on African American college students by shaping theories of intelligence. *Journal of Experimental Social Psychology, 38,* 113–125.

Aronson, J., & Inzlicht, M. (2004). The ups and downs of attributional ambiguity: Stereotype vulnerability and the academic self-knowledge of African American college students. *Psychological Science, 15,* 829–836.

Aronson, J., Lustina, M. J., Good, C., Keough, K., Steele, C. M., & Brown, J. (1999). When white men can't do math: Necessary and sufficient factors in stereotype threat. *Journal of Experimental Social Psychology, 35,* 29–46.

Aronson, J., & McGlone, M. S. (2009). Stereotype and social identity threat. In T. D. Nelson (Ed.), *Handbook of prejudice, stereotyping, and discrimination* (pp. 153–178). New York: Psychology Press.

Aronson, J., & Salinas, M. (2010). *On the role of stereotype threat in the real world of high stakes exams.* Manuscript in preparation.

Aronson, J., & Steele, C. M. (2005). Stereotypes and the fragility of academic competence, motivation, and self-concept. In C. Dweck, & A. J. Elliot (Eds.), *Handbook of competence and motivation.* New York: Guilford Press.

Beilock, S. L., Gunderson, E. A., Ramirez, G., & Levine, S. C. (2010). Female teachers' math anxiety affects girls' math achievement. *Proceedings of the National Academy of Science USA, 107,* 1860–1863.

Cohen, G., Garcia, J., Apfel, N., & Master, A. (2006). Reducing the racial achievement gap: A social-psychological intervention, *Science, 313*, 1307–1310.

Cohen, G. L., Purdie-Vaughns, V., & Garcia, J. (2011). An identity threat perspective on intervention. In M. Inzlicht, & T. Schmader (Eds.), *Stereotype Threat: Theory, process, and application*. New York: Oxford University Press.

Danaher, K., & Crandall, C. S. (2008). Stereotype threat in applied settings re-examined. *Journal of Applied Social Psychology, 38*, 1639–1655.

Cullen, M. J., Hardison, C. M., & Sackett, P. R. (2004). Using SAT-grade and ability-job performance relationships to test predictions derived from stereotype threat theory. *Journal of Applied Psychology, 89*, 220–230.

Dee, T. S. (2004). Teachers, race and student achievement in a randomized experiment. *The Review of Economics and Statistics, 86*(1), 195–210.

Dee, T. S. (2007). Teachers and the gender gaps in student achievement. *Journal of Human Resources, 42*(3), 528–554.

Dee, T. S., & Jacob, B. A. (2007). Do high school exit exams influence educational attainment or labor market performance? In A. Gamoran (Ed.), *Standards-based reform and children in poverty: Lessons for "no child left behind."* Brookings Institution Press: Washington DC.

Falk, A., & Heckman, J. J. (2009). Lab experiments are a major source of knowledge in the social sciences. *Science, 326*, 535–538.

Fryer, R. G., Levitt, S. D., & List, J. A. (2008). Exploring the impact of financial incentives on stereotype threat: Evidence from a pilot study. *American Economic Review, 98*(2), 370–375.

Gilbert, D. T. (1998). Ordinary personology. In D. T. Gilbert, S. T., Fiske, & G. Lindzey (Eds.), *The handbook of social psychology* (4th edition). New York: McGraw Hill.

Good, C., Aronson, J., & Harder, J. (2008). Problems in the pipeline: Women's achievement in high-level math courses. *Journal of Applied Developmental Psychology, 29*(1), 17–28.

Good, C., Aronson, J., & Inzlicht, M. (2003). Improving adolescents' standardized test performance: An intervention to reduce the effects of stereotype threat. *Journal of Applied Developmental Psychology, 24*, 645–662.

Good, C., Dweck, C. S., & Rattan, A. (2008). *Do I belong here? Middle school girls' sense of belonging to math.* Unpublished paper, Barnard College, Columbia University, New York.

Harrison, G. W., & List, J. A. (2004). Field experiments. *Journal of Economic Literature, 42*, 1009–1055.

Herrnstein, R. J., & Murray, C. (1994). *The bell curve: Intelligence and class structure in American life.* New York: The Free Press.

Inzlicht, M., & Ben-Zeev, T. (2000). A threatening intellectual environment: Why females are susceptible to experiencing problem-solving deficits in the presence of males. *Psychological Science, 11*, 365–371.

Keller, J., & Dauenheimer, D. (2003). Stereotype threat in the classroom: Dejection mediates the disrupting threat effect on women's math performance. *Personality and Social Psychology Bulletin, 29*, 371–381.

Kellow, T. J., & Jones, B. D. (2007). The effects of stereotypes on the achievement gap: Reexamining the academic performance of African American high school students. *Journal of Black Psychology, 34*, 94–120.

Levitt, S. D., & List, J. A. (2007). What do laboratory experiments measuring social preferences reveal about the real world? *Journal of Economic Perspectives, 21*(2), 153–174.

Linn, R. L., & Werts, C. E. (1971). Considerations for studies of test bias. *Journal of Educational Measurement, 8*, 1–4.

Martens, A., Johns, M., Greenberg, J., & Schimel (2006). Combating stereotype threat: The effect of self-affirmation on women's intellectual performance. *Journal of Experimental Social Psychology, 42,* 236–243.

Marx, D. M., & Goff, P. A. (2005). Clearing the air: The effect of experimenter race on target's test performance and subjective experience. *British Journal of Social Psychology, 44,* 645–657.

Marx, D. M., & Roman, J. S. (2002). Female role models: Protecting women's math test performance. *Personality and Social Psychology Bulletin, 28,* 1183–1193.

Massey, D. S., & Fischer, M. J. (2005). Stereotype threat and academic performance: New data from the national survey of freshman. *The DuBois Review: Social Science Research on Race, 2,* 45–68.

Mattern, K. D., Patterson, B. F., Shaw, E. J., Korbin, J. L., & Barbuti, S. M. (2008). *Differential validity and prediction of the SAT* (College Board Research Report 2008–4). New York: The College Board.

Mendoza-Denton, R., Purdie, V., Downey, G., & Davis, A. (2002). Sensitivity to status-based rejection: Implications for African-American students' college experience. *Journal of Personality and Social Psychology, 83,* 896–918.

McFarland, L. A., Lev-Arey, D. M., & Ziegert, J. C. (2003). An examination of stereotype threat in a motivational context. *Human Performance, 16,* 181–205.

McGlone, M., & Aronson, J. (2006). Social identity salience and stereotype threat. *Journal of Applied Developmental Psychology, 27,* 486–493.

Millsap, R. E. (2007). Invariance in measurement and prediction revisited. *Psychometrika, 72*(4), 461–473.

Mook, D. G. (1983). In defense of external invalidity. *American Psychologist, 38,* 379-388.

Murray, C. (2008). *Real education.* New York: Crown Forum.

Nguyen, H. -H. D., O'Neal, A., & Ryan, A. M. (2003). Relating test-taking attitudes and skills and stereotype threat effects to the racial gap in cognitive ability test performance. *Human Performance, 16,* 261–293.

Osborne, J. W., & Walker, C. (2006). Stereotype threat, identification with academics, and withdrawal from school: Why the most successful students of colour might be the most likely to withdraw. *Educational Psychology, 26,* 563–577.

Ployhart, R. E., Ziegert, J. C., & McFarland, L. A. (2003). Understanding racial differences on cognitive ability tests in selection contexts: An integration of stereotype threat and applicant reactions research. *Human Performance, 16,* 231–259.

Reardon, S. F., Atteberry, A., Arshan, N., & Kurlaender, M. (2009). *Effects of the California high school exit exam on student persistence, achievement, and graduation* (Working Paper 2009–12). Institute for Research on Education Policy and Practice, Stanford University.

Sackett, P. R. (2003). Stereotype threat in applied selection settings: A commentary. *Human Performance, 16,* 295–309.

Sackett, P. R., Hardison, C. M., & Cullen, M. J. (2005). On interpreting research on stereotype threat and test performance. *American Psychologist, 60*(3), 271–272.

Sackett, P., & Ryan, A. M. (2011). Concerns about generalizing stereotype threat research findings to operational high stakes testing. In M. Inzlicht, & T. Schmader (Eds.), *Stereotype threat: Theory, process, and application.* New York: Oxford University Press.

Schmader, T., Johns, M., & Forbes, C. (2008). An integrated process model of stereotype threat effects on performance. *Psychological Review, 115,* 336–356.

Schmader, T., & Stone, J. (2008). Toward a problem-focused approach to prejudice. *Psychological Inquiry, 19,* 108–113.

Shih, M., Pittinsky, T. L., & Ambady, N. (1999). Stereotype susceptibility: Identity salience and shifts in quantitative performance. *Psychological Science, 10*(1), 80–83.

Spencer, S. J., Steele, C. M., & Quinn, D. (1999). Stereotype threat and women's math performance. *Journal of Experimental Social psychology, 35*, 4–28.

Steele, C. M. (1997). A threat in the air: How stereotypes shape intellectual identity and performance. *American Psychologist, 52*, 613–629.

Steele, C. M., & Aronson, J. (1995). Stereotype threat and the intellectual test performance of African-Americans. *Journal of Personality and Social Psychology, 69*(5), 797–811.

Stricker, L. J., & Ward, W. C. (2004). Stereotype threat, inquiring about test takers' ethnicity and gender, and standardized test performance. *Journal of Applied Social Psychology, 34*, 665–693.

Walton, G. M., & Cohen, G. L. (2007). A question of belonging: Race, social fit, and achievement. *Journal of Personality and Social Psychology, 92*, 82–96.

Walton, G. M., & Spencer, S. J. (2009). Latent ability: Grades and test scores systematically underestimate the intellectual ability of negatively stereotyped students. *Psychological Science, 20*, 1132–1139.

Wax, A. (2009). Stereotype threat: A case of overclaim syndrome? In C. Hoff-Sommers (Ed.), *The science on women and science*. Washington, D.C.: American Enterprise Institute.

Wicherts, J. M., & Millsap, R. E. (2009). The absence of underprediction does not imply the absence of measurement bias. *American Psychologist, 64*, 281–283.

Young, J. W. (2001). *Differential validity, differential prediction, and college admission testing: A comprehensive review and analysis* (College Board Research Report No. 2001–6). New York: College Entrance Examination Board.

Zwick, R. (2002). *Fair game? The use of standardized admissions tests in higher education*. New York: Rutledge Falmer.

18 An Identity Threat Perspective on Intervention

■ GEOFFREY L. COHEN,
VALERIE PURDIE-VAUGHNS,
AND JULIO GARCIA

Kurt Lewin, the renowned experimental social psychologist, said that understanding the processes underlying a problem can help us to remedy it. He also said that one of the best ways to understand a phenomenon is by trying to change it. This chapter discusses how an understanding of "identity threat"—the psychological threat arising from possible devaluation of one's group—led to successful interventions that closed the achievement gap in schools, a pervasive social problem in the United States. The interventions include invoking high performance standards, encouraging optimistic interpretations of adversity, and buttressing students' sense of self-integrity and belonging. All the interventions were tested using randomized field experiments that assessed outcomes over long periods of time, sometimes years. Not only did the interventions lead to positive academic trajectories for ethnic minority students in general and female students in science, they also advanced a theoretical understanding of how identity threat compounds over time through recursive feedback loops. Because of the self-reinforcing nature of recursive cycles, subtle but well-timed interventions can have effects that appear disproportionate to their size and duration. Additionally, the research shows how making the jump from lab to field—from theory to application—can bring to light new theoretical principles related to psychological processes and intervention itself.

Keywords: Stereotype threat, academic performance, black–white test score gap, male–female science gap, intervention, affirmation

Across a variety of times and places people have faced negative stereotypes about their group's ability and belonging in society. Because they know that members of their group have faced prejudice and discrimination, and because they may have experienced these themselves, they may worry they could be judged or treated stereotypically (Steele, Spencer, & Aronson, 2002). This concern is understandable. It can be costly to trust someone who could later prove untrustworthy (Cohen & Steele, 2002). The emotional, psychological, and pragmatic costs of committing oneself to an endeavor or relationship, assuming fair treatment only to find otherwise, can be doubly troubling. Not only is there the loss of time and energy, but there is also the feeling of having been taken in. For this reason, in school and work settings in the United States, ethnic minorities may entertain the hypothesis that they could be stereotyped until they are provided with evidence to the contrary. Women in math and science may experience similar concerns (Davies, Spencer, Quinn, & Gerhardstein, 2002).

However adaptive and reasonable this response can be, it can prove costly. As other chapters in this volume attest, the concern that one may be viewed through the lens of a stereotype—stereotype threat—can raise stress, deplete mental resources, and undermine performance (Steele et al., 2002; see also Beilock, Rydell, & McConnell, 2007; Inzlicht, Tullett, & Gutsell, 2011, Chapter 7, this volume; Schmader, Johns, & Forbes, 2008). It can erode people's sense of comfort, belonging, and trust (Cohen & Steele, 2002; Steele et al., 2002; Walton & Carr, 2011, Chapter 6, this volume; Walton & Cohen, 2007), as well as lower their career aspirations (Davies et al., 2002). Structural factors are often seen as the source of inequality. However, inequality can also arise from differences in people's perceptions, their subjective construals (Ross & Nisbett, 1991). Groups may differ in their subjective construals at school or work because of real historical antecedents. But such construals can reinforce objective inequalities. When members of a group underperform because they perceive that they could be stereotyped, their educational, economic, and career opportunities diminish. Because inequality has psychological as well as structural causes, psychological interventions need to be considered along with structural approaches (Nisbett, 2009).

Research on stereotype threat has shown that it can occur regardless of the objective prejudice in an environment. The mere possibility that one could be seen negatively can prove threatening. All of us belong to groups that, in one setting or another, can cast us as outsiders. When we care about succeeding in the setting, the sense of being seen as an outsider can be debilitating. As research on stereotype threat demonstrates, such concerns can arise from widely known negative stereotypes about our groups (Steele et al., 2002). A white basketball player may worry about confirming, in the minds of others, the "white men can't jump" stereotype to such an extent that it undermines his or her vertical leap performance (Garcia, 2002). Likewise African Americans and Latino Americans at school or work, and women in math and science, may underperform because of the stress arising from possibly confirming a negative stereotype about their ethnic or gender group (Davies et al., 2002; Steele & Aronson, 1995).

Stereotype threat is an example of the general phenomenon of identity threat (Branscombe, Schmitt, & Harvey, 1999; Steele et al., 2002). *Social identity threat,* the group form of this threat, arises when people realize that they could be devalued on the basis of their group for any reason. Because the threat is directed at one's group, one need not experience it personally. For instance, African Americans and women felt threatened—displaying lower self-esteem and worse performance—when they thought that someone *else* in their group could perform poorly and thus lend credence to the stereotype (Cohen & Garcia, 2005). Like any psychological stressor, identity threat can depress cognitive functioning and emotional well-being, especially when chronic and experienced in a domain, like school or work, where outcomes have material and symbolic consequences.

■ MOVING FROM LAB TO FIELD: CONCEPTUALIZING IDENTITY THREAT IN REAL-WORLD SETTINGS

Laboratory research suggests several effective steps for reducing stereotype threat. Among these are exposing students to role models who disconfirm the stereotype through their competence (Marx & Roman, 2002), encouraging people to see performance gaps between groups as due to social rather than genetic factors (Dar-Nimrod & Heine, 2006), and having people call to mind an alternative, positively stereotyped identity they hold, such as "high-achieving college student" (Rydell, McConnell, & Beilock, 2009). A structural strategy to reduce stereotype threat is to ensure adequate representation of the stereotyped group in the classroom or workplace (Inzlicht & Ben-Zeev, 2000). The picture of stereotype threat emerging from these studies is of a process that is powerful but malleable. Although stereotype threat causes dramatic decrements in performance, small changes in the laboratory can free people of its effects. Clearly, it is possible to manipulate a person's subjective construal in the lab for the better. Such laboratory research, moreover, proved critical in the development of social-psychological interventions that closed achievement gaps in schools. However, in the field, unlike the lab, a blizzard of competing cues could offset the effect of any positive intervention. A solid understanding of how identity threat and intervention processes play out over time and interact with other factors in social environments is needed.

Figure 18.1 presents a model of the way in which psychological threats, including identity threat, affect performance (Cohen & Garcia, 2008). Threat acts as a restraining force (Lewin, 1951). It prevents positive forces in both the person and the environment from asserting their full impact on performance and learning. A student may have the ability to excel, but stereotype threat may prevent the expression of

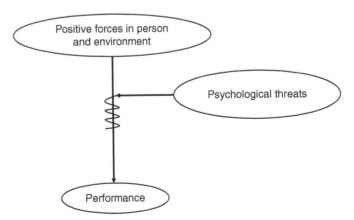

Figure 18.1 The interplay of psychological threat with other forces.

that ability, as when a skilled athlete chokes under pressure. Likewise, opportunities for learning may present themselves, but an intimidated student may fail to take advantage of them. Threat may also make negative factors gain a larger role in outcomes. For example, poor performance due to stereotype threat can make it more likely that a student will be assigned to remediation or held back in grade. Just as drag can prevent a car from achieving its top speed and efficiency, psychological forces can limit the efficiency of the school system. Effective social psychological interventions lessen threat, and thereby enable the positive forces to assert their impact more fully and help constrain forces that could have a negative impact.

Rather than being mutually exclusive, psychological and structural approaches are thus complementary (Garcia & Cohen, in press). Although both are necessary for optimal performance, neither is sufficient. For example, one popular psychological intervention is that of *attributional retraining* (Wilson, Damiani, & Shelton, 2002; see also Good, Aronson, & Inzlicht, 2003; Walton & Cohen, 2007). Students are taught to attribute setbacks to factors unrelated to the stereotype or a lack of belonging. Instead, they are encouraged to attribute them to common challenges inherent in school. Such interventions can dramatically improve performance (see Wilson et al., 2002). But they can prove ineffective and even counterproductive when unaccompanied by objective opportunities for growth. For instance, attributional retraining paired with poor instruction produced no improvement in performance for students with a history of failure. But when paired with high-quality instruction, it produced a level of performance on par with that of their peers without a history of failure (Menec, Perry, Struthers, Schonwetter, Hechter, & Eichholz, 1994).

One line of research explored the interaction between psychological and structural factors in a key educational situation—the feedback interaction between teacher and student. In this research, we explored the effects of identity threat in an interpersonal arena with implications for learning, rather than in the more common test-taking situation. Among the strongest predictors of student growth is the quality of feedback from mentors (Lepper, Aspinwall, & Mumme, 1990; Walberg, 1984). Such feedback is seen as a fundamental aspect of pedagogy by the educational community. If, as is often the case in today's schools, an African American student receives critical feedback from a white teacher, there is a potential for mistrust. The African American may wonder if the feedback reflects a genuine intent to help or if it instead reflects a biased judgment of his or her ability (Crocker & Major, 1989; see also Cohen, Steele, & Ross, 1999). When African American students were led to believe that a white college professor had given them critical feedback on an essay, they saw that feedback as relatively more biased than did white students and felt less motivated to revise their essay (Cohen et al., 1999). In a follow-up study, college science majors received critical feedback on a research presentation from someone they were led to believe was a male science professor (Cohen & Steele, 2002). Compared with male students, female students incorporated relatively fewer of the suggestions for improvement into a revision of their research presentation. In terms of Figure 18.1, critical feedback—a structural factor that should facilitate learning and motivation—had a positive effect only for the nonthreatened group. Even though our methodology ensured that nonstereotyped and stereotyped students received virtually identical feedback, the two groups perceived it differently. Contrary to a color-blind philosophy, uniform instruction did not have uniform effects.

How can we minimize the threat of negative stereotypes in order to convey feedback more effectively? In another experimental condition, we tested a theory-driven intervention designed to deflect the threatening characterization of the stereotype. Here, students received the same critical feedback as before, but now accompanied with the professor's assertion that he had high standards and his personal assurance that the student in question had the potential to reach those standards. The message, we thought, would invert the meaning of critical feedback in the eyes of stereotype-threatened students. They would see it less as a sign that the teacher had stereotyped them and more as a sign that he believed in their ability. Indeed, African American students receiving the feedback in this manner saw little if any bias and were as motivated as their white peers. Likewise, female science majors receiving this feedback incorporated significantly more of the feedback's suggestions for improvement. A recent field experiment found that the same intervention improved middle-school students' ability to learn from their teachers' feedback on their written work (Yeager, Purdie-Vaughns, Garcia, & Cohen, in preparation).

These studies reinforced the lesson that relatively small interventions, when attuned to important psychological processes, can have large effects (Ross & Nisbett, 1991). They suggested that theory-informed strategies could alleviate identity threat and close gaps in the ability to benefit from educational opportunity.

■ APPROACH TO REAL-WORLD INTERVENTION

Our intervention approach rests on three ideas (Garcia & Cohen, in press)—levers, recursion, and the dynamic nature of social systems. The first, *psychological levers*, are points in a complex system where targeted intervention can produce nonintuitively large and long-term effects. The lever used in many successful interventions concerns core psychological motives for belonging, self-integrity, and competence (Baumeister & Leary, 1995; Ryan & Deci, 2000; Steele, 1988; see also Sherman & Cohen, 2006). When they combat threats to such motives, even brief interventions can have large effects. In this way, social-psychological interventions accomplish what exceptional teachers and mentors do in more impactful ways in the real word (Cohen et al., 1999). They convey to students the message that they belong, have self-integrity, and can achieve a higher standard. These messages can prove especially important for socially stigmatized students, because they help negate a stereotype's characterization that they are seen as lacking ability and as not belonging. Indeed, when teachers have optimistic expectations for their students—higher than what is warranted based on students' prior records—this appears to especially benefit the achievement of minority students (Jussim & Harber, 2005).

Beyond psychological levers, the recognition of recursive cycles is also at the heart of our approach. In school, work, and many other real-world settings, processes can feed off their own consequences. Stereotype threat might lower performance. Lower performance in turn could increase stereotype threat, lowering performance still further, in a repeating cycle. In fact, rather than directly boosting performance, many social-psychological interventions instead interrupt the downward spiral characteristic of such self-exacerbating cycles (e.g., Blackwell, Trzesniewski, & Dweck, 2007; Cohen et al., 2006, 2009; Wilson et al., 2002).

A final key idea in our approach concerns the recognition of the dynamic or interactive nature of forces in a social system (Garcia & Cohen, in press; Ross & Nisbett, 1991). An intervention effect might act as the first spark in a chain reaction. For instance, a small intervention early in the year could raise children's performance. Because of this, their teachers may see such children as being more worthy of attention. The intervention effect could then be carried forward and even amplified by teachers' positive expectations (Jussim & Harber, 2005; Rosenthal & Jacobson, 1992). Such interactions can involve many social and psychological processes. Students who do better early on may come to feel efficacious in school, believe in the malleable nature of intelligence, and trust their teachers, all of which can contribute to better performance (Blackwell et al., 2007; Garcia & Cohen, in press; Tyler, 2004).

Because of recursive, interacting cycles, early outcomes have disproportionate impact. Early differences, even when slight, can snowball into large effects over time, as feedback loops both compound initial differences in performance and broaden their consequences (Caspi, Elder, & Bem, 1987; Cohen et al., 2009; Heckman, 2006). As one example, small early advantages in young athletes' size and coordination—even when due to random variability in when their birthdays fall relative to the start of the sports season—have sizable effects on their prospects of becoming professional athletes (Barnsley, Thompson, & Barnsley, 1985). A child who displays more early competence is likely to be perceived as more able, be given more opportunities to excel, and receive more mentoring. These in turn can advance the child's interests and self-confidence, which in turn can further their opportunities for growth. These recursive processes can play a larger role in domains like math and science, where subsequent learning builds on an earlier foundation of knowledge (see Blackwell et al., 2007). Small differences at an early age become magnified over time, making it increasingly difficult to catch up or enter a discipline later (Miyake, Kost-Smith, Finkelstein, Pollock, Cohen, & Ito, 2010).

The *identity engagement model* incorporates the notions of levers, recursion, and dynamic interaction (Cohen & Garcia, 2008; Garcia & Cohen, in press). It offers a model of how identity threat affects performance and learning in real-world settings over time. Figure 18.2 provides a graphic representation.

People's group identity will be psychologically engaged if they think it could cause them to be judged or treated negatively. For instance, most African Americans know that school and work are places where they could be judged negatively because of their race (Steele & Aronson, 1995; Walton & Cohen, 2007). People tend to

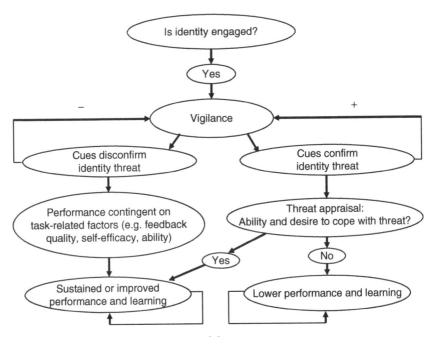

Figure 18.2 The identity engagement model

become vigilant when their identity is engaged (Kaiser, Brooke, & Major, 2006; Murphy, Steele, & Gross, 2007; Purdie-Vaughns, Steele, Davies, Ditlmann, & Randall-Crosby, 2008). They comb their environment for cues to discern whether their identity is in fact affecting how they are being viewed. A minority student, for example, might scrutinize a teacher's feedback for evidence of bias (Cohen & Steele, 2002; Crocker & Major, 1989). In this vigilance stage, people engage in what coping researchers call a primary appraisal, asking themselves, "Is there a threat?" (Lazarus & Folkman, 1984).

The cues can *disconfirm* the threat, as when a teacher provides critical feedback with an invocation of high standards and personal assurance. When this occurs, people tend to feel treated as individuals. Their performance depends largely on structural and personal factors, such as the quality of instruction and their skill. The positive forces can assert a relatively direct impact on performance and learning.

But if the cues *confirm* the threat, a threat appraisal phase follows. People engage in a secondary appraisal, asking themselves, "Do I have the desire and ability to cope with this threat?" (Lazarus & Folkman, 1984). The importance of this stage for intervention rests on the insight that, often, it is not so much a particular stressor that is disruptive, but rather the psychological reaction to it. For example, people perform worse under stereotype threat partly because they try to suppress thoughts about the stereotype. They expend mental resources that could otherwise help their performance and, ironically, become more vulnerable to the stereotype's rebounding into consciousness later (Logel, Iserman, Davies, Quinn, & Spencer, 2009; Schmader, Forbes, Zhang, & Mendes, 2009). One can lessen the impact of a stressor by altering psychological reactions. For example, one study altered college students' psychological reaction to test anxiety by informing them that arousal on standardized tests "doesn't hurt performance and can even help performance." This raised their actual scores on the math section of the Graduate Record Examination (GRE) by almost 1 standard deviation (Jamieson, Berry Mendes, Blackstock, & Schmader, 2010). The intervention, it seems, changed the meaning participants assigned to their bodily state. As a result, sympathetic nervous system activity correlated not with worse performance but better (Jamieson et al., 2010).

In our model, identity threat can escalate, with its consequences feeding off themselves and creating other vulnerabilities. Teachers may label underperforming students as at-risk and assign them to a remedial track, which could further undermine performance and increase disciplinary problems (Rosenthal & Jacobson, 1992; Steele, 1997). After performing poorly, students may worry still more about being stereotyped or seen as not belonging (Wilson et al., 2002). Left to itself, identity threat thus escalates and implicates a broader swath of outcomes (Garcia & Cohen, in press; Cohen et al., 2009). This could help explain the downward spiral in performance and disciplinary problems observed, particularly among minority students, at certain stages like middle school (Eccles, Lord, & Midgley, 1991; Simmons, Black, & Zhou, 1991). Interrupting the recursive and interactive process of identity threat early presents an opportunity to have long-term performance benefits. Even a small initial effect at the beginning of a recursive cycle could serve as a spark that yields benefits that compound and broaden over time (Cohen et al., 2009; Garcia & Cohen, in press).

■ FIELD-TESTED INTERVENTIONS

The vigilance stage, a phase when people assess their environment, lends itself to intervention. The meaning people assign to events, their subjective experience, can be manipulated (Ross & Nisbett, 1991). In the study described earlier, the meaning of critical feedback changed with an invocation of high standards and personal assurance. It no longer reflected a biased judgment but a belief in one's potential (Cohen & Steele, 2002). Vigilance-based strategies provide people with a hopeful narrative for understanding events in their lives, especially adversity.

In one of the experimental conditions in a study by Good et al. (2003), students were exposed to role models who discussed their initial difficulties after moving from elementary to middle school, but who reported getting increasingly better grades as they learned the ropes and kept working (see also Aronson, Fried, & Good, 2002). In another experimental condition, students were led to view intelligence as expandable rather than fixed (see Dweck, 1999). Both interventions lessened the tendency to see frustration in school as evidence of intellectual limitation. Compared with students in a control group, students in both conditions went on to earn higher statewide test scores. Indeed, girls particularly benefited, eliminating the gender gap in math scores. Similar positive effects of such interventions on grades were displayed in a New York City school by low-achieving African and Latino American students from economically disadvantaged backgrounds (Blackwell et al., 2007).

We explored an intervention conducted at the vigilance stage with our colleague Greg Walton (Walton & Cohen, 2007, 2011; see Walton & Carr, 2011, Chapter 6, this volume). We wondered if an intervention could reframe not the meaning of a single event, like the receipt of critical feedback, but one's entire college experience. As African American students may experience *belonging uncertainty* in school (Walton & Cohen, 2007), visiting and revisiting the question of whether they and members of their race belong, they may globalize the meaning of a setback in school. We tested a strategy addressing concerns about belonging (Walton & Cohen, 2007). It sought to shore up minority students' sense of belonging in school by breaking the false sense that their difficulties were unique to themselves and their race (Steele et al., 2004).

College freshmen were brought into the lab at the end of their first year, a time of consolidation. They were told they would be helping researchers interpret the results of a survey, a survey that we had actually administered to junior and senior students at their school. The results of the survey conveyed that although most first-year students had worried about whether they belonged during the transition to college, these worries subsided. Moreover, the survey concluded, the prevalence and duration of these worries did not differ "across demographic groups." At the heart of the intervention lay two messages: One's difficulties are shared (Schachter, 1959), and there is reason for hope (Snyder, 2000). To facilitate internalization of the message, students were asked to give a speech summarizing not only the survey results but their relevance to their own college experience, ostensibly to help incoming first-year students better understand the transition to college (cf. Aronson et al., 2002).

Relative to both a randomized control condition and campus-wide data, this intervention improved African Americans' grade point average (GPA), an effect that follow-up data indicate persisted through their final year of college (Walton & Cohen, 2011; Walton & Carr, 2011, Chapter 6, this volume). As African Americans benefited most, the racial achievement gap closed by roughly 50%. The intervention had changed the meaning they assigned to their school experience. African Americans receiving the intervention were less likely to globalize the meaning of adversity. On days of hardship, African American students in the control condition dropped in their sense of belonging. But those in the treatment condition did not.

Like the high standards and the assurance strategy, these interventions work by affecting primary appraisal–in this case, the meaning assigned to adversity. Interventions at the vigilance stage can be characterized as preventative. They help to prevent threat from arising or from growing so acute that it triggers a downward spiral (Garcia & Cohen, in press). Can interventions prove effective once such a cycle has taken hold? Can they shore up people's internal resources, so that they have the ability to cope more effectively with a threat (Sherman & Cohen, 2006)? Here an intervention acts like an anti-inflammatory. It lessens the psychological reactions that would otherwise inflame the threat. We directly tested this in a field experiment at a middle school with a roughly equal representation of white and black students (Cohen et al., 2006; Cohen et al., 2009).

The values people hold, such as those tied to their relationships or their religion, form an important basis of their sense of self-integrity. Calling up one's self-defining values acts to affirm a global view of oneself as virtuous, efficacious, and socially connected (Steele, 1988; see also Sherman & Cohen, 2006). This permits people to see a stressor from a broader perspective, lessening its impact on their sense of self and social worth (Schmeichel & Vohs, 2009; Sherman & Cohen, 2006). For instance, values affirmations reduce psychological stress and threat. When they had reflected on important personal values, people asked to give an impromptu talk in front of a difficult audience had lower levels of the stress hormone cortisol (Creswell et al., 2005). Laboratory studies have also shown that values affirmations can lessen stereotype threat (Martens, Johns, Greenberg, & Schimel, 2006). Anecdotally, some teachers have found that expressive writing, in which underprivileged children relate their troubles to, among other things, social values, can have dramatic positive effects on their engagement with school (Freedom Writers & Gruwell, 1999).

Using such findings as our starting point, children were randomly assigned either to a values affirmation condition or to a control condition. In the former, children completed packets inquiring about their values, such as relationships with friends and family, athletics, and music. After identifying their most important values, they wrote about why these were important to them in a series of structured exercises. Different versions of the intervention were repeated throughout the year. Although each administration lasted only 10–15 minutes, the activity tapped into an important source of meaning for these adolescents. Students in the control condition completed writing exercises focusing on neutral topics, such as an unimportant value or their daily routine.

The affirmation had a positive impact on affirmed African American students, the group under identity threat. They earned a higher GPA in the academic term in which the intervention commenced than did nonaffirmed African Americans. The lowest performing African Americans benefited most. In the affirmation condition, the number of African Americans earning a D or below in the intervention-targeted course was only 9%, whereas in control condition, the rate was consistent with historical norms, 20% (Cohen et al., 2006). Over their remaining 2 years of middle school, only 3% of affirmed African American students were held back in grade or placed in remediation, compared with 9% of nonaffirmed African Americans (Cohen et al., 2009).

Consistent with the idea that early performance outcomes can be carried forward through recursive cycles, the intervention's benefits persisted over the remaining 2 years of middle school, even with no additional administrations in the second year (Cohen et al., 2009). Its benefits rippled out to improve grades in core courses not originally targeted by the intervention. On the whole, the intervention closed the racial achievement gap by roughly 30% over 2 years in students' core courses of English, social studies, math, and science.

Although all students experienced a decline in GPA during middle school, the recursive nature of threat is suggested by the less pronounced drop in GPA of affirmed African Americans relative to nonaffirmed African Americans. For African Americans, the affirmation appeared to interrupt a recursive cycle. It made poor performance in the first few weeks of 7th grade less predictive of both poor achievement and a low sense of belonging for the remaining years of middle school

(Cohen et al., 2006, 2009). The intervention's positive effects on performance and learning in the classroom have been recently replicated with Latino American middle school students and female physics students (Miyake et al., 2010; Sherman, Hartson, Binning, Purdie-Vaughns, Garcia, Taborsky-Barba, Tomassetti, Nussbaum, & Cohen, 2011). The study offers several theoretical insights. First, social identity threat interacts with social experience to shape outcomes. It increases vulnerability to early failure and its recursive impact (Cohen et al., 2009). Such threat can be overcome when interventions interrupt a recursive cycle by combating threats to the motive to see oneself as virtuous, efficacious, and socially connected. Second, one thing that interventions can accomplish is to change the way people encode social experience. In contrast to their nonaffirmed peers, affirmed African Americans no longer globalized the meaning of early failure into a conclusion that they did not belong in school (Cohen et al., 2009). They were also less likely to harbor thoughts about the racial stereotype, as evidenced by a measure of the psychological accessibility of the stereotype given later in students' tenure in middle school (Cohen et al., 2006). Although social identity threat is a powerful process, it is malleable when acted upon by other powerful psychological processes. Finally, social identity threat makes people's sense of belonging more dependent on external contingencies, like adversity or early poor performance, something that these interventions remedy (Walton & Cohen, 2007).

Policy Box

Our results run counter to much conventional wisdom in education, social science, and social policy by demonstrating that social-psychological interventions, even when brief, can help remedy what are often seen as fixed disparities in real-world academic outcomes. Together with programs to improve the opportunities of at-risk students, such interventions can close racial and gender achievement gaps in classrooms.

Setting explicitly high standards, encouraging optimistic interpretations of adversity, and validating students' sense of belonging and self-integrity are among the effective psychological interventions that educators and policy makers can use. This is particularly so when dealing with members of academically at-risk groups, such as ethnic minorities in general and women in math and science. Because such students may worry about being devalued on the basis of their ethnic or gender group, their sense of belonging and self-integrity in such settings may be more uncertain.

To be successful, practitioners must understand the psychological processes that these interventions address. Such knowledge informs decisions about a range of an intervention's elements, such as its activities, timing, and the form of its integration into a classroom or work environment. Knowledge of processes also illuminates the structural factors in a school or work setting that threaten people's sense of belonging, self-integrity, and performance.

Institutionalized beliefs about school and work often presume that achievement is primary and that a sense of belonging and self-integrity is merely a reward for achievement. The reviewed research clearly shows that, to the contrary, such psychological states may be necessary preconditions for success.

■ CONCLUSION

Moving from laboratory research to real-world intervention can have both theoretical and applied implications. Because social identity threat, like other important psychological processes, interacts with other factors in a social system over time, its full character and impact become apparent only over long periods of time, a time scale difficult to observe in the lab (Cohen & Garcia, 2008). Moreover, when targeted at critical points in a recursive, interactive process, interventions can produce apparently disproportionate effects both in magnitude and in duration (Garcia & Cohen, in press; Ross & Nisbett, 1991). Indeed, interventions may sometimes have larger effects in real-world social systems like school or work. The recursive elements in them, rather than being noise that occludes effects, may trigger chain reactions that exaggerate small initial benefits (see Paluck, 2009).

Additionally, interventions can interact with preexisting positive forces in the social environment (Garcia & Cohen, in press). They can heighten their impact or dampen factors that inhibit their impact. Although social psychological interventions may be necessary for significant change, they are not sufficient. In the absence of positive environmental supports, like committed teachers, a psychological intervention is likely to have little or no effect. The interventions reviewed here have been tested in various schools and with various students, including economically disadvantaged Latinos (Sherman et al., 2011) and women in science (Good et al., 2003; Miyake et al., 2010). However, they have all been tested in relatively racially integrated schools, equipped with qualified staff and basic resources for learning. In such contexts, the interventions close achievement gaps by 30%–40%. It seems plausible that the interventions have relatively stronger effects in such identity-integrated settings, where concerns about being seen stereotypically prove most acute (see Inzlicht & Ben-Zeev, 2000).The efficacy of the interventions in predominantly minority schools and in disadvantaged schools has received less attention (for an exception, see Blackwell et al., 2005). We suspect that in school or work settings with few resources for learning, social-psychological interventions might improve student well-being but would have little impact on learning and performance. After all, the interventions will not teach a child to read, or provide the human and curricular resources that such a student needs to learn to read. But when coupled with such resources, psychological interventions can catalyze lasting positive change (Cohen et al., 2006; Garcia & Cohen, in press).

The interventions discussed here share an important quality. They are indirect in nature (Robinson, 2011). The intervention activities have an intrinsic appeal that, on the whole, is not directly linked to a desire to improve performance. Students are not told that activities are intended to improve their well-being or achievement. Instead students are involved in enjoyable activities, such as writing about values they cherish (Cohen et al., 2006, 2009), participating in fun tutorial sessions about the brain and its potential for growth (Blackwell et al., 2007; Good et al., 2003), or helping others in need (Aronson et al., 2002; Walton & Cohen, 2007). Indeed, the benefits of the affirmation exercise are lessened when it is presented as a means to improve self-integrity (Sherman, Cohen, Nelson, Nussbaum, Bunyan, & Garcia, 2009).

Indirect strategies are particularly important in situations where more direct approaches may increase threat. For instance, persuasive education that focuses people on the health and obesity consequences of bad eating habits risks stigmatizing and thus threatening those they are designed to help. For any intervention, the objective benefits to recipients may be offset by the consequences of being identified as "in need" (Schneider, Major, Luhtanen, & Crocker, 1996). Effective interventions circumvent this problem by making their support subtle or embedded in intrinsically appealing activities and social causes (see also Bolger & Amarel, 2007; Lepper et al., 1990; Robinson, 2011).

All the interventions discussed here are also grounded in hard-won understandings of motivational processes, the result of years of basic research. By contrast, interventions based on intuitive theories of motivation, such as praising children for their abilities, or doling out rewards and incentives, often backfire (Dweck, 1999; Lepper, Green, & Nisbett, 1973).

Understanding the effects of identity threat can help explain when and why people from all walks of life perform below their potential (Steele et al., 2002). Moreover, interventions minimizing the effects of identity threat can have a more global impact beyond achievement, including on health (see Inzlicht, Tullett, & Gutsell, 2011, Chapter 7, this volume; Walton & Cohen, 2011). Because inequalities in education correlate with inequalities in well-being and health, the effects of identity threat—and of interventions to alleviate them—reach beyond the classroom.

■ ACKNOWLEDGMENTS

Portions of the authors' research cited in this chapter were supported by grants from National Science Foundation (NSF/REESE program), Spencer Foundation, W. T. Grant Foundation, Nellie Mae Education Foundation, and Yale's Institute for Social and Policy Studies.

References

Aronson, J., Fried, C. B., & Good, C. (2002). Reducing the effects of stereotype threat on African American college students by shaping theories of intelligence. *Journal of Experimental Social Psychology, 38*, 113–125.

Baumeister, R. F., & Leary, M. R. (1995). The need to belong: Desire for interpersonal attachments as a fundamental human motivation. *Psychological Bulletin, 117*, 497–529.

Barnsley, R. H., Thompson, A. H., & Barnsley, P. E. (1985). Hockey success and birth-date: The relative age effect. *Canadian Association for Health, Physical Education, and Recreation, 51*, 23–28.

Beilock, S. L., Rydell, R. J., & McConnell, A. R. (2007). Stereotype threat and working memory: Mechanisms, alleviation, and spillover. *Journal of Experimental Psychology: General, 136*, 256–276.

Blackwell, L., Trzesniewski, K., & Dweck, C. S. (2007). Implicit theories of intelligence predict achievement across an adolescent transition: A longitudinal study and an intervention. *Child Development, 78*, 246–263.

Bolger, N., & Amarel, D. (2007). Effects of support visibility on adjustment to stress: Experimental evidence. *Journal of Personality and Social Psychology, 92,* 458–475.

Branscombe, N. R., Schmitt, M. T., & Harvey, R. D. (1999). Perceiving pervasive discrimination among African Americans: Implications for group identification and well-being. *Journal of Personality and Social Psychology, 77,* 135–149.

Caspi, A., Elder, G. H., Jr., & Bem, D. J. (1987). Moving against the world: Life-course patterns of explosive children. *Developmental Psychology, 22,* 303–308.

Cohen, G. L., & Garcia, J. (2005). I am us: Negative stereotypes as collective threats. *Journal of Personality and Social Psychology, 89,* 566–582.

Cohen, G. L., & Garcia, J. (2008). Identity, belonging, and achievement: A model, interventions, implications. *Current Directions in Psychological Science, 17,* 365–369.

Cohen, G. L., Garcia, J., Apfel, N., & Master, A. (2006). Reducing the racial achievement gap: A social-psychological intervention. *Science, 313,* 1307–1310.

Cohen, G. L., Garcia, J., Purdie-Vaugns, V., Apfel, N., & Brzustoski, P. (2009). Recursive processes in self-affirmation: Intervening to close the minority achievement gap. *Science, 324,* 400–403.

Cohen, G. L., & Steele, C. M. (2002). A barrier of mistrust: How negative stereotypes affect cross-race mentoring. In J. Aronson (Ed.), *Improving academic achievement: Impact of psychological factors on education* (pp. 303–328). San Diego: Academic Press.

Cohen, G. L., Steele, C. M., & Ross, L. D. (1999). The mentor's dilemma: Providing critical feedback across the racial divide. *Personality and Social Psychology Bulletin, 25,* 1302–1318.

Creswell, J. D., Welch, W., Taylor, S. E., Sherman, D. K., Gruenewald, T., & Mann, T. (2005). Affirmation of personal values buffers neuroendocrine and psychological stress responses. *Psychological Science, 16,* 846–851.

Crocker, J., & Major, B. (1989). Social stigma and self-esteem: The self-protective properties of stigma. *Psychological Review, 96,* 608–630.

Dar-Nimrod, I., & Heine, S. J. (2006). Exposure to scientific theories affects women's math performance. *Science, 314,* 435.

Davies, P. G., Spencer, S. J., Quinn, D. M., & Gerhardstein, R. (2002). Consuming images: How television commercials that elicit stereotype threat can restrain women academically and professionally. *Personality and Social Psychology Bulletin, 28,* 1615–1628.

Dweck, C. S. (1999). *Self-theories: Their role in motivation, personality and development.* Philadelphia: Taylor and Francis/Psychology Press.

Eccles, J. S., Lord, S., & Midgley, C. (1991). What are we doing to early adolescents? The impact of educational contexts on early adolescents. *American Journal of Education, 8,* 520–542.

Freedom Writers & Gruwell, E. (1999). *The freedom writers diary.* New York: Broadway Books.

Garcia, J. (2002). *When white men can't jump.* Tufts University.

Garcia, J., & Cohen, G. L. (in press). Social psychology and educational intervention. In E. Shafir (Ed.), *The behavioral foundations of policy.* New York: Russell Sage Foundation Press.

Good, C., Aronson, J., & Inzlicht, M. (2003). Improving adolescents' standardized test performance: An intervention to reduce the effects of stereotype threat. *Journal of Applied Developmental Psychology, 24,* 645–662.

Heckman, J. (2006). Skill formation and the economics of investing in disadvantaged children. *Science, 312,* 1900–1902.

Inzlicht, M., & Ben-Zeev, T. (2000). A threatening intellectual environment: Why females are susceptible to experiencing problem-solving deficits in the presence of males. *Psychological Science, 11*, 365–371.

Inzlicht, M., Tullett, A. M., & Gutsell, J. N. (2011). Threat spillover: The short-term and long-term effects of coping with threats to social identity. In M. Inzlicht, & T. Schmader (Eds.), *Stereotype threat: Theory, process, and application.* New York: Oxford University Press.

Jamieson, J. P., Mendes, W. B., Blackstock, E., & Schmader, T. (2010). Turning the knots in your stomach into bows: Reappraising arousal improves performance on the GRE. *Journal of Experimental Social Psychology, 46*, 208–212.

Jussim, L., & Harber, K. (2005). Teacher expectations and self-fulfilling prophecies: Knowns and unknowns, resolved and unresolved controversies. *Personality and Social Psychology Review, 9*, 131–155.

Kaiser, C. R., Brooke, V., & Major, B. (2006). Prejudice expectations moderate preconscious attention to cues that are threatening to social identity. *Psychological Science, 17*, 332–338.

Lazarus, R. S., & Folkman, S. (1984). *Stress, appraisal, and coping.* New York: Springer.

Lepper, M. R., Aspinwall, L. G., & Mumme, D. L. (1990). Self-perception and social-perception processes in tutoring: Subtle social control strategies of expert tutors. In J. M. Olson, & M. P. Zanna (Eds.), *Self-inference processes: The Ontario symposium* Vol. 6 (pp. 217–237). Hillsdale, NJ: Lawrence Erlbaum.

Lepper, M. R., Greene, D., & Nisbett, R. E. (1973). Undermining children's intrinsic interest with extrinsic rewards: A test of the "overjustification" hypothesis. *Journal of Personality and Social Psychology, 28*, 129–137.

Lewin, K. (1951). Field theory in social science; selected theoretical papers. D. Cartwright (Ed.). New York: Harper & Row.

Logel, C. E., Iserman, E. C., Spencer, S. J., Davies, P. G., & Quinn, D. M. (2009). The perils of avoiding negative thoughts: Thought suppression as a mediator of stereotype threat. *Journal of Experimental Social Psychology, 45*, 299–312.

Martens, A., Johns, M., Greenberg, J., & Schimel, J. (2006). Combating stereotype threat: The effect of self-affirmation on women's intellectual performance. *Journal of Experimental Psychology, 42*, 236–243.

Marx, D. M., & Roman, J. S. (2002). Female role models: Protecting women's math test performance. *Personality and Social Psychology Bulletin, 28*, 1183–1193.

Menec, V. H., Perry, R. P., Struthers, C. W., Schonwetter, D. J., Hechter, F. J., & Eichholz, B. L. (1994). Assisting at-risk college students with attributional retraining and effective teaching. *Journal of Applied Social Psychology, 24*, 675–701.

Miyake, A., Kost-Smith, L. E., Finkelstein, N. D., Pollock, S. J., Cohen, G. L., & Ito, T. A. (2010). *Reducing the gender achievement gap in college science: A classroom study of values affirmation. Science, 330*, 1234–1237.

Murphy, M. C., Steele, C. M., & Gross, J. J. (2007). Signaling threat: How situational cues affect women in math, science, and engineering settings. *Psychological Science, 18*, 879–885.

Nisbett, R. E. (2009). *Intelligence and how to get it: Why schools and cultures count.* New York: W. W. Norton and Co.

Paluck, E. L. (2009). Reducing intergroup prejudice and conflict using the media: A field experiment in Rwanda. *Journal of Personality and Social Psychology, 96*, 574–587.

Purdie-Vaughns, V., Steele, C., Davies, P., Ditlmann, R., & Randall-Crosby, J. (2008). Social identity contingencies: How diversity cues signal threat or safety for African Americans in mainstream institutions. *Journal of Personality and Social Psychology, 94*, 615–630.

Robinson, T. N. (2011). Stealth interventions for obesity prevention and control: Motivating behavior change. In L. Dube, A. Bechara, A. Dagher, A. Drewnowski, J. Lebel, P. James, R. Yada, M. Laflamme-Sanders. (Eds.), *Obesity prevention: The role of society and brain on individual behavior* (pp. 319–327).

Rosenthal, R., & Jacobson, L. (1992). *Pygmalion in the classroom*. Expanded edition. New York: Irvington.

Ross, L., & Nisbett, R. E. (1991). *The person and the situation*. New York: McGraw-Hill.

Ryan, R. M., & Deci, E. L. (2000). Self-determination theory and the facilitation of intrinsic motivation, social development, and well-being. *American Psychologist, 55,* 68–78.

Rydell, R. J., McConnell, A. R., & Beilock, S. L. (2009). *Journal of Personality and Social Psychology, 96,* 949–966.

Schachter, S. (1959). *The psychology of affiliation*. Stanford: Stanford University Press.

Schmader, T., Johns, M., & Forbes, C. (2008). An integrated process model of stereotype threat effects on performance. *Psychological Review, 115,* 336–356.

Schmader, T., Forbes, C. E., Zhang, S., & Mendes, W. B. (2009). A meta-cognitive perspective on cognitive deficits experienced in intellectually threatening environments. *Personality and Social Psychology Bulletin, 35,* 584–596.

Schmeichel, B. J., & Vohs, K. D. (2009). Self-affirmation and self-control: Affirming core values counteracts ego depletion. *Journal of Personality and Social Psychology, 96,* 770–782.

Schneider, M. E., Major, B., Luhtanen, R., & Crocker, J. (1996). Social stigma and the potential costs of assumptive help. *Personality and Social Psychology Bulletin, 22,* 201–209.

Sherman, D. K., Hartson, K. A., Binning, K., Purdie-Vaughns, V., Garcia, J., Taborsky-Barba, S., Tomassetti, S., Nussbaum, D., & Cohen, G. (2011). *Identity threat, self-affirmation, and academic performance*. Manuscript in preparation.

Sherman, D. K., & Cohen, G. L. (2006). The psychology of self-defense: Self-affirmation theory. In M. P. Zanna (Ed.), *Advances in experimental social psychology* Vol. 38 (pp. 183–242). San Diego: Academic Press.

Sherman, D. K., Cohen, G. L., Nelson, L. D., Nussbaum, A. D., Bunyan, D. P., & Garcia, J. (2009). Affirmed yet unaware: The role of awareness in the process of self-affirmation. *Journal of Personality and Social Psychology, 97,* 745–764.

Simmons, R. G., Black, A., & Zhou, Y. (1991). African-Americans versus White children and the transition into junior high school. *American Journal of Education, 99,* 481–520.

Snyder, C. R. (2000). *Handbook of hope: Theory, measures, and applications*. New York: Academic Press.

Steele, C. M. (1988). The psychology of self-affirmation: Sustaining the integrity of the self. In L. Berkowitz (Ed.), *Advances in experimental social psychology* Vol. 21 (pp. 261–302). New York: Academic Press.

Steele, C. M. (1997). A threat in the air: How stereotypes shape the intellectual identities and performance of women and African-Americans. *American Psychologist, 52,* 613–629.

Steele, C. M., & Aronson, J. (1995). Stereotype threat and the intellectual test performance of African Americans. *Journal of Personality and Social Psychology, 69,* 797–811.

Steele, C. M., Spencer, S. J., & Aronson, J. (2002). Contending with group image: The psychology of stereotype and social identity threat. In M. Zanna (Ed.), *Advances in experimental social psychology* Vol. 34 (pp. 379–440). New York: Academic Press.

Steele, C. M., Spencer, S., Nisbett, R., Hummel, M., Harber, K., & Schoem, D. (2004). *African American college achievement: A "wise" intervention*. Manuscript submitted for publication.

Tyler, T. R. (2004). Procedural justice. In A. Sarat (Ed.), *The Blackwell companion to law and society* (pp. 435–452). Malden, MA: Blackwell.

Walberg, H. J. (1984). Improving the productivity of America's schools. *Educational Leadership, 41,* 19–27.

Walton, G. M., & Carr, P. (2011). Social belonging and the motivation and intellectual achievement of negatively stereotyped students. In M. Inzlicht, & T. Schmader (Eds.), *Stereotype threat: Theory, process, and application.* New York: Oxford University Press.

Walton, G. M., & Cohen, G. L. (2007). A question of belonging: Race, social fit, and achievement. *Journal of Personality and Social Psychology, 92,* 82–96.

Walton, G. M., & Cohen, G. L. (2011). A brief social-belonging intervention improves academic and health outcomes of minority students, *Science, 331,* 1447–1451.

Wilson, T. D., Damiani, M., & Shelton, N. (2002). Improving the academic performance of college students with brief attributional interventions. In J. Aronson (Ed.), *Improving academic achievement: Impact of psychological factors on education.* San Diego: Academic Press.

Yeager, D., Purdie-Vaughns, V., Garcia, J., & Cohen, G. L. Wise feedback: Invoking high standards and assurance increases minority students' performance and motivation. Manuscript in preparation.

19 Conclusion

Extending and Applying Stereotype Threat Research: A Brief Essay

■ CLAUDE M. STEELE

This essay provides a capstone to this edited volume on stereotype threat by addressing three issues related to the original theory. First, stereotype threat arises when we could reasonably theorize that other people could see us stereotypically. But factors other than relevant stereotypes can make us feel this way. Thus, stereotype threat can be considered a specific instance of a more general "intersubjective" threat. The breadth of findings demonstrating stereotype threat effects reveal that this broader threat can play a bigger role in human social behavior than we have appreciated, and more basic theory and research on the role of intersubjectivity in psychological functioning is needed. Second, although critics have sometimes questioned the generalizability of stereotype threat beyond laboratory demonstrations, these questions of generalizability are better framed as a need to specify what moderates the effect. Because the experience of stereotype threat is conditional on a host of person and situation factors, it might not be meaningful to debate the generalizability of a unitary effect. Finally, policy questions regarding ways to reduce threat should be guided by answers about moderating variables. Situations in which threat is likely to be felt most strongly should be targeted for intervention, and successful intervention can be developed based on evidence of what alleviates threat.

Keywords: Stereotype threat, intersubjective threat, generalizability, moderation, policy

It's immensely gratifying to have been part of developing a fruitful set of ideas: formulating and clarifying the phenomenon of stereotype threat, trying to understand its generality and mediation, trying to find out where it is important in the real world, trying to find out ways of reducing its unwanted effects, and so on. Thus, I am proud to be associated with the work presented in this volume, work that has brilliantly explored these issues and others, and that far beyond any influence of mine, has developed a deep understanding of this phenomenon.

Research often produces the excitement of telling us more than we ever imagined we'd learn about a phenomenon. Empirical research is almost always frustrating.

But over time, it does reveal. That has certainly been my experience researching the phenomenon now known as stereotype threat. And the other joy of this effort has been the intellectual collaboration, direct and indirect, with so many of the contributors to this volume. For better or worse, talking is how I think—as these collaborators well know—and while not blaming them for my errors and poor judgment, I am indebted to them for so much of what I have been able to contribute.

A good theory, in addition to deepening understanding, also suggests how its understandings might be extended and applied. I will use my few words to discuss several such possibilities and the issues that arise in trying to pursue them.

■ STEREOTYPE THREAT AS A SUBTYPE OF INTERSUBJECTIVE THREAT

Stereotype threat can be thought of as a specific instance of a more general threat—that of being judged and treated negatively by others. One implication of stereotype threat research is that this general threat may play a bigger role in human social behavior than we've appreciated.

The capacity to sense threat of this sort arises from our intersubjective capacity. To communicate effectively, we have to have a sense of what others could be thinking and how they might react to what we say or do, as well as to features and events in the world around us. We need ongoing theories of others people's minds, and these theories influence how we think and behave. Stereotype threat arises when, because of circumstances and signaling cues, we could reasonably theorize that other people could see us stereotypically. The situational relevance of the stereotype increases our subjective sense that we could be judged negatively (in terms of the stereotype).

But, of course, factors other than relevant stereotypes can make us feel this way. We could have a bad reputation in some area. When in situations in which that reputation is relevant, we could feel a threat of being judged and treated in terms of it—a threat similar to stereotype threat. We could interact with people we know have very different values from our own, and again, worry that we will be judged through the lens of that difference. We could be with a person of some great distinction, wealth, or renown and worry that we will be seen through the lens of our relative lack. We could have done something we're not proud of and worry that we will be seen in terms of that failure or transgression. These intersubjective threats could cause anxiety, cognitive overload, physiological arousal, and distraction, just like stereotype threat does, and through these mediations, affect our behavior, performance, and relationships, just like stereotype threat does.

The point is that intersubjective threat of negative judgment may play a more pervasive role in human functioning than we realize. Stereotype threat research shows that behaviors we typically attribute to internal characteristics—as in attributing low test performance to characteristics like a lack of ability or motivation—are actually affected by this form of intersubjective threat. It's a small leap, then, to wonder whether other forms of intersubjective threat could affect other social behaviors.

Think of human relationships, and how much their quality can hinge on inter-subjective appraisals of how others in the relationship might judge and treat us. These appraisals can be more important than our dispositional liking or disliking of the people involved. Think of anger and aggression, and how much their likelihood depends on what we think others think of us. And again, appraisals of what others think of us can influence these reactions as much as our disposition toward anger and aggression. Think of intergroup conflict and discrimination: Research within the stereotype threat tradition by Philip Goff and me shows that the pressure not to be seen as racist can be a more powerful cause of racial avoidance than actual racial prejudice. Think of self-esteem and how it can depend on appraisals of how we stack up to others in our environment as much as on appraisals of our own strengths and weaknesses.

More basic theory and research on the role of intersubjectivity in psychological functioning is needed. I'd like to think that, among its contributions, stereotype threat research helps open this door. It reveals how our emotions, thoughts, and actions are shaped by appraisals of other people's possible emotions, thoughts and actions. It shows how much cognitive and affective processing is in significant part social in nature and, thus, how an important dimension of psychological functioning is social.

■ GENERALIZABILITY VERSUS MODERATION

There are a host of questions about stereotype threat's real-world applicability: Does it affect women's comfort and progress in science, technology, engineering, and math (STEM) professions? Is it a factor in mixed-sex math classrooms? Does it affect the performance of ability-stereotyped students on important standardized tests? Is it a factor in classrooms and schools in which ability-stereotyped students are the numerical majority? And so on. In trying to answer these questions, I have come to a belief about this strategy: It is generally best to regard these as questions about moderation rather than as questions about generalization.

The reason is that the conditionality of stereotype threat makes the generalization question not very meaningful.

Remember, stereotype threat is an intersubjective pressure. It's caused by situational cues and perhaps by individual dispositions that make the prospect of being negatively stereotyped (or of doing something that would confirm such a stereotype) plausible enough and important enough to be upsetting enough to interfere with a person's functioning in the setting.

This means that in almost any type of real-world setting in which this pressure could be relevant—classrooms, testing rooms, interpersonal interactions, etc.—it is possible to imagine either there being enough stereotype threat–inducing conditions to produce the threat, or few enough to prevent, reduce, or eliminate it. (This latter possibility is, after all, the hope of the intervention research reported in this volume.) That is, whether or not the effect occurs in a real-world setting, and the strength of the effect, should depend on the number and strength of the stereotype threat–inducing cues and conditions in the setting.

Let's say that a researcher finds no effect of stereotype threat on women's math performance in an all-women's math classroom. Does that mean that stereotype threat doesn't "generalize" to that situation? Not necessarily. It's imaginable that some such classrooms *could* have enough stereotype threat–inducing cues— pictures of male mathematicians lining the walls, heavy use of sports-based examples of math principles, frequent references to male-dominated hierarchies of math professionals, heavy emphasis on classroom competition, etc.—as to cause some stereotype threat—a sense of being vulnerable to gender stereotyping.

So, not finding an effect in some setting wouldn't be definitive proof that it couldn't occur there, that it couldn't "generalize" to that setting under even slightly different conditions. And finding a stereotype threat effect in a setting might be only trivial proof that it could "generalize" to the setting when, in fact, it rarely occurs there.

So, it seems more useful to approach the question of real-world applicability as a question of moderation rather than as a question of generalization. Generalization is a loose term; moderation is more precise. Moderation focuses attention on the relevant features of a setting and on the relevant dispositions of the people in it— that is, on factors that might determine whether or not the effect occurs in the setting, and, if it occurs, how strong and regular it will be.

■ HOW TO KNOW WHERE STEREOTYPE THREAT MAKES A DIFFERENCE? THE POLICY QUESTION

I will end by raising a question: How does one know where in the real world it is helpful—makes good policy or practice—to try to reduce stereotype threat? Stereotype threat research has had the good fortune of being looked to for its real-world implications. So, this is an important question to try to answer. My answer is straightforward and built on the last point: In deciding where stereotype threat–reducing efforts might have their maximum impact, use evidence of what moderates these effects as your guide. That is, target that part of the problem for which our knowledge of stereotype threat's moderation suggests this threat will be the strongest.

This can seem obvious. How else should one target an intervention? It's just that we may not think very much about this step—of going from basic science or theory to practice and policy. We may not even be aware we are making it. Going from the controlled world of the laboratory to the real world is something we often do intuitively. So, it is worth reminding ourselves that there are guides for taking this step, clues that point the way. To illustrate, I will describe how this strategy might work in relation to several areas in which stereotype threat research is seen to have application.

Achievement Gaps

Of course, there isn't just one achievement gap, there are several—racial, social class, and gender (mostly in advanced quantitative fields). And there isn't just one cause of these gaps. For example, racial and social class gaps in school achievement are caused most importantly by racial and social class differences in access to educational resources, as well as differences in peer cultures, family resources, etc. Thus, although stereotype threat can be a factor in any situation (depending of the particular features of the situation), a big part of these gaps has to be caused by identity-based differences in access to resources.

And this opens an important policy question: What part of these gaps might be reduced by efforts to reduce stereotype threat?

In answer: Perhaps it's the part of these gaps that *isn't* caused by differences in access to educational resources. In racially integrated schools, for example, racial gaps in achievement persist even when these schools have ample educational resources. To be sure, minorities attending better-resourced integrated schools often do better than minorities in poor segregated schools, but they rarely match their majority classmates in the integrated schools. These are racial gaps that can't be easily attributed to poor resources. Yet, they are big enough and frequent enough to contribute importantly to society's overall racial gap. And they have been long known about. The 1966 Coleman Report found that black K through 12 students got lower standardized test scores than did white students even in the better-off, integrated northern schools where better educational resources were expected to elevate all students' performance and wipe out racial differences.

Could these gaps be caused mostly by stereotype threat? Here is where what we know about the moderation of stereotype threat effects comes in. We know these effects are strongest for people who identify with the performance in question—in this case school achievement—and who are in situations in which they can worry about being stereotyped—in this case, being minorities in integrated schools where academic achievement is a central value. Both of these factors—as moderators—are more likely to be present in better-off, integrated schools with minority students from higher socioeconomic backgrounds.

It's reasonable, then, to think that stereotype threat could be a major cause of the racial gap in this kind of situation—better-off, integrated schools—and that such schools are places where practices that reduce this threat might have an especially big payoff.

Whether this hypothesis is correct, of course, is an empirical question. It's the means of getting to the hypothesis that I am stressing here. Knowledge of how these effects are moderated helps tell us which aspect of the racial achievement gap might be most improved by reducing stereotype threat.

Women in Math

Another example. In what part of women's math experience is it most important to reduce stereotype threat? Again, the moderation: This threat is strongest for women who are identified with math and operating at the frontier of their skills in gender-integrated situations in which a lack of fixed ability is a ready account of their math frustrations. In the real world, this would be classes and programs that involve difficult math and science curriculum—at any level of schooling—being taught in gender-integrated contexts, and where there is a more or less nativist understanding of the ability required to succeed.

In situations like these, it would not be unreasonable for girls and women to feel a threat of being stereotyped—the frustrations of the work will provide plenty of occasions for them to be stereotyped, the gender mix of the setting may make stereotyping seem more likely, the stereotype itself alleges an unfixable ability deficit, and so on. In situations like these, it seems especially likely that stereotype threat could hurt women's performance and persistence.

Thus, in situations like these, stereotype threat–reducing interventions might be especially valuable.

Again, whether this is so is an empirical question. This hypothesis—derived from the known moderation of stereotype threat effects—only suggests where the interventionist might begin.

High-stakes Testing

A last example. How should stereotype threat–reducing interventions be targeted to improve ability-stereotyped students' performance on tests? Again, a list of relevant moderators: Stereotype threat should be high for academically identified, ability-stereotyped students' taking difficult, high-stakes tests understood to be diagnostic of a fixed, global intellectual ability, and where the tests are made up of items not based on a curriculum the students have been explicitly exposed to. This list points to tests like the SAT—big, high-stakes, summary tests, culturally understood to be diagnostic of a broad intellectual ability that is difficult to modify. Possible remedies—suggested by the moderators—would be use of frequently administered smaller tests, tests directly tied to curriculum, so that they are achievement tests, not ability tests, and administered under a lower-stakes regime of, for example, being able to take the test repeated times. Here, the known moderation of these effects suggests both where the intervention should be targeted—at big, high-stakes tests—and how to do it—by breaking them into smaller, lower-stakes tests.

As scientists, we're trained to think hardest about internal validity. But in developing practice and policy, it's external validity that counts. Where does this threat make a difference in real life? Where is it critical to reduce this threat? Answering these questions is an important frontier of stereotype threat research, a big part of its future I hope. Almost 20 years after this research began, we know a lot about what moderates this threat, what makes it strong, what makes it weak. Just in time to take on this frontier.

■ CONCLUSION

As the chapters of this volume beautifully illustrate, research on stereotype threat is a powerful, bustling area of endeavor that continues to bear theoretical and practical fruit. It has developed nothing less than a comprehensive framework for understanding a very important dimension of human experience. I am grateful to have been part of the effort that accomplished this. And yet, I still regard the area as a growth stock, with the opportunity to make more, and equally profound contributions in the years ahead. I end by noting that an especially deep gratification for me are the great scientists who have been attracted to this work, and who, having achieved so much—as this volume reveals—are poised to achieve so much more.

■ INDEX

Page numbers followed by "*f*" or "*t*" refer to figures or tables, respectively.

Printed in the USA/Agawam, MA
November 25, 2016

643466.014